Also by Will Birch

No Sleep Till Canvey Island: The Great Pub Rock Revolution
Ian Drury: The Definitive Biography

Cruel to Be Kind

Cruel to Be Kind

The Life and Music of Nick Lowe

Will Birch

DA CAPO PRESS

Da Capo Press
Hachette Book Group
1290 Avenue of the Americas, New York, NY 10104
HachetteBooks.com
Twitter.com/HachetteBooks
Instagram.com/HachetteBooks

Printed in the United States of America

Originally published by Constable in the United Kingdom: August 2019

First U.S. Edition: August 2019

Published by Da Capo Press, an imprint of Perseus Books, LLC, a subsidiary of Hachette Book Group, Inc. The Da Capo Press name and logo is a trademark of the Hachette Book Group.

The Hachette Speakers Bureau provides a wide range of authors for speaking events. To find out more, go to www.hachettespeakersbureau.com or call (866) 376-6591.

The publisher is not responsible for websites (or their content) that are not owned by the publisher.

Library of Congress Control Number: 2019938961

ISBNs: 978-0-306-92195-7 (hardcover), 978-0-306-92197-1 (ebook)

LSC-C

10 9 8 7 6 5 4 3 2 1

For Mum

CONTENTS

'Rock and roll offers no precedent for Nick Lowe. You have to go outside rock and roll – to pop art, to the modern novel maybe – to find anybody who compares to Lowe. Oh, there are plenty of human ironists, lustful romantics and cheeky genre players making their way through record company corridors and into recording studios, but Lowe is all of these and more.'

Kit Rachlis, *Rolling Stone*, 1979

Nick Lowe is a god cast in marble at the foot of Mount Olympus, draped in purple velvet and holding a jade guitar.

laughingcrow, Elvis Costello Fan Forum, 2003

Introduction

Firstly, I should declare an interest. I have been a fan of Nick Lowe's music for nearly fifty years and he is, I would like to think, a friend.

For the record, other songwriters that ring my bell are John Lennon and Paul McCartney, of course; Jerry Leiber and Mike Stoller, creators of those mini-movie vignettes for the Coasters; Smokey Robinson, whose Motown classics are exemplified by 'The Tracks Of My Tears'; Ray Davies, for his proto metal rave-ups and dour views of English suburban life; and the immaculate Bob Dylan. There are many more, including Buddy Holly, Randy Newman, Joni Mitchell and Neil Young.

Unlike most of those famous names, Lowe is not an innovator, yet he has mastered multiple styles and his best work faithfully echoes the greats. If proof of his skills were needed, his original compositions have been recorded by a wide range of artists, from former *enfant terrible* Elvis Costello, to 'The Godfather of Rhythm and Soul' Solomon Burke; from household names including Engelbert Humperdinck, Diana Ross and Johnny Cash, to well-known vocalists such as Curtis Stigers, Tom Petty and Rod Stewart. In terms of musical and artistic credibility, Lowe is simply peerless.

Never a superstar, due to an unhurried work rate and a reluctance to play the fame game, he has nevertheless enjoyed hit records as an artist, record producer and composer. He came to prominence in the mid-1970s, firstly as one of the masterminds behind the famously independent Stiff Records, and secondly as a driving force in the mighty Rockpile. Front and centre in all things 'New Wave', he scored an international smash hit in 1979 with 'Cruel To Be Kind', one of at least three of his songs 'you know by heart', or so his publicist insists.

The influential music press of the day worshipped him and endorsed his every move, splashing his face across full-page features week after week. His natural wit and turns of phrase guaranteed him countless column inches, inclining him to weigh his review clippings rather than read them.

The plaudits weigh heavy; he has been the subject of three 'tribute albums'[1] and described as 'Britain's greatest living song-writer', and even 'a contender for greatest living Englishman', which he would no doubt find embarrassing. But he knows he's very good at what he does best, which is to create and perform exceptional music within his chosen genre-set – a mix of country, soul and pop that swings, and is more 'roll' than 'rock'.

Also, unlike almost any other British musician, he instinctively writes and sings timeless songs that sound American. A romantic explanation could be the fact that he is – as exclusively revealed in this book (please see the Appendix recounting his family history) – a third-generation descendant, the great-grandson no less, of an unlikely Euro-American love affair between an Austrian baroness and an American Civil War veteran.

'No shit!' he exclaimed as I unveiled the fruits of my research, causing him to envisage distant relatives with 'stovepipe hats and brocade waistcoats'. And that he is also distantly related, by marriage, to the inventor of the jukebox seems highly appropriate, for Nick Lowe is surely the human equivalent.

He is the assimilator, the thinker, the contrarian. At a pub in Goodge Street, wearing a fairly loud, chalk-checked suit, he asked the bartender for 'Half of bitter please, in one of those little jugs with a handle, if you have one.' This was at a time when most British men asked for a pint of beer in a 'straight glass', or sleever. I sensed he was either paying his respects to tradition – the gentlemanly half-pint – or this was simply his way of being different.

His choice of outfit was occasionally askew, perhaps deliberately so. When 'punk' broke in 1977 and the youth audience was suddenly polarised, he straddled the chasm of taste and opinion, his coiffure long and lank throughout the spiky-hair era, and he clung to his cowboy boots when everyone else was in plimsolls. Today, his postmodern quiff, heavy horn-rimmed spectacles and informed dress sense bear all the hallmarks of the ex-Mod. 'It's all smoke and mirrors,' he will say.

Never wanting to align himself with anything remotely in vogue, and unfazed by fashion, he remains defiant, his own man. I recall him once turning up to an appointment wearing a pretty cool, three-quarter length, black leather coat, twinned with socks and sandals – a controversial look, especially in Mayfair.

My first close encounter with him occurred in 1974 when my own group of the time were on a bill in London with the kings of the pub rock scene, Brinsley Schwarz, appearing that night under their code name, 'the Electricians'. Nick, his hair already showing signs of premature greying, was their charismatic, six-foot-something frontman. Backstage post-show, while other band members sat more or less alone with their guitars, he was pretty much the centre of attention for a giggle of girls whose adulation he appeared to enjoy. No doubt some of those same girls and many others around the world still carry a torch for Nick, probably with a supply of long-life batteries.

Unlike his buddy Elvis Costello, he is mysteriously absent from the Songwriters Hall of Fame, a state of affairs I imagine to be the result of some administrative oversight. Or perhaps it's simply the dearth of actual hits. He was, after all, the 'Jesus of Cool', a handy moniker from his debut album and a persona that distanced him from the commercial truth. And as 'cool' as he was, he could be a bit of a buffoon, unable to resist throwing zany shapes for press photographers.

Perhaps the powers that be perceive him to be nothing more than a joker, a musical parodist, a dilettante. But his followers know that's not the case, as do many national journalists and TV talk-show hosts who track his musical accomplishments and look forward to interviewing him. He has appeared on *The David Letterman Show* and Conan O'Brien's talk shows, and has been interviewed by *GQ*, the *New Yorker* and *Vanity Fair*, always charming his inquisitors with undeniable Englishness and storytelling flair. His yarns and personal recollections are heightened by a photographic memory, and as a modern-day entertainment raconteur he has few equals. As a Canadian columnist once wrote, 'Nick Lowe is one of the world's great interviews.'

And his story is as astonishing as his survival; it is not so much that he once battled the booze as embraced it with a thirst that would have killed lesser men. But his cast-iron constitution, infinite patience and playful sense of humour all form a defence mechanism that enables him to withstand the rigours of the road. His five decades in music have been a triumph of single-minded dedication to his craft over periods of charmed nonchalance.

Through it all he remains an upbeat, comfortable-in-his-own-skin kind of guy.

I felt compelled to write his story, not only to fill a yawning gap on the rock and roll bookshelf, but to also document a remarkable life. I had hoped he would one day publish his autobiography, but it was an impossible ask.

'Nick Lowe will not write a memoir' announced CNN in 2015, following his interview with reporter Todd Leopold. 'But the story may eventually get out,' it went on; 'there is a researcher working on a book.'

I guessed, and of course hoped, they meant me. They did. Then, a couple of years later, Nick told Graeme Thomson from the *Sunday Herald*, 'Actually, the writer Will Birch is doing a book about me. I sort of disapprove of it.'

I found this amusing; we had met regularly over lunches at which he was happy for me to interrogate him. And the louder I listened, the more he talked. But despite his helpfulness and generosity of time, it has still been a little strange for both subject and author to contemplate 'a biography'.

He is uncomfortable portraying himself as the hero of his anecdotes and unnerved by the dubious pleasure of seeing his stories in cold, hard print – 'without the hand movements'. I have assured him that there are still many fans out there for whom most of this will be new. He is not so sure. For my part, I was questioning the wisdom of reporting lurid tales of sex and drugs and rock and roll out of respect for his nearest and dearest. 'No, you have to,' he insisted.

In response to the inevitable question from my publisher, I hesitated to confirm that this was an authorised biography since Nick has at times been ambivalent towards the project. I think he would prefer to maintain a degree of mystique, rather than be seen to endorse every word. Furthermore, I didn't want my book to come over as some kind of sycophantic hagiography. The story has not been overly sanitised, which the term 'authorised biography' tends to imply.

I offered him the opportunity to read various chapters ahead of submission, and he initially declined. On reflection, this may have been a wise decision because once you start reading someone else's version of your life, which may contain the odd factual error, there is no end to it. But as publication approached, he did indeed review all of the key passages in which he speaks, for which I am grateful. He suggested a number of edits, which have been implemented, and I feel the text benefits from it.

More than once, the project was close to being pulled. At an early stage I was warned off by his then manager. An email informed me: 'A very subdued Nick Lowe is not ready to endorse or authorise any book about himself by anybody!'

I responded by assuring the sender that if Nick didn't want a book, I would desist, but I had to remind his manager that firstly, 'It's only a matter of time before someone else has a go at doing a book on Nick' (which would not require approval, and could not easily be blocked); and secondly, 'By the time *my* proposed book is published, we will all be pushing seventy years of age. PS: Please print this off and show it to Nick.'

That evening, the phone rang. 'Will, I am so embarrassed,' said the caller. 'I feel I am being misrepresented by my manager.'

Fortunately, I had witnessed this good cop/bad cop routine once or twice before. I knew how it went. If Nick was reluctant to commit, his manager was only too willing to ward off the foe. This time, however, things went in my favour and a planned trip to Oxfordshire to meet with Nick's sister would go ahead.

Penny had very good recall of her parents' lives but, like her brother, was sketchy on their mother and father's antecedents. A few key phrases aroused my curiosity: 'My grandmother was a Bluebell Girl, I think. My grandfather's mother was an Austrian countess and a pupil of Liszt. It was in the genes.'

Naturally I was intrigued, thus my research commenced forthwith.

PART ONE

Who Do You Think You Are?

CHAPTER 1

The Hero

15 April 1940, three miles off England's north-east coast

In the early hours of the morning a trio of Royal Air Force Hampden bombers from 49 Squadron are returning from a failed mine-laying expedition along Denmark's shoreline, a raging storm having hampered their mission.

Aircrafts one and two, piloted respectively by Flying Officer Forsyth and Flight Lieutenant Mitchell, make it back to RAF Hemswell in Lincolnshire, but Hampden L4043, piloted by twenty-four-year-old Squadron Leader Geoffrey Drain Lowe, is in trouble.

With his aircraft's instruments failing and navigation system shot, Lowe has only a basic compass for guidance. To his rear, Corporal George Appleton makes radio contact with base, but the bearings he receives prove unreliable. The Hampden is way off course and rapidly approaching the Durham coastline, its four-man crew contemplating a violent death in an interior so cramped that they call it 'the flying suitcase'.

With terra firma in sight, hopes are raised when they spot the flashing red lights of an unidentified landing strip. Lowe twists his plane towards the runway and instructs Pilot Officer Kennet Beauchamp to send an SOS on the Aldis lamp. The crew prays that its signal will be picked up, but there is no response. Beauchamp's only hope is to send a red flare from his Very pistol. Miraculously, it works.

Moments later, searchlights on the ground pick out the stricken aircraft, but as Lowe points it towards the glare, one of his two fuel-starved engines splutters and dies. Skilfully, he maintains height on the other, then – quickly assessing the situation – shouts: 'Bale!'

But none of the crew wishes to jump. With the Hampden now uncontrollable, Lowe has no option but to attempt a forced landing. As the plane dives towards the rocks below, he instructs his colleagues to collect in the well behind his pilot's seat for protection. When his one good engine finally stalls, he pulls the nose up and glides gracefully towards the sand, putting the plane down with a thud on Ryhope Beach, three miles south of Sunderland.

It's a little after 4 a.m. Airmen Lowe, Beauchamp and Appleton climb from the twisted aircraft virtually unscathed. Inside the wreckage, their twenty-eight-year-old rear gunner, Pilot Officer Anthony Bryan-Smith, is dead.

Less than a month after his crash landing, Squadron Leader Lowe was back in action, spearheading a formation of sixteen RAF Hampden bombers in an attack over Hamburg, Germany. Outwitting enemy fighter planes and anti-aircraft defences, he made two direct hits, causing fires and explosions on the ground. The ensuing commotion allowed his colleagues to move in and hit their target. Then, speeding away from the scene, Lowe manoeuvred his aircraft to enable his rear gunner to ward off the chasing Luftwaffe.

This description of a wartime event may read like a *Boy's Own* action strip, but the Hamburg mission of May 1940 was just one of many that Lowe survived, defying the unfavourable odds that faced every airman in RAF Bomber Command during the Second World War. The statistics are horrific – it is said that over fifty per cent of them died in the air, and only one in four emerged free of physical injury.

Geoffrey Drain Lowe was born on 31 May 1915 in Blackpool, Lancashire, a popular seaside town in north-west England. To step back for a moment through his family line, his mother Sybil, the daughter of Herbert and Emily Hobson, had married one Albert Drain Lowe in 1914. Albert, a motor mechanic by trade, was the son of John and Eliza Lowe, who met in the late 1870s when they both worked as Turkish bath assistants at Skelmorlie Hydro in Ayrshire on the west coast of Scotland. Skelmorlie, overlooking the Firth of Clyde, was a fashionable spa of its day. It was there that John Drain Lowe received training as a chiropodist and masseur. After they were married in 1881, John and Eliza set up home in Glasgow and later moved to 207 Central Drive in Blackpool, where Albert was born in 1892.

All of the Lowe menfolk, and indeed some of the women, have 'Drain' as their middle name. The story handed down was that they were originally the Drain family and a Scottish doctor by the name of Lowe had adopted and nurtured an earlier generation. Although the adoptees became 'Lowes', the doctor insisted that future generations retain 'Drain' in their name.

As a young man, Albert Drain Lowe joined the Indian Electrical and Mechanical Engineers, a body of mainly white soldiers protecting a corner of what was left of the British Empire. As a consequence, his son Geoffrey spent his early years in India but at the age of twelve was sent back to Britain and placed with friends of the family in Wales. Drain Lowe, as Nick's father Geoffrey became known, would never get over a sense of being abandoned by his parents. Whenever his parents came home Drain would be forced to listen to his father parade his spurious claims of rank in the subcontinent. Albert Lowe won't be the last military man in this story to affect officer status, but his son *would* achieve high rank.

Drain had his appetite for flying whetted ten years before his daring wartime raids. It was in Wales, while living with what were effectively his foster parents, that he first discovered the thrill of aviation. Cycling through a Pembrokeshire field one afternoon, he glanced upwards and saw a small aircraft that appeared to be in trouble. He followed its path as it fell to earth and landed in a field nearby. Apprehensive yet inquisitive, he pedalled as fast as he could towards the crashed plane, only to watch its pilot casually emerge from the cockpit and straighten his tie. Drain approached him nervously and they made conversation. 'Would you like to come up in a plane, maybe tomorrow?' asked the mystery airman.

Drain was soon airborne and, from that moment, hooked on flying. Aged sixteen, he was thrilled to be given a part-time job at the local airfield, sweeping up or making tea, but such mundane tasks were agreeable so long as he could wake up and smell the aviation fuel. On 6 August 1935, he joined the Royal Air Force, aged twenty, service number 37324. He spent his first six weeks at a training school in Brough, Yorkshire, and then several months at various RAF depots around the country. In June 1936, he joined 49 Squadron – a 'Bomber' squadron, as he noted with meticulous block capital letters in his RAF Pilot's Flying Log Book.

His Hawker Hind, with its superior Rolls-Royce Kestrel engine, would see him all right in the conflict that was to come, and the Royal Air Force became Drain's surrogate family as he rose through its ranks. He was now a pilot officer, and by 1938 would graduate to flying officer. These titles were superficial divisions designed to sort the men out from the boys and give them something to which they might aspire, but promotion also meant a raise in pay and the opportunity to get one step closer to the action. In September 1939 – by which time Drain had become a flight lieutenant – Britain was at war with Germany.

Following his dramatic raid on Hamburg, Drain was awarded the Distinguished Flying Cross in a ceremony that happened to coincide with his twenty-fifth birthday. Newly decorated, he was stationed at RAF Scampton in Lincolnshire when he met his wife to be, Corporal Patricia Thatcher. With her quick wit and musical leanings, eighteen-year-old 'Pat' had a knack for penning satirical verse. One afternoon, she posted on the officers' mess notice board an amusing poem in support of the death-defying pilots, including Drain, who were in the habit of urinating on the aircraft's tyres immediately before take-off, or 'watering the wheel', in the superstitious belief that it would bring them luck (as well as provide relief immediately before a mission of several hours' duration).

The commanding officers, or 'COs', disapproved of this ritual, mainly because, they said, the acid in human urine played havoc with the rubber composition of the tyres. But the officers were powerless to stop the practice, and even they had to suppress a chortle when they read Pat Thatcher's couplets, intended to be sung to the tune of Dvorak's 'Humoresque'.

> *Aviators must refrain from urinating on the plane*
> *It's not a very pleasant thing to do*

Aviators must refrain from urinating on the plane
The CO doesn't do it, nor should you

No one could fail to be amused by Pat's poem, especially Drain, who was quick to fall for the saucy young girl who had longed to become an entertainer.

Patricia Kathleen Mary Thatcher was born on 2 January 1922, at 15 Camborne Avenue in Ealing, west London. She had been inspired and encouraged to entertain by her own mother, Blanche, who had been a singer and dancer during the golden era of British music hall. Indeed, on his maternal side Nick Lowe comes from a line of musicians and performers, as well as having American and Austrian ancestry (as detailed in the Appendix).

Although Pat herself was a promising singer and dancer, her aspirations were cut short by the outbreak of war. With her dreams on hold, Pat Thatcher had joined the Women's Auxiliary Air Force.

Drain Lowe ascended the Royal Air Force ranks, becoming a squadron leader in March 1941 and, two years later, wing commander. On Sunday 6 June, 1943, while stationed at RAF Upper Heyford, he and sweetheart Pat were married at the church of St Michael at the North Gate in the nearby university town of Oxford. Four days earlier, Drain had been awarded the Air Force Cross for valour to add to his tally of medals.

Drain and Pat's first child, Penelope Anne, was born on 8 May 1944 in Market Harborough, Leicestershire. Penny was too young to know much about Drain's RAF career immediately after the war ended, and for years was unaware of his exploits with Bomber Command.

'They never really went on about things,' says Penny of her parents. 'But the way my mother tells it, Father would come back from a mission and he wouldn't phone her. He rushed off to the pub to get a few drinks down his neck before closing time.'

It is hardly surprising that a man who had narrowly escaped death throughout the war, and seen many of his amphetamine-stoked comrades perish in mid-air, sought to anaesthetise himself with a slightly less-contentious drug. But Drain Lowe never became a 'hopeless piss artist' like his father-in-law, the actor Louis Thatcher, of whom we shall learn a little more in the Appendix.

When the war ended in September 1945, Drain was stationed at RAF Blyton in Lincolnshire, and the following year was despatched to posts in Malta and Iraq. In June 1947, he was seconded to the Air Ministry, but he found the work tedious as it mainly involved training recruits at various air bases around the country.

In the summer of 1948, Pat fell pregnant with their second child. Inevitably, Drain was in the air at the time his son was born at the Rodney House Maternity Hospital in Walton-on-Thames, Surrey, on Thursday 24 March, 1949. The child became an immediate recipient of his family's customary middle name for its offspring and was christened Nicholas Drain Lowe.

Penny, now five years old, suddenly had a brother. 'I resented him bitterly for coming along,' she says, tongue slightly in cheek. 'I had been the centre of attention and suddenly there's bloody Nick in the way! I put a cushion over his face one day and sat on it, hoping to bump him off.'

Nick's pre-school years were spent in family quarters at RAF sites in East Anglia while Drain traversed the country in a Harvard NA-16, carrying out 'weather tests' for the Meteorological Office. Pat took charge of nurturing young Nick at home; if her own ambition of becoming a vocal starlet had been dashed by the Second World War, perhaps her son could live out her dreams.

Penny had shown no inclination towards music, but it was generally agreed that Nick had natural ability. His earliest memories are of listening to his mum's radio in the days before rock and roll, and hearing records by the likes of Danny Kaye, Frank Sinatra and Nat 'King' Cole. He remembers his mother as being 'theatrical and flamboyant, tactile'.

'Mum came from the wrong side of the tracks,' says Nick, 'whereas the old man had a semblance of a little polish. He had been to public school, Wellington, but not *the* Wellington. It was the duff one in Somerset.'

At the age of five, Nick was sent to Chinthurst, a primary school in Tadworth, Surrey, where his sister was also a pupil.

'Nick was a rather pretty child,' recalls Penny. 'Lots of blond hair, a chubby boy. I remember beating boys up on the common because they used to bully him. I often used to take them on, but Nick was too pretty for his own good. Not really pretty, but pretty compared to the rest of them. It was a golden age, but we were only there for a term or two.'

The year 1954 ended with the first milestone in Nick's musical life when his maternal grandmother, Blanche, bought him a toy ukulele for Christmas. Made of brown and cream-coloured plastic, its nylon strings were capable of producing mellifluous, Hawaiian tones, even in the hands of an amateur. But for Nick, who was still a small child, the instrument was essentially a prop. Although he was left-handed, it was his instinct to hold the instrument as a right-handed player would, with his left hand on the fret board – in the same manner as his future left-handed contemporaries Wilko Johnson, Joe Strummer and Elvis Costello.

'I never had to turn it upside-down or re-string it, but I couldn't actually play it. I posed with it.'

Although still an RAF officer, Drain's Air Ministry work was carrying him one step closer to civilian life. One faintly glamorous aspect of his job in the mid-1950s was that the RAF occasionally assisted filmmakers with the supply of planes for movies such as *The Dam Busters* and *Reach For The Sky*, but this was a hollow reward. During spells when he was required to work in London, he had to don a suit and bowler hat, and carry a rolled umbrella for the commute into town. Drain hated it and at the end of each day would pop into the licensed bar at Victoria Station for a pick-me-up or two as the train departures for Tadworth slipped by.

'When you think about it, it wasn't that long after the war,' Nick says. One minute he's bombing the Ruhr, and the next he's effectively a civilian. Some nights he would come in quite drunk, and would of course get grief off my mother. One evening – and I want to say I'd been left on my own for some reason although it's unlikely because I can only have been about six – the old man came back with three or four of his mates. They'd all punched out the tops of their bowler hats and conga'd into the house wearing them. Beers were produced and in no time the party was in full swing. I thought they were fantastic; they were really funny and made a great fuss of me.

'One of them was hideously burned. He had no face, no nose, little ears, no eyelids, no hair and no fingers either, just stumps. He spotted my little plastic ukulele and said, "I used to be good on this." I can see him now in his comedy bowler, picking it up and getting a decent tune out of it – something like "Show Me The Way To Go Home". They all joined in and it made a great impression on me, this poor, burned bomber guy, playing my ukulele. Mum appeared at some point and of course read Dad the riot act. "This is not on, making all this noise, waking up the neighbours," and finally, "I bet you haven't eaten anything." Dad came out with the immortal line, which forever became a family joke, "It's all right, don't worry about me, there's a spam sandwich in every half pint!"'

In June 1955, Drain took Nick to the Derby, which father and son reached on foot, walking the two miles from their home to the Epsom Downs racecourse. Nick's abiding memory of the event was not the world-famous horse race, but the appearance of 'Prince Monolulu', the omnipresent, gaudily dressed racing tipster, renowned for his cry: 'I gotta horse!' Considered for many decades to be 'the most famous black man in Britain', Monolulu's theatricality certainly made an impression on six-year-old Nick, as would an unrelated yet somehow complementary primeval yell from the family radio set.

Awopbopaloobop Alopbamboom!

CHAPTER 2

Two-way Family Favourites

Little Richard's 'Tutti Frutti' started 1956 with a bang.

Rock and roll was about to cause quite a commotion in the Lowe household, an environment that was otherwise accustomed to the sound of Doris Day or novelty records such as 'The Ballad Of Davy Crockett'. Nick recalls that whenever 'Tutti Frutti' came on the radio his mother would be horrified: 'It was certainly a lot blacker experience than she'd ever had before.'

But for Drain the year would be remembered for something rather more dramatic than the outbreak of rock and roll. Following the respite of the immediate post-war era, during which Europe was chiefly concerned with the rebuilding of lives and communities, the wider world had become more dangerous than ever. The Cold War, between the powers in the Western bloc and those in the East, was the permanent backdrop, and the Suez Crisis of 1956 – brought about by Egypt's President Gamal Nasser being intent on nationalising the Suez Canal – was the powder keg.

Nasser's ambitions were regarded as the single greatest threat to world peace and, as tension mounted in the Middle

East, the RAF was already on permanent alert before the Suez Crisis turned into an armed conflict in October. In Jordan, the young King Hussein was in the process of asserting his country's independence by distancing it from the slightest whiff of British interference. Under a 1948 treaty, Britain had been allowed to retain air bases in the region in return for training and subsidising the Arab Legion security force. But Hussein didn't want his people to think that Britain was pulling his strings. In March 1956, he dispensed with the services of the prominent British commander of the Arab Legion, Lieutenant General John Bagot Glubb (known locally as 'Glubb Pasha'). Hussein's supporters rejoiced, but calm in the region had to be maintained. Britain offered to provide RAF support in the interests of protecting the king from terrorist attacks and possible assassination.

When Hussein eventually accepted help, RAF Group Captain Geoffrey Drain Lowe was already on the spot, having been released from the Air Ministry the previous November. In his crisp RAF uniform decorated with numerous medal ribbons, and his chubby, confident face and handlebar moustache gleaming in the Jordanian sunlight, Drain commanded the unit that would oversee Hussein's security.

'Papa went ahead, and Mama and I followed on, after he was ensconced,' recalls Nick. 'That was always the way it went, we didn't all just turn up. There's a lot of work for the wife because they've got to unpack and organise the house. Two-and-a-half years later, you've got to pack it all up again and move down the road.'

In the spring of 1956, Pat and Nick joined Drain in Jordan, while Penny was sent to boarding school in England.

'Penny and I were a bit competitive. She was kind of jealous of me, I think, and she had good reason to be. She was farmed out very early to boarding school and I was with Dad. It was great being in Jordan at that age, fantastic, at the arse end of British involvement. We lived in what felt like a palace and were waited on hand and foot. They didn't seem like servants to me, because I was real good friends with all the cooks and the guys who helped my old man.

'King Hussein had been pulled out of Sandhurst double quick and sent back to Jordan to stabilise the country. Drain was given the job of making himself available to dispense advice when necessary on matters of protocol et cetera. He was to keep an eye on the lad in a semi-paternal role and make sure he was OK. To this end, Hussein was a frequent visitor to the house, which was an overgrown bungalow at the top of a hill overlooking the city of Amman. That's where the camp was, a runway and two squadrons of Venoms, I think. If I went back there now, our old house would probably look quite modest, but at the time it seemed like a palace.

'It was quite a treat when the King turned up. There would be an armoured car fore and aft, with him in a car in the middle. The Arab army soldiers would let me climb up onto the armoured car and fiddle around with the machine gun. There was a large veranda in front of the house and I can remember Hussein pushing my Dinky toys up and down it to me. He would often come to see my dad and they'd disappear into a room and have a chat about something. Ma used to say he visited because when he was at Sandhurst he'd got a taste for pork sausages and ham sandwiches, which of course being a good Muslim he was not supposed to have. But he could get 'em round at ours! He'd drop by for a sausage sarnie.

'On Sunday afternoons, when there was hardly any air traffic, they used to have a sports-car club. Some of the officers had cars like frogeye Sprites, TR2s and Austin-Healeys, and they would do time trials racing round the perimeter track. The old man was dead keen on this. He would be the timekeeper. It was a nice afternoon out. Hussein used to come up there with a fleet of Mercedes gull-wing 300SLs in gunmetal grey. He'd have these playboy mates with him, Monte Carlo style – you can imagine what it was like. He would race his pals and of course they'd invariably let him win, but he was actually a pretty good driver. The Sprites and the Triumphs didn't stand a chance, but no one cared.

'The Jaguar D-type car had won the Le Mans twenty-four-hour race about three years in a row and Jaguar presented Hussein with their new model, the XK140. This example had a D-type racing engine in it, not only that but this one was sprayed bright red and had tablecloth-white leather upholstery, white carpets, spoke wheels, a real 1950s, unbelievable thing.

'When Hussein took delivery of the Jaguar, he didn't like it as much as his Mercedes 300SL, so he decided to hold a raffle for the entire foreign community; embassy people, military advisors, government drones, aid workers and so on who were there at the time. Every item in the raffle was an up-to-the-minute, top-of-the-range mod con – a stereogram, a Grundig tape recorder, a golden hostess trolley and an electric toaster for all I know. And the top prize was the Jaguar. It was won by three old nursing sisters but they didn't want it so they gave it back to Hussein. This is where my story creaks a bit, but family lore has it as follows:

'One evening I heard the familiar sound of armoured cars labouring up the hill. I was mucking around in the front garden. I looked over the wall and sure enough saw the first armoured car come around the corner, followed by the bright red Jag driven by Hussein, with another armoured car right behind it. They pulled up and the King got out; he went in to see the old man, emerged about ten minutes later, jumped into another car and off they all went, leaving the Jag behind. The old man always said rather jokingly that Hussein charged him a pound for it, a token. I don't know about that, but Dad didn't have a car for the Sunday afternoon car club, so Hussein just laid it on him – partly because he liked him, I suppose, but also so that the playboy racers and his Mercedes had something a bit tastier to race against round the peri-track. They used to have these time trials, the Jaguar and the Mercedes, and sometimes Drain would win and sometimes he wouldn't. It was the most incredible motor, driving round that runway, just gunning it, but I think my VW Golf is faster, and it can certainly stop a whole lot quicker.'

Because Drain was the commanding officer, Nick realised he had a responsibility not to embarrass his father. 'I felt that quite strongly. If I did blot my copybook, Mama would say, "Do you realise how bad this makes your father look?" But I loved the fact that I was an RAF kid. I understood the way things were in that life, living in married quarters, as they called it. It was transient, and there were things you could and couldn't do. There was a little sub-code of how you should behave – like you do in everyday life, but in that closed military world there's another set of rules that come along, largely unwritten.'

As the Suez Crisis intensified, the families of British servicemen were evacuated from Jordan and, on 30 October 1956, Nick and Pat came back to England. 'We had to leave Amman pronto,' remembers Nick. 'Papa had to stay on at Mafraq, "under canvas" on a pretty hideous airstrip in the desert.'[2]

While Drain was 'sent to the desert to beat off the foes', Nick and his mother stayed with Blanche in Cameford Court, a pre-war art deco block of flats in Streatham, south London.

'Mama didn't really wish to return to those roots. It was quite cramped. Blanche's sister, my Great Auntie Kath, lived in another block across the road and was married to a policeman named

Hugh Blair. They had a budgerigar that Kath taught to speak, and even though Kath and Blanche had poshed themselves up a bit, the budgie had a working-class accent. He could even speak his address [adopts high pitched Cockney voice]: "Binkie Blair – Eight Hayes Court – Streatham – London!"'

Blanche's own theatrical career, and that of her late husband Louis, was the Lowe family's connection to showbusiness, and Blanche takes much of the blame for introducing Nick to the little plastic ukulele that would see its fair share of reflections in the full-length mirror. But it was Pat who introduced him to the songs of the popular crooners on the radio, and encouraged his musical leanings by showing him some simple chords. Fussed over and encouraged by his mother and grandmother in such claustrophobic conditions, Nick soon gained the confidence to entertain.

A little later on, some ten-inch LPs started to appear, by jazz-inclined singers such as Peggy Lee and Anita O'Day. Nick devoured these records and learnt all the songs, soaking up the accented rhythms and big-band sounds. Also among Pat's collection were two ten-inch albums by Tennessee Ernie Ford, containing songs such as 'Shotgun Boogie' and 'Fatback Louisiana USA'. Nick was enthralled.

'I'm not even sure if "Sixteen Tons" had come out at that point,' says Nick of the Ford discs. 'I had no idea it was country and western, but it was very strange, Californian country and western with all these jazz influences, fabulous music. I still love it.'

This is the point at which Nick's musical leanings were informed and enriched, and it coincided with the UK hit parade being shaken up by the two-pronged assault of Lonnie Donegan and Elvis Presley. Donegan, the Brit, yearned to recreate the sound of his American heroes, and with a cheap guitar for accompaniment came extremely close. One particular disc that captivated Donegan was Lonnie Johnson's 1948 US hit, 'Tomorrow Night'. There were few white singers on the planet that strove to emulate musicians such as Johnson, but Donegan was in exalted company. Some 4,400 miles away in Memphis, Tennessee, the young Elvis Presley was hooked on precisely the same blues ballad, employing it to serenade his sweetheart, Dixie Locke.

Elvis and Lonnie were independently inventing white rock and roll, and in a crucial pincer movement they captured the imagination of Britain's aspiring young musicians. But while the sexier Presley became the role model that launched a thousand hips, Donegan's skiffle – or 'Teddy boy jazz' – was the great enabler. Lonnie inspired Hank Marvin, John Lennon, Van Morrison and, indeed, Master Lowe, who caught the bug even though he was still in short trousers.

'It struck me how lucky I was to have that influence at that age. Lonnie had that attitude – he was kind of ugly, not a pin-up – but even though I was seven years old I thought he was way cooler than Dennis Lotis [a featured vocalist with the Ted Heath Orchestra who dabbled in rock and roll lite].'

By 1957, Cyprus had become the RAF's new Middle East headquarters. Once a crown colony of the British Empire, the Mediterranean island had a complex and troubled history. The United Kingdom had had its arm around Cypriot shoulders since the Cyprus Convention of 1878, following a discreet deal with the Ottoman Empire. Now, thousands of British servicemen were being sent out to the region to help quell the troubles brought about by the rise of EOKA (Ethniki Organosis Kyprion Agoniston), a nationalist paramilitary organisation headed by Colonel George Grivas, whose aim it was to disrupt British colonial influence and promote the union of Cyprus with Greece.

On 16 May, Drain left Jordan and relocated to Nicosia with 'The King's Car' in tow. A fortnight later he returned briefly to England and in the Queen's Birthday Honours on 4 June was appointed a Commander of the Order of the British Empire (CBE) in recognition of his Air Force work during and after the Second World War. On 27 June, the newly decorated Drain recorded in his log book that he was accompanied by 'Pat and Nickie' on a flight from Southend to Cyprus, via Malta.

The recently constructed RAF airbase at Akrotiri was under threat of Egyptian bombing raids in the wake of Suez and, although Nick didn't realise it at the time, his father was there as part of British Bomber Command, ready to fly combat missions if the need arose. Although a threatened air raid by the Egyptians failed to materialise, an event was about to occur that both Nick and Penny believe was the beginning of the end for their father's distinguished flying career. It was the afternoon of 27 November 1957.

'Drain had to go into Limassol for something-or-other and I went with him in the Jag,' says Nick. 'On our return, arriving at the main gate, the guard waved us straight through because he recognised the rotund, middle-aged gentleman with a handlebar moustache sitting at the wheel of a pillar-box red Jaguar. Drain was a stickler for procedure when it came to producing ID papers and the like, so the poor sentry received quite a bollocking for his oversight. Whenever I witnessed this sort of thing I was always profoundly embarrassed because I knew quite a lot of the young soldiers involved. They were teenagers doing National Service, and they were always nice to me – possibly because I was the CO's son – though I never really picked up on any of that. They were kind and a bit lonely. I didn't know this chap, but he got a right earful. Dad said, "You shouldn't just whisk me through because you recognise the car! You should ask me for my papers!" While he was in mid-flow there was suddenly a bloody great explosion in the distance. EOKA guerrillas had bombed an aircraft hangar. They blew up a Venom bomber and some Canberras. That unfortunate incident probably put paid to the old man making any further progress. With his blameless record, he should have gone on to achieve high office, but it was not to be. It was some kind of inside job they said, but he was the station master and it all stopped with him.'

Drain stayed in Cyprus for a further fifteen months, returning home by sea in February 1959. The trigger for his CBE was thought to have been his sterling achievements and leadership qualities in Jordan – after all, King Hussein had survived the troubles – but the honour had been dampened by the EOKA guerrilla attack at Akrotiri. A return to the dreaded Air Ministry beckoned. At forty-four, Drain's valiant work was almost done. What now for Nick's hero, barely into middle age?

CHAPTER 3

The Chord Master

While in Cyprus, Nick's parents gave him a real ukulele banjo. The four-stringed, round-bodied instrument was certainly a step up from the plastic ukulele Blanche had given him two years earlier and, although not a toy, it was supplied with a handy accessory known as a 'Chord Master'. This device could be attached to the banjo's neck and had a number of buttons that dampened the strings in various configurations, allowing the user to simply press one button to produce the required chord. This left Nick free to concentrate on strumming rhythmically with his right hand as he changed chords with his left index finger.

It didn't take him too long to consider the Chord Master 'a bad look', although it did come with a few chord diagrams, which were quickly figured out. He soon ditched the gadget and suddenly everything came into focus. His mother could play the guitar in a rudimentary form, although she would use only four of its six strings.

'She used to forget about the two thick ones, but nonetheless off the two of us would go. "Bring A Little Water Sylvie", "Rock Island Line", "Jack O' Diamonds", all those old Lonnie Donegan songs. Do you remember "Ol' Riley" from the *Skiffle Session* EP? And his version of "Frankie And Johnny" – it's like James Brown! Lonnie was the nearest you could get to rock and roll on the BBC British Forces Network.'

Like countless RAF families, the Lowes moved from one country to another as their head of the family was shifted between strategic posts. 'I thought my father was on the run from the police until I was about twelve,' cracks Penny. The British government did however acknowledge that uprooting the families of servicemen, before they'd even had a chance to acclimatise, played havoc with their children's education and consequently provided financial help with boarding school fees so that officers could be re-stationed at short notice without disrupting the schooling of their offspring. In April 1958, after four years of attending a variety of infant and primary schools in far-flung locations, Nick was sent to Suffolk to board at the Abbey, the preparatory school for Woodbridge.

'I was almost ten years old. I wish I could say "almost nine" – it sounds a little more pathetic. I'm embarrassed to admit that I schmoozed my way into Woodbridge. I'd been at army schools in Jordan and Cyprus that only operated from eight in the morning until midday, after which it got too hot. When I returned to England, although I could read well enough I might as well have been the village idiot in every other respect. Even though they specialised in forces' kids like me, I wasn't remotely academic enough to gain a place at Woodbridge. But I had been taught very well how to work a room.

'My mother claimed – though she was often prone to exaggeration – that following the interview at the school we were invited into the headmaster's cottage for a cup of tea. I, by all accounts, went immediately to work on his wife, offering such drivel as, "What a charming home. Tell me, did you choose the wallpaper yourself?" Then, glancing out the window, "And SUCH an enchanting view – it must be glorious in the spring." All this old flannel that I'd learned from dishing out the tea and cakes at Pat's bridge parties. Anyway, it worked. I got in because I was so super suede shoe.

'When I started at Woodbridge, I was desperately homesick for about a week. But then it stopped, as if someone had flicked a switch, and I never felt that way again.'

Armed with his banjo and the makings of a repertoire, Nick and an imaginary friend would spend all of their free time anywhere that provided a bit of peace and quiet. He confesses: 'I used to play the bloody thing every minute of the day.'

Nick was less keen when a real friend would turn up; school chum Roger Buswell remembers: 'I would get to the Abbey early in the morning on the bus, being a "dayboy", and Nick would be in the library practising on the banjo. As a boarder, he had access to the library out of hours and that's where he would be, on his own. All the breakfast stuff would have been cleared away, so he maybe had a good hour before school started. If I disturbed him, Nick would get annoyed and say, "Don't watch me." He was a really nice bloke, but he could get a bit annoyed if he wanted to be left in peace.'

During Nick's time at the Abbey, a number of significant events occurred in the world of popular music. These included the deaths of Buddy Holly and Eddie Cochran, both of whom would garner a loyal following among music-obsessed British schoolboys. The old cliché that rock and roll died the moment Elvis went into the army is repeatedly trotted out, supported by stories of Little Richard having entered the ministry and Chuck Berry being in jail, but many overlook the fact that the turn of that decade saw the emergence of Sam Cooke, Roy Orbison and Dion; the songs that emanated from New York's Brill Building providing hits for the Drifters and the Shirelles; Phil Spector and his 'Wall of Sound'; Detroit's Tamla Motown label; and the arrival of the Beach Boys – in other words, some significant advances on the music's early roots. In Britain, TV's *Oh Boy!* launched the careers of Cliff Richard, Marty Wilde and Billy Fury, all of whom imitated the American model with aplomb. It was the era that made the single greatest impression on Nick, and formed the basis of his musical taste and vocal style.

In September 1960, aged eleven, Nick went up from the Abbey to the main Woodbridge School, and was placed in School House, form 1B. The 'streaming' of pupils, based on academic ability, would not commence until year three, and being placed in either the A or B stream at the start of year one was 'arbitrary', or so the boys were told. Despite this supposed democracy, those placed in the B stream were largely given B-stream teachers and were constantly reminded of their status. 'One member of staff took delight in telling those of us in 1B that we were the lowest form of life in the senior school,' recalls one of Nick's contemporaries, Steve Hampson. 'It didn't bother us a jot though.'

It was here that Nick encountered headmaster Eric Ayres, an extreme disciplinarian who also taught Latin. This was a particularly difficult subject for Nick and his form mates, few of whom were academically inclined and 'sweated buckets' whenever Ayres swept into the room.

'Ayres was somebody you did not mess with,' says former pupil, Graham Chignall. 'I sat next to Nick and we tried to remain under the radar, as they say. Nick was left-handed, and when it came to handwriting he had a most unusual style, holding the pen above the line he was writing, in a long, loping manner. In those days, we used real pen and ink, so he would have had to wait until the ink dried before moving on down to the next line.'

Chignall also remembers French lessons during that first year: 'To encourage our appreciation of the French language and the history of France, we had to write an essay on an important French event. Nick presented a story on how the French got kicked out of Algeria by the FLN, a freedom movement, and how the Foreign Legion were beaten. Needless to say, that did not go down well, but Nick's ability to put pen to paper had already started.'

Lowe, Chignall, the Hampson brothers and many others had found themselves at Woodbridge because it was a boarding school that had a history of accepting the sons of senior RAF officers and, of course, the fees this attracted. The school also took in a lot of dayboys, who outnumbered the boarders and were generally more studious. This created very much a 'them and us' atmosphere.

Former Woodbridge boarder Tim Jenkins asks: 'Was it that we were jealous of the dayboys because they went home and had tea? Possibly. Were they jealous of us because, although they may have been keen on sport, they didn't have to come to school for sport on Saturday mornings? Possibly not, but the dayboys were the clever ones. They were more likely to go to university than us, but we got more involved in the activities, such as music, and maybe a dance at the weekends, with the local girls' school.'

As far as hobbies and pastimes were concerned, pop music, maybe with a little jazz or skiffle thrown in, was even bigger than soccer, competing only with 'the opposite sex' as the top extracurricular distraction. Exposure to the latest records was confined to the occasional TV show such as *Juke Box Jury*, viewed on School House's old brown Bakelite set with 'a very intermittent aerial', or listening to Radio Luxembourg on transistor radios that had to be smuggled into the dormitory after lights out. One of the biggest hits of the year, in fact the nation's number one at the start of Nick's first term at the main school, was 'Apache' by the Shadows, a record that was singularly responsible for selling more electric guitars in Britain than any other.

In the wake of the Shadows every school in Britain would boast its own beat group and Woodbridge would spawn more beat groups than most, often with Nick Lowe as the driving force. He had already observed from the side-lines that, however fragile a group's musical ability, its members would always be an irresistible focus of attention for most of the young girls in the audience. Thus, he wasted no time in forming his first combo. Nameless, they made their debut at the 1960 school Christmas concert.

'Nick decided he was going to be on the bill,' remembers Graham Chignall. 'He recruited myself on an old army side drum and Chris Haines on tea-chest bass to complete his musical trio. He had figured out the songs because he was "the lead singer" and the only one who really knew what we were going to be doing onstage. He didn't waste a moment and with his usual "Let's hit it, boys!" went straight into the first number. We played "Lively", the Lonnie Donegan hit, and for our finale, "When The Saints Go Marching In".'[3]

Nick was seen by many of his contemporaries as undoubtedly possessed with natural ability when it came to musical entertainment. Crucially, he also had an ear to the ground, always listening out for new developments in pop, helped by the American records he heard and digested at those overseas air bases. Around 1961, this translated into the dawn of the commercial folk scene in the USA and artists such as the Highwaymen, Peter, Paul and Mary, and the emerging Bob Dylan.

'I liked the Kingston Trio. I thought they were great and we did some of their things. One was called "The M.T.A.", about the bloke who was forever doomed to ride the subway.' Nick laughs: 'We also did "The Streets of Laredo".'

Although Nick was musically influential at Woodbridge and some would hold him in awe, he was average in class.

'I wasn't very academic at all. I was only really interested in music. I was pretty good at English; I just had a facility for it, and we had a couple of good teachers. Unfortunately, I can't remember my English teacher's name [thought to be Gary "Duck" Symmonds], but I can see him in my mind's eye. He wasn't very good at keeping order, but I seemed to be able to home in on him through the racket of missiles flying across the room. He interested me. And Proctor Robinson was a real character, like he'd stepped out of a play. He was extremely effete with a posh accent and he used to dress like a total dandy with bright green tweed suits and yellow waistcoats, but he never taught me. He didn't like the cut of my jib. There were some good teachers there, but unfortunately I had an inability to pass exams and apply myself, a real inability.'

In sport and outdoor activities, Nick was a bit of a buffoon. Tim Jenkins recalls: 'We were sent off to an army camp somewhere and there was Nick – a bit like a character in *Dad's Army* – never quite the tidiest member of the platoon, hair sprouting from under the beret, one sock down to his ankle, being shown how to fire a bazooka. He was a sort of cheeky chappie, slightly two fingers up to authority. I wouldn't say he lacked confidence.'

At twelve, Nick joined the school's Combined Cadet Force[4] and remembers being attracted mainly by the accoutrements: 'I was in the marching band, because you got to wear white gaiters, which I rather liked, and a little brass drum on your shoulder, so it was all about the look. And you paraded through the town on Armistice Day. I used to like the admiring gazes of the town girls. I played drums. You used to have to start on the cymbals, which I thought was a bit naff, and then you got a drum when one became available.'

*

Drain was now stationed in Germany with Bomber Command, where the RAF's V-bombers were being prepared for Quick Reaction Alert as the Cold War was gripping an anxious public's imagination. Nick would fly out to see his parents during his school holidays and remembers making his way to the airport, aged eleven or twelve.

'I would take the tube out to Ruislip Gardens and go to the guard house at RAF Northolt to get the mail plane out to Germany. I would have written instructions from my dear mama, and I would have to say: "I'm here to catch the 6.30 out to Wildenrath."

'On one occasion, it was Sean Tyla and I in the little twin-engine plane with all these sacks of mail. It was good fun. Sean's old man was in the army, stationed at Rheindahlen air base. It was like a town, with masses of married quarters. There were a couple of trips like that. Later they would get me on a BEA Viscount.'

Sean Tyla later became a professional musician and songwriter. He formed one of the early 'pub rock' groups, Ducks Deluxe, and later signed to Stiff Records alongside Nick.

At Rheindahlen, Nick and Sean, three years his senior, assembled a skiffle group in which Nick played his banjo, but with one string missing. They named themselves 'The Four Just Men', after the popular TV detective series, and played at the 'Teenagers Club' on the air base.

'Nick was technically barred from the club because he was too young,' recalls Tyla. 'But he was tall and looked older. He donned a pair of his father's sunglasses and we managed to sneak him in completely unnoticed. I believe we played "Michael Row The Boat Ashore" at least four times.'

In Germany, Nick also witnessed the parties that Drain and Pat would throw at their house, which had a cellar bar, 'a bit like a pub'. It was at these events that a precocious Nick was encouraged by Pat to perform whenever the opportunity arose.

'My folks were very sociable. Whenever they had parties, which was quite often, I was frequently wheeled out to do a few tunes. I loved it, crazy about it. In fact, I couldn't get enough. But thankfully one lesson they did instil in me was "leave them wanting more". Especially the old man – he would always give me "the look" when it was time to quit. One Christmas, about twenty years ago, my father came down from the attic, bent double under the weight of a 1950s Grundig tape recorder the size of a small family car. It used to go incredibly slowly, which meant he could load lots of his favourites onto it with little or no "fi" – things like Xavier Cugat's "Latin Holiday", or Gianni Marzocchi's "Espresso". He once told me that Chubby Checker's "Limbo Rock" was the best record ever made and he couldn't understand why anyone would ever bother to make another one. On reflection, I think he might have had a point.

'Anyway, he put this tape on and it was of me aged about eight going through my Lonnie Donegan repertoire. I had no idea that they were all Big Bill Broonzy and Lead Belly songs. As far as I was concerned I was just impersonating the top pop artist of the day and like thousands of other aspiring kids of my generation I found that these tunes were easy to play. The tape was interspersed with my mother compèring. She sounded like the Queen. In fact, she made the Queen sound like Barbara Windsor, as I recall. "And now, Nick will perform another favourite by Lonnie Donegan," and I'd sing "Bring A Little Water Sylvie", or "Jack O' Diamonds". There was much hilarity around the Christmas tree that year prompted by a squeaky-voiced nipper singing those grown-up songs. I obviously didn't have the faintest idea what they were about, or even care. What strikes me now is that I am still more or less doing that kind of music – Lonnie lives on!'

As an alternative to visiting Germany in the early 1960s, Nick would occasionally spend his half-term holidays in Hornchurch, Essex, where he would be sent to stay with his grandfather, Albert, now a widower in his seventies.

'Albert dressed like an officer – ramrod back, hair gassed back, a handsome bloke, meticulous and extremely well-dressed. He had a number of fairly young girls he used to go out with. He took me to a place in Ilford, The Room at the Top, a cabaret club over a furniture store, with his bird, and me in my school uniform. It was like a floorshow. "Good evening Mesdames et Messieurs." A table would be carried to the front of the stage, like in those old films. I was about thirteen. "I Remember You" by Frank Ifield was the big hit record. I used to get on all right with Albert, actually. He was quite stern, but nice to me.'

In October 1962, world news was dominated by the Cuban missile crisis, but Nick and his school friends were more concerned with the Cuban heel crisis. Fascinated by the latest male fashions, they coveted Italian-style tonic mohair suits with 'bum-freezer' jackets, dramatically tapered trousers, and 'winklepicker' shoes with side laces, but such attire was way beyond their reach. Nick had to make do with his school blazer on social occasions.

That autumn saw the arrival at Woodbridge of two new boys, both a couple of years older than Nick. Brinsley Ernst Pieter Schwarz, from the Weald of Kent, was a disciple of the Shadows and brought with him an electric guitar and amplifier, while Barry Landeman, from Cambridge, was a student of classical piano. They would both become significant musical allies. Brinsley was quick to form a school group, the Democrats, with Martin Hampson (bass) and Chris Webb (drums). Barry would listen to them practising in the school hall.

'I went in and said hello,' says Barry. 'I introduced myself to Brinsley and we got talking. My piano lessons were awful because the teacher was useless and there was only one piano in the entire school. I got pretty fed up with it, and when Brinsley and I started talking about forming a group, I offered to play the drums. I didn't have any drums but, at some point, Nick similarly drifted in and became attached. At the time, he was playing banjo. I was quite impressed, but obviously banjo didn't fit in. I think he said he was going to play the bass, but he didn't have a bass! It was all a bit off the cuff, but we'd decided we were going to form a band. After Christmas, I came back with a drum and a cymbal, and not long after that Nick turned up with a bass guitar he'd apparently made from scratch and gradually it came to fruition.'

Legend has it that Nick made his own bass guitar – loosely based on the futuristic 'Vox Phantom' – in Mr Johnson's woodwork lessons, during which other pupils were content to construct pipe holders and bookshelves. But the truth is that Nick had persuaded another boy to make the instrument for him. As he confessed to the *East Anglian Daily Times* some fifty years later: 'I managed to coerce someone who was good at it to make me a bass in the woodwork shop. You had to tune it with a pair of pliers, but it worked!'

Until such time as Nick acquired his prestigious Hofner Violin Bass, as favoured by Beatle Paul McCartney, his DIY instrument would suffice, even if he had to carry the pliers around in his pocket.

The early weeks of 1963 represented a watershed in UK beat music when the Fender-driven, instrumental sound of the Shadows was supplanted overnight by the vocal prowess of the Beatles. Fashions changed too, as the gravity-defying hairstyles of the rock and roll era gave way to floppy fringes. Nick and his group quickly adapted to the new mood and, with the addition of Phil Hall on rhythm guitar, they sought to master the Mersey sound. Vocalists were added, including Mike 'Eddie' Hollingsworth, who introduced songs from his 1950s rock and roll heroes such as Cochran and Holly, and Paul Woodcraft, who brought in some slightly more bluesy material.

As the boys moved up the school they were given a little more freedom to explore their surroundings on foot or bicycle, allowing them to indulge in typical teenage pursuits. Smoking cigarettes 'behind the bike sheds' was commonplace, while trips to the local cinema remained a rare weekend treat, as the nearest town was Ipswich, just nine miles away but an hour by bus. There was also some relaxation in the guidelines governing school uniform and appearance. 'Sixth formers were allowed to walk along with one hand in their pocket,' says Tim Jenkins. 'Prefects could put both hands in their pockets.'

There was naturally a rebellion against these petty rules and authority in general, at precisely the point where teenagers were starting to flex their muscle. Men's hair grew longer, aided and abetted by the Rolling Stones. Music was still 'ace' and by 1964 it was all about 'R&B', due mainly to the emergence of the Stones. Nick, however, adopted a preference for the more obscure Downliners Sect, whose debut album was released that year. 'We knew that one inside out,' he recalls. 'I learnt all my Bo Diddley tunes from them . . . black roll-neck sweaters.'

'The first time I recall Nick playing the bass, "in concert" so to speak, was at School Entertainments,' says fellow pupil David Hipkins. 'His band was called "R.A.B.L.", which stood for Rhythm & Blues Limited. Typically, the stage curtains would open up for each act, but I recall Nick and his group did it differently, walking in from the back of the school hall, through the audience, and onto the stage, talking out loud in fake American accents. It was quite an entrance – perhaps this was "Nick the showman" beginning his journey!'

Nick credits Chris Buisseret, an older Woodbridge pupil whose father taught mathematics at the school, with introducing him to the musical sounds coming out of America and showing him a few new guitar chords. He remembers Buisseret as being 'a fantastic guitar player who could play country and western'.

'Chris might well have taught me a couple of chords. I was in awe of him, but he was rather disdainful of us. I remember one day he came in the room – he was a prefect, quite a senior cove – and we were playing records by groups like the Fourmost, and he said, "You still listening to this stuff? This is nowhere!"'

Nick and his ever-evolving crew frequently changed the name of their group, eventually settling on 'Sound 4+1' or, when two singers were deployed, 'Sound 4+2' ('a joke-let'). In the school summer holiday of 1964, Sound 4+1 played in Germany. Nick had already gone out on the BEA Viscount to join his family at RAF Rheindahlen, where Pat was conveniently on the entertainments committee and arranged for the group to appear at a number of the air base's venues over a two-week period. The other group members – Brinsley, Barry, Phil and Mike, accompanied by Brinsley's parents and sister – made the journey to Rheindahlen, via Holland, in the Schwarz family's Commer camper van.

'It was completely bonkers,' says Barry. 'When I look at it now and think about what our parents allowed us to do at that age, it was crazy. There were seven of us in the van, and our equipment and the luggage.'

Nick's own family transport would change before too long. 'The old man had Hussein's Jaguar all though my childhood,' remembers Nick. 'He shipped it back to England from Jordan, then took it to Cyprus, but with all the shooting going on at that time, driving around in such a distinctive car made him a bit of a target. By the time he took the car out to Germany, it was starting to look a bit tatty. It was still magnificent in one sense, but I think it had been rather badly re-sprayed and one wing didn't quite match – that used to get on his nerves. Then one day he suddenly announced that he'd sold it because he felt a bit of a goon in it. "I'm too old," he said, so he sold it to a young fellow down the road.'[5]

By now, music had taken quite a hold on many of the Woodbridge pupils, who started to behave 'like caged animals, crazy for music'. The school had always encouraged concerts and recitals but weren't quite prepared for the way in which certain events were being hijacked; the School Entertainments seasonal concert was now almost exclusively an R&B revue.

'We got more and more involved with it,' adds Barry. 'There was one occasion where I produced the entire show and as a way of getting onstage we would appear under different names and play different things. Rhythm & Blues Limited probably came up through one of those. Nick and I once called ourselves the Dylivans, with denim caps, and played the Donovan song "Catch The Wind", with improvised lyrics all about having prunes for breakfast.'

Raising money for charity was often a good excuse for putting on a school show, sometimes with a pseudo-intellectual slant. 'A History of Music – a concert in aid of the Oxfam relief fund' – took the form of two boys playing piano and cello, presenting 'Classical Composers', while a further thirty-six pupils presented between them: 'Negro Spirituals'; 'Rhythm and Blues'; 'Trad'; and with a spoken contribution from one Nicholas Lowe – 'East Coast Jazz'.

In early 1965, Sound 4+1 changed their name to the Pad, based on a sign that hung from the door of the school study occupied by Mike Hollingsworth and Paul Woodcraft. Reminded of this, Nick exclaimed, 'Paul Woodcraft and the Pad! It's a really cool name. I quite like it – in fact I think "the Pad" should make a comeback.' In London, where the Pad surely aspired to perform, the club boom was at its height, with the Marquee and the Flamingo being among the most prominent venues. Nick and his pals were magnetised by the capital and they paid a tentative visit during a half-term holiday.

'We basically cruised the coffee bars in Carnaby Street and Wardour Street,' recalls David Hipkins. 'Soho seemed pretty edgy to us, but it all seems painfully innocent now. I do recall meeting up with Nick and Crispin Gillbard, who was also in School House, and the three of us getting into our first strip club for the princely sum of five shillings, which was quite a lot of money back then. We were into the Mod scene, but let's face it – it's difficult for public school boys to carry off the Rocker/Greaser thing.

'Nick was certainly a ladies' man. I have a memory of his dad collecting him from School House after he was caught by one of our masters behind the cricket pavilion, trousers around his ankles, with that particular master's daughter! It is not my place to identify the young lady in question, but I think Drain threw Nick's identity bracelet out the car window as they drove away. Perhaps my memory is somewhat coloured here, but given the nature of our boarding houses being stuffed with randy, pre- and post-adolescent school boys, this episode was certainly held in awe by most of us.'

By the summer of 1965, 'soul music' – as in James Brown, Otis Redding and Wilson Pickett – was making its way across the Atlantic. Barry Landeman remembers its impact on Nick: 'Brinsley and I still liked the Shadows and the Beatles and I suppose, by comparison, fairly middle-of-the-road stuff, but

Nick was a bit more edgy and I think he was probably the first of us to become interested in the stuff coming out of Stax and Tamla Motown.'

One of the last performances by the Pad was at a 'Beat Service' at the Landeman family's church in Cambridge. 'The trendy vicar had recruited us to perform religious pop songs to the congregation,' recalls Barry. 'We did an instrumental version of "Bésame Mucho" and Nick did the solo. We stuck it through Brinsley's reverb chamber and of course in the church it had this huge sound. It was a big moment for Nick to play the lead on his bass guitar. We were just trying things out, but of course we thought we were fantastic.'

Woodbridge was more a finishing school for quick-thinking under-achievers than a beacon of academic excellence, but it did produce some notable individuals who went on to make their mark in the world. As Nick would tell many of his old friends among the audience when he returned to the school in 2012 to play a fundraising concert, he knew he would never become a naval officer, or a great cricketer, or a captain of industry. 'But no matter,' he told us. 'Because I knew that when I left school I wanted only one thing – to become a rock and roll singer.'

PART TWO

Learning The Game

CHAPTER 4

Kippington Lodge

Nicholas Drain Lowe was more or less expelled from Wood-bridge towards the end of his final term. There had been earlier incidents and warnings. Nick's sister Penny recalls her mother being summoned to the school more than once to be told: 'Nicholas just won't work.' His results were abysmal and he failed all of his exams, although he had done quite well in English, perhaps based on his love of words and the ability to spin a yarn. Despite his academic failure he was extremely popular with pupils and masters alike, and is considered to have made a positive contribution to school life.

'I had an agreeable but undistinguished time at school,' says Nick. 'I spent most of it under the delusion that I was Jack the Lad and everyone loved me, but the reality was that I was a trappy show-off with a high opinion of himself. I was lazy and although – after a periodic strafing from Drain – I would attempt to buckle down and do some work, my interest in pop music and clothes would make sure that any new found academic zeal would not last long. After Drain died, I found my school reports among his papers. To my astonishment they all said in barely veiled terms,

"This child is hopeless . . . we can do nothing more for him . . . save your dough." He clearly decided to ignore this advice and I left at age sixteen without any qualifications.'

On 18 August 1965, Nick's grandfather died at the National Hospital for Neurology in Queen's Square, London. 'It was rather convenient,' says Nick of Albert's death, with a quip echoed more-or-less verbatim by Penny, as if it were some long-standing family adage. Truth was, having lived for years in Royal Air Force accommodation, Albert's son, Drain, had never had to buy a house of his own, but he was now on the verge of retirement. When he inherited his father's chalet bungalow at 27 Great Nelmes Chase in Hornchurch, along with £8,467 in cash and piles of brand-new shirts and unopened shoeboxes, it enabled him to provide his family with a permanent home.

Penny, who by now was working in London, remembers Hornchurch as a 'ghastly' place to live: 'There were all these awful women who walked around in curlers all day until their husbands came home in the evening.' Nick, on the other hand, enjoyed the benefits of the location. He got a job as a shop assistant in nearby Romford at the Smart Weston male boutique, an 'old blokes' shop' that nevertheless stocked genuine Levi's shirts, which Nick remembers being 'as stiff as boards, like wearing a wardrobe'.

In the summer of 1966, the Lowe family left Hornchurch and bought Northend, an £11,000 detached house in Sarratt, Hertfordshire, where Drain and Pat had friends. Having left the RAF with almost four thousand flying hours under his belt, Drain settled into retirement. He was soon faced with reality, however; his RAF pension was inadequate if he aspired to maintain the lifestyle to which he had become accustomed. It was time to get a job. He had already been involved in the making of technical and training films while in the Air Force, and he knew a little about the process, but the RAF's film division had recently been taken over by the Army Kinema Corporation and there were no openings.

'He started a very bleak period where he searched for work,' remembers Penny. 'He was applying for jobs that he could have done in his sleep, like being an air traffic controller at some little airport. He was very correct and what he couldn't get over was not the fact that he didn't get the job, but that people wouldn't reply to his letters. It was a very grim time. He had a pension from the Air Force but it was barely enough to put real butter on the bread. Nick saw it more closely because I lived in London.'

Nick remembers his father getting quite depressed: 'A lot of the people he'd met when he was a bigwig in the Air Force, including media people and documentary crews, had said to him, "Drain, if you ever need a job, call me." And when he called them, he got a rude awakening as to the way that showbusiness operates. It was, "Who? Sorry, tell him I'm out." He had no idea of how that world works, or how cavalier they all are. Then he met a bloke in a pub.'

Said bloke was the BBC's Ray Millichope, editor of *Not Only . . . But Also* and, later, *Monty Python's Flying Circus*. Millichope liked Drain's outgoing personality and hired him in some vague PR capacity, but the job didn't last long.

'He had to go up to town every day, to Soho, and he told me he used to get completely rat-arsed at lunchtime, taking people out to chat them up, and he was turning into an alcoholic. But he used to get me lots of tickets to *Top of the Pops,* and other BBC programmes. I saw Jimi Hendrix record a session for *Pop Inn*. But dad couldn't do the job any more. He was getting too pissed and he didn't like showbiz folk, and all the brown-nosing and what-have-you. He came back home.'

While living at Sarratt, Nick became the archetypal teenage layabout. He would lie on the floor with his ear pressed up to the radiogram speaker as *The Exciting Wilson Pickett* blasted out. He also invited his friends round to hang out and meet his grandmother, the resilient Blanche. Now in her seventies – she would live until 1972, when she was seventy-nine – she had survived on casual work including a fairly recent stint as hat-check girl at Streatham Locarno.

'Blanche was a bit of an eighty-a-day girl, never without a cigarette on, carpet slippers, she spoke like a female Max Wall. When I met Max years later, he reminded me of Blanche. They looked and sounded the same.'

'Nick used to come home with all these eerie people,' remembers Penny. 'They were Mods, I suppose. They wore parkas and they'd go straight into my grandmother's room and the door would shut and they would lie about in her room with the bright orange walls, watching telly and smoking themselves to death. I thought they were all peculiar. I don't remember them playing any instruments.'

After a brief spell working in a Lyons cafeteria, to which he would cycle eleven miles daily to wash up, clear tables and 'push huge stacks of breaded plaice into the deep fat fryer', Nick enrolled at Cassio College in Watford, where he hoped to resit his English exams. It was September 1966 and 'soul music' was hot.

'With the enthusiastic encouragement of a small gang of Mod girls who were on the hairdressing course at Cassio College, I was properly introduced to soul and R&B music for the first time. I also had a friend in my class – an arch Mod called Colin Bayley – who would turn up to college whenever he felt like it, dressed to the nines and always carrying two or three new releases for me to hear. "I Spy For The FBI", "Function At The Junction",

"Twine Time", "With This Ring" and "Show Me" were a few of the titles he blasted the student common room Dansette with. I was hooked.

'The Mod scene I got into was strictly suburban and I rarely ventured up to the West End because I couldn't afford it. Instead we would frequent local venues like the Trade Union Hall in Watford and Burton's in Uxbridge to see great bands like Cliff Bennett & the Rebel Rousers, Jimmy James & the Vagabonds, or Ronnie Jones and the Q Set. Then things started to change, with groups like the Herd, the Move, John's Children and, most especially, the Creation, who some years later I produced a few tracks for. I also did a bit of singing with a band around that time, just youth club stuff, but it was time for me to shape up and try to get a job.'

Nick emerged from Cassio College with a modest O-level in English Language, just enough of a qualification in the 1960s to perhaps become a cub reporter. He discovered, however, there was a catch-22 situation; you couldn't be a reporter unless you were in the National Union of Journalists, and you couldn't be in the NUJ unless you were a journalist. The only way to get in was for someone to lift the fence up for you, so you could scuttle under. The person who 'lifted the fence up' for Nick was the then well-known broadcaster James Mossman, whose son Andrew had also attended Woodbridge. Mossman senior introduced Nick to the editor of the *Middlesex Advertiser and County Gazette*, published by the King & Hutchings newspaper group.

'Given that "famous pop star" was not an option,' says Nick, 'I'd decided to become a journalist. Not just a journalist, but a war correspondent. How hard could it be? I could read and write, plus I'd been raised in a military environment. Not only that, I'd also had an opportunity to study some of the top bods in the game at close quarters. These fellows were fairly regular visitors to our houses in Jordan and Cyprus whenever they came out to cover the various international crises that were bubbling at the time, and they needed to get Drain's help with passes and accreditation papers, or any other greasing of the wheels required to get the job done. My dad liked these people and I did too. I liked how they talked to me as if I was an adult, how they let me sit with them while they discussed their adventures in the desert or the latest political gossip. I also liked the way they could knock back a bottle of Scotch and it not have any apparent effect, how they smoked, how they leant back in the chair and crossed their legs, and of course what they wore. The belted safari jacket was a favourite, made of a cotton fabric known as Aertex, sun-bleached to a kind of off-white stone colour. They had the sleeves half rolled-up, and often teamed that with a pale blue shirt and scuffed desert boots. It was a look I knew I was destined to carry off. All I needed was to learn how to type.

'I landed a job as editorial assistant at the *Middlesex Advertiser* in Uxbridge, but unfortunately it didn't require me to wear a belted safari jacket. My duties in the news room included sweeping up, making tea, slipping out to buy the sub-editor's cigarettes – sixty a day – and listing the late-night pharmacies in the Raynes Park area. Putting away a bottle of Scotch would have seriously impaired my ability to answer junior readers' letters in my guise as "Tufty the Squirrel". It didn't take me long to realise I didn't have what it took to be a top newshound. If I needed any further proof, I was in no doubt after they sent me to review a film at a press showing in a fancy West End cinema, the Columbia, which later became the Curzon Soho. "Film Critic" – this was more like it! I thought I'd take the opportunity to impress my sister, who was much more successful than I, with this unexpected promotion. I called her affecting what I thought was an insouciant tone and the conversation probably went a bit like, "Yeah reviewing a movie . . . oh I don't know, hang on I had it here somewhere . . . ah here it is . . . 'Herbie the Love Bug' . . . not sure, I think it's a talking car." She saw through it of course, but was decent enough to play along, even after I told her it started at nine in the morning.

'We got to the cinema early to find the place already full of hacks, ciggies on, double whiskies in hand, ticking off their racing selections – real old-fashioned stringers. Glamorous it was not. The rep from the film company approached wearing a professional smile and asked us if we wanted a drink. My sister, who had some experience in this sort of situation, ordered a gin and tonic, so I did too. I'd never had one before, and finding it surprisingly easy to ingest, followed it swiftly with another four or five. The next thing I knew, I was alone in the empty auditorium, being prodded awake by the now unsmiling company rep. "Out!" she said. With my increasingly ferocious hangover, I returned to the office to make something up about the film I hadn't seen. It came out as if I was reviewing Laurence Olivier in *King Lear*; "The scene where Herbie drives himself into the hotel swimming pool masked, I felt, a deeper, more nuanced paradigm apropos the relationship blah blah blah", that kind of bollocks. It was my first and, as it turned out, only journalistic effort. Then I got the call from Brinsley.'

Since leaving Woodbridge school in 1965, Brinsley Schwarz had attended sixth form studies at the Skinners' School in Royal Tunbridge Wells, and formed a pop group called Three's A Crowd with bassist Dave Cottam and drummer Pete Whale. In 1967, Brinsley's group changed its name to Kippington Lodge, named after his parents' home near Sevenoaks in Kent, which was the property of the local preparatory school where his father, Wim, was a mathematics teacher and his mother, Joan, the matron. Kippington Lodge, the house, was large enough to accommodate a rehearsal space and numerous guests, including various transient musicians of Brinsley's acquaintance. Moreover, its pastoral setting seemed conducive to creativity.

The group attracted the attention of co-managers Irving Press, who was an optician, and Malcolm Glazier, a record plugger. In the summer of 1967, Press and Glazier signed up Kippington Lodge and sent a demo tape to record producer Mark Wirtz, then enjoying success with 'Excerpt From A Teenage Opera', a 45 rpm disc attributed to Keith West, who was also a member of the underground group, Tomorrow. Wirtz auditioned Kippington Lodge and quickly arranged for them to sign to EMI Records' Parlophone label, also home to the Beatles. The group's first session at Abbey Road studios that September failed to result in anything that sounded remotely like a hit, so Wirtz recommended they record 'Shy Boy', a song co-written by his prodigy, Keith West. It was recorded mainly with session musicians, one of whom fabricated an organ sound on his guitar. To recreate the effect onstage, Brinsley called upon his former Woodbridge alumnus, the keyboard-conversant Barry Landeman.

'I got a telegram from Brinsley,' recalls Barry. 'Did I want to come and join them on organ? Within a week I had upped sticks and relocated to Brinsley's house. My parents – bless their hearts – let me take the very expensive family piano with me. Brinsley and his roadie turned up in the van and we carted the piano down to a music shop and swapped it for a Hammond organ! We installed it in Brinsley's parents' dining room. They were tolerant and supportive of him; this is why he had the electric guitar way back when, and why we had gone to Germany in 1964. They just made things possible. I stayed there and lived with them.'

'Shy Boy', with Brinsley's song 'Lady On A Bicycle' on the flipside, was released in October 1967 in a bid to compete with the likes of Status Quo, Marmalade, the Herd – all Marquee-friendly groups that in the wake of *Sgt. Pepper* populated the hit parade with whimsical pop, dressed up in satin blouses with ludicrously expansive collars and post-Mod bouffant hairdos. The heavy-duty antidote to all this frippery (although they dressed similarly) was proto-power trio, Cream. When Cream appeared at Brighton Top Rank in January 1968, Brinsley and Barry were in the audience and were knocked out by the musicianship. Kippington Lodge now wanted to progress in a more serious musical direction, but bassist Dave Cottam wasn't convinced. Following the inevitable disagreement over 'musical policy', he resigned, leaving a vacancy for a new bass guitarist. Brinsley immediately thought of Nick.

In the period between Cottam's departure and the release of the group's next single, Nick agreed to give it a go. On a freezing cold Sunday in February 1968, he left his family home in Sarratt on the back of a motor scooter piloted by friend John Spackman. Nick had little more than the £10 note that Drain had pressed into his hand, and a further £10 in savings. 'It was quite a lot of money, if you were careful,' says Nick. 'I didn't really drink or take drugs, although I was dying to try them.'

Unbeknown to Nick, the editor-in-chief at King & Hutchings had told Drain and Pat that if things didn't work out for their son in the pop game, there would still be a newspaper job waiting when he returned. But Nick had no intention of returning to journalism, or any kind of nine-to-five existence, no matter how challenging life in a third division EMI pop group might become; this was his big break and he had his pride. With his fertile imagination and the facility to coin a snappy turn of phrase, journalism's loss would be pop music's gain. And, of course, life in the modern beat group was exceptionally groovy.

'They invited me to join and I went to live at the Lodge with Brinsley's family. His parents, Joan and Wim, must have been saints. I'm ashamed to say I was not a very considerate house guest. Among, I'm sure, many unsavoury habits, I was a keen smoker and would leave my cigarette butts all over the house, standing on their ends to burn out rather than use an ashtray. They never said anything to me but eventually, after a few months, it was evident that I'd understandably outstayed my welcome and I found myself down the road in Tunbridge Wells looking for somewhere to live. The summer of 1968 was glorious and the Pantiles was, and I presume still is, the beautiful and historic heart of the town. On Saturday mornings, the Duke of York pub was where all the young people headed, and a very good time was had by all. I don't know how, but after one of these expeditions I fell in with a bunch of like-minded people and was invited to stay in a flat right on the Pantiles above Strawson's Antique Shop. It could not have been a better result. I was the lowest head on the totem pole, sleeping on the floor, but when someone left you moved up, perhaps to the sofa, and eventually an actual bed. I was mostly broke, but so was everyone else I knew. It was heaven.'

There is some difference of opinion as to whether Nick actually possessed a bass guitar when he joined Kippington Lodge. 'I have a vague idea he may have had a guitar that wasn't his,' says Barry. 'It may have been the Gibson Les Paul with a pickup missing. There was something very shady going on, and where it came from I don't know, but I remember Nick tried to sell it to Eddy Grant from the Equals at a café in Denmark Street. Later I went with him to a shop in Tottenham Court Road where he bought a Gibson SG bass, because Brinsley at that point had a Gibson SG guitar. Matching guitars were cool.'

Following the failure of their second single, 'Rumours',

recorded prior to Nick joining, Kippington Lodge released their third, 'Tell Me A Story', composed by Barry. This time, the group were actually allowed to play on the record rather than use session musicians. In a sense, they'd proved themselves and Parlophone continued to promote them with little classified ads in the music press, if not full-on record promotion. The group's 1968 recordings and publicity photographs suggest a post-psychedelic pop group reminiscent of the Herd, but despite their heavily orchestrated recordings and Nick's Andy Bown hairstyle, Kippington Lodge simply lacked teen appeal. Their next single, 'Tomorrow Today', was also a flop. Unable to keep up the payments on his Hammond organ, Barry quit the group early in 1969 and accepted an offer to join pop harmony band Vanity Fare.

To find Barry's replacement, the group placed an ad in the *Melody Maker*, which resulted in the recruitment of Yorkshire-born organist, Bob Andrews. With a flair for R&B and soul, his musicianship hardened the group's sound and he soon moved south to share a flat with Nick. The fifth and final single by Kippington Lodge, a cover of the Beatles' 'In My Life', released in April 1969, features Bob's Hammond organ to the fore. Its B-side, 'I Can See Her Face', marks Nick Lowe's singing and songwriting debut on record, and his lead vocal strives to emulate Traffic's Steve Winwood. The single bombed.

Although it was rare for Nick to make a trip back home to visit his parents, they were always on his mind, particularly Drain, who was becoming tired of his job on the periphery of television.

'I remember going back home with our roadie, John Seymour, when we were picking up some piece of equipment from Watford. We went round to see my folks, a surprise visit. Although he was pretending not to be, I could tell that Drain was real down. So much so that when I got back to Tunbridge Wells, I went and bought some writing paper and sat down and actually wrote him a letter. My mama kept it and showed it to me shortly before she died. It may have been written in a haze of marijuana smoke, but it was quite heartfelt. I told him: "I know I hardly see you any more, but you're the greatest, and you'll find something. You're too good for those bastards." Apparently, the old boy was quite moved by it. He eventually found work elsewhere, and with Pat's help developed a highly polished look, as if someone had buffed him up. His hair looked like a 45 rpm record, and of course he had his handlebar moustache and some good shirts. But his war wound gave him gyp. It was a knee injury he incurred when he fell off a table. New Year's Eve, 1943.'

Eryl Holt, then fourteen years old, was working as a waitress at the Carousel, a Tunbridge Wells café above which Nick and Bob now shared a flat.

'They said they needed a cleaner and quick as a flash I said I would do it. It was five shillings per bedroom and seven-and-six for the bathroom and stairs. I became the envy of everybody because I had a legitimate reason to go round there and I heard all the good gossip about what was going on. These guys talked to me, and because I was a bit younger I wasn't seen as a predator. Nick always had charisma, right from the very first moment I saw him, in silhouette, walking down a narrow street in Tunbridge Wells.'

Eryl also remembers the night that Kippington Lodge came dangerously close to losing their bass player. In addition to the ballroom tours backing artists such as Billie Davis and J. J. Jackson, the group's most prestigious live work was their regular support slot at London's Marquee Club. On 5 July 1969, just a few hours after the Rolling Stones had performed their famous free concert in Hyde Park, the Kippingtons opened for the organ-based trio,

Village, at the Marquee. 'Nick got electrocuted while playing,' recalls Eryl. 'He fell down, writhing on the stage. Faulty wiring was blamed.'

'I had one hand on my bass strings and the other reaching for the mic, and about to say, "How're ya doing, London?" says Nick. 'But as soon as I grasped the mic, a circuit was created and I was in big trouble. According to witnesses, I leapt about four feet in the air and was flung across the stage where I crashed into the amps and lay writhing and twitching on the floor, unable to let go of either my bass or the mic. In my head, I knew exactly what had happened. It was very unpleasant but I was strangely calm. I couldn't see anything – it was like looking through frosted glass. All I could hear was a deep electronic drone note. Nevertheless, I clearly remember a voice talking to me – my voice – speaking very calmly and saying things like, "This isn't very nice, is it? Never mind though, it'll all be over in a little while . . . you won't survive it I'm afraid . . . this is a serious, serious jolt . . . your heart won't be able to cope for much longer." And then in the same conversational way, "How old are you? Twenty? Twenty-one? That's a shame, I thought you might go on to do something pretty good in the future, a few hits maybe, see the world a bit. Still, you've had a pretty good time and if you've got to go – well, at least it's on the stage of the Marquee." It was that matter of fact. There was no panic, no fear.

'In the club, meanwhile, there was mayhem – people shouting, girls screaming – while, onstage, attempts were being made to reach the plug board behind the amps in order to kill the power. People were naturally reluctant to prise my hands off the metal until finally Bob Andrews aimed a kick at the mic-stand, which did the trick. However, not realising he'd been successful he launched a follow-up kick, which missed his target but booted me in the chest so hard that – as they told me at the hospital later

– he'd started everything back up again and probably saved my bacon. An ambulance came and they put me on a stretcher and took me to the Middlesex Hospital. They fixed my hands, which were quite burnt. I couldn't believe it. I was so happy to be alive that I discharged myself and found the others, who were in the Ship pub near the Marquee drinking large brandies. I'd never been so pleased to see anyone. The club manager asked if we still wanted to do our second set, which of course we did. "And here he is, back from the dead, Lazarus!" We were only paid half our fee though.'

The following month, Kippington Lodge undertook a four-week residency in Margate, during which drummer Pete Whale became isolated from the others following a disagreement over musical direction. It was decided that Whale would be fired after the final Margate show. On the journey home, while the group members were trying to pluck up the courage to tell Whale he was out, he suddenly uttered, 'It's great to be in a band. I'm really looking forward to the future.' His colleagues were filled with guilt at the thought of sacking him, when Nick suddenly spoke out: 'Sorry Pete, but you're not in the group any more.' Whale went quiet for ten minutes and then said, 'Well, never mind, I still feel really good about the future!'

Kippington Lodge had already had talks with their prospective new drummer, Billy Rankin, whom they first saw playing with the Martin James Expression in a talent competition at Dowgate Hall in Tonbridge. 'I thought Kippington Lodge were fantastic, even if they'd gone a bit progressive,' says Billy. 'They used to play "Nights In White Satin".'

Rankin joined the group in September 1969, by which time Kippington Lodge were beginning to question their future as a minor EMI recording act with a trail of failed singles to their debit. As the 1960s were drawing to a close, the UK's live music circuit was changing dramatically, with an emphasis on the burgeoning college circuit. This development may have escaped the attention of Kippington Lodge's agent at Arthur Howes Associates in Regent Street.

'We used to go there to see our booker, Roger Easterby,' recalls Nick. 'We'd be sitting in the waiting room among comedians and strong men, plate spinners and midgets. I'm exaggerating slightly, but only a little. We were just another turn on their books.'

Also, a change of mood was permeating popular music, with Creedence Clearwater Revival leading the charge in America. In the UK, progressive bands such as King Crimson and Yes were coming to the fore, but the record that majorly influenced ear-to-the-ground music fans at this time – including the members of Kippington Lodge – was *Music From Big Pink* by the Band.

'We were also very into Crosby, Stills & Nash. I loved their first album and we developed this look, a sitting-on-stools look, and I remember we used to go round to Brinsley's house to hear his stereo. It was a treat – two speakers! We figured times were changing.'

The group needed a new name and image. As Brinsley Schwarz recalled, 'We agreed that we'd all try to think of a name and then we'd meet and choose one of them. But when we met, I was informed by the others that they had already decided. We were going to be called "Brinsley Schwarz". I opposed it, but I was gradually talked round.'

On 16 October, Billy Rankin scoured the classified advertisements in the *Melody Maker* seeking out work for the re-branded group he had recently joined. One ad leapt from the page. It read: 'Young progressive management company require young songwriting group with own equipment.' Sensing a promising opportunity, Rankin urged Schwarz to make the call, the out-come of which was to burn the name 'Brinsley Schwarz' into rock and roll legend, and shape its leading light's destiny.

CHAPTER 5

The Hype

The *Melody Maker* advertisement led Brinsley Schwarz to the door of twenty-seven-year-old Dave Robinson who, with his partner Dorothy 'Dot' Burn-Forti, headed up Famepushers Limited. Robinson, born in Dublin in 1942, had been a road manager for the Jimi Hendrix Experience and had managed the Irish group, Eire Apparent. He was now seeking to discover rock's next sensation. Having auditioned the dozens of groups that had answered his ad, Robinson decided that Brinsley Schwarz were the best of the bunch, not least of all because they owned their own van, they said, and their bass player was a songwriter of promise.

The Famepushers organisation itself had been founded on the fragile business infrastructure of two young entrepreneurs, Stephen Warwick, a former film sound editor who had worked on some early James Bond movies, and 'Eddie Molton', a mystery man who operated under numerous aliases in order to stay one step ahead of the bank managers he skilfully manipulated. The two men were in the process of setting up a number of companies to promote their various pipedreams, including 'The

Pleasuredome' – a combined pirate radio station and leisure resort for 'heads', housed on a rusting wartime sea fort in the Thames estuary, and *Bridge-o-Rama*, a film tracking the events of 'The Omar Sharif Bridge Circus', with the involvement of Sharif himself. Famepushers was another of their companies, but one that might connect the pair with the cash-soaked world of rock music.

When the group met with Robinson, Nick thought that the talkative Irishman was just the type of manager they needed. 'Both Dave and his girlfriend seemed like real exotic creatures to us. Very hip, cool threads, they were *nice* people. Dave had done some serious shit, like Hendrix, whereas we were still playing the Radio 1 Club.'

Robinson informed them that his objective was to find a group who wrote their own songs, and through honest hard graft, and Famepushers' contacts, would work their way up the ladder. It would be a mistake to promote the group aggressively, Robinson told them, without a trace of irony. 'You might find it extremely difficult to live up to the hype,' he explained, unaware of the extraordinary events that lay ahead.

Dave and Dot were cordially invited to Tunbridge Wells, where a friend of the group laid on a sumptuous feast in honour of its guests. Although the food was 'terrific', Nick's flat had condensation running down the walls and the group 'lived like pigs'. The van they claimed to own was actually rented and, worst of all, they already had a manager who appeared to own all of their equipment. To Robinson, things were starting to look a little less attractive, but for the bass player's songwriting talents.

On 1 December 1969, Famepushers wrote to Nick's parents:

I understand that you have discussed with
your son Nicholas his intention of coming
under our management for the furtherance
of his musical career. By law, as Nicholas
is under twenty-one years of age, the
signature of his guardian or guardians is
required on his contract which we are
enclosing. We think that both himself and
his group show very good potential in the
popular music field, and have no doubt that
they will be a success.

Nick's parents endorsed his contract and the group set off on their adventures with Famepushers. On 14 December, they played London's Country Club as the support act to Formerly Fat Harry. Checking out the headline act that night was twenty-two-year-old Andrew Lauder from the A&R department of United Artists Records. He had arrived early and watched, half-interested, as the members of Brinsley Schwarz filed onstage in scooped-neck T-shirts, velvet bell-bottom trousers and snakeskin boots, then the height of fashion.

'The promoter, Stuart Lyon, told me they used to be Kippington Lodge,' says Lauder. 'That didn't exactly get the pulses racing, but I liked them. They sounded a bit like the Band, and they'd obviously listened to a lot of the same music that I liked.'

A few days later, Lauder received a telephone call from Dave Robinson, who was seeking a record deal for his new protégés. This was a conflicted period for the group; as 'Brinsley Schwarz' they were struggling to get work, while at the same time fulfilling their contractual obligation as 'Kippington Lodge'. They had to decide whether to hang on to their bread and butter engagements and survive, or persevere with their new approach and starve. Nick was in no doubt. He'd had enough of appearing on teenybopper radio shows, and wanted to play underground clubs and colleges.

'I didn't particularly want to embrace the hippie thing,' he says. 'But I recognised the nice, well-turned ankle of a college girl when I saw it.'

Dave Robinson also recognised where the future lay and started planning recording sessions for the group, taking the ambitious step of hiring Olympic Studios in Barnes, south-west London, where artists such as the Rolling Stones and Jimi Hendrix had recorded. Then he booked rooms for the group at the nearby Red Lion public house. It was an extravagant way in which to commence their recording career and he had to rely on a few favours. Robinson's ideal producer for Brinsley Schwarz was Animals and Donovan hit-maker Mickie Most, who was gently persuaded to record some tracks with the group.

'We were doing very few gigs at this time,' says Nick. 'We weren't doing much self-composed material but we did have one terrible thing called "Life Is Dead", which was one of mine.'

Bob Andrews elaborates: '"Life Is Dead" was a rotten song that we would never have put on an album. It was a twenty-minute progressive dirge. And to us, Mickie Most was a pop person, so we gave him a hard time.'

Nick adds: 'We understood this to be a test recording, but Mickie said, "This song is much too long, it should be three minutes." We thought it was shocking that he was gonna machete his way into our intricate arrangement and axe the fifteen-minute guitar solo.'

Most declined further involvement with the group, so they went back into Olympic Studios with Dave Robinson in charge of production. But with the bills mounting and Famepushers' bank balance dwindling, Robinson's initial notion of slowly building the group's career was starting to look a little idealistic.

Eddie Molton wanted to know why it was taking so long to get Brinsley Schwarz off the ground and he called an immediate meeting with Robinson and Burn-Forti. Also present were Stephen Warwick, John Eichler, who was Warwick's former associate in 'the film division', and Famepushers' press officer, Ricky Blears.

'How quickly can we get Brinsley Schwarz a record deal?' asked Molton.

When Blears advocated showcasing the group at a prestigious venue, Robinson suggested the Speakeasy, a West End club frequented by music biz types.

'Not big enough,' decreed Blears.

'Why not the Royal Albert Hall?' asked Eichler.

'Too ordinary,' responded Blears. 'Where is the biggest and the best venue in the world? The rock and roll Mecca, where the group could play a gig and attract a lot of press?'

'The Fillmore East, New York,' replied Robinson.

'In a couple of hours, we'd talked it up from the Speakeasy to the Fillmore,' recalls John Eichler. 'Then it became, "Let's see if we can charter a little plane. Let's see if we can get a bigger plane. Let's see if we can fill it up with journalists." Dave said he had a mate at Aer Lingus whom he could contact and everybody went, "Yeah!" Ricky Blears was very good at dealing with the press and proposed a competition with the *Melody Maker*. We had to get some serious dosh, some American dosh. There was a lot of stadium rock going on at the time and "hype" wasn't such a dirty word. We didn't think of it as such. It was a laugh. We laughed ourselves stupid.'

The sheer audacity of launching a totally unknown and inexperienced British group in New York energised everyone in the organisation, but it fell to Dave Robinson to make it happen. Not only was he expected to secure a recording contract for Brinsley Schwarz, but also an engagement at a prestigious venue across the Atlantic and a huge favour from an inter-national airline.

This was rather a big ask, but it *was* the dawn of a new decade and it seemed to Famepushers that anything was possible. After all, man had recently walked on the moon and the Beatles were disbanding, obviously creating a void in pop that was waiting to be filled by Brinsley Schwarz.

Winning over Aer Lingus was relatively straightforward; for a mere seven grand they would supply a return charter flight to New York on the basis of the publicity that flying 'a planeload of journalists' across the Atlantic would attract, but the Fillmore booking was less straightforward. The venue's promoter, Bill Graham, was a fearsome character whose well-publicised motto – 'Though I walk through the valley of the shadow of death, I fear no evil, for I am the meanest son of a bitch in the valley' – struck fear into the hearts of managers and agents.

Robinson was undeterred and phoned Graham's west coast office incessantly until he finally got through to the self-confessed son of a bitch. He sensed that Graham wasn't going to stay on the phone for too long, so he had to make an impression.

'Brinsley Schwarz are going to be massive!' he exclaimed excitedly. 'Don't pass up the opportunity of having them play the Fillmore!'

Bill Graham's eyes were glazing over. Thinking it would see off the mad Irishman, he quickly terminated the conversation with, 'Look Dave, any time you're in San Francisco, drop by.'

No sooner had Bill Graham replaced his telephone receiver than Robinson was on his way to the airport. Early the following morning, he arrived at Winterland Productions on Market Street, San Francisco. When Graham showed up at midday, he was astonished to find Robinson waiting for him in reception, less than twenty-four hours after their telephone conversation. Graham agreed to a five-minute meeting and Robinson launched into his spiel.

'Bill, I have to have this gig. The press wants to see Brinsley Schwarz in the right setting.'

Graham promised to give the matter due consideration and Robinson flew home. A week went by without a response, but then the call came. 'Yes,' said Graham. 'There's a weekend in April at the Fillmore East. I've got Van Morrison and Quicksilver Messenger Service. Brinsley Schwarz can open.'

Robinson now concentrated his efforts on Andrew Lauder at United Artists. 'Brinsley Schwarz are making their world debut at the Fillmore East in New York, with Van Morrison and Quicksilver Messenger Service! It's all set up!' Lauder instinctively knew what was coming next.

'Dave still needed a record deal,' he recalls. 'Deadlines were suddenly imposed. The album was pretty much recorded and Barney Bubbles [the graphic designer Colin Fulcher] had done the artwork. I suddenly had to make a decision. I quite fancied going back to New York, although the whole promotion smelt of disaster because the chances of those things working are slim. My colleagues at the record company asked me for my view of the album and I said I found it likeable.'

Martin Davies, head of business affairs at United Artists, summoned Robinson in to discuss a deal. In the light of the New York campaign and the fact that the album was ready to go, Lauder and Davies offered the group a £22,000 advance against an 8 per cent royalty. The proposal was music to the ears of Molton and Warwick; with the Fillmore launch fast approaching they reminded Robinson that firm deals now had to be struck with Aer Lingus, Head Limousines and the Grand Metropolitan hotel chain, with comprehensive credit facilities throughout.

But even if all of this could be achieved, unimaginable problems lay ahead for Brinsley Schwarz and their intrepid managers.

The Fillmore dates were set for Friday 3 and Saturday 4 April, 1970, two houses per night. In the weeks leading up to the shows, the US launch of Brinsley Schwarz in front of the world's press was routinely referred to at the Famepushers office as 'The Hype'.

Ricky Blears notified the newspapers and on 18 March, the *Sun* reported the upcoming event under the headline A JUNKET FOR THE MONSTERS. Its writer, Mike Nevard, described it as 'the most expensive opening night in pop history . . . for four British popsters who have not yet been heard on record – and who have not been heard much anywhere . . . their backers describe them as "the monster group of the seventies".'

Dave Robinson was expected to organise the logistics, including rehearsal time and equipment rental in New York; seats at the Fillmore; photo passes for the journalists; and a fleet of limousines to ferry the entire party around Manhattan, not to mention firming up the flights and the record release date. It was decided that the British journalists would fly out on the Saturday to catch that evening's first show, then on the Sunday, after some free time for sightseeing, they would attend a press reception at the Royal Manhattan Hotel before returning home on an overnight flight.

'It was presented to the group as a fait accompli,' says Nick. 'We thought it was the greatest. We were gonna go to the Fillmore and we'd be famous – end of story. We could short-circuit all those unpleasant miles in a Transit van and the horrible club dates – we wouldn't have to do them! Of course, we were very inept; we'd been playing Goudhurst Village Hall two days before we left for the States. All I knew was that I wanted to climb on a big plane to North America and get down to the groupie club.

'We had a rehearsal just before the trip and our backers came down. They were horrified because we weren't doing any of the new tunes from the album that featured our Crosby, Stills & Nash harmonies. We could do these when we were sitting round in a circle, or in a studio, but when it came to getting up onstage and opening our mouths and singing through amps, well, we didn't know how to do it. Steve and Eddie were appalled that we couldn't do the harmonies live. We could only do our Kippington Lodge stuff like "Life Is Dead" or "I Can See Her Face", which was my heavy metal re-write of "Hush" by Billy Joe Royal.'

It was Famepushers' intention for the group to fly over a week ahead of the shows to acclimatise 'like footballers' and rehearse at the Fillmore using specially hired equipment. With ten days to go before departure, Robinson needed to apply to the London branch of the Musicians' Union for the group's work permits and then to the US Embassy for visas. It was this final detail that proved the most irksome.

'In the euphoria and excitement, little oversights were made,' says Brinsley Schwarz. 'Dave's ability to transcend normal thought may have left his administrative capabilities lacking. One of us had a drugs conviction but that didn't really hinder it.'

On Monday 30 March, already behind schedule, the Brinsleys went to the US Embassy to get their visas. It was here that Robinson encountered his first major stumbling block. The work permits hadn't come through and, therefore, visas would not be issued. With the Fillmore engagement just four days away, cancelling was out of the question, especially as United Artists had yet to part with a large portion of the group's advance. It quickly occurred to Robinson that the boys might take an unscheduled holiday in Canada – Toronto to be precise – just across the border from New York State. Once admitted into

Canada, posing as tourists, they would simply fly down to New York and commence rehearsals.

'In Toronto, they didn't like the look of us at all,' recalls Nick. 'We all had long hair when it used to cause grave offence. Bob said, "We're only gonna be here for an hour, we're just going over to the American Embassy to pick up some visas then we're off to New York." They let us in for twenty-four hours. We got a cab over to the Embassy, filled in the forms as best we could, handed them in and waited to be called. We were around 150, 151, 152, 153 – it went up to 300, with women dressed in black with crying children. We were worried that we'd miss our plane, but they were paying us a little extra attention. Eventually they called us over and the guy screamed at us. "Who do you think you are, trying to fool us? We've got a million dollars' worth of computer back there! Just to check up on your type. You wanna get into the United States? No chance!" Then he threw our passports across the room. We were slack-jawed. Robbo gathered us up like a mother hen.

'There were three days to go before the show. We went and got a hotel and sat and waited while Dave was on the phone, talking to the heavy mob in New York, to see if they could pull some strings. Our one-day visas ran out and we were afraid to leave the hotel in case they deported us. We waited while the days ticked by until the very day of the first show when we were told they'd managed to sort something out. We could go to the Embassy and pick up our passports. But that day, there was an air traffic controllers' strike and there were amazing photographs in the papers of jets queuing up to take off at all the major airports. Also, with the delay at the Embassy we'd missed our flight, so we had to rent a light plane, with a Japanese pilot. He took off from Toronto and touched down briefly in Buffalo, just across the border to get his papers checked. We said, "It's OK, we've got our passports here, with our visas." He said, "Oh don't worry, just wait in the plane." Nobody even looked at our passports.

'I remember the incredible sight as we flew into New York. It seemed like we were flying through the skyscrapers! We landed at a little airstrip somewhere in Queens. The important thing was there was a big limo there to meet us, and the driver handed us joints. He was a head with a hat on, and a uniform, and we got extremely stoned on this very strong grass, another sensible move on the day of the show. He took us into Manhattan, to the Fillmore where we saw our plight for the very first time. We'd ordered up lots of state-of-the-art equipment – another bad move – Fender Dual Showman amps that delivered a very loud ding around the auditorium. We had no idea how to operate them.'

When Brinsley Schwarz walked on stage for the first of four shows over two nights, nobody in the audience knew or cared that it had been a dramatic touch-and-go situation for five days, or that they had made it to the Fillmore with only forty-five minutes to spare. Unbelievably, however, the group's difficulties in getting to New York were about to be dwarfed by the experience that awaited the press entourage the following day.

The Famepushers itinerary stated that the journalists' flight would leave London at 10.40 a.m. and arrive at John F. Kennedy airport at 2 p.m. local time. It was a tight schedule that didn't allow for any delays. However, the Aer Lingus Boeing 707 which was due to fly the party across the Atlantic had been delayed on its way to London from Paris. After a three-hour wait a substitute aircraft was found, but it developed a mechanical problem over the Irish Sea, and after some frantic fuel dumping made an emergency landing, coming to a halt a few feet short of the River Shannon.

'They asked us if we would mind getting off,' recalls John Eichler. 'Ricky Blears and I were supposedly the senior people on the plane, so they took us into the VIP lounge and told us that the 707 had lost its brake fluid and had to land relying solely on reverse thrust. It was very dodgy. They threw open the bar and we drank the free booze until it was coming out of our eyes.'

At 4.30 p.m., the plane was declared airworthy and the party re-embarked for the onward flight to New York. As soon as the pilot turned off the no-smoking signs, the drinks continued to flow and the cabin filled with marijuana smoke.

'When that plane took off, it was the biggest drugs party that has ever taken place in mid-air,' says underground press writer Alan Marcuson. 'It was pandemonium and the air hostesses completely freaked out.'

On eventually arriving at JFK, the journalists, now seriously inebriated, faced the task of clearing immigration. 'I seem to remember not going through Customs,' says Andrew Lauder. 'It was as if somebody had dropped someone a bribe and suddenly a hole in the fence appeared. It felt as if I'd walked through a back door and straight into a limousine.'

Amid the general chaos, each member of the party jumped into the first stretch limo he or she could find. With less than an hour to go before Brinsley Schwarz were due to take the stage at the Fillmore, any ideas of freshening up at the hotel were shelved as the convoy of twenty-two cars raced towards the city, accompanied by motorcycle outriders (rumoured to be actors in uniform).

At 8.15 p.m., the convoy screeched to a halt outside the Fillmore to unload the shaken Brits, now at the end of a seventeen-hour ordeal. Inside the theatre, Dave Robinson was attempting to delay the show so that the press wouldn't miss the start of Brinsley Schwarz's performance. When Robinson received the news that the UK contingent had finally arrived, he terminated his confrontation with Bill Graham and, as the journalists got to their seats, the Brinsleys were walking on stage.

The group performed a nervous thirty-five-minute set comprising five Nick Lowe compositions: 'Indian Woman'; 'What Do You Suggest'; 'Rock And Roll Women'; 'Ballad Of A Has-Been Beauty Queen'; and their progressive dirge, 'Life Is Dead'.

Writer and broadcaster Charlie Gillett was not convinced: 'Unfortunately, Brinsley Schwarz were totally unimpressive live. If the band had been as good as the build-up, it would have seemed like a wonderful stunt, but the gig was a disappointment.'

And although the programme stated: 'Their first Fillmore appearance will provide part of the material to be included in a documentary on the group, for airing on British television', Bill Graham had forbidden the Famepushers camera crew from filming the performance.

As Brinsley Schwarz left the stage to polite, muted applause, most of the British contingent considered that they had now fulfilled their obligations to Famepushers and strolled out onto the New York streets to sample the invigorating nightlife. Back inside the Fillmore, the group's feeble performance was immediately overshadowed by the professionalism of Van Morrison and his thoroughly road-drilled band.

'Van Morrison was a hero,' says Nick. '*Moondance* had just come out and he had the band that was on the record. I'd never seen anything as good as that, except maybe Cliff Bennett and the Rebel Rousers some years earlier. I watched Van's show, or as much as I could stand, because they were incredible, and I had a mounting sense of dread that we'd made a terrible mistake.'

The following day, a very hungover collection of journalists attended a press conference at the Royal Manhattan. Ricky Blears recalls: 'The band, disappointed by their poor performance no doubt, decided that the best way out for them was to get completely stoned and stagger about in a speechless state, because they thought that's what pop groups did. I had great difficulty in getting them out of bed. The American press decided the whole thing was a complete shambles.'

The return flight to London was a profound anti-climax. On board, the Brinsleys sat sheepishly amongst the media folk as Nick reflected on having achieved his ambition to visit 'the groupie club' that he'd heard so much about from Dave Robinson. 'I hadn't wanted anything to interfere with that. But in order to get down to the groupie club I had to endure four shows. The club was called Nobody's and there I met the girl of my dreams. She followed me around all the next day, a real nuisance.'

As the plane sped homeward, there was a growing mood among members of the establishment press that they would not, and could not, be bought; no matter how extravagant Famepushers' hospitality, they were under no obligation to say wonderful things about Brinsley Schwarz. By the time the Boeing 707 made its early morning descent to Heathrow through heavy cloud and driving rain, the printing presses of Fleet Street were about to rattle with the story of one of the greatest public relations disasters in modern entertainment history.

'They say pride comes before a fall. I remember a week before we went,' says Nick, 'I was lording it in front of my contemporaries, saying, "Of course we're going to 'the States' next week, and when we come back from 'the States' . . ." We reconvened a week later in Wardour Street to watch the rushes of the film they'd made, by which time the reviews had come out in the *NME* and the *Melody Maker*, all of which were ghastly, saying what inept twerps we were. For a sensitive, naive young man it was devastating. As we walked into the viewing suite, all heads turned.

Everyone was holding *NMEs* and *Melody Makers*! To make matters worse, the film seemed to consist of hours of blurred footage of one of the gang touching up air hostesses. We were a laughing stock. Dave Robinson was very positive though. He didn't see the bad press as bad. "They don't mean that," he would say. "What they really mean is, you guys were great!"'

For the foreseeable future, the Brinsleys were out in the cold, but their agent, Tony Howard, noticed an increase in bookings. On the product front, Dave Robinson was able to secure a contract with Capitol Records for the USA, and a publishing deal with Chartwell Music, the proceeds from which helped to pay off the group's debts.[6] More importantly – and most ironically – having been shunned by the media, Brinsley Schwarz turned their back on the whole showbiz ethos and threw themselves into their music. In the aftermath of perhaps the least successful major launch of a popular music act, Brinsley Schwarz would turn their name around and become a symbol for anti-hype.

CHAPTER 6

Despite It All

The album *Brinsley Schwarz*, released on 17 April 1970, contains seven songs, six of which are credited to Nick Lowe, the other being a band composition. The music is heavily influenced by the sound of Crosby, Stills & Nash, whose debut album had dominated their turntable the previous year. Nick, Bob and Brinsley had pretty much perfected their three-part harmonies, with Nick's lead vocal echoing some of David Crosby's more bluesy moments. The instrumental improvisation and occasional 'progressive rock' flourishes are typical of the period.

The album's centrepiece is the seven-minute 'Lady Constant', a composite of stolen hooks, formerly the property of 'CSN'. Today, it might be considered a clever parody of the post-Woodstock, Californian vibe, but it was written by an earnest twenty-year-old living in Kent, a county popularly known as 'the garden of England', and it demonstrates how easily Lowe was able to leave listeners wondering where they'd heard a particular song before.

The album isn't all pastiche and derivation though; 'Mayfly' sounds truly original both in Nick's melody and Brinsley's harmony guitar motif in the extended fade, and 'Shining Brightly' is catchy and upbeat, even if its purple lyrics about 'Appalachian snow princesses' could easily have been lifted from a Redbone outtake.

The group had recorded no obvious singles, but they did appear on TV's *Top of the Pops* that May in 'the album spot', performing 'Shining Brightly'. Nick recalls visiting the Speakeasy the night before the TV show and meeting 'this really fantastic groupie, quite well-known at that point', but groupies were rarely seen in the presence of Brinsley Schwarz, sales of whose album fell quickly into decline. But no matter, for earlier that month they had been introduced to the enigmatic American songwriter Jim Ford.

'Dave Robinson was in the States on one of his money-raising exercises,' Nick continues. 'He heard about Jim Ford from Sy Waronker, the boss of Liberty Records. Sy said, "I'll invest in your group, but in return I want them to work with Jim Ford. He's a wayward genius, but you've got long hair so you'll be able to communicate with him." John Eichler went to pick Jim up from the airport. He arrived with a big Stetson on, rose-tinted shades, jeans with creases in and round-toed cowboy boots. I thought cowboy boots had to be pointed, but real cowboys wear the round-toed, comfortable variety and they also put creases in their jeans, because it's smart. Ford was the real thing, or as near to the real thing as I'd ever encountered. He was otherworldly and very charismatic. He turned up with a $3000 guitar, an astronomical sum for 1970, but it seemed he could barely play it, and yet it was so mean, the way he hit the thing. I'd never heard anybody who played like Jim Ford.

'He was totally unimpressed by us, but he was making the best of a bad job, I suppose. "Ju Ju Man" may have been one of the ones we recorded with him, plus "36 Inches High", "I'm Ahead If I Can Quit While I'm Behind" and "Harry The Hippie".

He told a lot of terrible stories and he would bend the truth a bit, but this one I believe. He told us he used to live with Bobbie Gentry, when she was a telephonist with RCA, and he claimed she stole "Ode To Billie Joe" off him. It sounds like a typical Jim Ford song, and in the light of what Bobbie Gentry has done since, it makes sense. He was a blues guy, but he'd stick extra bars in. We were very conventional young kids and we knew it went verse, chorus, verse, chorus, a little solo, and we said, "Er, Jim, last time you played that little bridge bit it went like this . . . now how does it go?" But Jim Ford's songs made a tremendous impact on me. Along with guys like Dan Penn, Spooner Oldham, and Joe South, he's the last piece of the jigsaw.'

Back at the Famepushers office, Molton and Warwick were in dire financial straits; their assistant was instructed to post out cheques at the last possible moment. Dave Robinson wasn't taking any chances and left the building, taking with him what little was left in petty cash. He drew up a survival plan for Brinsley Schwarz in which it was decided that the group would vacate their lodgings at the Red Lion, find a large house in a semi-rural location and adopt a communal lifestyle. No. 10 Carew Road, Northwood, Middlesex, was ideal; it had previously been an annexe to a private girls' school and had enough space to accommodate Robinson and the group, including Brinsley's family, plus a rehearsal room, sleeping quarters, kennels and a small office.

'It seemed like a palace to us. It was a huge, 1920s suburban house with a big back garden. The rooms were studies, where the sixth-formers used to live, and there were a few big bedrooms, where the teachers lived. We had no beds, so we slept on the floor.'

Eryl Holt, who would help out at Northwood, recalls: 'It was very much a commune with a veggie garden, which the wives and girlfriends tended, and there was a brief stage where everyone went around with nothing on. I got myself a very thick woolly jumper.'

Following the Brinsleys' exodus, Edward Molton disappeared, but not before making one last attempt to salvage his own relationship with the group. On 4 August 1970, he wrote to Nick's parents:

> It is an irretrievable fact that the group Brinsley Schwarz, of which your son is a member, have broken their contract with Famepushers Limited. This has allowed Dave Robinson, who as the managing director was always in very close contact with the band, to take over the management of Brinsley Schwarz. We obviously have your son under both a management contract, a production contract and a publishing contract, and I want to apologise in advance for any problems I may cause in trying to assert our legal rights.

Pat and Drain didn't reply, but that November the *Sunday Times* published an exposé of Molton and Warwick in its 'Insight' column. It included a report on the disastrous launch of Brinsley Schwarz, succinctly informing its readers:

> 'Hype' is the superlative sales promotion of a mediocre product. Famepushers paid no major bill – the debts of the trip added up to almost £13,000. It has been left to the group to pay off these as they can, yet the group had turned over earnings of almost £25,000 to Famepushers. What has happened to this is unclear.

The closing quote in the article was from Molton himself, exuding optimism (a few days prior to his disappearance): 'If creditors will be patient, they will be paid.'

The success or otherwise of the Jim Ford sessions led Brinsley Schwarz to record with another singer on the Liberty label, P. J. Proby, who was managed by United Artists boss, Martin Davies. Proby had failed to achieve any substantial UK chart success since 1965.

Nick recalls: 'Martin said, "Look, it's sort of all over for P. J. Proby, but I think he's a great artist. Before we do anything hasty, we should get him in the studio and see if he can come up with something new. I envisage a country rock sound. You guys are the country rock blokes, so how about it?" We were knocked out because Proby was the nearest thing to a bona fide pop star that we'd ever met. We told Martin we'd been working with Jim Ford and suggested that we try some of Ford's material. We weren't really aware that Proby had already done 'Niki Hoeke'. It turned out that Proby and Ford knew each other. They are, in fact, very similar.

'We sent Proby a selection of Jim Ford tunes that we'd learnt up. We were assured that he would be au fait with the songs when it came to cutting time. The day came and we waited for Proby to turn up. We were on evening sessions at Olympic. First of all, a roadie arrived with tons of guitars, all belonging to Proby – every type of guitar you could imagine, plus boxes of percussion instruments. We thought, "Bloody hell, he's taking this very seriously." About two hours later the great man arrived, wearing a cowboy hat. On his arm was the extremely attractive actress, Angharad Rees. It seemed that she was absolutely less than happy to be there.

'Proby had immense charm and charisma and had probably told Angharad something like, "I've just gotta drop some stuff off at the studio, honey." The next thing that emerged was that

Proby had obviously not listened to the songs at all and, to make matters worse, they were difficult songs with irregular bars and intervals – typical Jim Ford songs. We knew them inside out – we'd learnt every nuance – but it was hopeless to expect Proby just to dive in and start getting them straight away. He had no idea, but he put up a good show.

'The first thing we did was "Ju Ju Man". The lyric goes: "I was just sixteen years old, Maggie's hair was as black as coal." The first thing that Proby did was to sit down and rewrite it. Then he read it out, "I was just sixteen years old" – and by this stage he was getting tearful and saying to Angharad, "Honey, I'm gonna show you what I can do for you." Angharad was yawning at the back. He carried on, "I was just sixteen years old, Angharad's hair was flaxen gold!" Proby rewrote the whole song, substituting "Angharad". It's a beautiful name but let's face it, it doesn't exactly roll off the tongue like "Maggie", does it?

It was now time for Brinsley Schwarz to record their second LP, entitled – perhaps appropriately in the light of the Fillmore debacle – *Despite It All*. Again, Olympic Studios were used, with Dave Robinson co-producing. Bob Andrews's 'Piece Of Home' is the only non-Lowe composition among the album's eight songs. It is an eclectic mix that reveals a young fan's appreciation of various musical styles.

In the four or five decades that have elapsed since these recordings were made, there is hardly a popular music genre that Nick Lowe hasn't tackled. Country music is represented here by the waltz-time 'StarShip', with pedal steel guitar from B. J. Cole, close harmonies, and a western vocal twang; folk gets a look in on 'Ebury Down', with its finger-picked guitar and li-li-li chorus; and 'Old Jarrow' is an astonishing Gaelic hoedown.

Elsewhere, 'the Crosby, Stills & Nash sound' that had characterised the group's debut album is supplanted by 'the Van

Morrison sound'. This of course involves saxophones, which are provided by David Jackson from the 'prog rock' band, Van der Graaf Generator. The horn riff of 'Funk Angel', played by Jackson but possibly hummed to him by Nick during the warm-up, is an amalgam of several sax figures from Van Morrison's *Moondance*, while Nick's chord changes for 'The Slow One' veer quite close to those of Morrison's 'Caravan'.

'Love Song' is the first recorded glimmer of Nick's grasp of three-minute pop, with a catchy chorus, much repeated for commercial appeal. It was doubtlessly mooted as a possible single, but the actual 45 was 'Country Girl', which reflects the group's newfound confidence. It takes its spirit from the Byrds' Bob Dylan-composed 'You Ain't Going Nowhere', but is in fact more immediate.

To fill out the sound on *Despite It All*, Schwarz had overdubbed many of his guitar parts, and in order to replicate this in live performance it was decided that an additional musician would be required. An advertisement was placed in the good old *Melody Maker*.

'We got a lot of replies,' Nick says, 'and kept a note of all the applicants and those of us who answered the phone were instructed to write in a book what their first impressions of the applicant were. Brinsley's wife answered when a chap called Ian Gomm phoned. It was noted that he liked a lot of the artists that we liked; that he could sing; and that he had the right kind of guitar. We decided that as well as playing with them, we would have a little talk with them. The night before the auditions, Billy Rankin and I had stayed up tripping. We had a very nice time. The next morning, as we were coming down, the guitarists started arriving. They all turned into various farm animals as far as I was concerned. There was a goat and a pig and a turkey before Ian Gomm. When Ian arrived, he had red hair. Nobody thought he would have red hair, plus a sort of car coat and suedette shoes, an extremely normal look. He sang a couple of tunes and I said, "Right, you're in, you've got the job." Brinsley hit the roof.

'Ian also had a very dry sense of humour, although he looked completely wrong. I guess we were looking for a laid-back guy with cowboy boots, been places, done things, would know a couple of semi-famous American singer-songwriters, maybe had something to do with John Sebastian or knew one of the guys in NRBQ. I thought Ian Gomm was completely right, but Brinsley and Bob didn't see it at first. They hadn't been up all night like Billy and me. Then I suddenly thought I may have made a horrible mistake, but it was too late, he was in.'

Ian Gomm joined Brinsley Schwarz in September 1970, just as *Despite It All* was nearing completion. He brought to the group a keen knowledge of pop and electronics, and was 'handy with a screwdriver'.

Brinsley Schwarz had now moved on from their country-rock phase and, as a result of investigating the musical roots of their heroes, the Band, become infatuated with obscure rhythm and blues. They also kept tabs on the happening American acts, as reviewed in *Rolling Stone*, and Dave Robinson would be dispatched to London to pick up the latest imported records.

'Dave used to feed us stuff. Tracy Nelson, Area Code 615, Clover,' Nick says. 'He used to give us records he'd brought back from America, like the first Little Feat record, and say, "Everyone's talking about this, although I haven't heard it myself." I owe Dave a lot. He had his ear to the ground and he turned me on to new stuff. He knew a lot of hip people and he had very fertile ground to put his seeds in. I can't minimise his contribution.'

The five-piece Brinsley Schwarz were now living their music round the clock and developing a unique stance; whereas nearly every other group in the UK was using massive banks of amplifiers and playing at ear-splitting volume, Brinsley Schwarz acquired the smallest amplifiers they could find and turned the volume *down*.

'The Brinsleys were the quietist band I'd ever heard in my life,' says Martin Belmont, who would soon replace Mick Hince as the group's roadie. 'That was their whole thing. They took a perverse pride in it. The Brinsleys were the complete antithesis of what was going on elsewhere, with quiet, simple songs with great lyrics, mostly written by Nick. But no one person was more important than the whole.'

The German club scene soon beckoned and Brinsley Schwarz undertook a three-night residency at Frankfurt's Zoom Club. Dave Robinson drove the group in his new car, a Daimler Majestic Major, affectionately dubbed 'the Daimlerooni'. Nick relieved the tedium of the journey with a strong dose of LSD, but suffered a bad trip.

'I fell asleep in the back of the car. I woke up feeling paralysed. I couldn't speak and I couldn't move and I remember feeling very panicky.'

As the group became more introverted, rejecting ambition and volume, the pressure was now on their creative linchpin to devise new songs appropriate to this low-key approach. In Nick's mind, nothing flashy or overtly commercial would fit the bill, but he struggled to write within this tight, self-imposed framework. Crumbling under the weight of introspection and pummelled by liberal doses of psychedelic drugs, he felt the first tremors of an impending nervous breakdown. Although he was essentially the group's lead vocalist and songwriter, and 'stood in the middle', Nick was also the most irresponsible and out of control. He remembers gigs where he would sit in the dressing room after the show, unable to help with the gear. And when it was time to leave, he would often hear someone say, 'Who's got Nick?' They would put him in the van, where he would quietly sit.

'I was as good as gold but unable to speak. I was completely gone. Ian Gomm didn't really understand what had happened to me and it was lovely having a really sensible person like him in the group.'

Schwarz remembers Ian Gomm's relative naivety: 'Ian kept asking, "What's wrong with Nick?" The rest of us sort of knew. If Nick talked at all, it would be about the meaning of life, knowing the truth, having the answer, and his own insignificance in the scheme of things.'

When Nick's unpredictable behaviour began to affect his onstage performances, his colleagues became even more concerned. Some nights, he would suddenly change a song halfway through or cease playing altogether.

'We'd be playing along and everything would suddenly go high and clicky,' recalls Schwarz. 'We'd look round and Nick would have his hands in the air, no bass. We'd shout out, "Nick! Play!" He'd say, "No man, it sounds great without me!"'

'It was at a naval establishment in Plymouth,' recalls Nick. 'There were all these officer cadets dressed in uniform. The ladies were in ball gowns. I really thought we were playing on the deck of the *Victory* and it was the Napoleonic Wars. I was hallucinating like mad. Billy Rankin was in the same state as me, but when he tried to stop playing his drums, it did get a little thin. But they loved it. We went back a year later and played a sensible show. We were good the second time, but I remember the guy saying, "Frankly, we were rather disappointed this year. Last year you were much better!"'

On one occasion during this period, Nick was simply incapable of taking the stage. 'It was at St Albans Civic Hall,' says Bob Andrews. 'I played the bass and sang some of the songs from *Despite It All*. Ian sang some of his songs and Brinsley did a couple. We got through it, but Nick was certainly physically unwell. As a group, we were very insular. With most groups it's "Us Against the World", but we were even more so, hardly acknowledging "The World" at all. Nick had a very large imagination, but he was poorly and very fragile. He didn't get out of bed for a couple of days. There was a period when it got very black and existential. He had nothing to say.'

Following the previous year's sessions with Jim Ford, the unconventional Kentuckian had become Nick's favourite songwriter, and '36 Inches High' his favourite Ford song. Its imagery – the soldier on a big white horse, the flags of war, the silver pistol – conjures up visions of the American Civil War. And although there is clearly no historical link between Nick's antecedents and '36 Inches High', the mysterious song affected him profoundly, and he soon adopted the term 'Silver Pistoling' to describe the LSD experience.

'It was the terrible, bad trip song. Panic, third eye, I was having a very bad time on acid.'

As one of the group's roadies, Malcolm Addison, observed, 'Nick used to hold his fingers to his head, like a gun, and sing, "Silver pistol to blow my brain." He used to do that a lot.'

Despite Nick's hallucinatory nightmares, the work continued to flow in, including a return to Germany where the group had secured a week's residency at the Blow Up Club in Munich. On the way to Harwich, where they were due to catch their ferry, Robinson crashed the Daimlerooni. 'We'd been delayed at a petrol station and Dave had to step on the gas,' recalls Ian Gomm.

'He lost it on a curve and we ended up in an old lady's garden. The car was on its side, a write-off. We would have been killed had it not been such a well-built car.'

It was in Germany that a number of strange, almost surreal incidents deeply affected the group, and Nick in particular. His expression 'Silver Pistoling' was in constant use and, after a show at the Blow Up, Nick and Bob were invited to the sparsely furnished Bavarian house of a member of the German progressive rock group, Amon Düül II. After conversing with the German musicians, Nick decided to take a look around and went wandering off on his own, through long corridors and huge, empty rooms. He eventually came across a glass ornament case and in it were displayed two silver pistols. 'It did him in,' says Schwarz. 'I think he was already verging on insanity.'

Nick really went in on himself as the Brinsleys made for home via Frankfurt, where they played once more at the Zoom Club. 'We said, "Enough is enough," and played our Shadows-style instrumental, "Rockin' Chair",' says Schwarz. 'It was an anti-encore. Then we drove home via Dover. I remember Nick and myself were in the front of the van, completely wasted and mentally exhausted. I was driving and the others were asleep. I said to Nick, "I've really had it. I don't know how much more of this I can take." And Nick replied, "Me neither. Why don't you drive into a tree?" For a brief moment I contemplated it, to get it over with.'

While Brinsley Schwarz had been suffering their doom-laden tours of Germany, exacerbated by Nick's lysergic excesses, they were not to know that their musical attitudes would soon be skewed by the arrival in London of an American group called Eggs Over Easy. Comprising Jack O'Hara, Brien Hopkins and Austin de Lone, all multi-instrumentalists and accomplished singers, 'the Eggs' were in town to make a record with ex-Animal and former Jimi Hendrix manager, Chas Chandler. Following contractual difficulties with their American record label, they were encouraged to stay in London and kick their heels until their business problems blew over. Holed up in Kentish Town on '$100 a week to drink beer', they learnt about a local pub called the Tally Ho that hosted jazz bands. As legend has it, Jack O'Hara wandered up to the pub one Sunday evening and enquired about the possibility of some gigs, telling the barman, 'Sure we play jazz.'

In May 1971, Eggs Over Easy commenced a residency at the Tally Ho, augmented by former Animals drummer John Steel, and slowly built a following. Then, on 15 June, they appeared at the Marquee, as a trio, opening for rock duo, Hardin & York.

'Dave Robinson was in the club, and came backstage to introduce himself,' recalls O'Hara. 'He said, "You've got to meet the band," and immediately drove us to Northwood in the dark. Nick was the only one awake, but the next morning we met the others. Dave said we reminded him of Clover. My impression of the Brinsleys was that they were very Grateful Dead-influenced, and they also liked the Band. We were like genuine Americans to them and they were enamoured of the culture that came natural to us.'

'The Eggs told us they were playing this pub in Kentish Town,' recalls Nick. 'It was a wild neighbourhood, certainly not the chi-chi spot it is now. Billy Rankin and I, being the unattached ones, girded our loins and went to the Tally Ho the following night. There was quite a small audience, but Eggs Over Easy were really great. At first it was a groovy little thing, rather Hogarthian, with snotty-nosed urchins hanging round the door and a Sikh bus driver doing a wild frug-a-go-go routine. But within a few weeks it was discovered by the clique. The beautiful people. Eggs Over

Easy played very quietly. They also had small amps, which was quite unusual then. Coincidentally, we'd recently adopted a similar approach and seeing the Eggs doing it was confirmation that it was the right thing to do. They also performed covers effortlessly, like "Brown Sugar". It seemed unbelievable to do a song that had just been in the charts. So hip. They had a very good look as well – like trainee novice monks.'

Dai Davies, who had interviewed Brinsley Schwarz for *Top Pops and Music Now* and would later become the group's manager, recalls Nick's reaction to discovering Eggs Over Easy: 'I remember Nick telling me in awe that the Eggs could call on over a hundred songs – fifty originals and fifty unashamed covers. This impressed Nick no end. People would call out for songs and the Eggs would respond. They were remarkable – a living jukebox! The Brinsleys immediately decided they too would do pubs. Nick, abetted by Dave Robinson, had made the decision and the rest of the band fell in, probably thinking it was a democratic process.'

The idea of playing pubs fitted in perfectly with the Brinsleys' reaction to the Fillmore stunt, although it would be some months before they had built an extensive enough repertoire to take the plunge. 'It was Nick Lowe and Dave Robinson who were fanatical about the anti-hype approach,' adds Davies. 'The adjective "real" was bandied about a lot. It was an us-and-them philosophy.'

Nick was about to become a central figure in the emerging pub rock scene, but although he enjoyed a return to his musical roots in the Guinness-fuelled atmosphere of the Tally Ho, he was still suffering from self-neglect and an over-exposure to psychedelics. With some gentle prodding from Dave Robinson, he sought medical help.

'I finally lost my mind through taking LSD and if it hadn't been for the other guys in the group I don't know what would have happened. I had to be literally led around for six or nine months. I was also in a terrible state. I didn't speak and I was covered in lice and I had gonorrhoea. I was a horrible hippie case and my mind had really gone. I certainly thought I was never going to be mentally well again, and as a matter of fact, I don't think I'll ever recover from it. I know quite a lot of people that this happened to and I've learnt to recognise it in others. They're rather nice people. You can spot them. We know what it's like to be totally alone. But I'm better now. The only help I had was when I was taken by Robbo to see Sam Hutt, these days known as country singer Hank Wangford, who at that time was sharing a flat next to the Royal Albert Hall with Roger Chapman from Family and Jenny Fabian. Sam had Indian drapes in his waiting room and was playing "Workingman's Dead".

'Basically, I went to see him because I had the clap. He examined me and asked, "What's that in your hair?" I said, "You may as well have a good look at me because I'm alive with shit, but you might have to fumigate your surgery afterwards." Sam asked me what was wrong. I blurted it out. I told him I felt like I was looking at myself doing stuff and that I couldn't seem to drop back into my own self. He knew I'd been tripping. He mixed up a powder with a pestle and mortar and put it into little packets. I don't know whether it was a placebo or not, but I felt better. Sam Hutt got me good. Then I discovered alcohol. I hadn't really been interested in it, although in New York I'd had several drinks of the Southern Comfort and Coke variety in the groupie club. But like a lot of people who'd been through the same experience as me, a drink was a good antidote.'

Now lice-free and with newly combed hair, Nick confidently fronted Brinsley Schwarz for the group's first appearance at the Tally Ho on 19 January 1972. They slipped into the groove with ease and a fortnight later returned to the pub to commence a run of twelve consecutive Wednesday nights.

'We were such outcasts. But when we started playing this funny pub, a bit of credibility started to come our way.'

Coinciding with their Tally Ho residency, Brinsley Schwarz released their third long-player, *Silver Pistol*, its title a nod to Jim Ford, two of whose songs – 'Niki Hoeke Speedway' and 'Ju Ju Man' – are included. The album, which had been recorded the previous summer at Northwood, has a naive charm, with a deliberate down-home feel and DIY quality. The group even recorded in their garden and on one track, 'Egypt', Nick's black Labrador, Poacher, can be heard barking in the background.

Silver Pistol sees the flowering of Nick's songwriting, especially on 'Nightingale', a light and tender ballad. Guitar solos and overdubs are kept to a minimum throughout, enhancing the low-fi listening experience, and the influence of the Band permeates every track – from Brinsley's approximation of the Robbie Robertson guitar sound on the title track, to Nick's Dylanesque warbling on 'The Last Time I Was Fooled'.

Another act that the Brinsleys were heavily influenced by was Clover, whose singer, Alex Call, had perhaps the biggest effect on Nick's vocal style in this period, particularly if one listens to Clover's song 'Mr. Moon'. Very few British musicians were this deeply immersed in what would come to be known as 'Americana'.

By the time that *Silver Pistol* appeared in the shops, Brinsley Schwarz had moved on. During the lengthy gap between its recording and release, the group's music veered closer towards the roots of rock and roll and rhythm and blues, reflecting their new status as leaders of the barroom revolution. In April 1972, they commenced the recording of *Nervous On The Road* at Rockfield Studios, and it was there that they ran into the Welsh rocker and reclusive record producer, Dave Edmunds.

'There were more myths about Edmunds than was humanly possible,' says Martin Belmont. 'He had a big house in Monmouth, his chemical intake was massive, he would drive his Jaguar at ninety miles an hour through country lanes on Mandrax and whisky with his vintage Gibson 335, out of its case, on the back seat. In the studio, he would listen to playbacks at a deafening volume and squeeze the EQ up so far that people's trousers would rustle.'

'I thought Edmunds was really cool,' says Nick. 'He used to arrive at the studio to start work late in the evening just as we were packing up. There would be a scrunch on the gravel as he pulled up in the Jag, and he'd get out carrying various bottles and bags, and in he would go. He would work all night and these unbelievable noises would come out. I went out of my way to meet him, but he was very secretive, like a hermit. Then one time he came in while we were recording and listened to one of our tracks and asked us if he could have a tinker with it. Dave Robinson, who was our producer, looked a bit tense, but we all thought it was a good idea. Our recording was very tiresome, but Edmunds got a few Revoxes going, patched in some echo effects and suddenly the thing was jumping. In next to no time, he had transformed our leaden sound into an all-singing, all-dancing groove. We were a bit slack-jawed and saucer-eyed at this, although Dave Robinson got a bit cross. He said, "You can't have that, it's not real!" "Real" was the word we bandied about! I'm not blaming Robbo, we were all learning. When Edmunds and his engineer Kingsley Ward left the room we immediately disconnected all their tape echoes and returned to our mundane, lumpen thump. That's when I thought Edmunds might be the guy to produce our next record. I rather set out to get him to do it because I thought he could really sort us out.'

Nervous On The Road opens with 'It's Been So Long', a breezy little number from the pen of Ian Gomm. The sound throughout the record is basic, but Nick's songs are strong enough to withstand any amount of under-production, notably the shuffling 'Surrender To The Rhythm'; the pleading, aching 'Don't Lose Your Grip On Love'; and the title track, which summarises Nick's state of mind as he recovered from the effects of LSD. The Bob Andrews and Nick Lowe collaboration, 'Happy Doing What We're Doing', is a succinct mission statement reminiscent of the Lovin' Spoonful's 'Jug Band Music', complete with a superb 'minimal' guitar solo.

'We went over the top with our minimalist approach,' says Nick. 'It was aggressive. Solos had to be really, really pathetic. It could never be thin enough.'

It was now two years since 'The Hype' and, on 7 May 1972, Brinsley Schwarz performed in torrential rain at the Bickershaw Festival as one of the opening acts for the Grateful Dead. In the audience was Declan MacManus, a seventeen-year-old aspiring songwriter, who was then living in Liverpool. MacManus – destined to become 'Elvis Costello' – was a fan of Brinsley Schwarz, and as one half of a duo called Rusty, performed several Nick Lowe songs from *Silver Pistol*.

On 27 July, when the Brinsleys played Liverpool's Cavern Club, MacManus sidled up to Nick in the Grapes public house and offered to buy him a drink. MacManus recalls there being 'a barrier' between himself, who was 'just an amateur musician', and Nick, who was in a professional recording act.

As any bespectacled budding musicologist was no doubt aware, London's pub rock circuit was gradually expanding with new venues such as the Hope & Anchor and the Kensington coming on stream. A number of roots-rock combos appeared almost overnight, including Ducks Deluxe, with former Brinsleys roadie Martin Belmont on guitar alongside Sean Tyla, whom Nick had first met on his way to Germany back in 1961; Bees Make Honey, led by bass-playing advertising executive Barry Richardson; and Kilburn & the High Roads, fronted by charismatic polio victim, Ian Dury.

'Pub rock was an attempt to revive what had been going on before,' says Dai Davies. 'With Dave Robinson and Nick Lowe being around, there were many attempts to philosophise about it. It wasn't enough just to turn up in pubs and play – you had to have accompanying theories! The theory was that we were recreating what had made the Stones and the Who great.'

While the Brinsleys never played on a bill with the Stones or the Who, they did appear with London's other seminal rock group, the Kinks. This occurred on 9 June 1972 at Cambridge Corn Exchange, where both acts had to share the 'dressing room'. This took the form of a portable cabin, without a roof, positioned close to the stage. By the time the Brinsleys had finished their set, the Kinks had arrived, and, as Nick recalls, 'It was all go in the stockade. We felt quite drab sitting there watching these exotic flowers. Around show time there was a lot of trouble with the PA system. I went outside to smoke some grass, then Gomm and I decided to watch the Kinks from the back of the hall. On they came and it sounded terrible. Feedback, everything goes off, then on again, bloody awful. They persevered for a while with Ray Davies trying to keep it all going. "Here's one you all know, sing along!" Eventually they had to leave the stage. I was thinking, "What a shame", because I was extremely stoned and felt a lot of goodwill towards them. Anyway, the roadies were trying to fix the sound – "Not that one Jeff, try channel 24!" More noise. They went back on again, but it still sounded awful, then the sound went off completely, followed by all the lights in the place, so now it's pitch black. You couldn't see a thing. The crowd were quite calm, but it *was* Cambridge.

'Me and Gomm wanted to go and tell them everything was cool and groped our way forward through the crowd to get backstage. There was no security in those days, just a couple of trestle tables and a curtain. When we finally made it to the stockade there were all these voices in the dark, arguing about the sound. Now, every band has catchphrases and in-jokes, and our favourite at that time came from some band we'd opened for, whose manager we had overheard talking on the phone to somebody about his "boys". "Well, I've seen the place," he said, "and I'm telling you now, the boys won't be happy – I'll ask them, but I'm telling you right now they will NOT be happy!" We adopted this, and would trot it out whenever we'd arrive at one of the shitholes we had to play. All someone had to do was stand looking doubtfully around the room and say, "Well, I'll ask them . . ." and we were in hysterics.

'Anyway, we were in the stockade with the Kinks, in the dark, and Gomm says, "Well, I'm telling you now, the boys won't be happy." I thought that was just what the Kinks needed to hear, so I repeated it. Then there was a sound, like a large animal running through the undergrowth, and furniture being upturned, and I felt this wind go past me. Suddenly there were two hands clamped around my throat, and I went crashing backwards into the trestle table piled with Watneys beer and bowls of peanuts. There was food everywhere. I'm on the ground with the hands clamped round my neck, and he's saying, "The boys won't like it?! I'll show you how much they won't fucking like it!" And I'm on my back being strangled by this person on top of me. I was very stoned and I'd gone from goodwill towards the Kinks to fighting for my life. Just as I think I'm about to pass out, on come the lights and I look up to see Ray Davies, my boyhood hero, his face contorted with rage, staring down at me with flecks of foam at the sides of his mouth. He was beyond fury, white-faced. I could hear someone behind us saying, "Come on, Ray, leave him, he's not worth it." He let me go and they all trailed out to go back onstage. I'm lying in this pool of beer, and peanuts, and cheese and onion crisps. It rather put a downer on the rest of the evening for everyone.

'There is a slight epilogue to this in that many years later the phone at home went one night, and it was Ray Davies. He asked me if I wanted to produce his brother, Dave. I said, "Well I wouldn't rule it out, Ray, but do you know we have actually met before?" Of course he said he didn't remember, but he thought we might have met at some cocktail party. "Yeah, yeah." I tried to gently remind him of it. "The Corn Exchange, Cambridge, ring any bells?" He had no memory of it.'

'Pub rock was the regrouping of a bunch of middle-class ex-Mods, who had been through the hippie underground scene and realised it wasn't their cup of tea,' as Nick once said. He could easily have been describing Alan 'Bam' King, former guitarist with definitive 1960s Mod group, the Action, and later, English hippie ensemble, Mighty Baby. King was now in the process of forming Ace, a group that would have one of pub rock's rare commercial successes with 'How Long', written and sung by future Lowe-collaborator, Paul Carrack.

Another former member of Mighty Baby was guitarist Martin Stone, who hovered on the fringes of the pub scene, and with songwriter Phil Lithman formed a country blues duo named Chilli Willi & the Red Hot Peppers. In 1972, 'the Willies', as they were affectionately known, recorded the album *Kings Of The Robot Rhythm*, on which Nick Lowe, Bob Andrews and Billy

Rankin performed session duties. *Robot Rhythm* was released on the independent Revelation label, in a sleeve designed by Barney Bubbles, and is an early example of the packaging for which Bubbles would later become celebrated.

Chilli Willi gradually expanded to a quintet, adding multi-instrumentalist Paul 'Diceman' Bailey, bassist Paul 'Bassman' Riley and drummer Pete Thomas. In early 1973, they hit the London pub scene where they encountered a young man who would soon usurp John Coleman, their existing manager.

'We were summoned to Coleman's flat in Kensington,' recalls Riley. 'In walked this chap in an Afghan coat, a tank top and enormous steelworker's clogs. Most notably, he had a back-beard haircut – that style where you have long hair at the back but it is cut very short at the front, so it looks, at first glance, as if you've got short hair. His name was Andrew Jakeman and he seemed rather keen.[7]

'When he became our roadie, the burden of responsibility for maintaining the infrastructure of the group suddenly became his. But he started to try and make something of it and we said, "Hang on, this geezer is all right." Also, Jakeman didn't mind turning around to people and going, "Fuck you!" That was a phrase I could understand. I'd had it up to here with hippies by this time, and all that "OK man, that's cool, never mind" kind of bollocks. Jakeman started to get things done.'

Andrew Jakeman soon befriended Barney Bubbles and together they forged a creative partnership. When Jakeman became Chilli Willi's manager, he imposed on the group a strict work regime. Eventually, Revelation went bust and when John Coleman left London, Jakeman acquired the lease on his flat at 48 Queen's Gate Terrace. The address would become the Chilli Willi headquarters, from which Jakeman would run 'Downhill Management' and distribute a band newssheet entitled *Up Periscope*.

By 1974, Jakeman's image had changed; gone were the back-beard haircut and the Afghan coat, to be replaced by a much snappier look, in preparation for the day he would unveil his new persona as 'Jake Riviera' and offer his management services to Nick Lowe.

CHAPTER 7

Nervous on the Road

In early 1973, the lease on 10 Carew Road expired and Brinsley Schwarz were forced to seek alternative accommodation. They soon discovered Wilton Park Farm in Park Lane, Beaconsfield, to where they transferred their operation. Musically, the Brinsleys were in a rut and Nick, now partially recovered from his psychedelic nightmare, was feeling a certain amount of frustration.

'I'd started to think that what we were doing was real old-fashioned. I remember wanting to do Gilbert O'Sullivan's "Get Down". It had a good tune, it had been number one in the nation, and we'd only do it once. But I ran into some serious flak from the others and that made a real impression on me. From this minor thing, a huge row blew up and I said to them, "You don't get it."'

Despite Nick's desire for his group to out-hip the competition by unleashing an unexpected, middle-of-the-road pop song on its audience, he was starting to lose interest in being their de facto leader. At that time, Brinsley Schwarz were in the process of recording their fifth LP, *Please Don't Ever Change*, and were guaranteed to pack any pub venue with their hugely entertaining repertoire, but they were trapped by their self-imposed, purist stance.

'I enjoyed being the big fish in a small pool, I can't deny that,' says Nick. 'Being the darlings of the pub rock scene had a certain cachet, but it was going nowhere. My theory is that when they let the groups make their own records it all went horribly wrong. They let them write their own songs and more or less produce their own records when they knew bugger-all about it. This new multi-track recording thing had just come in. Those three factors are the reason why those records sound so awful and why there's no great legacy from pub rock.'

Brinsley Schwarz suddenly got a huge, unexpected break when they were offered the support slot on Paul McCartney's UK tour. The Brinsleys had recently played a benefit show in aid of Release – an 'underground' charity organisation that started in 1967 to provide free legal advice to people arrested for drugs offences – at London's Hard Rock Café, where McCartney was present, along with members of his band, Wings. Following the Brinsleys' set, Paul jumped up onstage and asked if Wings could borrow their equipment to perform an impromptu set. Through Dave Robinson's friendship with former Grease Band guitarist Henry McCullough, now a member of Wings, a meeting with McCartney's manager was set up. After a couple of false starts it was agreed that the Brinsleys could join the Wings tour on the proviso that they would be prepared to travel on McCartney's tour bus.

Suddenly, pub rock's top outfit had been booked to open for the world's most famous pop star. The tour commenced on 11 May 1973 at Bristol Hippodrome and would wind up two weeks later with a series of shows at London's Hammersmith Odeon. Each night, Dave Robinson studied McCartney's performance and was amazed by his professionalism, and how the Wings set kept improving on a nightly basis. He tried to impress upon the

Brinsleys the need to constantly work on their own show, but Nick and the band seemed to prefer the comforts of the pub.

Irrespective of Nick's reluctance to take charge, his towering height and strong facial features gave him a certain aura. He was a focal point in the eyes of fans, especially one Hermine Demoriane, a tightrope walker, who later recalled in her memoir:

> I get to the front row, face to face with my favourite Brinsley, the bass guitarist. He's so close that unless I lift my chin up I can only see his crotch . . . I like him very much . . . how am I ever going to get over having that great big lump of flesh, be it called Nick Lowe, in my bed?

Not long after the Wings tour, Dave Robinson ceased to manage Brinsley Schwarz and Dai Davies took over.

'Dave Robinson and the Brinsleys had been living in each other's pockets for three years,' says Davies. 'They were getting a little less purist and now wanted to become successful. Success was all right for Ronnie Hawkins or Lee Dorsey. It was a laudable thing! Nick Lowe, who did all of the thinking for everybody, reached a point where he wanted to make classic pop records and be in a successful pop group, although he had to invent an ideology to justify it.'

Please Don't Ever Change was released in October 1973. The title is taken from their charming version of the Crickets' 'Don't Ever Change', a hit of 1962, the year in which much of Nick's pop sensibility is grounded, although his five original songs reflect a more esoteric appreciation of rock's roots; 'I Worry ('bout You Baby)' has echoes of Fats Domino, as if written two decades earlier; the Ska-infused 'Why Do We Hurt The One We Love?' sounds like a pop standard from its opening bar; and 'Play That

Fast Thing (One More Time)' would go on to become a barroom favourite. But the album, produced by the group with engineer Vic Maile, was really no more than a holding plan until they could get into the studio with Dave Edmunds.

On 6 November, Brinsley Schwarz appeared on BBC Two's *Old Grey Whistle Test*, performing 'Surrender To The Rhythm' and 'One More Day'. Nick chose this high-profile TV appearance to unveil a new look, and on the day of the show had his hair dramatically cut into a spikey Mod style. He had failed to forewarn the group of his image change. 'I was really pissed off,' says Ian Gomm. 'Most of us still had long hair and Nick made us look like a bunch of old hippies.'

Nick had been encouraged to 'youth up' by a German woman he had recently met named Ulla Heathcote, an acquaintance of the aforementioned Hermine Demoriane. Ulla was a successful fashion designer and scene-setter who showed him around London and introduced him to new experiences.

'Ulla used to get on my case. "Wear this, do that." There was a bit of resentment among the group because she would turn up in her sports car and whisk me off to nightclubs and parties. She said, "What are you doing this old man's stuff for? You're not a bunch of old men, you're only twenty-four or twenty-five." Up until then, we'd wanted to be old blokes, like the Band.'

At the start of 1974 – while the UK was contending with the 'three-day week'; fuel shortages; television that shut down around 11 p.m.; and pubs that were forced to adhere to strict closing hours – Nick commenced keeping a diary in which he would record his thoughts and experiences. Within three months he had given up and confesses to being 'too undisciplined'. The diary is lost.

Nick's good intention was probably disrupted by the Brinsleys' new adventure that March, when Dave Edmunds was hired as musical director for the film *Stardust*, starring David Essex and Adam Faith. The script called for a pop group to warm up the crowd before Essex appeared onstage. Edmunds put forward the members of Brinsley Schwarz.

'Much to my astonishment,' Nick says, 'Edmunds phoned me up and told me he was producing Del Shannon. He wanted me to come and play bass. I was thrilled that Edmunds had asked me, but it was also a thrill to work with Del. Then Edmunds got us in *Stardust*. David Puttnam was the producer and we stayed at the Post House Hotel in Manchester. Having a room with a TV and a kettle, plus UHT milk and a WC, was un-dreamt of. We were there for three glorious days and the bar was open all night. Keith Moon and his mates were there, with grade-A babes. Our job was to play live to these kids before David Essex came on, but they booed and howled at us.

'The night before the filming we got drunk with Keith Moon, who sent out for copious quantities of curry, which he dumped over actor Karl Howman's head, a very seventies thing. The next day we had to be on call at six in the morning, even though they don't want you until six in the afternoon, but we failed to get up. I had this irate phone call from David Puttnam, who was beside himself with rage. "You get up and you get down here now!" he yelled. I still used to react to grown-ups telling me off. He put the fear of God into me. I jumped out of bed and was the first one down there. He was seething and things didn't improve when Dave Edmunds, who had one line in the film, which I think was "Fuck Off", managed to persuade them to open the bar so he could get a Bloody Mary. I said to Puttnam, "Have a heart, we've never done anything like this before, we can't help it if we were up late." It was the straw that broke the camel's back. Puttnam screamed, "Look, I know what your name is, and yours, and yours, and believe me, I will see that none of you ever works for me again." He was completely right.'

Shortly after the *Stardust* episode, Dave Edmunds agreed to produce the next Brinsley Schwarz album. He noted that the Brinsleys were strongly influenced by the Band and concerned with 'keeping it real'. Authenticity was their preoccupation, thus they were wary of using studio effects, or double-tracking the vocals to fatten the sound – an approach that resulted in some of their early recordings sounding rather flat. Edmunds pointed out to them that if they really wanted their records to sound 'under-produced', then they had to be recorded in a certain way, which was exactly what the Band did. With all of this in mind, Edmunds set about introducing some production values to the forthcoming record.

'Whereas we were intimidated by the recording studio, Dave treated it with contempt,' says Nick, describing Edmunds's approach to making records. 'He was fearless and he got us to do little tricks that had never occurred to us, such as double-tracking only selected lines, radical pushing up of faders, guitars surging, echoes keeping the mix moving all the time.'

The result was the Brinsleys' most polished album, *The New Favourites Of Brinsley Schwarz*. Recorded during April and May 1974 and released that summer, the record kicks off with massive power chords, redolent of the Who, announcing the opening bars of '(What's So Funny 'bout) Peace, Love And Understanding'.

The song's lyrics seem to take a sly poke at those who thought it simply hilarious to utter, 'Yeah, peace and love man,' whenever they spotted a longhair in loon pants. Now, 'the hippie' was answering back, and his detractors' feeble joke became a tiresome cliché. This may have been on Nick's mind when he sat down to write the song and ask his rhetorical question. After all, what exactly *was* wrong with peace and love, surely the universal goals of civilisation?

Nick has since described composing the song as 'the seismic moment' of his early songwriting career. 'When the title, "What's so funny 'bout . . ." sprang into my head, I simply couldn't believe my luck. I knew I was onto something.'

The words may have been subconsciously influenced by the Gaylads' 1970 Ska classic, 'Peace Love And Understanding', as it boomed out of a north London jukebox around the time the Brinsleys were packing them in on the pub circuit. Tune-wise, Nick has always acknowledged the influence of Judee Sill's 'Jesus Was A Cross Maker', and the role it played when he was putting the song together. 'I pinched her ginchy little lick,' he confesses.

As he would later tell *A.V. Club*: 'It was originally supposed to be a joke song, but something told me there was a little grain of wisdom in this thing, and not to mess it up. Just to keep it real simple, and don't be too clever with it. Because I thought I was hot stuff back then, when I really, really wasn't. I had a lot to learn. As I said, this was the first decent, proper, original idea I'd had, and something told me just to take it easy. And I'm glad I did, because otherwise that song would have died when Brinsley Schwarz died. Not the guy, the group [laughs].'

'What's So Funny 'bout . . .' would later be recorded by Elvis Costello and performed onstage by Bruce Springsteen, achieving almost anthemic status, a modern-day hymn no less. And thanks to the song's inclusion on the multimillion-selling movie soundtrack album *The Bodyguard*, sung by Curtis Stigers, it would one day help to sustain Nick's musical career well into the twenty-first century. But in 1974, only a few thousand fans heard it.

Further strong Lowe songs can be found on *New Favourites*. 'Ever Since You're Gone' is a Chitown-tinged soul ballad, with just a hint of Boz Scaggs in the vocal delivery, and 'The Look That's In Your Eye Tonight' is a waltz-time paean to the lover he reluctantly has to leave. The latter is easily as good as some of the material that was coming out of Nashville's hit factories at the time and consolidated his skills as a songwriter. These early songs confirm just how long he's been close to the top of his game, and how under-appreciated his earlier work was at the time.

The lighter numbers on side one, 'The Ugly Things', and 'I Got The Real Thing', are joyous power pop with Beatles-like chord changes and harmonies. Side two is less remarkable, but entertains with covers of the Hollies' 'Now's The Time' and Otis Clay's 1972 soul classic, 'Trying To Live My Life Without You'. The remaining R&B-flavoured songs exhibit New Orleans, Motown and soul influences, reflecting the diversity that characterised the London scene. Sadly though, the Brinsleys' sixth and best album was another commercial flop.

No sooner had Dave Edmunds mixed the record than he decided it was time to air his studio tan. Save for a couple of isolated shows, he hadn't toured in five years, but he enjoyed the company of Brinsley Schwarz so much that he considered them his ideal backing band. A dozen or so venues were booked for the 'New Favourites Tour' that June, but what none of the seasoned players had anticipated was the threat posed by the tour's opening act, Dr Feelgood.

The Feelgoods had hit London the previous year, tearing up the circuit with a ferocity that hadn't been witnessed since the early days of the Rolling Stones. So powerful was their onstage presence that the musical sea change they unwittingly set in motion would help to bring about the demise of Brinsley Schwarz and their pub rock contemporaries.

'Dr Feelgood blew us off stage every night. And Dave Edmunds got his illnesses. At Bristol, he wouldn't go on – "My hands won't work". We believed him, but the Feelgoods were fantastic – no contest. They made us look real pedestrian and kind of old.'

Brinsleys fan Declan MacManus, recalls seeing the tour: 'Dave Edmunds was absolutely howling, and so loud. He was the loudest thing I'd ever heard in a club, playing through a Fender Dual Showman, flat out. I suspect he was being propped up at the microphone, but he seemed to have amazing powers of recovery. Five minutes before he went on, he didn't seem to be with-it at all. Then he'd get up and do it.'

For a group that had been obsessed with the music of the Band, Brinsley Schwarz were dumbstruck when their American musical heroes paid them a visit that September. The Band were in England to play Wembley Stadium, midway down a bill headlined by Crosby, Stills, Nash & Young. A few days before the concert, the telephone at Wilton Park Farm rang, and Brinsley answered.

'It was Martyn Smith, phoning from Warner Brothers,' he recalls. 'He said, "Do you mind if the Band come up and rehearse?" I took it that he'd said, "*a* band". He said, "No man, *the* Band! Now!" I said, "Fine!" Then I put the phone down and told the others that the Band were coming to rehearse. They said, "Sure."'

It transpired that some days earlier Bob Andrews had called Martyn Smith because he had wanted to meet his idol, Band organist Garth Hudson, and Smith had arranged the best possible introduction. Once convinced that the Band's imminent arrival was not a hoax, the members of Brinsley Schwarz hurriedly began making preparations. 'Billy made sandwiches,' recalls Martin Belmont. 'And Nick started hoovering the rehearsal room in readiness for their arrival. And Nick is a man who loathes the sound of a Hoover.'

Soon the Band's equipment arrived, followed by a stretch limousine. 'Five cardboard cut-out figures got out,' recalls Andrews, recounting the mass outbreak of hero worship.

'We were crazy for the Band,' say Nick. 'We didn't believe they were coming to our place. We thought it was a wind-up, of course. Someone was having a joke. We had a dormant farm with lots of outbuildings, and our rehearsal room was a barn on concrete blocks to keep the rats out. The Band turned up and we just sat on flight cases outside. They brought their own guitars and Garth's Lowry organ and used our amps and drums. It was a lovely warm evening. We stayed away from them because we didn't want to crowd them. They stayed for an hour or two. I remember Levon [Helm] and Rick [Danko] looking around the old farm implements in the yard and the stables. Then right at the end, Garth [Hudson] was playing his Lowry, making incredible music that sounded like it came from the spheres and we were all leaning on the organ listening to him. Suddenly Bob couldn't contain himself any longer and said something to the effect of, "This is a dream come true. You don't know how incredible you are." It was a sweet speech. Sadly, it freaked Garth out. The spell was broken and he just said, "I guess it's time to leave." He was confused and embarrassed by this kid telling him how great he was. It was a shame. Bob got the piss taken out of him for it, but if he hadn't said it, I would have done.'

Several souvenirs from the Band's visit were retained in the hope that some of their magic might rub off on the Brinsleys. Ian Gomm kept the empty orange liqueur bottle from which Richard Manuel had been drinking, and Schwarz, besotted with Robbie Robertson and desperate to learn a few of his tricks, held on to his idol's guitar lead. 'I'd spent years trying to perfect the Robertson sound,' says Schwarz. 'As soon as he plugged into my amp, which he'd decided to use, he sounded just like Robbie Robertson! It really pissed me off.'

*

After *New Favourites* failed to sell in quantity, Brinsley Schwarz thought they might wriggle out of their United Artists contract. There had been some interest from Island Records, whose A&R man Richard Williams took his boss, Chris Blackwell, to see the group play live at the Nag's Head, High Wycombe, but nothing came of it. Around this time, someone floated the radical idea of the group relocating to America, where their music might be more appreciated, but United Artists was reluctant to fund such a risky enterprise. Paradoxically, as their frustration grew, Brinsley Schwarz became so popular on the London pub scene that they resorted to using spoof names to control attendances. Only the most ardent follower would decode 'Reg Lowe & the Electricians'.

But it was all getting rather desperate; United Artists, keen to recoup some of their outlay following a string of unsuccessful albums, persuaded the group to cover some Beatles songs, the intention being to issue them under a pseudonym to overcome any prejudice that might have existed at the all-powerful BBC Radio 1. Consequently, a single that coupled the Lennon/McCartney compositions, 'I Should Have Known Better' and 'Tell Me Why', was credited to 'Limelight'. To all intents and purposes the Brinsleys had become masked men.

A last-ditch attempt to make a hit record – and perhaps one that could find favour in the USA – involved the American producer Steve Verroca. Recording took place at Rockfield in two seven-day sessions, three months apart.

'Steve Verroca was a good producer, but I was too young then to give him what he wanted, vocally. Verroca said, "Now Nick, I want you to understand, this guy is at the end of his tether. But, he's still got a couple of cards left to play." I didn't know what he was talking about – *the guy is at the end of his tether but he's still got a couple of cards he can play?* What? He then explained: "The song. You're about to do the vocal on the song. You are *the guy in the song.*" I'd never before been asked to consider being a character. I thought it was incredible to be taken seriously like that, and asked to play the part.'

The master tapes of the Verroca album were thought to have been lost, but the tracks eventually saw a release in 2017 as an album entitled *It's All Over Now*. Its contents include covers of Tommy's Roe's 'Everybody', William Bell and Judy Clay's 'Private Number' and the Bobby Womack-composed title track. An attempt to record Bettye LaVette's 'Let Me Down Easy', featuring a Bob Andrews lead vocal, ended up, according to Nick, 'like a Troggs tape'.[8]

'We'd been to the pub, I think. Bob was singing and I actually fell asleep. You hear him singing, and then you hear me letting out this strangled cry and lots of banging, as Bob clocked me one. You can hear my bass still playing, but I'm clearly fast asleep.'

Nick's original material includes 'God Bless Whoever Made You' – co-written with Ian Gomm and later covered by Jona Lewie; 'We Can Mess Around With Anything But Love'; 'As Lovers Do'; and 'Cruel To Be Kind',[9] a blue-eyed Philadelphia soul pastiche that Nick confesses was written with one ear on 'The Love I Lost' by Harold Melvin & the Blue Notes.

'Cruel To Be Kind' would one day underscore a pivotal moment in Nick's career and introduce his music to a much wider audience, but that would have to wait another five years.

In the autumn of 1974, Andrew 'Jake' Jakeman, who was still managing Chilli Willi & the Red Hot Peppers, began to spend all of his spare time around the Brinsley Schwarz operation.

'I met Nick at the Marquee,' said Jake. 'He was there with Billy Rankin to see some band and they were speeding out of their lids. I went back to Beaconsfield with them in Billy Rankin's Ford Anglia that had a three-litre Zodiac engine in it. It was the most scary drive! Billy kept saying, "It's all right, man, the pills cut through the booze, no problem!" I went out and stayed at their house and talked to them, because we all knew each other, and I suggested to Nick that I would look after them.'

When the Brinsleys undertook an eight-date Dutch tour in November 1974, Jakeman tagged along, making himself useful and assuming a quasi-managerial role. But for guitarist Ian Gomm, the aspiring Jakeman blew it the moment they landed back at Heathrow Airport.

'We were on the public concourse,' recalls Gomm. 'Jake started shouting loudly, and threw his briefcase in the air. It slid across the floor, towards a crowd of people. Shortly after that incident, he said he wanted to manage Nick and I as songwriters.'

It was United Artists' managing director Martin Davies who had suggested that Nick Lowe and Ian Gomm might wish to be retained as an in-house songwriting and record production team, having realised that their group was likely to disband. As part of the package, Martin Davies proposed Jakeman as the duo's manager.

'Jake could see the potential,' continues Gomm. 'But I didn't like the way he inveigled his way in, and homed in on Nick. I thought he was leading him astray. So I turned it down. I didn't want Jake to manage me, but Nick loved all the drama.'

'I thought, "Excellent! Here's a bloke who doesn't mind",' says Nick. 'Jake and I just hit it off and we liked each other. He was much more worldly than I, which I found attractive. He'd lived in France; he knew about wine and food, and films. I figured he was someone I could learn a lot from. Also, I liked the fact that Jake was a party animal, but he was a bit of a handful for Brinsley. It was Brinsley's group, which was rather convenient for the likes of me and Billy. Brinsley used to make it all run well, but to get him to embrace certain styles or ideas, we had to go through a rather elaborate deception. If we could make him think it was his idea, then it got done. Jake would say, "Come on guys, let's do this, shape up!" And you could sense Brinsley thinking, "Hold on, mate, not so fast, I'm the leader here."'

Before long, Nick fell into the habit of crashing on Jake's couch at Queen's Gate Terrace, rather than return to the Beaconsfield commune after an evening's cavorting in Kensington. Many hours were spent at the Churchill Arms public house, where they would discuss their future plans, perhaps working together to shake up the music business. This was a decisive turning point for Nick and his would-be manager, and one on which both of their careers now hinged. Jake was Nick's number-one fan, and Nick would benefit from the fact that Jake was a human dynamo – 'the manager from another planet' – and hungry for success.

In January 1975, Jakeman launched 'The Naughty Rhythms Tour' in an attempt to bring Chilli Willi & the Red Hot Peppers to the masses. But the UK trek, which also featured Kokomo and Dr Feelgood, had the opposite effect and hastened the end of Chilli Willi.

The Feelgoods dominated the action and broke through on a national scale. Jakeman quickly sensed that the original pub rock groups were becoming redundant. In Jake's eyes, Dr Feelgood were the unstoppable force that would transform live rock and roll in the UK, and he was more right than wrong. Most importantly, he knew that Nick Lowe was a genius who needed no more than a swift kick up the arse every ten minutes. Nick knew it too, and from this point he and Jake were bonded. They would remain friends and business partners for an incredible four decades.

*

As 1975 dawned, Nick was about to enter a world of personal and musical mayhem, fuelled largely by a cocktail of off-the-shelf depressants that came in a tall glass bottle, and under-the-counter stimulants that were often wrapped in origami. His senses would also be awoken by exciting developments on the music scene, but first there was the small matter of winding down the operation to which he had been attached for the past six years – the cult-heroic but under-achieving group, Brinsley Schwarz.

Following a UK tour, on which they opened for folk-rock musician Al Stewart, the Brinsleys' farewell show on 18 March at London's Marquee Club was an emotional occasion. Delivering two sets for their hardcore fans, Nick – somewhat tongue-in-cheek – announced various songs as their 'hit singles'. They played 'Country Girl' (twice), encored with 'Brown Sugar', but omitted their current and farewell 45, 'There's A Cloud In My Heart'. Brinsley himself thought it was the best gig they had done for years, and hoped that they might continue, but for Nick it was time to move on. He sensed that something new was coming, musically, but his colleagues still didn't 'get it'.

'I don't really remember us having the conversation, but I suppose there was one. I definitely disappointed Bob and Brinsley and probably they were right to feel let down. I don't think I behaved altogether very well. It was all to do with hanging around with Jake, and spending more and more time at Queen's Gate Terrace, and I began to think that the Brinsleys thing was all a bit yesterday. I really wanted to be shot of it, but I think I jumped ship in a rather undignified fashion. I ran away from some loose ends, which I'm not very proud of, and I realised, of course, that I'd have to find somewhere to live. I was terrified. I didn't know anyone outside our little scene, except for Jake. Initially, I went to share a flat in Fulham with my sister.'

'I was working for *The Economist* in London,' recalls Penny. 'Nick was homeless, so I duly found a flat in St Olaf's Road, Fulham, which I could afford, and off we went. I remember giving Nick some money for the deposit to go and get a television set on hire purchase. But I will never forget Jake coming round, just to talk to me about how much money I needed from Nick every month. Although everything was in my name, Nick was going to pay me half. I wasn't terribly business-like, and I was going through it, and I said, "Well, the mortgage is x, and the electricity is y, and that's roughly what it is every month." To which Jake replied, "I hope you're not ripping him off, trying to make a few quid out of him." I had to remind Jake that Nick was my brother, and that that was the most unpleasant thing I'd ever heard.'

For Nick, sharing a flat with his sister was 'a bad idea' from day one. Penny had a high-powered job and needed to go to bed early on weeknights, but no sooner had she retired for the night than Nick would stagger back from the Nashville pub, which was within walking distance, with several musician friends in tow. They would proceed to 'get the guitars out', and Penny would emerge from her room, 'covered in face cream', and address the drunken throng.

'Sadly, everybody came back to ours,' says Penny. 'Those smelly, unwashed people. I was the one who had to go out and earn a crust, and I only had the weekends to do the housework. I'd go into the sitting room and there would be all these bodies everywhere. Dave Robinson would be there, and I said, "For God's sake, Dave, it's nearly ten o'clock, you should be up and about by now." He looked at me, holding my can of Pledge, with horror. And they would smoke pot. There were little old ladies who lived in the block and I could smell it down the street. And Nick would be in his scuzzy old bedroom for hours, composing new songs on his Revox.'

Nick comments: 'The way my brother-in-law tells it, my sister screamed at the cream of English music who were sitting around – Ian Dury, Elvis Costello, Graham Parker – and she would shout, "Right, you lot can all fuck off!"'

There were, however, advantages to living in London, such as being able to network with other musicians, hang out at the key nightspots and generally promote oneself, not forgetting, of course, that in the mid-1970s, the capital was still rather quaint.

'London back then was a dreary, drab old place,' recalls Nick. 'There were no flat white coffees or lattes, nothing like that. That's when London belonged to me, when it was a dreary old shithole. But it was my shithole.'

Following the Brinsleys' break-up, United Artists had exercised its contractual option on Nick's solo services and may have envisaged him as 'some kind of Rock Lite *artiste*, like James Taylor or John Sebastian, quirky and be-denimed'.

But this was nothing like the image that Nick adopted that year; with his hair trimmed short and a trilby on the back of his head, he hit the London hotspots as a songwriter-about-town. Demo cassettes bulged from the pockets of his natty three-piece suit as he exploited his 'have I got a song for you' routine, like some old-time Tin Pan Alley hustler. He was otherwise unemployed, spending most of his time in the company of Jake, whose managerial role had recently been cemented on a handshake.

CHAPTER 8
The Wilderness Year

I'm a fan. I'll write songs about pop music.

The two men were now inseparable and whiled away the hours over the record player at Queen's Gate Terrace, although Jake found it hard to sit still for long and took a job as tour manager for Dr Feelgood, then basking in the success of their debut album, *Down By The Jetty*. About to embark on their 'Speeding Through Europe' tour, the Feelgoods played some warm-up dates in Holland, and Nick went along for the ride. At Boddy's Music Inn in Amsterdam he performed alongside members of Dr Feelgood, the Kursaal Flyers and the recently disbanded Chilli Willi, as 'Spick Ace & the Blue Sharks'. It was suggested that the makeshift combo record an EP with the working title 'All Meat Diet', but the Spick Ace project was short-lived.

'I feel the hand of Jake on that. I think it was essentially the Feelgoods and a few floating people who were in town. It was a jolly up. We were having a laugh.'

*

Andrew Jakeman's entrepreneurial skills were starting to make ripples. United Artists, the record label to whom the Feelgoods had recently signed, regarded him as something of a golden boy. But this was also the label from which Jake was hoping to extricate Nick. Visiting the UA offices, where he would make full use of the mail room and photocopying facilities, Jakeman casually mentioned that Nick was cutting a tribute to chart-topping teen sensations, the Bay City Rollers. He was half hoping that UA would consider it a ridiculous idea and shred Lowe's contract. At first the label thought it was just another of Jakeman's pranks, but their chortles were silenced when Nick delivered 'Bay City Rollers We Love You' the following week.

> *I'd like to buy a white guitar like Woody's*
> *Play it up high, with some other guy,*
> *singing Bye Bye Baby, Bye Bye*

It was certainly a highly commercial novelty, its sound reminiscent of songwriter and producer Mike Batt's 'Wombles' hits, complete with 'Glitter Band' drums. Recording at Vic Keary's Chalk Farm Studios, Nick slowed the tape down in order to record his vocal, so that when it was played back at normal speed his voice would sound higher and younger, perhaps in order to appeal to the pre-pubescent Bay City Rollers fans. To ice the cake, Nick recruited children from the nearby Haverstock Hill School to provide the sing-along backing vocals under the tutelage of their music teacher, Penelope Tobin.

> *Derek, Alan, Eric, we love you*
> *Les and Woody do you feel the same way too?*
> *You're making all our dreams come true*
> *Bay City Rollers we love you*

The guitar solo picks out the melody in a lower octave, reminiscent of Hank B. Marvin on some 1962 Shadows hit. Although meaningless to its intended audience, this was a cool production touch that would resonate with older listeners, should they ever get to hear it. Subtle references aside, United Artists loved 'Bay City Rollers We Love You' and scheduled its release!

A second track was required and 'Rollers Theme (Instrumental)' would typify the throwaway flipside of the era. In Japan, the disc was packaged in a picture sleeve bearing a Peter Max-style illustration of 'the Rollers'. Attributed to the pseudonymous 'Tartan Horde', the record label informed customers that the songs had been written by 'Terry Modern' and that this was a 'Modern Boys Production'.

'I used to listen to the hit parade avidly and I think the Wombles sound was what I was subconsciously trying to emulate. I also thought the Rubettes were great, and the Bee Gees, and Abba, no problem at all. I was listening to that stuff so that I could steal from it. It was a "nudge-nudge wink-wink" thing for your friends. If it was too similar to something else that you claimed to be your own, that wasn't on, but if you did a giant lift, aggressively, like you'd so obviously borrowed a middle eight from somewhere, it didn't seem to matter.

'There comes a time when you just cannot keep up with all your influences, and suddenly even the stuff that you thought was really cool for a while, like that week you thought the much-maligned Electric Light Orchestra were hot, all meshes into one big splodge of influence. Even though my stuff sounds familiar – even I've heard it before – it's because I come from that era when two verses, a chorus and a middle eight is how a song goes, using as few chords as possible. In retrospect, I think I thought those seventies hit-makers had this great thing going on, but they were not dealing with it properly. They could have made it much more subversive. The Rollers thing seems like nothing now, but it was quite shocking back then to find you could do this. It wound people up, making these awful records. I had fun doing them but they were purposely, knowingly bad, to get me out of my record deal.'

The Tartan Horde disc represented a win-win situation for Nick; if successful, much-needed cash would be generated. If it were a flop, he might be released from his United Artists contract so that a new, more lucrative deal could be sought elsewhere. Whatever the outcome, Lowe's name would not be directly attached to the Rollers project, and, at the very worst, he might gain kudos as the shadowy mastermind behind the tacky tribute.

Much to everyone's surprise, 'Bay City Rollers We Love You' sold well in Japan, then the world's fourth largest market for recorded music, and far from losing Lowe his contract, United Artists demanded a follow-up.

Various recording sessions took place over the next year as Jake and Nick pieced together their plan for world domination. But before any of their creative jewels could be presented to the wider audience, they faced the challenge of making a suitably naff single to follow 'Bay City Rollers We Love You', in order that Nick might be dropped by United Artists.

With its conga rhythm and sing-along chorus, 'Let's Go To The Disco' was a strong contender, guaranteed to flop if sprinkled with not quite enough fairy dust. Strategic incompetence was the name of the game, and Nick enlisted Dave Edmunds to carefully fashion the non-hit. It was recorded at Rockfield, in a two-day session that also yielded a superfluous cover of Dr Feelgood's 'Keep It Out Of Sight'. The result, attributed to 'The Disco Brothers', was then delivered to United Artists. It did the trick, although the release of 'Let's Go To The Disco' would be shelved for twelve months, by which time United Artists had finally dispensed with the culprit's services.

During his stay of execution, Nick signed a music-publishing contract with Peter Barnes's Rock Music Company, securing a modest but useful advance. He immediately sought to fulfil his songwriting obligations by presenting a quarter-inch home demo tape of 'Television' to the Kursaal Flyers. Although not a hit, it did result in what is thought to be the third[10] recorded cover of Nick's career when it was included on *The Great Artiste*. Nick was not so successful, however, with 'Fool Too Long', which he pushed in the direction of Dr Feelgood. It had been recorded at Dave Robinson's 8-track studio above the Hope & Anchor, and from the same session came 'Everybody Dance', co-written with the American guitarist and Roogalator main man, Danny Adler. Nick had seen Roogalator on the pub circuit, having been tipped off by former Chilli Willi bassist Paul Riley, who was now a member of Adler's blues-driven combo.

'Danny Adler and Roogalator, on their night, were really sensational,' says Nick. 'They were like Captain Beefheart, with a funky weird groove. Danny called it "Roogalation" and nobody else has come up with a better word for that groove. He was a much better musician than all of us, but his one foible was that he took it too seriously. No one could get his arrangements. By the same token, if I'd sat and listened to him, my thing would have been better too.'

'Nick liked our sound,' says Adler. 'We were different from other things around and he was really into my guitar style. In fact he used to ask me to teach him various licks. He needed a B-side for something and had some lyric fragments for "Everybody Dance". He was trying to do it as a cod-disco funk thing. I suggested we do it in a reggae groove, and he gave me a co-writer credit.'

Although the basic track for 'Everybody Dance' was laid down at Dave Robinson's studio, the equipment developed a malfunction and the recording had to be completed elsewhere. Searching for somewhere inexpensive, Robinson called in at Pathway Studios, a basic 8-track facility in nearby Newington Green. Pathway was to play a key role in Nick's career as a budding record producer, but for the moment he was creatively directionless.

Some of the recordings made in this period would one day be released on a ragged compilation entitled *The Wilderness Years*. Nick's self-deprecating sleeve note includes a brief comment about each track, and while he glosses over the pure pop sensibility of 'Bay City Rollers We Love You', he rightly dismisses several throwaway songs, 'So Heavy' being a case in point. Another Rollers tribute cut, the dub style 'Allorolla', he describes as 'ludicrous', and of the obscure 'I Got A Job', he writes: 'A song I can remember neither writing nor recording, truly the flagship of *The Wilderness Years.*'

The year 1975 was a period of great frustration for Nick. Most days he would wake up with an empty diary and a sore back, having kipped on his manager's couch once too often, but the devil found plenty of work for their idle hands. Pranks were the order of the day and at Dingwalls Dance Hall in Camden Town, the hip hangout for musicians, journalists and seasoned groupies, Jakeman mentioned to anyone within earshot that Nick had been selected to replace Peter Gabriel in the progressive rock band, Genesis. The lines were now being drawn; Genesis – for all their commercial success with concept albums, lengthy instrumental workouts and artsy costumes – represented the old guard (despite being about the same age as Nick). Nick felt that a musical revolution was in the air, although the detail was hard to pin down.

'Jake kept saying, "There's something coming and we've got to do it, whatever it is." I felt that the music was about to change. Things were certainly getting faster. Pop journalism was changing too. No one swallowed that line: "And Nick's dislikes are – phony people and girls who wear too much make-up! Favourite meal? Chinese!" By now, pop music had been around the circuit and we were the first generation to benefit from that. We were hip then, in our own little world. We were looking to make a mark. The *NME* and the *Melody Maker* were big sellers. I'd open them up each week and it would be like my personal diary. I'd say to myself, "Now, let's see what I got up to this week." We got such a kick out of doing things a little bit skew-whiff. We liked being perverse, and then we got more and more emboldened when we saw it ruffle a few feathers. That was a terrific thrill after being seen as a bit of a loser. I got much more arch under Jake's influence and I thought, "Look, we don't need to be underlings in this pop business. We can be tastemakers here. This is our time."

'The way I saw it was I'd done my apprenticeship playing the clubs in Germany, up and down the motorway with the Brinsleys, and suddenly I was at the front of the queue. It was as if someone was saying to me, "OK, you're the new generation, you've learnt your craft, now what have you got?" I looked around and I didn't like anything. I wanted to make some mischief and a name for myself. I didn't want to be Mike Batt, or Jonathan King, or in a supposedly hip group like Bad Company. I could feel something was brewing that had come out of pub rock. Just to see Ian Dury and the Kilburns, or the Feelgoods, you knew that even though it was old stuff they were doing, the way they were telling it was brand, brand-new.'

By mixing with influential writers and photographers from the music press, and feeding them titbits, Jakeman was a one-man publicity machine. It was a facility that would stand him in good stead during the gradual coming together in London of a few like-minded individuals who had been quietly working on a broadly similar musical blueprint. Through the pub rock network and, crucially, Dave Robinson's studio at the Hope & Anchor, two musicians gravitated towards Nick's world: the aforementioned Declan MacManus (or 'D. P. Costello' as he was now styling himself) and Graham Parker, a twenty-four-year-old petrol pump attendant from Camberley, Surrey.

Heavily influenced by Bob Dylan and Van Morrison, Graham Parker was a supremely gifted songwriter who had been honing his craft in a series of amateur groups since his teens. Inspired by Dr Feelgood's performance on the 'Naughty Rhythms Tour' at Guildford Civic Hall, he was ready to make his move. Answering an ad in the *Melody Maker*, Parker hooked up with slide guitarist Noel Brown, and following a lead from Noel's friend, Paul Riley, was soon recording demos with Dave Robinson. It was evident that Parker possessed a rare vocal and songwriting talent. Robinson played the demos to writer and broadcaster Charlie Gillett, and within days Parker's 'Between You And Me' was aired on Gillett's BBC radio show.

Listening in that Sunday was Phonogram A&R man Nigel Grainge, who offered Parker a recording contract on the strength of hearing that one song. 'I heard the magic,' says Grainge. 'Then I went to hear him rehearse with his band. It was mind-blowing.'

Dave Robinson, now orchestrating Parker's career, suggested that Nick Lowe should produce. 'I didn't know who the fuck Nick was,' says Parker. 'All I knew was that he called himself "Tartan Horde" and had a minor hit in Japan. I thought of him as a quirky guy who might write a novelty song now and again.'

Apart from self-producing his Bay City Rollers tribute disc, Nick had never occupied the studio hot seat before, but he would

be in reasonably familiar surroundings; his former colleagues –
Bob Andrews, Brinsley Schwarz and ex-roadie Martin Belmont
– were now three-fifths of Parker's sensational new backing
group, the Rumour, that also included drummer Steve Goulding
and bassist Andrew Bodnar.

Explaining Nick's appointment as producer, Belmont quips,
'Well, first of all he was cheap! He'd never produced anything,
but Dave was savvy enough to realise that Nick was the man for
the job. He was a feel producer who would be able to catch the
spontaneity. There would be no "take ten".'

Nick hadn't seen Brinsley or Bob since the break-up of their band
earlier that year, but bruised egos were not allowed to stand in the
way of the task in hand – to deliver a great Graham Parker debut
album. Parker's musicians were electrifying, and his key songs
– 'Back To Schooldays', 'Soul Shoes', 'Howlin' Wind' and 'Don't
Ask Me Questions' – simply trumped everything that the pub rock
scene had promised. Eden Studios engineer Mike Gardner would
take care of the sound, and really all Nick had to do was show up
and summon some great performances from the players.

Nick's production technique essentially involved taking the
more forceful musicians into his confidence and assuring them that
they were making history. At the same time, he would encourage
the whole band with expansive arm movements and lashings of
enthusiasm. Spontaneous magic was the objective, never mind
the technical niceties of the mixing desk. Playback volume in the
control room was loud, although not quite at Edmunds-level,
and every now and then, Nick would hit the talkback button to
communicate with the musicians on the other side of the glass.
'Dreadful,' he might whisper after a particularly rocking take.

At first, the less-seasoned players were not sure how to
interpret Nick's ironic commentary, but the good humour soon
became infectious. If stuck for a witty riposte, Nick would simply

fall back on some good old public schoolboy humour, singling out any individual musician he considered strong enough to take his mock criticism. 'Look,' he might say to the drummer in an exasperated tone, 'you're wasting *your time, the school's time, and your parents' money.*' The whole band would be rolling around in fits of laughter as the atmosphere in the studio became relaxed and creative. The proof of Nick's unorthodox approach lay in the grooves of *Howlin' Wind,* the Graham Parker album that would one day find itself at number 54 in *Rolling Stone*'s list of 'The 100 best albums of the last 20 years'.

While Nick was producing Parker, Andrew Jakeman continued to tour manage Dr Feelgood, who had recently signed to CBS Records for North America. In January 1976, the corporation held its annual sales conference in San Diego, California, where the Feelgoods were invited to perform. The incoming president of CBS, Bruce Lundvall, had taken a shine to the little ole R&B combo from Canvey Island and granted them an almost unlimited touring budget. 'Obviously we loaded it up,' says the band's manager, Chris Fenwick. 'If someone wanted to make themselves busy, there was plenty to do.'

One of the Feelgoods' closest friends, happy to roll his sleeves up, was 'guitar roadie' Nick Lowe, who checked in at San Diego's Rivermont Hotel as 'Dale Liberator, equipment handler'. His presence on the jaunt was not entirely unrelated to the fact that Beserkley Records, a San Francisco-based independent label, had expressed interest in signing him, now that he had been dropped by United Artists. Although there were enquiries from one or two other companies, including Nigel Grainge's Ensign label, Jakeman was taken with Beserkley's flair, and the Feelgoods' Californian trip provided him with the perfect opportunity to take a detour to San Francisco.

Following the CBS conference, which turned out to be a pleas-
ingly hedonistic few days, the Feelgood party transferred to Los
Angeles, where they paid a visit to West Hollywood's Starwood
Club to see blues legend, John Lee Hooker. Upon leaving the
venue, their hire car was stopped on Santa Monica Boulevard
and its occupants ordered by two police officers to get out of the
vehicle and 'up against the wall'.

Chris Fenwick remembers Nick's reaction: 'He said to one of
the cops, who was holding a gun, "Do you mind if I smoke a
cigarette, old boy?" He was doing the "Limey abroad" routine,
but the cop yelled, "Don't move!" Some illicit smoking material
was found in the glove compartment and Fenwick, as driver,
was hauled off to jail. The night's events would be recalled some
years later in Nick's lyrics for Dr Feelgood's Top 10 hit, 'Milk
And Alcohol'.

Following Fenwick's release, and during the lengthy period
in which he was required to attend a drugs rehabilitation course
in Los Angeles, the core of the British contingent was holed up
in Laurel Canyon at a bungalow they rented from Skip Battin
of the Byrds. Nick spent much of his time sitting on Battin's
veranda writing songs. These included 'Heart Of The City'
('where the cars are the stars'), an upbeat item much in the spirit
of Jonathan Richman & the Modern Lovers' 'Roadrunner', which
had recently appeared on *Beserkley Chartbusters Vol. 1*.

'Without a doubt, I was absorbing all that stuff,' confesses Nick,
when asked if he had consciously 'borrowed' from the Richman
cut. 'There was a time when I used to do it on purpose. In the
same way that people nowadays sample their records, I used to
steal so that people would say, "Oh yeah, he's with-it! What a
good sample! He knows a good record when he hears one."'

Nick also became excited when he discovered that Clover,
the American band that had been such an influence on Brinsley

Schwarz, were appearing at the Palamino, a country-and-western stronghold in North Hollywood. Former Chilli Willi drummer Pete Thomas, now living in the USA and playing in singer John Stewart's band, was also in town and organised the trip to see Clover.

'We couldn't believe the distances,' recalls Nick. 'It said North Hollywood, so we thought, "OK, we're in Hollywood, how far can it be?" It took us an hour-and-a-half to get there. It was like going from London to Birmingham, just to get to the Palamino. Clover were totally bemused by us turning up. The Feelgoods obviously had their Canvey Island accents and the guys in Clover couldn't understand a word they said. But they realised we came in peace.'

'We were in matching green suits,' recalls Huey Lewis, then vocalist and harmonica player with Clover. 'And Nick and Jake and the Feelgoods were in charcoal grey. Nick says, "Hi, we are fans of yours," and we reply, "Do you wanna jam?" Nick says, "Sure, how about 'Wine And Cigarettes'?" We were amazed he knew it.'

When it was discovered that Clover were about to play some shows near their home town of Mill Valley, just outside San Francisco, Nick and the gang headed north. At River City, a club in Fairfax, near Mill Valley, Nick met twenty-year-old Shirley Alford, whom he would soon have the pleasure of introducing to Dr Feelgood vocalist, Lee Brilleaux. Shirley recalls, 'At the end of their set, Clover announced that they were happy to welcome their friends from England, Dr Feelgood! "So, please put your hands together for Lee Brilleaux!" I don't remember what they played, but my memory is of Lee getting up there and playing a harp solo that had jaws agape.'

The following night, Clover were booked to play a private function in Palo Alto, south of San Francisco. The British visitors and members of Clover made their way there in a makeshift convoy. Again, Brilleaux repeated the magic.

'At the end of the evening, Nick and I walked out to get into my car,' continues Shirley. 'It was an old MG. Lee had climbed into that tiny space behind the seats where you could maybe fit one suitcase, and he said, "I'm gonna ride back with you two, all right?" Nick ordered him out of the car.' Despite this, Shirley was reunited with Lee in San Francisco that May, and they later married.

By the time Andrew Jakeman met with Matthew 'King' Kaufman at Beserkley Records in San Francisco, Nick's interest in signing to an American independent label was starting to wane.

'My stock wasn't all that high and Beserkley was the final nail. One night, Jake said, "Look, I think we should forget about this and invent our own record label. London is where it's at, and we know all the key people in the music press."

'Writers like Nick Kent and Charles Shaar Murray were our mates and would write about us in the *NME*. The power of the music press was considerable. We knew that if we put a word in Nick Kent's ear on Tuesday, it would be on the streets of Preston on Thursday morning. We could by-pass all the record company press departments who took two weeks to set up an interview. We were hanging out with the scribes, and the good ones too. They all wanted a bit of it. It was terrific. We could set up our own thing and have it just the way we wanted it.

'So, I think when Jake saw what Matthew Kauffman was doing, it brought it home. Of course, Beserkley Records were in San Francisco, far enough away not to be a nuisance. Also, Jake thought they were a bit airy-fairy, west coast hippie, even though they had short hair and winklepickers. But we wanted something nastier, so we could start hammering at the door.'

*

In March 1976, Graham Parker & the Rumour hit the road as the support act on Thin Lizzy's UK tour. Nick, still somewhat directionless, was hired by Parker and his band to act as tour manager, a task to which he was ill-suited.

'My short career as tour manager ended when I got all the accounts wrong. I was about £125 out, which was a lot of dough. Dave Robinson fired me. I got the band out of bed though.'

A positive outcome of the tour, however, was Nick's latest song, 'So It Goes'. It may have been subconsciously influenced by Thin Lizzy's 'The Boys Are Back In Town', which Nick had heard every night on the tour, although he acknowledges Steely Dan's 'Reeling In The Years' as the true source of 'the chord trick' he had deployed. Its title was also the name of a new music programme about to air on Granada Television, but lyrics that referenced US diplomats and 'discussions with the Russians' were perhaps too obscure for a TV theme tune.

With 'So It Goes' marking a return to creative form, Nick went into Pathway Studios, where he had overdubbed 'Everybody Dance'. Pathway was ideal, mainly on the basis that it was affordable, but it also included in its £8 per hour rate the services of resident engineer, Barry 'Bazza' Farmer.

'The recording of "So It Goes" and "Heart Of The City" took about four hours,' says Farmer. 'Nick played a Fender Telecaster to convey the songs to drummer Steve Goulding. Nick was one of the best producers I'd worked with in terms of dealing with the music. He did two or three takes and then it was down, which was great for the immediacy.'

The Pathway session of 28 June 1976 produced the magic, and had cost just £45, paid for by Nick's publisher, Peter Barnes. Jakeman was delighted and thought that the two songs would provide the perfect vehicle with which to launch not only Nick's solo career, but also their new, as yet unnamed record label.

A master plan was evolving; Nick would handle the music and oversee record production; graphic designer Barney Bubbles would create the look of the brand; and Jakeman – who had now reinvented himself as 'Jake Riviera' – would take care of marketing.

'We had discussions about Jake's name,' recalls Nick. 'I think he thought that "Jake Jakeman" was too ho-hum, and it was a time when people were starting to make up outlandish names for themselves. I also remember discussing the name for the new label. Jake said, "Stiff Records", but I thought it should be a name that was much more like a noise, like those old-fashioned labels such as Chant. Jake wouldn't have it. He thought "Stiff" was the one. I said, "OK, but when it comes to the company name it should sound like a big corporation trading in oil, or a James Bond villain's type of organisation, something like "Zirco", a mysterious multi-national set-up." We hit on the word "Global", then "Riviera Global", to make it sound bigger than it really was. We talked about it endlessly. We'd go up to the Churchill pub, then back to the flat and stay up all night, drinking cider and smoking pot. We put a lot of thought into it.'

'Stiff Records' had now been conceived, but although it would be hot on advertising slogans, such as 'The World's Most Flexible Label', 'Undertakers To The Industry' and 'If They're Dead We'll Sign 'Em', the new label had neither premises nor infrastructure. Attention turned to Dave Robinson, who had recently vacated his room at the Hope & Anchor and was renting offices at 32 Alexander Street in west London, from where he managed Graham Parker & the Rumour.

Jake accepted Robinson's invitation to move his business operation to Alexander Street and, on 13 August 1976, Stiff Records was launched with the release of Nick Lowe's 'So It Goes' c/w 'Heart Of The City' (catalogue number BUY1). Funding for the label's first pressing arrived in the form of contributions from friends, including Dr Feelgood's Lee Brilleaux. Humorous phrases adorned the product, including 'Electrically Recorded' and 'Mono Enhanced Stereo', but distribution arrangements were almost non-existent. Fans could, however, buy the record direct from Stiff's offices, and personal callers were not discouraged.

One of the first customers to turn up at Alexander Street was Declan MacManus aka D. P. Costello, whose mission was, in fact, twofold: to buy a copy of 'So It Goes', and to pitch his own music to Stiff.

'I took the afternoon off work – headache or something – and went to Stiff,' he recalls. 'I had my little cassette, and a Bohemian girl named Suzanne Spiro opened the door. When I told her that I wanted to buy Nick's record, she said, "There's nobody here." She didn't seem like a record company person, she could have been selling me a scented candle. I tried to hang around, but then I had to leave. I walked to Westbourne Park tube station with my guitar slung over my shoulder and unbelievably ran into Nick, who was on his way to the office. I remember his words and I was kind of flattered. He said, "So you're going to tread the boards again?" He used that old phrase, "tread the boards", and it really stuck in my mind.'

On 21 August, Nick was booked to play Mont-de-Marsan in south-west France, at an outdoor event billed as the 'First European Punk Rock Festival'. Although punk rock, as a musical movement, was starting to make a ripple in New York and London, the genre had yet to be defined quite as rigidly as it would in the months to come. In the mind of free-thinking promoter Mark Zermatti, 'punk' could encompass the street rock of the Hammersmith Gorillas; the jazz blues groove of Roogalator; the proto-punk of

Eddie & the Hot Rods; and Nick Lowe's eclecticism. Also on the bill was an unknown quartet called the Damned. Their guitarist, Brian James, was an 'obscurist music fan' who had heard about Jake Riviera and Stiff via the Bizarre record shop in Paddington, which was conveniently close to the Lisson Grove dole office.

The Damned's drummer Rat Scabies (Chris Millar) had secured their Mont-de-Marsan appearance through Mark Zermatti's cohort, Larry Debay, who ran Bizarre.

'We'd only done about two gigs,' recalls Scabies. 'But the Sex Pistols were gigging by now and we'd done the 100 Club and things were starting to look a bit lively. We all met at Victoria coach station and Jake came up to us and said, "Right, you're the Damned, get on the bus." He knew who we were and we were quite impressed by that. But our fellow travellers appalled us. I was expecting it to be punk, but there was nobody under thirty-five, except for us. We met Sean Tyla and Larry Wallis and Nick Lowe, who wore an Eddie Cochran T-shirt.'

In September, at Riviera's behest, the Damned went into Pathway Studios with Nick as producer to record 'New Rose'.

'Nick was the producer because he was Jake's mate,' continues Scabies. 'If Jake thought he was OK, that was OK with us. Jake could control us, there was a bit of a dad element to it. We were all quite young and he took care of things. But he could also be as badly behaved as us.'

Studio engineer Barry Farmer recalls: 'The Damned were just normal guys, with not much experience of recording, but one day some TV cameras turned up, and it was almost as if someone had flicked a switch, and it was, "OK boys, time to go mad!" As soon as the camera crew left, it was back to work and they settled down.'

'They seemed like a garage rock group to me,' says Nick. 'They owed more to the Stooges and the MC5, but when I actually got the bonnet up, so to speak, and took a look under the hood they also had a sort of glam rock thing going on, a bit like the Sweet. They didn't take themselves at all seriously and yet they thought they were shit-hot. They were a bit of a handful, quite difficult to control. I thought they were against the same things that I was against at the time, but I was quite shocked to find that amongst the things they were against was people like me.'

Although it is a myth that Nick sped the tape up before recording the lead vocal as it would have been 'totally unnecessary', the Damned's astonishingly fast and powerful 'New Rose' holds the distinction of being the first British 'punk rock' single, released three weeks ahead of 'Anarchy In The UK' by the Sex Pistols.

'Stiff put the single out,' says Scabies. 'And there was a bigger response than they could handle, so they gave it to Andrew Lauder at United Artists to distribute. Jake made us ring the office every day to see what was going on. Suzanne Spiro told us we'd gone into the charts at 65 or something. I was amazed.'

Stiff's publicist Glen Colson sums up Nick's evolving role at the label: 'He was the house producer really. Jake loved Nick because he adored Brinsley Schwarz, and he would have done anything for Nick. In those days, Nick was more of a friend of Jake's who was gonna do the producing. His solo career was on the back burner. He made the Damned into magic. Anything that he touched turned to gold, not in sales terms, but in magic terms. He'd walk in and, if there were no lyrics, he'd go in the toilet and come back out with them. Nick was the man who was gonna do it.'

Following Nick's Californian trip earlier in the year, Clover had been persuaded to relocate to the UK, where they would be co-managed by Jake Riviera and Dave Robinson. The Stiff crowd were all fans of the American group's music, but the timing was far from ideal.

'The day we landed in London, Johnny Rotten was all over the *NME*,' recalls Huey Lewis. 'Punk had hit, and the game was on. At this point we were a long-haired country-rock band, so they decided to groom us for the American market. We went into the studio with Nick, and we cut about twenty songs. Then we went on the road supporting Linda Lewis, and Nick was our tour manager.

'Nick showed us how to tour, British style, and became our mentor. He told us, "Right, this is how proper touring goes – you put your toothbrush in your pocket, you put your skinny jeans on, and you buy a three-pack of clean underwear every three days. We meet in the bar at seven, we get in, we do our thing, and we get out. And there's no whining and no whingeing."

'That was the deal, and Nick taught us. We learnt our trade in London.'

Dave Edmunds had now relocated to the capital from Wales, following a messy divorce, and was living in a tiny flat in West Kilburn with his girlfriend, Lesley. It was there that Nick started to ply Dave with song ideas. When a new song was 'blessed' by Dave, the pair hit the town to celebrate their mutual creativity.

'We hung out only in a tentative way at first, because I was in awe of him,' says Nick of the virtuoso musician six years his senior. At the Speakeasy, where Nick was having to nurse a single drink because he was broke, he was approached by Gerry Beckley, one third of the popular vocal group, America, 'suntanned, shirt slashed to the waist, looking quite prosperous, like he'd just walked off Venice Beach'.

Nick hadn't seen Gerry since the Brinsleys lived at Northwood and Gerry's parents, and indeed those of his musical colleagues, were members of the US Air Force stationed at nearby Ruislip. Gerry offered to buy Nick a drink, and they were soon re-bonding. Before long, Edmunds had quietly slipped away and Gerry was suggesting he and Nick 'visit some friends in Mayfair'.

On arriving at a top-floor apartment in Curzon Place, they entered a darkened room, and sitting around the table, cross-legged, were Harry Nilsson, Kit Lambert, Derek Taylor, Ringo Starr and Keith Moon. They all greeted Gerry like a long-lost brother, then Ringo and Keith popped round to the Playboy Club to get some more champagne. A guitar was passed around, and Nick hoped he would get an opportunity to entertain these rock-biz titans with the song that Edmunds had blessed earlier that day. But every time the guitar travelled in Nick's direction, someone else grabbed it.

'I'm The Invisible Man, until finally, I get the guitar. "I've got one, I've got one." But I couldn't remember how it went. "Let me start again . . ." I did a very duff, toe-curling performance, and realised that I'd completely blown it, whereupon Gerry very nicely offered to find me a cab. I said goodbye and nobody noticed, but before leaving I went over to Harry Nilsson, who was falling asleep, and I tapped him on the shoulder and said something really daft, like, "I know you think I'm dumb, but one day I'm going to make something of myself." It was a terrible speech and that was the last I saw of Harry until about 1987.'

Dave Edmunds had been a musical legend since his adolescence in Cardiff, where in 1961 he formed his first group, the Raiders, while working in a local music shop. His blond hair and good looks gave him the air of a future pop star, while musically he had studied and mastered the styles of rock and roll guitar maestros such as Scotty Moore and James Burton. In the mid-1960s, he formed Love Sculpture and scored a hit with his interpretation of Aram Khachaturian's 'Sabre Dance', a dazzling instrumental that showcased his mastery of the instrument. And in 1971, his version of Smiley Lewis's 'I Hear You Knocking' was a million selling top-five hit in the USA. More hits followed, such as 'Born To Be With You', which demonstrated his ability to replicate Phil Spector's 'Wall of Sound'.

Edmunds was a multi-instrumentalist and self-taught recording engineer who had unlocked the secrets of ear candy record production. No wonder Nick was in awe; he saw Edmunds as a mysterious, glamorous figure, and sat quietly in the studio like a star-struck pupil watching Dave stack vocal harmonies and overdub guitar parts to make the recording whole. Whereas most recording engineers would treat the studio with respect and tweak the knobs gently, Dave worked the mixing desk with abandon, ramming up the faders while switching the tape machine off with his elbow.

'There was nothing subtle about it,' says Nick. 'He had little respect for the equipment and taught me lots of stuff, including a refusal to be intimidated by the technology. After all, it's just a bloody tape recorder! Simply use it to record the noise you want to make. His influence was very hard for me to shake off, but eventually I managed to win his confidence.'

Dave welcomed Nick's friendship not least of all because, having moved to London, he knew no one. Edmunds felt that his life was in crisis, emotionally and financially. He had lost his house and the connection to his daughter. Hooking up with Nick and Jake, and various acquaintances from the Stiff scene, helped him to regain his self-confidence, although he was still keeping much of the pain to himself.

Despite his predicament, Dave Edmunds still had his fans, the most fervent being Robert Plant, whose world-famous band, Led Zeppelin, had recently launched their own record label. Plant turned up at Rockfield one day and suggested to Dave that he might consider signing with Swansong. A meeting was set up with the band's manager, Peter Grant, whose coarse London accent rang in Edmunds's ears: "'ere Dave, the boys wanna sign you, but no fucking lawyers, OK? I'll take care of you.'

Edmunds was soon contracted by Swansong to deliver four albums in as many years, the first of which – *Get It* – was nearing completion. He had also assisted Nick on various studio projects and collaborated on songs, an early example being 'As Lovers Do', recorded at Trident Studios in 1975. As a songwriter, Dave was far less prolific than Nick, who could knock out an Edmunds-friendly tune on demand. They had already collaborated on a number of songs specifically crafted for the Edmunds oeuvre – a look back *at*, but an update *on*, the American music he'd enjoyed as a youth.

Although many of Nick's songs were built on the standard rock and roll chassis, they sounded fresh and modern. 'I Knew The Bride', which musically and lyrically is a homage to Chuck Berry, sails dangerously close to Berry's 'You Never Can Tell', describing the proud dad who gave his daughter the down-payment on 'a lovers' nest'. Another song from this period, 'Here Comes The Weekend', is a Lowe/Edmunds co-write that was 'scribbled down on the back of a fag packet in the dressing room of the Nashville', and showcases Dave's faux-Everly Brothers harmonies.

'Dave was so great at harmonies. Also, he had a thing about changing the sound of his voice on a certain part that would sound really phony on its own but great in the mix. He would go: "Eee-argh" or "ur-ghh" to make unusual but tuneful sounds. I saw him do this quite a lot. Also, he would be playing guitar and switch the tape machine into record with his foot.'

Collaborating with Nick saved Dave from lapsing into retro rock, and Dave reciprocated with studio wizardry and musicianship. It was the ideal partnership: creative, pragmatic and, most of all, fun. Before long, they were toying with the idea of forming a band that would be capable of taking Dave's rocking music to the world. An embryonic line-up had played London's Hope & Anchor in September 1976, with former Chilli Willi bassist Paul Riley and drummer George Butler, but when Nick decided he wanted to be the bass player, Riley was offered the job of live sound engineer, or 'the consolation prize', as Riley puts it.

'Dave and I used to talk about getting this fantastic group together,' recalls Nick. 'We would meet at the Churchill and have these conversations. "Wouldn't it be fabulous if we had . . .?" then we'd sober up and go off the idea. Then Dave would get the horrors and say, "No, no, no, I'm giving it all up." Then the next night it would be, "But, supposing we did get a group together, we'd need Terry Williams on drums." No one else would do – he had that powerhouse style – but then we'd say, "No, no, no, we can't get him, he's still with Man. It's ludicrous even talking about it. But then of course we'd need another guitar player. There's this Scottish bloke in Fatso who's good – Billy Bremner – but supposing he'd be the bloke, there's no use talking to him if we can't get Terry Williams."

'We went to see Billy Bremner with Fatso at the Nashville. He was very funny, and we soon became inseparable. He was such a sports fan and we'd start going to the racetrack, and we became mad boxing fans. He got us in to see all these fights beamed in at Leicester Square Odeon in that lovely pre-satellite TV age. Then we actually started to rehearse and it sounded fantastic.'

Bremner, who 'could sing like Little Richard', was soon enrolled, and when Man unexpectedly disbanded in December 1976, drummer Terry Williams became free and the line-up was complete. For the next four years the quartet would tour the world and thrill audiences with their no-nonsense, faster-than-the-speed-of-light rock and roll. Headline acts for which they were booked to open trembled at the thought of having to follow the band known as 'Rockpile'.

PART THREE

The Lost Weekend

CHAPTER 9
The Go-To Guy

At the start of 1977, Nick was tasked with producing the debut album of Declan MacManus, or 'Elvis Costello' as Jake Riviera had rebranded him. It had also been Jake's idea to give the twenty-two-year-old a pair of outsized horn-rimmed spectacles to amplify his more geek-like physical attributes. Married, with a two-year-old son, Costello worked as a computer operator at the Elizabeth Arden cosmetics factory in Park Royal, west London, but was now forced to take time off work or simply go missing in order to fulfil his obligations as a Stiff Records recording artist. 'Elvis' couldn't believe his luck when he found himself recording alongside members of Clover and producer Nick Lowe.

'When they told me that Nick was going to produce it, I thought that was just fantastic,' Costello told me over lunch at his Kensington hotel. 'It was unimaginable that I was going into Pathway, a studio that was even to that degree professional, and there was Bazza, the recording engineer, who knew what he was doing, Nick with his humour, and musicians like Micky Shine and John McFee.

'Nick's role was to say, "Not that, that." He's since said a few times that I had these weird vocal ideas which he thought might not work, but they did work. The other thing that people don't remark on very often is that it's Nick and me singing on a lot of the backgrounds.'

With Costello's *My Aim Is True* nearing completion, life suddenly became hectic; not only was Nick producing Elvis, the Damned and 'Go The Whole Wide World' art-school urchin Wreckless Eric (Eric Goulden), but there were also preparations for the live debut of 'Dave Edmunds' Rockpile'.[11]

The new quartet appeared at London's Nashville Rooms on 21 February 1977, for the first of four consecutive Mondays. Nick and Dave shared lead vocals and Billy was permitted to cameo his sly take on Elvis Presley's 'Mess Of Blues'. Rockpile was a smash, and audience numbers grew week on week. Nick Kent, the ace reporter from *New Musical Express*, would later describe Lowe as a 'lean, determined young man whose position between guitarists Bremner and Edmunds was re-emphasized by all these slight, almost machoid gestures, the clenching of fists, the taut jutting chin, the mean look, the constant speed-freak chewing'.

For anyone waiting for a super-group that would meld the traditional values of rock and roll with a contemporary twist, Rockpile was the dream combo. As far as Nick's own recordings were concerned, the on-demand availability of Pathway Studios had facilitated not only the recording of some lightweight material, such as the surf instrumental 'Shake That Rat' and a sequel to 'Bay City Rollers We Love You' entitled 'Rollers Show', but also his most recent composition, 'Marie Provost'. Inspired by the tragic demise of silent movie starlet Marie Prevost,[12] it is described by Canadian writer John Mackie as 'a black humour masterpiece'.

Marie Provost did not look her best
The day the cops bust into her lonely nest
In the cheap hotel up on Hollywood West
July twenty-nine

It may have been an appetite for showbiz gossip that caused Nick to dip into a reprint of *Hollywood Babylon*, Kenneth Anger's 1959 compendium of Tinseltown scandals. As Anger tells it, rather sensationally, the ill-fated and overweight actress's dead body was eaten by Maxie, her pet dachshund. Although blood-shed was evident in her apartment, a more plausible account of the tragedy was that Marie had fatally passed out on her bed following a lone drinking binge, and the dog was merely attempting to awaken her by nipping at her ankles. Notwithstanding a mis-spelling of the poor girl's name, artistic licence allowed Nick to imagine the song's punchline:

She was a winner
Who became the doggie's dinner

Nick's then girlfriend, Valerie Boyd, recalls him slaving over the lyric, writing and rewriting, until every line was as snappy as 'that hungry little dachshund'.

Another Pathway recording from this period, 'I Love My Label', was apparently co-written by Lowe with someone called 'Profile', deemed to be Jake Riviera. The song is often described as 'a jingle for Stiff Records'.

'A strange, grumpy northerner named Stan Shaw played the organ,' Nick says. 'He used to say, "I only play a Vox me, none of that fancy gear." And I did the piano, brow furrowed, tongue poking out the corner of my mouth.'

*

To promote *Get It* in the USA, Dave Edmunds was booked to open for hard rock band Bad Company, fronted by former Free singer, Paul Rodgers. Nick, Billy and Terry were acting as Dave's anonymous backing group, so the Rockpile name was parked pro-tem. The tour opened in Denver, Colorado, on 25 April 1977.

'It was a great eye-opener,' says Nick. 'I didn't think it was possible for a group to make enough noise for people to hear music in basketball arenas, but they went nuts for us.'

Dave's roots-rock musical approach was, however, slightly at odds with the macho posturing of Bad Company, and ticket sales were not quite hitting their target. The promoters arranged for an additional opening band – the Outlaws – to be brought in and Edmunds's involvement was suddenly marginalised.

Nick considered Bad Company to be 'on the way out and very boring'. It was winding him up to the extent that he got 'extremely drunk' in San Diego and wrecked the dressing room. He concedes that he and Edmunds appeared to be quite pleased with themselves, and that the headline act may have found this irritating, because Rockpile were an extremely hard act to follow.

'Our ranka-danka business was really kicking ass and the punters loved us. Then Bad Company cut our time down, which was the worst thing they could possibly have done, because we would just do our best songs and then leave the stage with much hand-wringing, exaggeratingly staring at our wristwatches and shaking our heads slowly. Bad Company let us stay on the tour a bit longer, but they gave us about a foot of stage. So, off the tour we went.'

Jake Riviera was strangely absent when all this occurred, and one can only imagine the carnage had he been present. Riviera was otherwise engaged in trying to establish a reliable distribution outlet for Stiff Records in the UK as Elvis Costello's debut album was being prepared for release. Riviera had also accompanied the Damned on their recent American tour, during which he spread the word on Stiff from coast-to-coast, almost certainly with a US distribution deal in mind.

Notwithstanding the precise details of Edmunds's contractual arrangements, a note on the *Get It* sleeve states: 'Dave Edmunds is an Advancedale Artist', implying that he was a client of Stiff's management arm. Swansong Records boss Peter Grant may have seen things differently and he maintained a fatherly, vice-like grip on Dave's activities. This was obviously a diabolical conflict; Edmunds was 'officially managed' by Grant, and recorded for his record label, yet he was also a prominent member of Rockpile, who were looked after and, to all intents and purposes, administered by Jake Riviera. The highly combustible situation would become the basis of a three-year stand-off between Grant and Riviera, and, as legend has it, prevent the release of any product involving Nick Lowe and Dave Edmunds under the 'Rockpile' trademark.

'I remember the screaming rows that Jake used to have with Peter Grant over Rockpile,' says Elvis Costello. 'It was a power struggle to get them established as a recording act. I was in the office the day Jake threw the bottle of cider through the window. I was there when he broke his toe kicking the filing cabinet. The good cop/bad cop rants were very entertaining. It was like our side against these fat cats.'

Edmunds and his musicians came home from America at the beginning of June, by which time Stiff had released *Bowi*, Nick's four song extended play disc, named in response to David Bowie titling his latest release *Low*. This joke was fairly typical of Stiff's early marketing flair. In addition to 'Marie Provost' and 'Shake That Rat', the EP also included the moody, atmospheric 'Endless Sleep', of which road manager Dez Brown recalls:

'Nick's instrumentation consisted of a Senior Service cigarette lit by a Swan Vesta match, a Fender Telecaster guitar and a cider bottle, possibly Bulmer's, banging on a cardboard box.'

An astute cover of Sandy Posey's 1966 US hit 'Born A Woman' completed the *Bowi* track listing. Composer Martha Sharp's song, which Nick first heard on the *Cruisin' 1966* compilation album, contains some of the most succinct and perfect rhyming couplets in all of pop:

> *It makes no difference if you're rich or poor, or even if you're*
> *smart or dumb*
> *A woman's place in this old world is under some man's thumb*

Sharp's lyrical skill set a standard to which Nick's words would now have to aspire, and his singing on the track, with its aching, Anglo-American twang, combined with a straight-ahead, no frills instrumental setting, would become the template for his best power pop recordings.

In its inimitable style, Stiff Records advertised *Bowi*, and therefore 'Born A Woman', in the radical feminist magazine *Spare Rib*, whose editors may have failed to spot the relevance.

If you're 'Born a woman', Sharp tells us, 'you're born to be lied to, stepped on, cheated on, and treated like dirt', before delivering the song's incisive sign-off, 'when you're born a woman, you're born to be hurt'.

Within two weeks of returning from the USA, Nick was back in Pathway recording more new songs including 'Shake And Pop', 'Music For Money' and 'I've Been Taking The Truth Drug'. Another new song, 'I Love The Sound Of Breaking Glass' – co-credited to Andrew Bodnar and Steve Goulding from the Rumour – had been inspired by the room-trashing incident in San Diego.

It also reflected the mood of David Bowie's aforementioned *Low* album (which coincidentally contained a track entitled 'Breaking Glass'), especially the futuristic 'Sound And Vision'.

Modern sounds were certainly filling Nick's head when 'I Don't Want The Night To End' was transferred to 16-track tape at Basing Street Studios, and he asked the sound engineer to make Pete Thomas's closing drum fill sound like 'oil drums falling down a fire escape'.

Nick's growing reputation as the go-to guy for 'bash it down and tart it up later' record production – said to be the basis of his 'Basher' nickname (although Nick would later tell writer Paul du Noyer that it originated from a friend's send-up of typical RAF wartime lingo, as in: 'Hello Basher, it's Ginger here, afraid Nipper's gone over the side, bail out!') – soon found him inundated with offers of studio work. Most of these opportunities were declined, but during the summer of 1977 there were two jobs he simply couldn't refuse.

First, there was the production of *Be Seeing You*, the new album from Dr Feelgood, then reclaiming their status as the UK's premier R&B turn following the dramatic departure of their key songwriter, Wilko Johnson.

'Gypie Mayo was a fantastic guitarist,' says Nick of Johnson's replacement. 'And Lee Brilleaux's natural charisma and charm was such that people automatically deferred to him. He naturally assumed leadership and nobody minded. I encouraged them to write.'

Nick's presence, combined with his skills as a song doctor, certainly inspired the Feelgoods to complete their own compositions, including the chart hit, 'She's A Windup'.

As soon as that record was finished, he got the call to rescue *Stick To Me*, the third album from Graham Parker & the Rumour. This was an emergency re-recording that had to be completed in a six-day window following the disintegration of the original master tapes.

Parker recalls: 'While we were recording with the first producer, Bob Potter, we spotted all this black stuff coming off the tape recorder heads. The album couldn't be mixed, and we had another Scandinavian tour coming up so, at Dave Robinson's suggestion, Nick was the man who was gonna do a quick fix on it.'

In and around these frenzied sessions, Nick worked on what would become his next single for Stiff, a cover of the Gerry Goffin and Carole King classic, 'Halfway To Paradise', which had been a UK hit for Billy Fury in 1961. Trivia fans may be interested to know that the title scribbled on the Pathway tape box reads: '1/2 way to being cool', and according to Dez Brown, the multi-tracked harmonies were the work of 'The All Dave Edmunds Male Voice Choir'.

Musical compatibility notwithstanding, the relationship between Lowe and Edmunds was about to become less than harmonious. Nick had just given an interview to Nick Kent, in which he blithely announced that he had 'quit Rockpile'. Kent's article entitled THE ROCKPILE TAPES appeared in the *NME* in late July 1977.

Investigating the story, Kent had spoken with Dave Edmunds, who was dumbfounded. 'If only Nick would give me a reason,' he pleaded to the writer. 'I've phoned him up, we've been in touch. I mean, he's still my best mate, him and Jake [Riviera] both, but yes, I'm confused and I'm angry because I've still not received one good concrete reason for him leaving, from his lips.'

Kent's article informed *NME* readers that Nick had unexpectedly 'thrown the switch on Rockpile's natty assault-programme', walking out just as the band was on the brink of success. Kent perceived this as 'the new-attitude Nick Lowe with newly developed ego drive, in the mood to deliver some good copy'.

Nick's stance was certainly cocky and self-assured. 'I can write these hard rock songs two-a-penny,' he told Kent. 'Playing bass is nothing to me – anyone can do that. I'm a songwriter. Period. If this was the sixties, I'd be one of those Tin Pan Alley junk-pop tunesmiths knocking out an album's worth of tunes for the Peters and Lees of my time. I could write for Peters and Lee. Christ, I could write any song to order. If the Clash want new songs, or the Jam, say, I could churn 'em out. That's what I'm good at.'

He then added: 'I want to be a commercial success. I want to sell records. I want to be rich, of course, and I want to get the girls. I'm still in it for all the "boilers" I can get.'

When told about Nick's pronouncements, Edmunds responded: 'The way he's going he's just going to be a huge cult figure. And he's that already!'

Nick maintained that he was 'just a hack tunesmith', but Kent disagreed and heaped praise on Nick's songwriting, with a special mention for 1971's 'Nightingale', which Kent described as 'a dazzler'.

Kent then proffered the theory that Lowe's reasons for leaving Rockpile 'can only have been hastened by the insights he had into the workings of Swansong Records by dint of Edmunds' association'.

Well, maybe. On the afternoon that Nick nailed 'Halfway To Paradise' at Pathway, just a day or two before his interview with Kent, Dave Edmunds arrived late at the session, having come from a meeting at Swansong. 'Dave was in a damned good mood,' recalls Dez Brown. 'I think he'd picked up the advance for his next album.'

Dave gave his all at the session, only to be demeaned by Nick, who suddenly found Rockpile 'too one-dimensional and restricting'. Nick was displaying his rarely exhibited ruthless streak, emboldened by his growing status as the hip 'Mr Fix-It', a tumbler or two of vodka, and a certain amount of encouragement from Jake Riviera. But Kent's perception was correct; Nick had started to 'despise' Swansong, and fingered label boss Peter Grant for 'running it like the Roman Empire', ruled over by a team of heavy-handed minders.

'I was drunk most of the time,' recalls Nick. 'I was definitely walking in a path of righteousness that only a large amount of stimulants can persuade you you're on. I had two careers happening. Rockpile was going like mad in America, even though I'm not really sure how much I wanted that side of things to work. I was much more interested in the cottage industry of Stiff Records; that was more interesting than the chance of becoming like one of the groups we were opening for. I wasn't a very nice person back then, but I really thought, "Hang on, it's my turn now," because I had all this stuff going on in the UK with Stiff. "Who's next? Step forward. It's me."'

Kent also made the point that Nick had been less than productive of late, other than his studio work with the Damned, Elvis Costello, Dr Feelgood and Graham Parker. 'For all his activity over the last year or so, Nick Lowe hasn't seemed over concerned about his own career.'

Of course, Nick's record release schedule was entirely his own prerogative, and maybe the time wasn't right to be focusing on a solo album. But, all bragging aside, his newest song, 'Tonight', would have suited Peters and Lee perfectly well.

Although the *NME*'s Nick Kent knew that Stiff was planning a national tour for the coming autumn – Dave Edmunds had told him as much – what he probably didn't know was that the relationship between the label's two head honchos was quickly festering. Behind Stiff's 'all-for-one' public image, conflicting initiatives were tearing its proprietors apart; Robinson was busy guiding the career of Graham Parker and dealing with the indifference of Parker's American record label, Mercury, while Riviera was focused on securing a US deal for Costello. It is of course ironic that their respective protégés – both of whose records had been produced by Lowe – were frequently subjected to lazy comparisons in the music press. But to the untrained ear there were distinct similarities; Parker and Costello were both steeped in classic American rhythm and soul, and expressed themselves in angry, staccato voices and deeply bitter wordplay.

'It's obvious we both liked Van Morrison,' says Costello. 'I never thought any more of it, but Graham and I always seemed to get lumped together. He wore shades. I wore glasses. I've always thought the comparison did neither of us very much use. Graham wrote some terrific songs, but I don't think he got full credit.'

Parker responds: 'At the time I felt that I'd made it, but I kept being reminded that there was this other guy who was apparently the same. He started selling more records than me, and when he did something, it made major press. I'd first seen Elvis in 1975, with Flip City, but he didn't have my aggression or energy. Now he was onstage giving it stick. Knees bent and screaming. That was probably my contribution – balls to the wall.'

As plans for the Stiff tour got under way, Riviera was in negotiation with Columbia Records in New York. Their A&R executive, Gregg Geller, had first become aware of Stiff the previous summer when his then boss, Steve Popovich, handed him a copy of 'So It Goes'. Geller loved the record and kept an eye on UK music press reports of Stiff's activities from his desk at the CBS HQ in New York. When Geller visited London to attend the company's convention at the Mayfair Hilton in late July 1977, he stepped out onto Park Lane and was immediately confronted by Elvis Costello, busking with his guitar and a portable amplifier.

Costello's sidewalk session did the trick; ambushing Geller and the CBS suits was Jake Riviera's most inventive campaign yet, especially when Costello was arrested for disturbing the peace and taken into police custody, only to emerge later that evening to perform a blistering set at Dingwalls, to where the American contingent had been directed. Geller took a copy of *My Aim Is True* back to New York and before long a draft contract was drawn up and sent to Riviera's American attorney.

Although Pathway and its ace recording engineers Barry 'Bazza' Farmer and Chas 'Chazza' Herrington had served Nick well, the studio's cramped, funky conditions and 8-track tape recorder were hardly state-of-the-art. Not averse to embellishing his songs with instrumental overdubs, or the kind of cool audio effects he had witnessed Edmunds deploy at Rockfield, Nick gradually moved his operation to the more sophisticated Eden Studios in Chiswick, where some of the Pathway recordings would be 'goosed up'.

At Eden, engineer Roger Béchirian transferred the Pathway tapes to the 16-track format and set up the studio for Nick's next sessions that August through September. Present at one of these sessions was Gregg Geller.

'I was back in London and Jake whisked me off to Eden Studios,' he recalls. 'Nick was mixing "I Love The Sound Of Breaking Glass". I knew relatively little about Nick at that point, but I liked "So It Goes", and Graham Parker's album, and Elvis's just-released debut, both produced by Mr Lowe. But none of this prepared me for "I need the noises of destruction". That simple line caught my ear as we entered Eden that day, and it has been rattling around in my head ever since.'

Nick remembers playing the song to Geller 'at earth-shattering volume', which seemed to do the trick; Geller wanted to sign Nick to Columbia, just as he had recently signed Costello. There was now a real imperative for Nick to record more tracks and collate his work into one cohesive long-player. With this in mind, he recruited Messrs Belmont, Andrews, Bodnar and Goulding from the Rumour to help him cut 'No Reason' and a cover of Jim Ford's '36 Inches High'. And with three members of Ian Dury's band – Norman Watt-Roy, Charley Charles and Johnny Turnbull – plus Steve Nieve from Costello's Attractions, he recorded 'Nutted By Reality', a phrase he had recently heard Larry Wallis utter.

Two final songs – 'Tonight' and 'Little Hitler' – would complete the record, both cut with drummer Pete Thomas. On guitar and backing vocals was Dave Edmunds, with whom Nick had patched things up following the recent *NME* interviews. Before long, Dave and Nick would be back on the road.

In early September, the UK music press announced 'Stiff's Greatest Stiffs Live', a tour on which five Stiff acts – Elvis Costello, Nick Lowe, Ian Dury, Wreckless Eric and Larry Wallis – would play twenty-four concerts, commencing 3 October. The tour was to coincide with a batch of new releases, including the new Elvis Costello single, 'Watching The Detectives'; *New Boots And Panties* from Ian Dury; and Nick's debut album, which Stiff's press release referred to under its working title, 'Wireless World'.

Stiff envisaged a package tour reminiscent of a 1960s-style revue, fast moving, with short sets and shared equipment, its programme held together by zany compères Les Prior and Kosmo Vinyl. 'Each act will play a 30-minute set, with the running order changing nightly,' said Stiff.

The Naughty Rhythms Tour, masterminded by Jake Riviera in

1975, had been the blueprint, but in an all-Stiff show each artist would be vying for his label's as well as the public's attention. This, it was hoped, would result in some seriously competitive stagecraft, but not all of the acts were match fit and the revolving bill concept started to look shaky. Wreckless Eric's group lacked the power to close the show successfully, and Nick preferred an early slot to allow plenty of time for a post-set drink. Larry Wallis would fare little better. Conversely, Costello and Dury would both deliver riveting performances. The music formerly known as pub rock was about to re-emerge as New Wave.

Ten days before the tour opened, Jake Riviera and Dave Robinson had a major disagreement at the Stiff HQ. Label manager Paul Conroy arrived at the scene to find the street littered with broken glass and empty cider bottles that Riviera had thrown through the window during the blazing row. STIFF's RIVIERA IN MYSTERY SPLIT announced the *Melody Maker* in its next edition, but this time it was not one of Jake's publicity stunts.

A pragmatic settlement was quickly reached; Riviera would leave Stiff and take Lowe and Costello to a new label, and Robinson would continue with what remained, essentially Ian Dury and Wreckless Eric. The tour would still go ahead. Glen Colson was instructed to ensure that it got plenty of press coverage on the opening night to help sell out the rest of the shows.

At High Wycombe Town Hall, Nick took the stage wearing his new fluorescent green 'Riddler suit' dotted with question marks, which had been created by Jake's American girlfriend, the seamstress Tony Laumer, whom he would marry in 1978. Sporting an incongruous, twin-necked guitar, Nick opened with two of his more cynical songs, 'Shake And Pop' and 'Music For Money'. His backing group consisted of Larry Wallis and drummer Pete Thomas (on guitars); Terry Williams and guitarist Dave Edmunds (on drums); plus keyboard player Penny Tobin.

'It was more important to have something that looked strange,' says Nick.

Over the previous two years he had built an enviable reputation as a record producer and songwriter-about-town, but was a reluctant Live Stiff, and characteristically modest about his role in the proceedings.

'I enjoyed wearing the Riddler suit, but I viewed my own musical contribution as an irritating interruption to the day. I didn't take it very seriously. I had to be there, but Elvis and Ian were so fantastic that I didn't really see myself as a contender.'

Costello is of the opinion that if Lowe and Edmunds had chosen to put their best case out front, they certainly could have headlined. 'They were playing this low-key game, constantly switching instruments and being deliberately perverse in hiding their pop potential,' he says.

It is true that Edmunds would join Nick in the front line to perform 'I Knew The Bride', but was otherwise hiding behind a drum kit. Nick viewed Dave as 'a great drummer, but he lacked the stamina to play drums for the whole set'.

Adversely affecting the stamina of many of the team was 'The 24-Hour Club', whose more determined members – primarily Larry Wallis, Dave Edmunds and Pete Thomas – sought to brighten up their leisure time by seeing just how far the weekly allowance of £50 would stretch, if thrown in the general direction of a bar. As the coach rolled through the English countryside, Nick was a permanent fixture at a table seat, holding court with a bottle of vodka and a strong cigarette permanently on the go, declaring that everything was 'marvy' and treating those within earshot to a 'mile melter' – a well-honed story, guaranteed to make time fly during an interminable road journey.

Backstage, Jake Riviera was haranguing college social secretaries and demanding sandwiches and drinks for the musicians.

'There was certainly a fiery atmosphere when Jake was around,' recalls Glen Colson. 'He would arrive at about ninety miles an hour, have a bit of a scream up, put everybody on edge, and then leave.'

Offstage, tension was building between Lowe and Edmunds, with Dave being disappointed that Nick didn't always attend the after-hours drinking sessions. Although he was an occasional member of the 24-Hour Club, Nick was trying to keep his head down in order to control his own excesses.

'Dave had been getting very drunk. We'd all been doing it, but Dave's hangovers were now so dreadful that he couldn't really perform the next night. I sensed he was going to blow me out, or let me down. I could see it coming.'

After his hermit-like years in the recording studio, Dave Edmunds enjoyed being part of the Stiff circus, and banged on about it to anyone with a spare hour to kill. It was as if he had been radicalised by the new scene he found himself in. 'All I want is to be with Jake and Nick and Stiff Records,' he repeated, seemingly unaware that 'Jake-Nick-Stiff' was history.

Meanwhile, the Stiff tour was captured on film by director Nick Abson, but the scenes of petty rivalry, backstage debauchery and Nick's newly discovered Essex accent were embarrassing. Ian Dury reckoned the film would 'never see the light of day' and it's true that the results have never been released in any authorised form.[13]

Concentrating his efforts on finding a new UK record label for Costello and Lowe, Jake Riviera had discussions with former United Artists executives Martin Davies and Andrew Lauder, who were now looking to launch Radar Records. Having negotiated a licensing agreement with WEA (the international conglomeration of Warner Brothers, Elektra and Atlantic), Radar's initial roster would consist of three ex-Stiff acts, two of whom – Elvis and Nick – were now contracted to the recently incorporated Riviera Global Record Productions Limited, and a third – the Yachts – who were not. In Radar's new Covent Garden offices, Lauder presided over the release schedule and ever-loyal graphic designer Barney Bubbles set up his drafting table.

By now, the ink was dry on Costello's US contract with Columbia and *My Aim Is True* was scaling the US Hot 100. Added to the original track listing was 'Watching The Detectives', which Nick had produced at Pathway using the Rumour's rhythm section.

'Steve Goulding and Andrew Bodnar had a very clear space in which to play,' says Costello. 'The reggae thing was sort of implied. It could have been done like Neil Young's "Down By The River", but they did it so great, and then Nick wound up the sound so fantastically on Steve's drums. We were really into having that explosive dub sound. It's an amazing intro and it gave me a lot of confidence to realise you could make pictures with sound, like a movie. But Nick was so modest, sort of like, "Oh, it's kind of you to say it's good." Come on now, you've just produced "Watching The Detectives". That's when we started making records by the way.'

One of the more connected persons that Jake Riviera had met on his American trip was New York photographer Roberta Bayley, whose camera lens had captured not only the growing pains of Blondie, but the truly iconic monochrome shot of the Ramones that graced the cover of their debut album. In November 1977, Bayley came to London to take photographs of some American acts that were breaking through in the UK, including Blondie, the Runaways and Johnny Thunders' Heartbreakers.

Elvis Costello had commenced the recording of his next magnum opus, the game-changing *This Year's Model*, and Nick was once again in the producer's chair.

'Elvis had rented this fancy guitar, a Rickenbacker or something,' recalls Roberta Bayley. 'Jake was like, "You've gotta get pictures of Elvis with the guitar," so I took the pictures. I don't want to sound like Yoko Ono, but I pretty much had no idea who Nick Lowe was – I might have had the *Bowi* EP – anyway, he was at the control board, drinking heavily, and that's when we met.'

When Jake departed for San Francisco and the opening of Costello's maiden tour of America, Roberta moved into the Queen's Gate Terrace flat. She remembers Nick bringing home tapes from the studio, and thinking and rethinking the running order of the songs on his album in progress. 'He would make lists and then rip the paper up and throw it out the window – the whole drama – but that's what he loved to do. I remember Fay Hart came home with the Dead Boys record, and Nick calmly walked over, took it off the turntable and chucked it out the window.

'Fay was sleeping on the couch, I was sleeping in Jake's room, and Nick had his own room. Nick and I went to see the Runaways at Hammersmith Odeon, and then, after a week or so, the inevitable happened . . . you know, I found him charming. I was bowled over and as madly in love as you could get in three or four days, and during that period where Nick and I were having this torrid love affair, he brought two different girls back to the flat. He'd just go to his room, and I'd just go to mine. I was trying to be very modern, and thinking, "OK, we're not going to say anything because why would I get angry? I've only just met this person." I thought it was going to be the great romance of the century, but obviously Nick had other plans.'

After her brief time with Nick, Roberta returned to the USA. When Costello's show reached New York, Nick was in town to perform with Elvis at the Ukrainian Ballroom, located in the then edgy East Village.

'Nick was like a cult guy who hadn't yet broken through over here,' says Bayley. 'But everybody who was cool, like four hundred people in the United States, knew who he was.'

Among the four hundred, and also at the Ukrainian show, was Columbia's Gregg Geller, now about to sign Nick Lowe to a US record deal.

On 17 December, Elvis Costello & the Attractions appeared on NBC's *Saturday Night Live* and pulled a stunt that helped to secure their reputation as the new bad boys of British rock. Performing 'Less Than Zero' under the TV studio's blazing lights in front of pre-rehearsed camera angles, Costello stopped abruptly mid-song and, veering wildly off-script, suddenly blasted out 'Radio Radio'. Squeezing out the song's confrontational line about wanting to bite the hand that fed him, he had thrown down his gauntlet. He had planned the stunt in the band's dressing room. 'We'll start off with the one they've done all the camera angles for,' he told the Attractions. 'And then we'll change songs just like Jimi Hendrix did on the Lulu show!'

Nick was nearby, in his capacity as hanger-on. 'We discovered that *Saturday Night Live* was largely not live at all. We were young and full of piss and we thought, "Right, we'll show 'em! They think it's live and spontaneous. Let's see how they like this!" It was fantastic to watch all these hipster New York types running around like headless chickens. That was the way we were back then, happy to throw a hand grenade at some perfectly nice people who were only trying to do their job. We got a lot of pleasure out of messing it up and they squirmed like mad! I went back to the hotel and wrote "American Squirm". I don't think it's my finest hour, but it's amazing how popular the song is in America. You would think they'd be quite cross about it.'

In late 1977, a young American singer named Rebecca Carlene Smith arrived in London to record her debut album for Warner Brothers Records. She had reached this point via a network of musicians and industry advocates including Rodney Crowell, Emmylou Harris and Martyn Smith, the Welshman who in 1974 had arranged for the Band to rehearse at the Brinsley Schwarz commune. Martyn Smith had recently co-managed a late incarnation of the Flying Burrito Brothers with industry veteran Ed Tickner, and it was Tickner who had walked their pretty, young protégée into Warners.

Martyn Smith and Ed Tickner conceived the idea of launching her in Europe as 'blueblood country' and suggested that she should become known professionally as 'Carlene Carter'. Martyn Smith was to be Carlene's 'executive producer' and proposed hiring Dave Edmunds to be hands-on in the studio.

'I didn't want to do the kind of country music that was happening at that point in time,' Carlene told me over the phone from her home in California. 'I was looking for something a little more edgy, but without going into a full LA rock thing. I was a big Edmunds fan, and I loved "I Hear You Knocking". So, I went into Eden Studios with Dave, and the first words out of his mouth were, "Do you know [country singer] George Jones?"

'I was like, "Yeah! He comes to our house for dinner with his wife, er, Tammy, Wy . . . Tammy Wynette I think her name is." Dave gave me a handful of George Jones songs he wanted me to do, and we did some recording with Terry on drums and Billy on guitar. But Dave wasn't really getting what I wanted to do. I stopped recording with him, but we remained friends.'

With studio time booked, a solution was required. Following discussions between Martyn Smith and Graham Parker's manager Dave Robinson, it was decided that the Rumour would be the ideal musicians to work with Carlene, with senior band members Bob Andrews and Brinsley Schwarz sharing production duties. During the course of Carlene's recording sessions, Nick stopped by to provide some bass and backing vocals.

'I'd just returned from the CBS Convention in New Orleans, with Martin Belmont. Both of us were a bit disgruntled to find our friends and colleagues knee deep in this fantastic gig, working with Carlene.'

Twenty-two-year-old Carlene had no shortage of country credentials; already twice divorced with a daughter, Tiffany Anastasia, by her first husband, Joseph Simpkins Jr, and a son, John Jackson, by her second husband, Jack Wesley Routh, Carlene was the daughter of singer and 'Ring Of Fire' co-writer June Carter and fifties honky-tonk star Carl Smith, who was a member of both the Grand Ole Opry and the Country Music Hall of Fame. Carlene's maternal grandmother was Mother Maybelle Carter, a founding member of the world-famous Carter Family, who made their recording debut in 1927 and are universally recognised as the first vocal group to become country music stars. June Carter, having divorced Carl Smith in 1956, and a second husband, Edwin 'Rip' Nix, a decade later, was now married to country music's foremost international superstar, Johnny Cash. This was a musical dynasty forever without equal, and the 'Carter–Cash' clan of the 1970s was the living embodiment of entertainment tragicomedy.

For many young, male songwriters, such as Carlene's former boyfriend, Rodney Crowell, or indeed Nick Lowe, the prospect of bonding with Carlene and perhaps sneaking through a back door into 'The House of Cash' would have been an intoxicating proposition, not that there was the slightest whiff of professional opportunism on Nick's part; Carlene was strikingly beautiful, musically talented and, most importantly, shared his lust for life.

But crucially, when Nick gazed at Carlene, he saw a reflection of himself, complete with comparable strengths and weaknesses. Carlene, too, liked what she saw that day at Eden Studios.

'He was playing bass in the control room and I remember he was dishevelled, pretty drunk, and funnier than shit, but he played great. He said, "Hey, CC," and no one had ever called me that before. I fell madly in love with the guy immediately. It was pretty amazing. I actually said to my sister, "Rosie, I'm gonna marry that man."'

CHAPTER 10

Trying to Mate in a
Horrible State

In February 1978, almost a decade to the day since Nick left home to become a professional musician, Radar Records released his single, 'I Love The Sound Of Breaking Glass'. While preparing for the launch of an accompanying album that had been eighteen months in the making, Nick was suddenly despatched to Finland. With assistance from guitarist Martin Belmont and drummer Terry Williams, he was instructed to record with 'Finland's Eric Clapton', Albert Järvinen.

When reporter Allan Jones arrived to cover this slightly bizarre story for *Melody Maker*, Nick told him that he had decided to flee the UK because he couldn't face glimpsing the press reviews of *Jesus Of Cool*. But the fact was, Jake Riviera – who had become acquainted with Järvinen while tour managing Dr Feelgood in Scandinavia – had arranged the trip to prevent Nick from 'blabbing' about his new album to the journalists that frequented the London clubs.

'Nick was very much the man about town,' says Martin Belmont. 'So any plan Jake had to maintain the Lowe mystique,

Nick would blow in a couple of evenings at Dingwalls with a hearty, "Good evening bartender, more ale for my friends!"'

After the initial sessions with Järvinen, during which 'American Squirm' and three other tracks – 'I've Been A Fool Too Long', 'Television' and a cover of the Visions' 1963 song, 'Cigarette' – were recorded, Riviera flew out to Finland to check on progress. Nick begged his manager to be allowed to return home, but his plea was greeted with the retort: 'No, you're staying here for another week, and then you're going to do some gigs with Albert's band!'

The subsequent tour involved driving for hours over snow-covered mountains and iced lakes 'like a scene from *Doctor Zhivago*', until the band happened upon some gigantic dancehall. Nick found the Finnish landscape 'a bit Hansel and Gretel', but the pain could be dulled to a certain extent by drugs and alcohol.

One of the British contingent had imported a ludicrously large amount of an illegal substance but getting the Class-A material into the country had been child's play compared to finding some local vodka with which to wash it down. The liquor stores were government controlled with variable opening hours that seemed to change arbitrarily, and the thirsty musicians would trudge around in the snow looking for a store that was open so that they could buy several bottles of the stuff.

'If you're taking cocaine, you have to drink,' explains Belmont. 'It's a scientific fact. If you're taking "that much cocaine" you need to drink "this much vodka" to stay balanced. It's the theory of relativity.'

When Nick returned to London he found himself – as if by destiny – on *Top of the Pops*, resplendent in the Riddler suit and miming to his Top 10 hit, 'I Love The Sound Of Breaking Glass'. Carlene Carter accompanied him to the TV studio and, after the show, he asked her if she would like to go on a date, maybe out for dinner somewhere.

'I said, "Yeah",' recalls Carlene. 'He picked me up at the Kensington Hilton, where I was staying, and the first thing he said was, "I quit drinking today." And he proceeded to tell me that the doctor said he had to slow down, and it had scared him. He's telling me all this stuff just when I was hoping to have a few cocktails.'

Lowe and Belmont encountered more inclement weather in March 1978 when they accompanied Elvis Costello & the Attractions from New York State to Canada for Costello's appearance at Toronto's El Mocambo. On the Buffalo-to-Toronto leg, they stopped off at Niagara Falls for a photo opportunity with Chalkie Davies. The weather was so bitter that most of the party refused to leave the warmth of the van, whereas Nick took great pleasure in standing outside in the blizzard without hat, overcoat or scarf. 'He doesn't feel the cold,' said Davies, although Nick did insist on wearing his 'musical pullover' (a maroon V-neck emblazoned with a series of musical notes, knitted for him by Brinsley Schwarz's mother, Joan).

When *Jesus Of Cool* was released the reviews were mixed, with the *NME*'s Nick Kent writing: 'Though it often tends to portray its creator as a scheming pop jack of all trades, it is at its strongest when it proves Nick Lowe to be the master of subversive pop.' *Melody Maker*'s Allan Jones was more positive, describing the album as 'a masterpiece of contemporary pop, certainly I can think of no one so dedicated right now to the very idea of pop'. In *Sounds*, Peter Silverton expressed his concerns: 'It still seems at times that there's not been quite enough effort – maybe Nick's deep down scared of laying down his art to the world – what happens if only a few critics pick up on it yet again?'

After boldly walking out on Stiff alongside Elvis Costello the previous year, Nick certainly didn't need *Jesus Of Cool* to flop, and a concerted effort had been made to produce a commercially viable album, albeit one with some inherent weirdness. The record was moderately successful, peaking at number 22 in the UK album chart, which was a huge improvement on the sales of Nick's earlier albums with Brinsley Schwarz. A little commercial success would do no harm to Nick's status as the critics' darling. Robert Christgau, 'Dean of American Rock Critics', called the album 'an amazing pop tour-de-force'.

Despite hit records, Lowe remained the ultimate cult artist. In the USA, where he was now signed to Columbia Records, his album was renamed *Pure Pop For Now People* (which had been the slogan on the *Bowi* EP of the previous year), so squeamish were the Americans over anything that might have been construed as blasphemous.

'They were coy about *Jesus Of Cool* as a title,' Nick says. 'It was a phrase Tim Lott had used in a retrospective review of *Silver Pistol*. He was slightly critical, but stated that Brinsley Schwarz "did have in their ranks a bona fide Jesus of cool in Nick Lowe". We thought it was ludicrous, but could be useful. It seems like nothing now, but at the time it fitted perfectly. It was Jake's idea to pinch it. The Americans wanted a different title. Jake loved it. "Two album titles? Yes please!" It was right up his street. It was also a good story for the press – "Sorry! Too hot to handle!"

'It goes back to what I was saying about us being the first generation of fans who were suddenly not only making records, but running around record companies too. As kids, we'd been avid readers of the backs of record sleeves – for example, do you remember the ad for Emitex? Apparently, it was the ONLY way to clean your records, obviously gospel. Now we could design our own alternative record covers, maybe with intentional mistakes in order to make "rare" artefacts, with Porky Peckham's scratching in the run-out grooves.[14] We were having a game with it.

'The *Jesus Of Cool* sleeve photographs, of which there were many, were taken by Chris Gabrin in a single session. Jake said, "Grow a beard, don't wash your hair," then halfway through the session, "Shave your beard off, wash your hair." The session took bloody ages. There were a lot of borrowed guitars, and we also scrounged loads of clothes from various people. I think that some of the clothes even belonged to other workers in the building – men and women. We were almost stopping people in the street – "He's about your size, can we borrow that jacket?" We were in a room full of people half-dressed.'

America, squeamish or otherwise, was still in thrall to the Beatles and the pop culture they invented, and the 'British Invasion' of the mid-1960s had left an indelible legacy from which the touring bands of the 1970s benefitted. All things 'Swinging London' were still hard currency, and many of the teenage girls who had lined up to see *A Hard Day's Night* were now in their late-twenties, unattached, and helplessly drawn to any 'cute' young male with a guitar and a British accent. In the stadiums and arenas, the superstars of rock were distant and unattainable but, on the club circuit, pop music's lower order was conveniently accessible. 'Boilers' – as touring musicians were wont to refer to a certain variety of female fan – were a-dime-a-dozen, although the boiler would often leave her passing playmate with an unwanted souvenir.

Rockpile had by now reunited and were perfectly positioned to ride this wave. In April 1978, they set off on a seven-week US tour, bottom of the bill to Elvis Costello & the Attractions and 'Spanish Stroll' hit-makers, Mink DeVille. Promoting *Pure Pop For Now People*, they were billed as 'Nick Lowe with Rockpile', and for this tour at least, Nick would 'stand in the middle'.

By opening the show, Rockpile had an important role to play, especially when the tour hit the American Midwest; audiences on the east and west coasts were populated by 'proto punks' who were hip to the new scene, but in cities such as Kansas, most of the crowd were simply confused. 'Short hair? Cheap suits?' DeVille and Costello were perhaps a little too cutting edge for these people, whereas Rockpile, with their straight-ahead brand of rock and roll, provided an important link between what the audience could understand and a band that 'looked like it had come from Venus'.

Although Rockpile were the perfect warm-up act, some fans thought they appeared onstage way too early. 'People were still gathering at the theatre, unprepared to be hit by the full force of this band,' says Elvis Costello. 'On their days off, Rockpile would play club shows. At the Whisky a Go Go in LA they played one of the top five shows I've ever seen. They were so unbelievable.'

'Unbelievable' doesn't begin to describe Rockpile when operating at maximum velocity. The shorter set demanded of them on a three-act bill allowed them to focus on their strongest numbers. Invariably they would open with 'So It Goes', then launch straight into 'Fool Too Long' before the audience had time to draw breath. 'I Knew The Bride' and 'Down Down Down' maintained the pace, with 'They Called It Rock' and 'Ju Ju Man' providing the denouement. 'Heart Of The City' was the inevitable encore and audiences went nuts.

As the tour rolled on, Nick grew to love the USA and became semi-seriously dismissive of anywhere with 'not enough neon'. But the American concert circuit was also the devil's playground and Rockpile, along with Costello's Attractions, hit it hard. Night after night, various members of the touring company would 'ski down mountains of cocaine into lakes of vodka', only to find themselves in hangover hell.

Girls were plentiful and, as Nick attests, there was 'bags of sex'. According to one former lover, 'Nick found it difficult not to give in to every woman who wanted to sleep with him, which was in fact every woman who met him.' Rockpile's in-house comedian Billy Bremner, with whom Nick often shared a motel room, cheekily dubbed him 'the range rider'.

Nick's new best friend, Carlene Carter, was on a US mini tour when a road-scarred Rockpile returned to London in July 1978. That summer, Jake and Nick vacated the flat at Queen's Gate Terrace – which would be taken over by Elvis Costello, temporarily estranged from his wife, Mary – and moved into their newly co-owned house in Melrose Terrace, Shepherd's Bush, formerly the home of record producer Tony Visconti and his wife, the singer Mary Hopkin. They were soon joined there by their respective girlfriends, Tony and Carlene, and the building became party central.

On the ground floor was 'UK Pro', a small but handy 8-track recording studio. 'The soundproofing was extensive,' recalls Paul Riley, who would later become its in-house recording engineer. 'Visconti just wanted a facility at home where he could overdub and mix. He had poured in a lake of concrete where the floor used to be and installed two layers of soundproofing to appease the neighbours.'

Nick and Jake saw the potential of the tiny studio, which they would rename 'Am-Pro' (short for 'Amateur and Professional'). It was an inexpensive facility for making demos and modest, independent recordings.

Eden, however, remained the studio of choice, budget permitting. It was there that Dave Edmunds put the finishing touches to his next album, *Trax On Wax 4*, and Nick commenced production of Elvis Costello's *Armed Forces*. 'It's a cross between Kraftwerk and Abba,' he excitedly told me during a break from recording, wearing, I observed, shoes without socks.

The album's hit 45, 'Oliver's Army', was very nearly ditched; none of the band liked the recording until Nick offered to 'buy the song' from Costello, at which point Steve Nieve ran to his piano and added the Abba-inspired hook. The sessions also yielded Costello and the Attractions' version of what would become Nick's signature song, '(What's So Funny 'bout) Peace, Love And Understanding'. Archly attributed to 'Nick Lowe and His Sound', Costello's cover recording would first see the light of day as the flipside of Nick's next 45, 'American Squirm'.

In September, Rockpile undertook a brief UK tour to warm up for an American marathon, opening for Van Morrison in thirty cities across seven weeks. On Van's nights off, Rockpile supplemented their income with more sold-out club dates. On 25 October, they played the Bottom Line in New York City, where they were joined onstage by 'origin of the species', Keith Richards.

Just the previous day, the legendary Rolling Stone had escaped a prison sentence in Toronto for possession of heroin. Having been handed down a twelve-month suspended sentence, he returned to the Big Apple and after a quick wash and brush-up at his Lower Manhattan apartment, hit the town.

'We were backstage before the second house,' recalls Nick, 'and the rumour was circulating that Keith had turned up. We were thinking, "So you get out of jail in Canada and head straight for the Bottom Line to see Rockpile? I don't think so." But you could sense he was in the building. There was an electrifying buzz coming through the walls. He was with Barbara Charone and she came backstage and asked us if he could come and meet us. Obviously, we said yes but decided it would be inappropriate to offer him any refreshment so the crew kept the Class-As out of sight.

'Suddenly, there he was. Dave Edmunds had known him from way back and was always a bit snooty about Keith's collection of Chuck Berry's licks, which was a bit rich coming from the guitarist in Rockpile. This dated back to the early 1960s when Edmunds's band supported the nascent Rolling Stones on what must have been their first and only run of gigs in Wales. In those days, a guitarist's standing rested solely on his ability to replicate Chuck's trademark "monkey beat" rhythm, and the word up and down the valleys, possibly initiated by Edmunds himself, was that the Rolling Stones' bloke, monkey beat-wise, was wanting.

'Anyway, I asked Keith if he fancied doing a couple of numbers with us. He wanted to go somewhere quiet to "talk" about it, so he and I squeezed into a broom cupboard next to the dressing room. To my astonishment he produced an enormous bag of illicit substances and started digging in. Most of it went on the floor. Edmunds then turned up and we agreed to do "Let It Rock" with Keith. We ran through it in the dressing room and an argument broke out between Dave and Keith over precisely how Chuck's opening riff should be executed.

'Then a change came over Keith. From being a perfectly rational, lovely bloke he morphed into a shambling caricature of himself before our very eyes, just as likeable but virtually incapable of playing a note. Perhaps it was something he ate. Dave had his doubts, as did I, as to whether he'd last until the encore, but the word was well and truly out that Keith Richards was in the house. If he didn't appear there would have been an eruption. The problem was that he was showing every indication of being unlikely to remain conscious for long, so we agreed that he would come on for the number at the start of our set. Come show time, we walked out onto the stage and the crowd went insane. There was a little amplifier on the floor we'd provided for Keith and off we went. The place was jumping, but suddenly

I noticed all the bottom frequencies went out of my bass sound. Then it switched to a screaming treble. I looked round and there was Keith, fiddling with the controls of MY amp. He obviously thought it was his. The guitar break came along and Edmunds shouts, "Take it away, Keith!" and I could sense Bremner muttering under his breath, "And don't bring it back." A very wonky solo followed but the crowd was going crazy – as if it was the Beatles or, er, the Rolling Stones. At the end of "Let It Rock" he stayed on and tried to play two or three more songs with us, but by this time Dave had had enough. I wouldn't have cared what Keith did – the fact remains that he had escaped the clutches of the Mounties to see Rockpile at the Bottom Line, but all Dave could see was that bloody guitar player from the wassa-names . . . can't play Chuck Berry for toffee, then or now . . . muscling in on his act. Completely unmoved by the majesty of the occasion, he gave Keith a withering look and shouted to our road manager the immortal line, "Dez! Get this cunt off the stage!"'

By December, the members of Rockpile were back in London and ready to start recording. Every evening, Monday through Friday, they would convene at the Swan public house, or 'The Pelican' as Nick referred to it, a couple of hundred yards down the road from Eden Studios in Chiswick.

It was hard to pull yourself away from the pub while Billy Bremner was telling yet another joke, such as the one where you were asked to think of a sentence containing 'blue suit' and 'cosmic ray'. 'I am wearing my blue suit,' deadpanned Billy, 'cosmic ray one's at the cleaners.' The laughter was accompanied by yet another round of drinks and Rockpile had the perfect excuse – they were 'the graveyard shift', waiting for the studio's daytime client to finish his session and pack up. 'Just one more, if I must,' said Nick, slurping his large vodka and Slimline tonic, or a 'vab and slab lab tab' in Bremner-speak. Nick figured if he could hang it out at the pub long enough, he wouldn't have to exchange pleasantries with 'the day shift'.

It was the same most weekday evenings that winter as forthcoming albums from Nick and Dave were recorded in tandem. Solo albums were the order of the day until the band could release its music under the 'Rockpile' brand, to which end Jake Riviera was still in torturous discussions with Swansong label boss Peter Grant. Although Grant was still Dave's 'official manager', Jake was doing all the heavy lifting.

Invited to a meeting at Grant's East Sussex country estate, Jake planned to tell the Led Zeppelin mogul that he envisaged Dave and Nick doing 'a Beatles in reverse' – that is, making a Rockpile album *after* a series of solo releases. But on arriving at the estate in a limo laid on by Grant, Jake was kept waiting for two hours 'on the wrong side of the moat'. Eventually, the drawbridge was lowered and Grant emerged in his dressing gown, brandishing a large bottle of cocaine. 'What's your problem, son?' he asked Riviera, menacingly. 'Would you like me to give you a million dollars?' And this was the way it would continue until Edmunds had fulfilled his four-album Swansong contract.

The Eden recording sessions were officially scheduled to end at midnight, but usually extended into the early hours of the following day. There was no one around from the studio's office staff to keep tabs on overruns, and house engineer Roger Béchirian turned a blind eye to the proceedings, rolling his eyes but digging the vibe. As the electricity bill soared, Edmunds ramped up the playback volume from loud to even louder as 'Queen Of Hearts', a Hank DeVito tune, blasted out of the giant speakers. With his hands on the mixing desk and 'riding the faders', Dave emphasised the acoustic guitar hook that punctuated the chorus. Nick looked on, impressed.

On the night I visited, a little magic was being made, but whether magic could always be made under such conditions was a moot point. As the little hand of the control room clock edged further south, returns were diminishing. Billy was on his last cigar amid overflowing ashtrays, and Terry had split. Nick was slouched over the desk, head in hands, evaluating the night's work, while Roger tidied the tape boxes and annotated the session. Dave, who appeared to be a little more awake than most, said his goodbyes and left. Greeted by birdsong as dawn rose over Acton, he threw his guitar into the back of the Jag and made for home, knowing he'd got a couple more keepers in the can.

Back in 1973, Anglophile and hit songwriter-in-waiting Chrissie Hynde had left her native Akron, Ohio, and travelled to London with $200 in cash, a suitcase full of clothes and the notion of one day forming her dream rock and roll band. In the five years that followed, she survived on a succession of part-time jobs and some simple good fortune during the occasional 'no-fixed-abode period'. Ear-to-the-ground, she soon encountered an informal network of key individuals in and around the music scene. Among the many were the NME writer Nick Kent; Malcolm McLaren and Vivienne Westwood; future members of the Sex Pistols and the Damned; Motörhead's Lemmy Kilmister; guitarist Chris Spedding; and, fortuitously, Nick Lowe.

By 1978, Hynde had hooked up with bass player Pete Farndon who told her about a guitarist, in his home town of Hereford, by the name of James Honeyman-Scott. Together with drummer Gerry Mackleduff, Farndon and Honeyman-Scott helped Hynde record a six-song demo that included a version of Ray Davies's 'Stop Your Sobbing'.

Guitarist 'Jimmy Scott' made a real impression on Chrissie Hynde. She wanted him in her band, but he had gone back to

Hereford and was disinclined to return to London. But one thing Hynde *had* learnt about Scott during the demo session was that he was a major Nick Lowe fan.

Chrissie Hynde confesses: 'I don't think Jimmy wanted to leave his job in Hereford, or his girlfriend, but I knew he wouldn't want to turn down an opportunity to work with Nick. I thought that if I could get Nick to produce our first single, Jimmy would definitely join my band. It was a ploy, my secret weapon.

'Pete and I dropped the demo tape through Nick's letterbox, then we hung around Oxford Street until we thought, "Well, he must have listened to it by now." We called Nick from a phone box and the first thing he said was, "Oh, hi KH [which was Nick's term of endearment for Chrissie], I definitely want to get in on this Sandie Shaw song." By which he meant "Stop Your Sobbing". I'm not sure he loved the other tracks because he didn't really like angry stuff – that whole punk thing was where my head was at – but the Kinks song was very sweet and I was now able to say to Jimmy, "Nick Lowe's gonna produce it."

'I called Jimmy, but before I could tell him the news, he said, "I've been listening to the demos and I want to join your band."'

In late 1978, Chrissie and her as yet unnamed outfit went into Eden Studios for a one-day session with Nick to record 'Stop Your Sobbing' and 'The Wait'.

'Nick had his own language in the studio – "Make it sound like dinosaurs eating cars!" And he used the word "proper" a lot. After we left, Nick added background vocals. I think he also had Elvis Costello in the studio, who made a few suggestions, and Nick is singing on the record, which obviously thrilled us.'

Upon recruiting drummer Martin Chambers, Chrissie's group became the Pretenders. With razorblade cheekbones, skinny legs and all, they personified the look of the day and launched their career with the Lowe-produced 'Stop Your Sobbing'. Original songs such as 'Kid' and 'Brass In Pocket' followed. The timing was perfect; on the east and west coasts of America, the music of Elvis Costello and Graham Parker – with Nick Lowe as catalyst – was starting to gain traction, and the Pretenders caught the slipstream. They went on to become an international hit machine as record-buyers gradually caught up.

'A very big chunk of what the Pretenders are would not have existed without Nick,' says Hynde. 'I'm not saying that I wouldn't have got a band together – I might not have done – but meeting Nick was a catalyst for many, many aspects of what this band was. All roads lead back to Nick.'

His idiosyncratic skills in record production and man-management were quickly evolving. He had an ability to identify the alpha male among the musicians. It might not have been the artist whose name appeared on the record; it could have been the drummer or the bass player, or 'some quiet guy sulking in the corner'. Nick simply did what needed to be done to make the players come up with a great performance.

'I was good at finding out who you had to suck up to, or bully. It depended on what they wanted and I had to identify what it was I had to do. If they needed a court jester, I became one; if they wanted a grim-jawed, gimlet-eared, "I've heard it all before, kid" type of guy, I could do that too. If there was someone who couldn't get his song on the record, I might say: "Why don't you come a bit early to the session tomorrow and we'll go through the song and see if we can't work on it?" knowing full well that the song was beyond help. The trick was to make him realise his song was beyond help!'

*

Throughout this hectic period, Nick and Carlene saw as much of each other as their respective schedules would allow. Carlene's daughter, Tiffany, then aged six, recalls a lot of 'going back and forth' between Los Angeles, Nashville and London, often accompanied by one of her nannies. Carlene calculates that she herself made seventeen round trips between Los Angeles and London in the twelve months from mid-1978, 'to see my boyfriend'. Carlene accepts that Nick was seeing other girls on and off, and there were a couple of incidents that still amuse her.

'He was coming to LA, and he called me from San Francisco the night before. He asked me to pick him up at the Tropicana Motel and then we would go to my house. I drove there and as I was walking by the window of his room I looked in and he was sitting on a girl's lap. I knocked on the window and put my thumb up in the air. There was a look of sheer terror on his face. On another occasion, I was playing the Keystone Club in Berkeley, and Nick came along. I was onstage with the Clover guys and I could see Nick at the bar. He was hitting on some girl like crazy and she was giving him her phone number. When I got offstage somebody gave me some roses. We were walking down the street, and Nick said, "I can't help it if women find me irresistible." I whacked him round the head with the roses. He called me "The Flying Fist of Fury". Anyway, after I caught Nick in the room with that girl he came up to my house and we were sitting on a piano stool looking out at the lights of Hollywood, and I said to him, "Nick, I know you'll do what you want to do, and I will always love you, but you're not gonna disrespect me like that." And he said, "I know, I know, I wanna do it right, I think we should get married." And I went, "What?!" I wasn't expecting that.'

CHAPTER 11

Seconds of Pleasure

When a band is about to break, it's the best time you will ever have. It's way better than when you actually become famous.

With an average age of thirty-two, and jokingly referred to by insiders as 'Dad's Army', Rockpile were nothing less than a mutual admiration society. Their respect for each other's musicianship just about comes across in the documentary *Born Fighters*, which was filmed by director Peter Carr during the making of Dave Edmunds's *Repeat When Necessary* and Nick's *Labour Of Lust*.

Following a brief synopsis of the duo's lengthy musical careers up to that point, the cameras turn to Nick's place where he and Dave are running through 'How Do You Talk To An Angel' and 'Born Fighter'. Carlsberg Special Brew and Black Tower Liebfraumilch are much in evidence as Nick tells Dave, 'Because this stuff we do is simple, it comes out as rock and roll; there's no way you can write an up-tempo beat item with three chords and it doesn't come out as rock and roll; it's impossible for it to come out otherwise.'

Nick's philosophical remarks, delivered in a Thames Estuary tone of voice, uncannily foreshadow the *Spinal Tap* mockumentary's Nigel Tufnel.[15] When the action switches to Eden Studios, Nick is giving a running commentary on the rudiments of rock recording for the benefit of the uninitiated viewer.

'In this business where you've got to have your records come out of the radio at you, the whole game is to try and make your record sound louder than anyone else's. For me, the secret is to get the drums sounding loud, and then you have to have a good vocal performance.'

As Billy Bremner adds a soaring harmony to 'Born Fighter', Nick reiterates his point: 'High voices for some reason have always been very commercial sounding, they come out of the radio very well.'

While Edmunds perfects his guitar solo for the track, Nick talks about the dynamic between himself and Dave: 'I always think that our relationship is distant, even though we are very close friends. Sometimes I get surprised about feeling affection towards Dave. He's not the most lovable creature in the world, for God's sake, even though he's a great guitarist and singer. He's like a sort of elder brother. I'm much more demonstrative than Dave is, I get more excited much quicker than Dave does, then I tell him he's old and boring.'

Nick's comments are playfully facetious, but as he takes another sip of wine he adds: 'See, the thing is, you can't do this sort of thing unless you're . . .'

Edmunds has now returned to the control room and has clearly heard this line before. Aware of the film crew's proximity, he quickly interjects with a loud cough over the words 'on drugs'. Then, affectionately, he says to Nick: 'Hey, calm down, champ. You've got a big fight coming up.'

A few nights later, ace guitarist Albert Lee shows up and is captured on film adding his trademark sound to 'Sweet Little Lisa'. Albert is everyone's favourite guitar hero and his lightning licks leave onlookers dazzled. Nick, more dazzled than most, remains silent during the playback, seemingly unmoved, while Albert sits close by. All is quiet. Then, as soon as Nick is certain he has the floor to himself, he gently addresses Albert: 'Listen . . . you've obviously read my pamphlet.'

Albert chuckles as Nick contemplates another bottle of sweet German wine and an un-tipped Senior Service, one of the stronger cigarettes on the market. It now seems as if Dave has to really be on his toes to prevent Nick from monopolising the proceedings with humorous remarks, but it is an atmosphere of friendly competition. And while Edmunds has superb technical skills and is a master of the studio console, Lowe dominates the songwriting department with his inherent ability to scribble down a good line. And it is 'the song' upon which this enterprise ultimately depends. Dave has usually recorded a couple of Nick's off-the-peg items for each release, and there was even a time when they successfully wrote together; their earlier composition, 'Deborah', captured the essence of the Everly Brothers in an updated setting.

The central section of Carr's film, in which Edmunds tackles 'Endless Grey Ribbon', celebrates the band's love of country music, with its Tennessee twang and the potential for building ethereal harmonies. Nick and Dave demonstrate their effortless vocal instincts, and with Billy adding a high harmony from the top of his register, they achieve a golden blend. The mood is broken, however, when Dave returns to the control room, having recorded his lead vocal, only to hear Nick utter to camera: 'I was just explaining about what a bad singer you are.'

Dave, who must surely be used to Nick's ironic remarks by now, appears genuinely hurt. 'I can always depend on Nick to let me down,' he mourns.

Towards the end of the film, Nick and Dave are sitting at a table, engaged in a fairly tedious 'meaning of life' discussion. Dave is bright and lucid, whereas Nick once again has his head lowered and is running his hand up the back of his neck, in customary fashion when worse for wear.

'I wanna get out before I start sliding downhill,' he says. 'I can think of lots of different things to do. I'd go and work with my dad. I'd be as happy as a sandboy, strumming in the evenings until it runs out of fun. As soon as it stops being fun, I'm off.'

Dave tells Nick he has a 'terrible attitude' and is talking rubbish.

Nick continues: 'My whole life is ruled by gloom. The songs I do are inspired by gloom. In 1978, more than any time, you've got to fly close to the wind, drive yourself heavy.'

When Dave tells Nick that he should have a day off and unwind, Nick isn't listening. Instead, he's describing his father's wartime activities in the RAF. 'That's what he did for five years, and every night he got back, and he's a fantastic guy, my old man.'

Born Fighters was aired on Granada TV on 11 August 1979. Nearly four decades later, when asked if he had watched the film recently, Nick replied, 'I'd rather nail my feet to the ground and stare at the sun.'

Among the tracks recorded for *Labour Of Lust* was 'Cruel To Be Kind', written by Nick during his time with Brinsley Schwarz. Released as a single in 1979, it became a worldwide hit, helping to establish 'Nick Lowe' as a commercial proposition and build faith with the big record companies. Music industry insider Kal Rudman, publisher of the *Friday Morning Quarterback* 'tip sheet', predicted that 'Cruel To Be Kind' would rake in 'elephant dollars' ('or rhino bucks', replied Nick). But the fact that the song was even recorded for *Labour Of Lust* was down to one man.

'It was disconcerting at first to find that, after listening to all of my demos and works in progress, Gregg Geller – who was head of A&R at Columbia and had already signed Elvis Costello – appeared to be mostly interested in "Cruel To Be Kind". I was a bit embarrassed by the song actually, because since it was written in 1974 I'd reinvented myself as a cutting-edge, thrusting new-waver. Gregg had heard the Brinsleys' demo, on which Ian Gomm had helped out by showing me the tricksy G9sus4 chord, which is a feature of the song, but way beyond my musical ken at the time. I thought the tune was a bit old school and not in a good way. I was saying, "But don't you want to hear 'Up Against The Wall'?" or some old rubbish I'd churned out that I was trying to punt, but Gregg had the bit between his teeth and was quietly insistent that "Cruel" would be on any list of potential material for my next record on Columbia.

'Gregg Geller is a gentleman; more like a Harvard professor than the picture of what "New York A&R man" conjures up. His tweedy look belies an encyclopaedic knowledge of blues, soul, country, folk, jazz and pop. He is proper cool and I was extremely lucky to have attracted his attention. He's still a much-loved friend, but back then that gentle but steely pressure he exerted on me to cut "Cruel" was irksome indeed. I was no match for him, of course, and his persistence finally won out, thank God. I told the others, "Look boys, I'm sorry, we've got to do it. Mr Geller says so." Edmunds grabbed it by the throat and once we got those harmonies going it turned out great. Gregg was proved right. I am extremely grateful to him for twisting my arm – it's a good song that has lasted, and it's still my calling card.'

Nick wasn't the only artiste in the Riviera Global camp to enjoy commercial success in this golden period. Dave Edmunds reached number two on the UK singles chart with his cover of Elvis Costello's 'Girls Talk'. Costello's own version was little more than a sketch when he gifted it to Dave, perhaps aware of the production magic that Edmunds could bring to it. The outcome enhanced Costello's reputation as a coverable songwriter, although Dave introduced the song at one concert with the quip, 'Here's a song by Elvis Costello, and he thanks you from the bottom of his wallet.'

Costello himself was busy racking up the hits with 'Oliver's Army', 'Accidents Will Happen' and 'I Can't Stand Up For Falling Down', all bearing the label copy 'Produced by Nick Lowe', while Nick himself grazed the singles charts with the world-weary 'Cracking Up'.

It was a run of hits that rewarded manager Jake Riviera for his industrious tenacity and inspirational dedication during and after the pub rock era. Now at his commercial peak, Riviera would stop at nothing to harangue and motivate Columbia Records in the USA to get behind his artists, whether that involved 'tap dancing on Al Teller's desk' – Teller was president of Columbia – or some inventive, outrageous prank.

The relatively conservative record execs often failed to appreciate Riviera's sense of humour; at one point, when Jake sensed that the label was not giving Costello's latest release enough of a push, he visited a New York hardware store and purchased a crate full of shovels. These he despatched to Columbia's head of promotion with the message: 'If you are trying to bury Elvis Costello, perhaps you could make use of these.'

It seemed totally natural to Jake and Nick that they should be having hit records, although when this happened they didn't experience nearly the level of elation they had expected.

'For a while it seemed that everything we recorded was a hit. When I've seen those history of rock programmes I've been astonished to discover how high some of those records got. "That got that high?!" Today, chance would be a fine thing, but back then I never even used to notice. I just thought, "It's time for the hits now." It seemed like everyone had a hit record in them, but I knew that sooner or later the public's taste would change.'

In the USA, 'Cruel To Be Kind' was followed up with Nick's version of the Mickey Jupp song, 'Switchboard Susan', or 'Switchbox Susan' as many American fans still yell out for to this day. The song's opening line – in which the singer pleads with a telephone operator, 'give me a line' – is followed by the snakiest of guitar licks as Terry's snare drum shot heralds the ultimate Rockpile groove. The song is then littered with more ingenious puns and innuendo, including a reference to getting 'an extension' (that has little to do with the communication device invented by Alexander Graham Bell).

Nick had discovered the number when he produced one side of Jupp's Stiff Records album *Juppanese*, for which Rockpile were hired to furnish their instrumental prowess. But Jupp hated the way 'Switchboard Susan' had turned out.

'Mickey Jupp is touched with genius but he could be a difficult and contrary man. We were all staying in this hotel by Worthing railway station. I nearly had to throw myself across the tracks to stop the train and prevent Rockpile from leaving town. But "Switchboard Susan" had a cracking backing track, so I offered to buy it off Mickey and he agreed. Then I stuck my vocal on it.'

In other *Labour Of Lust* songs, the pleasures and perils of the rock and roll life are reflected in Nick's on-tour scribbling. Like many writers he has denied that his songs are autobiographical, but some of these pearls were undoubtedly prised from personal experience. 'Big Kick, Plain Scrap' namechecks 'the Crest motel' with multiple 'on drugs' references; 'Skin Deep' captures a couple avoiding eye contact while 'belly to belly'; and the self-explanatory 'Dose Of You' tells of a bad infection getting worse.

Such tales of intoxication and casual sex were certainly road-related. 'I'm sure that touring was the frame of reference for some of those songs,' admits Nick. 'It's all pretty brutal, that's the nature of it. There's not much poetry involved.'

There is some poetry, however, in 'Endless Grey Ribbon', in which a long-distance truck driver is contemplating a bed of white linen at the road's end. Of this atmosphere-charged song, Nick modestly remarks, 'It's a little over-crafted, like so much of my stuff back then, but what the hell? You gotta start somewhere.'

Two further songs in the *Labour Of Lust* collection are notable for their quiet, confessional vocal; 'Basing Street' delivers the confidential lowdown on a midnight stabbing in a west London turning, and 'You Make Me' conveys a deeply personal message. The whispered vocal technique came about by chance when the members of Rockpile were sharing hotel rooms and Nick would get back to his bed after a few drinks and not want to disturb his sleeping bandmate. Carrying a song idea in his head, he felt compelled to pull out an acoustic guitar but 'croak very quietly'. Without a tape recorder to hand, Nick called his home telephone back in London and quietly sang 'You Make Me' down the phone line onto his answer machine for fear of forgetting the tune. On playing it back a few weeks later, the intimate vocal sound struck him as 'really cool', and it was replicated in the recording studio.

Nick had now set to one side his blue Fender bass and was using a Hamer eight-string model when Rockpile returned to the US tour circuit in the summer of 1979. This time they would be the opening act for Blondie, who had just enjoyed a number one hit with 'Heart Of Glass'. Blondie's drummer, Clem Burke, had been attuned to all-things-Nick since visiting London in 1976, just as the musical tide was turning.

'After hearing "Heart Of The City" I became very aware of Nick as the producer of both the Damned and Elvis Costello,' says Burke. 'Then came *Jesus Of Cool* and it seemed as if Nick was everywhere. Rockpile were at the peak of their powers when they toured with us – a force of nature playing with an intensity that was fitting for those New Wave and punk rock times, almost like the Ramones but with more accomplished musicians. They were the world's greatest rock and roll band at that time. I think Nick may have been a bit more sussed than the other three and more in touch with what was new and happening on the music scene, but there was an empathy between all of us on the tour. They realised that opening for Blondie gave them the opportunity to play to a wider audience since we were enjoying a run of great success with our album *Parallel Lines*. I, for one, was a fan and I enjoyed hanging out and having a drink or two with the guys.'

'Blondie got that number one record, but they weren't quite prepared for playing bigger places,' says Roberta Bayley. 'Rockpile were often blowing them off stage, and at Oakland lots of people started leaving the venue before Blondie came on. Blondie thought I was a traitor because they were paying for me to be there, as their photographer, but I was hanging out with Rockpile. It was embarrassing if you think about it, and I got kicked off the tour.'

Tour manager Andy Cheeseman had the job of keeping Rockpile in line on the Blondie tour. He recalls Nick being 'easy-going', and Dave cooking the band's lunch on the tour bus, earning him the nickname 'Microwave Dave'. They would also play cards for hours on end – games like Last Card or Switch.

'They were usually well-behaved before a show,' says Cheeseman. 'But on a scale of one to ten, I'd say it was about a five or a six. Soundchecks were cursory, maybe two numbers, and

I would be sent to the liquor store to get the vodka if a promoter refused to supply spirits on the rider. The band were easy to tour manage, but Jake was the hardest part of it. He was on the road with us quite a lot, particularly in New York or Los Angeles, the fun places.'

The Blondie tour took a short break after playing the Greek Theatre in Los Angeles, and it was in LA that Nick and Carlene took the opportunity to tie the knot. The wedding ceremony took place on 18 August 1979 at Carlene's home on Queens Road, off Sunset Boulevard. This was to become the set for video director Chuck Statler's 'Cruel To Be Kind' promo (which would be among the 208 video clips broadcast by MTV on its launch day in 1981). On the day before the wedding, Statler filmed Nick and Rockpile miming to 'Cruel' at the Tropicana Motel, and interspersed it with footage from the ceremony itself. Cameos include Dave Edmunds as 'the chauffeur', Terry Williams as 'the photographer' and Billy Bremner as 'the chef'.

Clover bassist John Ciambotti gave Carlene away, and Jake Riviera was Nick's best man. Pat and Drain flew out for the occasion and appear in the video production singing along with friends and family, including Carlene's daughter, Tiffany.

Two days later, Rockpile were back in New York for a sell-out show at the Palladium, where Andy Warhol was spotted in the audience, no doubt tapping his toe to 'Born Fighter'. In early September, Nick and Carlene honeymooned on the island of Saint Martin in the Caribbean, after which Rockpile set off for Australia.

In October 1979, Nick commenced the production of Elvis Costello's next album, *Get Happy!!* It would appear in the UK on a new label, F-Beat, following Costello and Lowe's departure from Radar. The sessions took place, rather unusually, in Holland.

'We went to Hilversum,' recalls Costello. 'It wasn't like we were in Amsterdam – we were in the middle of nowhere with zero nightlife and in this very BBC-like studio where you couldn't turn the volume up beyond a certain level. But one crucial, liberal mistake they made was to deliver us a bottle of iced vodka and a tray of Heineken at six o'clock every evening, and that was just for starters. You can imagine what happened next.'

What happened next was that a huge number of songs were captured, mostly inspired by the 1960s soul music that Costello had recently become hooked on, following his visit to Rock On Records in Camden Town where he binged on Stax 45s. Many of Costello's tracks, however, had to be completed in London after the Attractions outstayed their welcome in the Netherlands. But Elvis was at his most prolific, to the extent that the twenty-track *Get Happy!!* was swiftly followed by the release of the twenty-track *Taking Liberties*, a goldmine of demos, covers and outtakes, mostly produced by Nick and 'Balanced by Roger Béchirian'.

In other news, Warner Brothers Records released Carlene Carter's *Two Sides To Every Woman*, produced by Lance Quinn and Tony Bongiovi. *Billboard* listed it in its 'Pop' category and the harder rocking tracks certainly pulled Carlene further away from her country roots. Nashville's music community may have fancied her as a standard bearer for the Carter–Cash continuum, but it was too soon for Carlene to simply toe the family line, however much she adored the musical tradition. Instead, she rebelled, and aligned herself with the tougher music that was coming out of London.

'Carlene seemed to be running away from destiny,' says close observer Paul Riley. 'She could have been a huge country star, but it was as if she was doing her darnedest not to be one. You can see why, especially when most of your family are country stars, it's expected of you to follow that path, but it's a bit like going into the family business when all you want to be is a rock and roller. Aligning herself with Nick's world avoided the formulaic musical solutions waiting to compartmentalise her.'

In live performance, Carlene certainly possessed the power to shock, and was not averse to upsetting the apple cart; at New York's Bottom Line on 8 October 1979 she introduced her song 'Swap-Meat Rag' with the memorable comment, 'If this don't put the cunt back in country, I don't know what will.' There was a smattering of laughter from the audience, but also much embarrassment, most of which emanated from the table occupied by Johnny Cash and June Carter, who had quietly snuck into the club hoping to surprise Carlene after the show.

'Mama and John came backstage and John was so red-in-the-face mad at me,' Carlene would later tell writer Michael Simmons. 'The first thing I said was, "Mama, Mama, I'm so sorry I said that word!" and she goes, "What word, honey?"'

Carlene's folks quickly forgot about her inelegant announcement, but in the wider world it made *Playboy* magazine's 'Quotes of the Year' – and what a year it had been. As Christmas approached, Nick and Carlene were ensconced at Melrose Terrace in London when word came that Johnny and June would soon be passing through town, en route to a vacation in the Middle East. Where better to stay than with the Lowes?

As Nick recalls: 'A convoy of taxis pulled up outside our modest terraced house in Shepherd's Bush. One cab had Johnny and June in it, and the other two cabs carried their luggage. Most people jump to attention a bit when the in-laws come to call, but if they're Johnny Cash and June Carter you'll find as soon as they walk in the door, your house has shrunk to a quarter of its size. I couldn't believe they were there. I'd come down in the morning to find John sitting in our little kitchen in his dressing gown, drinking a cup of coffee with a guitar across his lap and

June, similarly attired, but with a diamond or two glamming up her look, scrambling eggs on the gas hob.

'Looking back, it's hard to understand why I was so surprised to find that John was such a music fan, by which I mean that he enjoyed listening to and talking about music quite as much if not more than making it. I suppose in my naivety I thought that because he was so great he didn't have to listen to records as obsessively and forensically as me and my mates did in order to make sense of it. How and why the groove works? How the tune is arranged? Why this vocalist puts the lyric across and why that one doesn't? All that kind of stuff – but I was wrong – in this respect at least, he was just the same as we were.

'John liked a drink back then too, and some of my fondest memories are of when these two interests combined and he would produce a large bag of cassettes from which he'd make a selection, then jump up with a "Now this you gotta hear" and attempt to find a track lurking somewhere on a tape of twenty or thirty other tunes. He'd accomplish this with one hand, while in the other his wine glass, plus its surging contents, hovered threateningly over the glowing valves of the sound system. He played me Bob Luman, Johnny Horton, who he used to go fishing with, and Ferlin Husky. I remember he made comments like, "That's Grady Martin," or, "This doesn't sound like Nashville, I think they cut it at King." Man, what a treat.

'Shepherd's Bush nowadays is a leafy, residential part of London, but in the 1970s it was a fairly down-at-heel, working-class area with a multi-racial makeup, you might say – a significant proportion of which was Irish. Once or twice, John and June went for a walk around the neighbourhood. On these occasions, there was no nonsense about going incognito – baseball cap, shades, hoodie, that kind of malarkey. They would turn out fully loaded, John in black coat and boots, June in mink and diamonds, including, I recall, a magnificent Russian-style mink hat. They'd keep to the side streets, away from the crowds, but they'd soon be recognised and when it happened they were never mobbed for autographs or otherwise hassled at all. Mostly people were just thrilled to see them and shake hands and say "Hello". Sometimes they'd shout down to them from upper windows "What about ye, Johnny?", "Fair play to yez." The two of them were unfailingly kind and friendly, especially June, who had a joke and a giggle for everyone. They were sheer class. Two of the best people I've ever known.'

On 26 December 1979, Nick enticed Cash into the recording studio on the ground floor of the house. Forsaking traditional Boxing Day arrangements, Elvis Costello, Dave Edmunds, Martin Belmont and Pete Thomas all turned up for the session. Cash and Costello duetted on 'We Oughta Be Ashamed', and Cash sang Nick's 'Without Love', later to be released on Cash's *Rockabilly Blues* album.[16]

This would not be the last Nick Lowe song to be recorded by Johnny Cash, or indeed the only time that June Carter visited Melrose Terrace. Carlene had been rushed into hospital with what turned out to be an ectopic pregnancy.

'I didn't know I was pregnant and I found out the hard way,' says Carlene. 'I went to the hospital in excruciating pain, but they thought I was some neurotic, crazy American and turned me away. Finally, Nick had to take me in the middle of the night. The next thing I knew, I was waking up in a hospital ward, completely out of it, with a scar across the bottom of my tummy.'

Nick called June Carter, who immediately caught a plane to London where she elected to stay at the Lowe household and, while there, take on some domestic chores.

'Look, you won't even notice me,' June told Nick. 'If I get

in your way, just tell me, because I know you're working late every night.'

'Yes, correct,' thought Nick, who was 'working his ass off' in the studio, and living a lifestyle he didn't particularly wish his mother-in-law to witness. Although he appreciated the help, he had to escape. It was too early to head for the studio, so he visited a betting shop in Shepherd's Bush. Pulling from his pocket one of Billy Bremner's racing tips – 'a dead cert, probably a horse race cross-collateralised with some snooker final' – he put £5 on a horse which romped home first at 8–1. When he returned to Melrose Terrace with his winnings, he realised he'd forgotten his keys.

'I rang the bell and June came to the door with a huge smile on her face. "Hi, honey, hi!" She was wearing a kind of turban on her head, with an incredible jewelled brooch on the front. It looked like the Eye of Zoltan. And she was wearing one of Carlene's aprons and a pair of pale blue Marigold rubber gloves. The memory I have is that she wore her diamond rings over the top of the Marigolds, which as ridiculous as it sounds, she might have done for purely practical purposes.'

It was generally agreed that Carlene's next album would involve Rockpile, and that Nick should produce, although he'd been most reluctant. 'I decided I was going to write a song that Nick couldn't say no to,' says Carlene. 'Something that would make him say, "This is a perfect Rockpile song." The song was "Cry" and Dave and Billy and Terry went to Nick and said, "Come on, mate, we can't let her record this with those Americans, she needs *us*."'

The sessions spanned late 1979 through early 1980, and although it was recorded piecemeal, *Musical Shapes* is a cohesive collection, showcasing Carlene's rocking songs, perfectly complemented by Billy Bremer's guitar skills, Terry's swinging drumbeats and a standout duet with Dave Edmunds on 'Baby Ride Easy'.

For Rockpile, 1979 ended with a performance at 'The Concert for Kampuchea', where they were joined onstage at Hammersmith Odeon by Robert Plant for a version of Elvis Presley's 'Little Sister'.

The following year would see more touring and a great deal of recording; Riviera Global and its clients monopolised the Eden Studios diary throughout 1980, and some significant albums were made there that year. These included *Trust*, the fifth in an unbroken run of Elvis Costello albums produced by Nick. At this point Elvis and the Attractions were, to put it kindly, 'burnt out', following relentless roadwork combined with the usual rock and roll madness.

'The exhaustion had set in around that time,' says Costello. 'We went down to Devon to rehearse in our lawyer's cottage. We drank a load of raw scrumpy and vodka, and by the end of the recording sessions I was even taking downers [Seconal] and drinking whisky, which made me very bleak. I just thought the whole thing was shit. There was too much negativity, we were drunk and hungover, full of self-pity, but the record contains two or three of the best performances the band ever cut. "Shot With His Own Gun" came out good. But Nick was disenchanted. I think he thought we weren't trying, and I remember Jake got very angry.'

'It was a very blurry old time,' recalls Nick. 'I seemed to never be out of Eden Studios. I was either there or on a tour bus. We loved Eden – it all worked – and there were a lot of hit records flying about. Elvis Costello . . . Dave Edmunds . . . I don't remember ever getting very excited about it, although going to America and hearing "Cruel To Be Kind" on several radio stations in LA was a trip. Whenever I hear one of my records on the radio now, I think there's been some kind of mistake.'

*

199

In June 1980, Nick was reunited with Dr Feelgood to produce *A Case Of The Shakes* at Eden, where one had to squeeze past countless boxes of wine piled high in the corridor throughout the sessions.

'I've been to the doctor for a check-up,' said Feelgood vocalist Lee Brilleaux. 'He said I should cut back on the beer and spirits, but apparently it's OK for me to drink white wine.'

Everyone appeared to be following Lee's doctor's advice and the studio was swimming in Chablis as the brutal, rocking sound of 'Drives Me Wild' and 'Best In The World' poured out of the giant speakers.

'I like the sound Nick got on that album with the big clattering drums,' said Feelgood guitarist Gypie Mayo. 'He went for a Sandy Nelson kind of sound. Nick's thing was, "Keep it raw; keep it spontaneous. You are Dr Feelgood. You are not the Doobie Brothers!"'

It was also during 1980 that Jake Riviera became involved with Squeeze, famous for hits such as 'Cool For Cats' and 'Up The Junction'. The group's relationship with their existing manager, Miles Copeland, had recently deteriorated when his other clients, the Police, fronted by 'Sting' with Copeland's brother Stewart on drums, became his priority act.

'When we first met Jake, I knew we were in for a fun ride,' says Squeeze co-leader Chris Difford. 'He was full of excitement and passion about our music and introduced the idea of Nick producing us. We leapt at the chance and walked into his house in Shepherd's Bush ready to show him our wares. I had met Nick once before, when he was in the Brinsleys. They played at a pub in Abbey Wood where my first band was supporting. He was very brotherly to me and encouraged me to write more songs, which was big of him considering the songs we were playing were mostly not mine.'

Jake Riviera suggested to Squeeze that they might consider replacing their departed keyboardist, Jools Holland, with Paul Carrack, formerly of Ace. Jake also proposed to Squeeze that they make a double album, with a different producer for each of its four sides. On paper, Jake's 'million-quid quartet' comprised Paul McCartney, Dave Edmunds, Elvis Costello and Nick Lowe. Had it come off, it would have done none of his three management clients any harm to be credited alongside the former Beatle, but McCartney declined, and so it was Nick who was first to enter the ring with Squeeze.

'Jake would come down to light the blue touch paper, but it was Nick who we looked up to,' says Difford. 'We listened to his tales of Johnny Cash, and touring with various bands. He was a master storyteller, but we ended up in the pub and little got done.'

Dave Edmunds was next to accept the challenge, producing a few tracks for Squeeze. When those sessions faltered, it was left to Elvis Costello to pick up the production pieces. 'Working with Elvis was challenging for me,' says Difford. 'I would watch his face as he read my lyrics, to see if I would get the grin of approval.' Either way, Costello – assisted by engineer Roger Béchirian – produced what still stands as the greatest Squeeze album, *East Side Story*.

The year's biggest challenge, however, was the making of the first official Rockpile LP, almost certain to be green-lit now that Dave Edmunds was in the process of finalising his contractual obligations to Swansong. Riviera's face-off with Peter Grant was still ongoing and became infused with drama when Jake issued his office staff with instructions of what action they should take, should he fail to return from his next visit to Grant's HQ.

'I remember Jake coming back from one meeting with Peter Grant and the word "gun" was mentioned,' recalls Andy

Cheeseman. 'Jake believed Grant's hype and I think it was also a case of him trying to prove that he was really fighting for his artist, and was prepared to die, if it meant getting Edmunds off Swansong. I guess Peter Grant was doing whatever he had to do to keep the Led Zeppelin boys happy, but I don't remember any great A&R input from them. I got the impression that signing Dave was a bit of a vanity project for Swansong.'

Seconds Of Pleasure, the 'debut album' from Rockpile, was announced with ads in the American music press carrying the copy line: 'Four promising solo careers bite the dust'. Whether or not this was Jake Riviera's way of winding up Peter Grant, or indeed Dave Edmunds, anticipation among Rockpile fans was high; perhaps the album would fuse the magical elements of *Labour Of Lust* and *Repeat When Necessary*, in other words, Nick's arch lyricism and pop sensibility set to Dave's production skills and rock and roll groove. Laden with vocal harmonies and a thousand ringing guitars, it would be the ultimate ear candy. Dream on.

'If ever there was a "erm, will *this* do?" moment, that was it,' says Nick. '"How many tracks have we got now? Eleven? Oh good." I wanted to do poppier stuff and shock people by doing it. It seems ridiculous to say that now, but I liked the Hollies and the Fortunes. We erred on the side of Dave, but Rockpile was a missed opportunity. It was all a little bit fraught.'

Seconds Of Pleasure had all the characteristics of a contract-filler – before the ink was even dry. Recording had been rushed, but it wasn't all bad. To dissect its contents, 'Wrong Again (Let's Face It')', sung by Dave, demonstrated to its writers, Messrs Difford and Tilbrook from Squeeze, that anything was possible in the big happy Riviera Global family.

'Teacher Teacher', sung by Nick and written by Kenny Pickett and Eddie Phillips of 1960s psychedelic rock group, the Creation, is about the nearest the album gets to real commerciality. A souped-up version of 'Heart', sung beautifully by Billy Bremner, is one of the better Lowe-composed songs on the record, but it is the magnificent 'Now And Always' that towers over the entire album. Clocking in at around two minutes, it could easily have sat alongside 'Learning The Game' in Buddy Holly's late-1958 New York portfolio, such is its grace and simplicity.

With the exception of 'You Ain't Nothin' But Fine', also sung by Bremner, and 'When I Write The Book', which like 'Heart' would become a staple of Nick's live shows in the years ahead, most of the other tracks on *Seconds Of Pleasure* are perfunctory rock-a-boogie cover versions, and precisely what Rockpile needed to move away from if they were to compete in the 1980s marketplace. An accompanying EP of Nick and Dave performing some Everly Brothers songs was a pleasant bonus.

'Rockpile couldn't get arrested at radio in the States,' says industry veteran Jerry Jaffe, who had seen the Brinsleys at the Fillmore in 1970, and first met Nick when the group played Amsterdam in 1973.

'In fact, it was Nick who told me, "You should be in the music business." I was a teacher at the time and he encouraged me. I've followed his career ever since. When it was my job to get Polydor's acts played on American radio, I would plan my promotional field trips around Rockpile's tour itinerary. I think I was at more of their shows than the guys from Columbia Records. Rockpile were on the verge of becoming very popular, but American radio looked on them as being an offshoot of punk music. Even though they were older and their music was based on a purely American sound, there was this connotation that they were "punk", as far as the radio programmers were concerned.'

Nevertheless, *Seconds Of Pleasure* hit number 27 on the *Billboard* 200 chart, and its lead 45, 'Teacher Teacher', would reach a respectable number 51. A twenty-date US tour to promote the album included three sold-out nights at New York's Ritz. Afternoons in the city were spent in the bar of the Gramercy Park Hotel, where Nick would 'lay down his Amex card and the drinking would commence'.

According to F-Beat's Andy Childs: 'Rockpile were sensational at the Ritz, in contrast to the slight disappointment of their album. You couldn't discern any disharmony within the band, although Nick would sometimes spend long periods alone in his hotel room, somewhat distant and reclusive.'

The Rockpile tour wound up on the west coast in mid-December 1980, by which time the band was ready to take a breather.

For the stars of Riviera Global, 1980 climaxed with a concert on 27 December at Birmingham's cavernous National Exhibition Centre, where they were billed alongside acts from the happening 'Ska revival' movement – the Selecter, Madness and UB40.

About an hour before show time, the giant doors of the arena's loading bay opened to admit a mighty Silver Eagle tour bus carrying Elvis Costello & the Attractions, Squeeze and Rockpile. To observers gathered backstage, it was a highly theatrical entrance; marching slowly, six feet in front of the enormous bus, like some sombrely attired funeral director, was Jake Riviera. With barely concealed pride and avoiding eye contact with onlookers, he guided the vehicle into its designated parking bay. Then the musicians disembarked in various states of disorientation, with Nick and Elvis both sweating profusely. Who was to know that it would soon be the end of the road for Rockpile?

CHAPTER 12
Cracking Up

When the records were suddenly not hits, it was as if, 'Where's my hit-making machine? My hit-making machine done bust.'

Nick and Carlene, with Tiffany and her nanny in tow, had by now moved into Bank Lodge, a large double-fronted house in Wellesley Road, Chiswick. It was conveniently situated for Eden Studios; the approach road to the M4 motorway and thus London Heathrow Airport; and the Pilot public house just across the street.

The year 1981 would be tour-free for Nick – his first, and last, almost for ever. His break from the road was mainly due to rumblings in the Rockpile camp; irrespective of the possibility of further recordings from the band, Nick had for some months been piecing together his next solo album using assorted musicians including drummer Bobby Irwin. By the end of January, he had ten backing tracks in the can, and Columbia Records was expressing its delight at the prospect of releasing some new Nick Lowe product in the USA.

On the evening of 6 February, I visited Riviera Global's Acton offices for some obscure reason. Nick was present, and as we strolled up Horn Lane to the Duke of York for 'an early one', he matter-of-factly announced that Rockpile had broken up that day. 'What?' I exclaimed. Then, after a pause for thought, I responded with some pseudo-philosophical 'what is it with groups?' type rhetoric. Apparently, there had been a 'band meeting' in the Pilot a few hours earlier. I was obviously interested to learn more. It transpired that there had recently been some kind of disagreement between Dave Edmunds and Jake Riviera over the signing of a document that gave Riviera's production company permission to deal with Columbia Records on behalf of the group.

The said legal document – 'an inducement letter' – had in fact been executed by all of the band members in October of the previous year. The signing took place at a London rehearsal studio on the eve of their UK tour to promote *Seconds Of Pleasure*. With very little understanding of the agreement, as was quite often the case in those days, the four musicians had signed and carried on carousing. Why not? The business relationship between Rockpile and Riviera, which was largely founded on trust, had served all parties very well for several years.

But Dave Edmunds wasn't happy. In the absence of a contract that might have given him a degree of comfort as Rockpile's album began to climb the US charts, he felt powerless. Discussions with Riviera soon followed, but were fruitless. Edmunds was in Eden Studios mixing the Stray Cats when he got the call telling him 'the band's over'.

The irony for Edmunds was that having delivered *Twangin . . .* – his fourth and final album for Swansong – he was now out of contract and theoretically free to make records with or for anyone, including 'Rockpile', but the band's power base – essentially Nick and Jake – had seemingly lost interest.

'I loved Rockpile, but I saw it as a stepping stone,' Nick would confess many years later. 'My heart wasn't really in it.'

A planned Scandinavian tour was quickly cancelled due to 'Nick Lowe's sickness'. Billy and Terry were suddenly out of work, although they would both resurface in fresh surroundings, such were their considerable skills. Terry went on to drum with Meat Loaf and, later, Dire Straits. Billy worked with Shakin' Stevens, and would soon add his signature guitar sound to the Pretenders' hit, 'Back On The Chain Gang'. Meanwhile, the cognoscenti would remember Rockpile as one of the world's great live bands. During their four-year lifespan, they became a crowd-pleasing opening act, and headliners often found it hard to follow their 'amphetamine-fuelled Chuck Berry music with attitude'. There was also the occasional clash of opinion between Nick and Dave.

'Edmunds suggested we should try doing "Shake And Pop" another way, and came up with "They Called It Rock" as a title. I thought that was just about the worst title for any song about anything, and he thought "Shake And Pop" was the worst. Also, I got to loathe playing rock and roll music too fast and too loud. All the swing went out of it. Although we were a force to be reckoned with on a good night, we were lazy. When we suddenly had to turn in something a bit classy, nobody was prepared to put the work in, including me. It meant we had to talk to each other and communicate, to decide what we were going to record. That's the hard part of it, really. It was great not having too much responsibility until suddenly it was: "OK boys, the contracts have all been worked out, you can now record as Rockpile! Let's go!" Then it was: "Oh, I think I liked it much better when we couldn't!"'

*

For reasons that I didn't fully comprehend, I suddenly found myself thrown into the Riviera Global maelstrom, to witness first-hand the frenetic activity of a powerhouse pop organisation that punched above its weight. It started with a phone call from Jake on 25 February 1981. Would I like to come round for dinner? I accepted, of course, and turned up proffering a rather gauche wine. 'Ah yes, I remember,' said Nick, unwrapping my chilled bottle of H. Sichel's finest Blue Nun and enthusiastically reaching for a corkscrew. After some good-humoured banter, we sat down to eat, and it was over dessert that Jake whacked me round the ears with his left-field proposal.

'How would you like to come and manage Carlene?'

His words took some time to sink in. Carlene sat opposite, possibly awaiting my response, although behind her dazzling smile I sensed some indifference. Perhaps Jake perceived that I was at a loose end; my own band, the Records, was halfway through recording what would be our third and final release for Virgin, and we were no longer touring. Or perhaps Jake needed a middleman to absolve potential conflicts of interest in what had become a complex web of management, music-publishing and record-production interdependence.

I needed time to think about it. Jake already had his work cut out looking after Elvis and Nick, and may have needed an intermediary. I sure as hell knew that 'managing Carlene' in a Riviera Global environment would involve very few creative or business decisions from me. I would probably end up driving the minibus, which of course became the case. Still, it was a great experience and I was a major fan of all things 'Riv Glob'.

Bear in mind that out of a small suite of offices in unfashionable Acton, Jake ran a number of cool enterprises. Firstly, there were the F-Beat and Demon record labels, overseen by former United Artists and Radar A&R guru Andrew Lauder. Just inside the

Horn Lane front door, passers-by could get a tantalising glimpse of a staircase lined with framed 'gold discs' – all fake, of course. Those attributed to 'sales in Australia and New Zealand' were hung upside down.

As well as the record labels, Jake had also masterminded the careers of Nick Lowe and Rockpile; Squeeze and its hit songwriting team, Difford and Tilbrook; Elvis Costello & the Attractions; Clive Langer, who would score some two-dozen hits as co-producer of Madness; Roger Béchirian, producer of the Undertones' chart smashes; and the genius-like graphic designer, Barney Bubbles. It didn't get much hotter than that in 1981. After prevaricating for a couple of weeks, I agreed to give it a go. At the time, Carlene was recording tracks at Am-Pro for her follow-up to the rocking *Musical Shapes*.

It was fun hanging out at the studio, where a copy of *Teach Yourself Rock Bass* was pinned to the wall, with a label on the cover stating: 'Studio Copy – Do Not Remove'. Bobby Irwin, Paul Carrack, Martin Belmont and James Eller pounded out Carlene's backing tracks while Nick directed proceedings from behind the mixing desk using his various 'production tools'.

'Ssshh! Here he comes now,' he would crack, as a member of the band – having just performed a tricky vocal overdub – returned to the control room to hear the playback. Everyone was sending each other up in a generally happy although not particularly 'relaxed' atmosphere; most of us were permanently over-refreshed.

Of Nick's studio style, Paul Riley – often the recording engineer on those sessions – remarks: 'The first production tool of Nick's I ever noticed is he would go to the grocers and get a jar of orange juice and go to the off licence and get a half bottle of vodka, then he would come to the studio and pour half of the orange juice down the sink and fill the jar up with the vodka, and have a packet of Senior Service or Capstan Full Strength cigarettes on the go. He would have the talkback mic on one finger and the jar in the other hand, having a really good time and projecting it upon those who were on the other side of the glass. He had a great way of vibing them all up, and I think it was mainly that device that enabled him to do a lot of editing, as it were, on the fly. Quite often a guitarist he was talking to would be sitting there thinking that this was his big moment, and Nick would say, "OK, what I want you to do in this bit is go Chong! Chong!" They thought they were going to embroider the track, but Nick just wanted a little daub.'

The general consensus among Nick's musical colleagues is that he was extremely skilled in the art of creating a good atmosphere in the studio to extract performances out of people. Some say he was at his best when he'd had a few drinks; he needed to drink 'to be Nick' and overcome any lingering introversion. After a glass or two he would 'come alive' and be hugely entertaining, with humorous expressions and a good vocabulary.

In between Carlene's sessions, Nick was laying down more material at Eden Studios for his own upcoming album. A typical session would see upwards of a dozen people in the control room in the early hours of the morning, only four of whom were actually contributing to the task in hand. Everyone else seemed to be there for the crack. In the midst of this, Nick would be glued to his producer's chair, dying for a piss, but totally engrossed in directing a guitar part and simply unable to leave the room.

The jollification continued night after night, and I don't recall anyone ever saying, 'Right, everybody out! This is work!' Recording engineer and occasional guitarist Aldo Bocca, who experienced the madness amid the music, recalls, 'It was a five-year party. Some of us stopped drinking for ten years after that.'

Looking back some three decades later, did Nick think that this was simply 'the way it was' back then, or did the partying get in the way of the music?

'I think it definitely did,' he confesses. 'It's an interesting thing to ponder. I have often thought about this. There seemed like an endless supply of material to record, even if some of it wasn't very good. "Here's an idea, let's tosh this up!" Rather than taking some care over it and rejecting the weaker stuff.'

In May 1981, Elvis Costello & the Attractions went to Nashville to make *Almost Blue*. Being a collection of country cover versions, it was a special project that called for the services of famed C&W producer, Billy Sherrill. This was therefore Costello's first album without Nick in the chair. 'With the benefit of hindsight, it would probably have been better to have done it with Nick, or Cowboy Jack Clement, somebody more down to earth than Billy Sherrill,' says Costello. 'The Nashville record was too conceptual on my part, in that I wanted to go to the heart of the beast.'

Never mind, for Nick there was just as much fun to be had elsewhere. That summer was taken up with the completion of Carlene's *Blue Nun* album and her rehearsals with the 'CC Riders' – namely Belmont, Carrack, Eller and Irwin – for some live work in the UK and Europe in the autumn. In and around this, Nick flew to Texas to produce the Fabulous Thunderbirds' album, *T-Bird Rhythm*, and continued to work on his own recordings.

On the domestic front, life at Wellesley Road was relatively swinging as Nick and Carlene celebrated their second wedding anniversary. Together, they looked like the king and queen of downtown pop. She was drop-dead-gorgeous and knew her way around a country song, while he was this slightly grizzled English singer-songwriter who could have composed for her all day and all night. For a while it appeared to be a professional, reciprocal marriage made in honky-tonk heaven, a bit like a hip Tony Hatch and Jackie Trent.

'Yes! I think we loved the idea of each other. Both Carlene and I were very keen on our own trip, and we were very aware that we made an interesting couple. But on many issues, we didn't really see eye-to-eye at all. I couldn't sit down and talk to her about the Scottish devolution debate, and I was always interested in that sort of stuff. But we were in love with the idea of each other. We thought we made a great couple. Remarkably, we didn't work together much, although we used to get the guitars out in the evening and we did write a few songs, nothing really good though. We each had a slightly different take on it, and it never seemed worth arguing about. I never understood any of her lyrics. There's a kind of lyric writing that American songwriters do, in the country area, a bit folky, the sort of thing you hear on Bob Harris's radio show . . . Americana, new country. Carlene more or less invented that, and I've heard people in Nashville say that *Musical Shapes*, the record that she did with Rockpile, was the template for what they're still doing. Gear it up from the Flying Burrito Brothers and turn up the sex.'

Carlene and Nick appeared to be on the case, but behind the public facade their music-making took second place to endless partying. In Carlene's case, she didn't seem to want success at that time in her life; true, she wrote a lot of songs, and there were standouts like 'Do It In A Heartbeat' and 'Cry', but to those around her at that time she came across as an heiress who couldn't care less.

'She wasn't hungry enough,' says Nick. 'I guess she wasted her opportunities. It's easy to see that now, but I think I knew it then as well. She did have money of her own, I don't quite know where it came from, but we never had any financial troubles. And I was earning quite a lot at that point.'

'That was an interesting thing about our life together,' says Carlene. 'I never knew how much money we had. We gave ourselves an allowance and I never questioned it. If I made money it went in our account, and if Nick made money, well, I don't know where it went [laughs]. There was one time when I was flush and he needed money to get on the road, and he did the same for me the next time. It was very much a marriage of support for each other. We were young, we had money in our pockets, and a really nice house. My first car there was that 1960s Vauxhall Wyvern. There were tons of things I would do that he didn't care to do, like drive, which is just as well because he might have killed himself back in those days.'

'I can't remember ever having a serious conversation with Carlene,' continues Nick. 'We didn't even talk about our careers, other than she would come in and say, "That motherfucker hasn't given me my cheque yet and I did that gig three months ago," stuff like that. But there were never any long dark nights of the soul. No one said, "My records aren't quite deep enough, I'm going through the motions on this one, what do you think I should do?" We never discussed that. We were too busy having fun, like two crazy kids with a dream.'

In October 1981, Nick and a large group of friends decided to go on a lads' weekend to Harlingen, Texas, to attend a convention organised by 'The Confederate Air Force'. Those in attendance included Pete Thomas, Bobby Irwin, Bill Kirchen and Andrew Lauder. For Nick, it was an opportunity to spend time with his dad under a flight path full of American military aircraft from the Second World War, all beautifully restored and maintained. Paul Tibbets, the man who dropped the bomb on Hiroshima from a B-29, sat in its cockpit and gave talks. Also, a Japanese kamikaze pilot, who had survived because his aircraft had stalled, appeared in full uniform and signed autographs. Nick lapped it up.

'Tennessee Ernie Ford was the voice of the Confederate Air Force. He used to do his commentary over the loudspeakers. You'd have a Spitfire and a Messerschmitt screaming over the heads of the crowd and old Ernie would be announcing, "And the might of Hitler's Germany was vanquished by those death-defying airmen . . ." They had a B-17, the Flying Fortress, which they would land on one wheel, and Ernie would be saying, "Here he comes now, he's coming in, I don't think he's gonna be able to do it, folks."

'We were all agog. When I think back on it, "health and safety" would never have allowed anything like that to happen here. The pilots would re-enact the Battle of Midway about thirty feet above the heads of the gawping crowd, where there were babies on shoulders. Why there hasn't been a major disaster at one of these things I do not know. But if you liked old warplanes, which a few of us did, it was really fantastic. You could get right up close to the planes and it was very, very dangerous. Those who attended automatically became a colonel, and you could buy quite an agreeable uniform to strut around in.'

As their third Christmas as a married couple approached, Nick and Carlene considered their options for seasonal festivities. While Carlene was keen to spend the holiday with her family, perhaps at Cinnamon Hill, the Cash estate in Jamaica where Johnny and June would be staying that year, Nick steadfastly refused to be anywhere other than with his parents in England. Carlene and Nick had a narrow escape; on Christmas Eve 1981, armed intruders held up Johnny Cash and his family at gunpoint in their Jamaica home. The house was ransacked and Cash was robbed of money and possessions. Fortunately, no one was badly hurt.

Nick's great-grandfather, Don Clan-Alpine Thatcher, c1890. (Courtesy of Missouri History Museum)

Nick's mother, Patricia Thatcher, in RAF uniform, c1940. (Courtesy of the Lowe family archive)

(above) Geoffrey Drain Lowe, with daughter Penny and son Nicholas, 1949. (Courtesy of the Lowe family archive)

(right) With father and mother in Amman, Jordan, 1956. (Courtesy of the Lowe family archive)

The young Nick in Cyprus, 1957.
(Courtesy of the Lowe family archive)

Nick at Woodbridge School, Suffolk, 1960. *(Courtesy of the Lowe family archive)*

Group Captain Geoffrey Drain Lowe CBE, DFC, AFC, alongside a Royal Air Force Canberra bomber, 1957.

(Courtesy of the Lowe family archive)

Sound 4+1 play Rheindahlen air base, Germany, 1964. *(l–r)* Nick, Mike Hollingsworth, Barry Landeman, Brinsley Schwarz, Phillip Hall. *(Courtesy of Barry Landeman)*

Nick with his first bass guitar, made in the school woodwork shop. *(Courtesy of the Lowe family archive)*

The Pad relax before a 'Beat Service', Cambridge, 1965. *(l–r)* Barry Landeman, Paul Woodcraft, Brinsley Schwarz, Nick, Phillip Hall. *(Courtesy of Barry Landeman)*

'Licence To Rave' – the Pad play Woodbridge School, 1965. Nick is far right with his Hofner Violin 'Beatle bass'. *(Courtesy of Barry Landeman)*

Kippington Lodge onstage, France, 1968. *(l–r)* Barry Landeman, Pete Whale, Nick, Brinsley Schwarz. *(Courtesy of Barry Landeman)*

Brinsley Schwarz, Amsterdam, 1974. *(l–r)* Brinsley Schwarz, Billy Rankin, Bob Andrews, Nick, Ian Gomm. *(© Gijsbert Hanekroot)*

Nick performs with Elvis Costello & the Attractions, Buffalo, New York, 1978. *(l–r)* a piano tuner, Steve Naïve, Nick, Pete Thomas, Bruce Thomas, Elvis Costello, Martin Belmont. *(© Chalkie Davies)*

Rockpile, 1978. *(l–r)* Dave Edmunds, Terry Williams, Nick, Billy Bremner.
(© Keith Morris Archive)

Keith Richards sits in with Rockpile at the Bottom Line, New York City, 1978.
(© Roberta Bayley)

The Riddler suit, designed and made by Tony Laumer, *The Midnight Special* TV show, Los Angeles, 1978.
(© *Michael Ochs Archives/Getty Images*)

On the US tour circuit with Rockpile, 1978.
(© *Roberta Bayley*)

With Carlene Carter, London, 1979.
(© Roberta Bayley)

With Jake Riviera and Dave Edmunds, 1980. (© Roberta Bayley)

Nick and Carlene, 'king and queen of downtown pop'. *(© Keith Morris Archive)*

The Cowboy Outfit, 1984. *(l–r)* Nick, Bobby Irwin, Paul Carrack, Martin Belmont.
(© Keith Morris Archive)

(above) With Elvis Costello, 1986.
(© Keith Morris Archive)

(right) With 'Superman's girlfriend', Margot Kidder, 1987. *(Courtesy of the Lowe family archive)*

Little Village
play Farm
Aid, Irving,
Texas, 1992.
(l–r) Nick,
Jim Keltner,
John Hiatt,
Ry Cooder.
(© Ebet Roberts)

With Tracey MacLeod, 1990.
(Courtesy of Tracey MacLeod)

With songwriting
legends, Spooner
Oldham and Dan
Penn, London,
1998. *(Courtesy of the
Lowe family archive)*

Nick 'has his ear bent' by Ian Dury, Walthamstow Stadium, 1999. *(© Andy Phillips)*

'Guitar-Bass-Drums', Great American Music Hall, San Francisco, 2008.
(© Ken Friedman)

At the concert in aid of the Richard de Lone Special Housing Project, San Francisco, 2008. *(l–r)* Jim Keltner, Richard de Lone, Nick, Ry Cooder. *(© Ken Friedman)*

With T-Bone Wolk and Daryl Hall, London, 2008. *(Courtesy of the Lowe family archive)*

With former Fabulous Thunderbirds guitar slinger, Jimmie Vaughan, 2009. *(Courtesy of the Lowe family archive)*

The band line-up for 'Costello Sings Lowe/ Nick Sings Elvis', San Francisco, 2010. *(l–r)* Bill Kirchen, Austin de Lone, Ruth Davies, Elvis Costello, Nick, Bob Andrews, Paul Revelli, Derek Huston.
(© Ken Friedman)

Bobby Irwin, Nick, Curtis Stigers, with Rat Scabies lurking, Brentford, 2008.
(Courtesy of the Lowe family archive)

Nick's musicians and co-producer aka 'The New Firm', London, 2011. *(l–r)* Geraint Watkins, Bobby Irwin, Steve Donnelly, Matt Radford, Neil Brockbank and inset, Johnny Scott.
(© Dan Burn-Forti)

(*above*) Nick, Roy and Peta, wedding day, Kew Gardens, September 2010. (*Courtesy of the Lowe family archive/Adrian Harvey*)

(*left*) With Canadian singer-songwriter, Ron Sexsmith, London, 2011. (*Courtesy of the Lowe family archive/Colleen Sexsmith*)

(*below*) 'The headmaster of British rock' plays his old school, Woodbridge, Suffolk, 2012. (© *Tim Jenkins*)

Nick performs at his sister Penny's birthday party, with Roy on drums, Oxfordshire, 2014. *(Courtesy of the Lowe family archive/Andrew Meyler)*

With Andy Fairweather-Low and Paul Carrack at a fundraiser for musician Henry McCullough, London, 2015. *(Courtesy of the Lowe family archive)*

With his 'Holiday Revue' co-performers, Los Straitjackets, New York, 2017.
(© Jim Herrington)

Nick is reunited with his 1970s band-mates, Billy Rankin and Brinsley Schwarz, at his '50 Years in Entertainment' party, London, 2018. (Courtesy of the Lowe family archive/ Bella Riza)

A family holiday, Italy, 2018.
(Courtesy of the Lowe family archive)

'Nick had never had a Christmas that was not at home, even if it was only with us,' says his sister, Penny. 'And every now and again Carlene would say, "I'd quite like to be in America this year." And Nick would say, "Well you go to America, honey, I'm going to Sarratt." He was completely selfish.'

'There was no compromise with my brother-in-law,' adds Penny's husband, John Perriss. 'When it came to something like that, it was always on his terms. Carlene probably thought Nick would have liked to be around Cash, especially as a songwriter. I thought it was all rather strange.'

Carlene became long-suffering in this respect, but she was always agreeable to visiting Nick's parents for Sunday lunch. Nick was reluctant to hang out at the Cash place, as Carlene explains: 'He was very conscious of not wanting to appear to be pushing his songs, although he would have loved to write for John [Cash]. When it came to Christmas, Nick didn't want to join the circus. But I always loved our Christmases with Nick's folks. They were so kind to me, and Pat would say, "Oh Carlene, my little petal."'

The couple's indulgencies knew no bounds during this period and out of necessity their lifestyle was simply transferred to the Hertfordshire countryside. They would usually arrive late, and Pat would observe that Carlene had caught another cold, and suggest she had a little lie down on the sofa to see if she might feel a bit better.

As John Perriss recalls, 'Nick would say, "I tell you what, babe, we'd all feel a bit better if we went out for a walk." We'd walk around the village, talking a load of old bollocks, and the further we walked the higher they got. When we got back, Pat would say, with wonderful naivety, "Carlene darling, that walk has done you the power of good, you seem so much fresher and brighter, and that cold of yours has gone." Carlene told Pat that she thought it was the country air.'

*

February 1982 saw the release of *Nick The Knife*, its sleeve bearing an illustration of Nick by the artist Ian Pollock. 'It was the result of a memorable drinking session with Nick,' says Pollock. 'I was too intoxicated to draw him, so we lounged back at his magnificent house. The result is a compilation of all of the photographs I took of him, embellished by a little lager and an enthusiastic presentation of his collection of model aeroplanes.'

Nick purchased the portrait from Pollock for £150 and hung it over his fireplace at Wellesley Road. At one of Carlene's barbecue parties, famed security man Paddy Callaghan was on the door, and enquired about the portrait's origin. When told that it was 'a work by the artist Ian Pollock', Callaghan asked, in a sinister tone, 'Does Nick want me to have a word with him?'

Nick The Knife gave an indication of the direction Rockpile's sophomore album might have taken had it ever been made. These were the songs that were on Nick's mind as his former band was going through its death throes, and at least four of them would no doubt have complemented the various rock and roll classics from Dave Edmunds's record collection.

The swampy 'Stick It Where The Sun Don't Shine' – which would become a much-loved feature of Nick's live show in the coming years – hijacks Creedence Clearwater Revival's 'Green River' riff and berates a nameless individual who loved to 'tittle-tattle'. In a promotional interview for *Nick The Knife*, he told journalist Martha Hume that he first heard the 'Stick It' phrase on US television the previous year.[17] 'It was a brand-new expression to me,' he said. Hume thought the song sounded 'as if the Everly Brothers had suddenly got mad'.

The up-tempo 'Burning' continues the lust-on-the-road report-age, while 'Couldn't Love You (Any More Than I Do)' is a powerful ballad, made delicate by Nick deploying his 'little man you've had a busy day' vocal persona. Collaborations include 'My Heart Hurts' and 'Too Many Teardrops', both co-written with Carlene, who remembers working on the latter on the night of her first date with Nick.

'One's Too Many (And A Hundred Ain't Enough)', co-written with Kim Wilson of the Fabulous Thunderbirds, takes its title from a line in the 1945 movie *The Lost Weekend*, and neatly acknowledges the level of drinking that had become the nightly norm at the turn of Nick's decade. As Elvis Costello recalls: 'One very dark night I knocked on Nick's door in Chiswick after some misadventure. I turned up for a cup of tea. It was about five in the morning and he and Kim were there writing "One's Too Many", and they were having this big debate as to whether they could have the word "beholden" in the song.'

'Let Me Kiss Ya' demonstrates the commercial potential of Nick's writing in a pop-funk era bookended by Michael Jackson's *Off The Wall* and *Thriller* albums. Although it's a hook-laden recording, reminiscent of a Jackson 5 hit, it might have benefitted from a little more vocal and production sheen. There was often a temptation to under-do the studio gloss in the name of authenticity, and gratuitous overdubbing was shunned. As one observer commented: 'Nick prefers to use some reverb and a tambourine – it's the musical equivalent of two coats of varnish and a bit of beading.'

A re-treated 'Heart', done in light reggae style with dub effects is, at its core, one of Nick's strongest songs. It occasionally features in his live set to this day, as does 'Raining Raining', a perfect pastiche of Smokey Robinson-era Tamla Motown, and sounding like a song that the Temptations had carelessly left off their *Wish It Would Rain* album.

When a US tour to support *Nick The Knife* was booked, Nick was suddenly in need of a backing group. Who better than the

CC Riders? After all, they were conveniently available, now that Carlene's *Blue Nun* album had exhausted its promotional potential. Briefly billed as 'Nick Lowe and the Chaps', but soon rebranded as 'Nick Lowe and His Noise To Go', the quintet flew to the USA to commence a coast-to-coast tour in large venues, opening for 'Shake It Up' hit-makers, the Cars.

Sharing the Noise To Go spotlight was Paul Carrack, set to become Nick's vocal foil in a role similar to Dave Edmunds's in Rockpile. Jake Riviera had been looking out for Carrack since the days of Ace, and was in negotiation on his behalf with Epic Records in the USA. When the Cars tour ended, some UK dates were played, including a well-received show at Hammersmith Palais with the Blasters in support. Plans were then made for Nick to produce Carrack's *Suburban Voodoo* album. It would contain a number of Lowe/Carrack co-writes, including 'I Need You', for which Martin Belmont also earns a writing credit. In October 1982, the song reached number 37 on the *Billboard* Hot 100, and a US tour suddenly saw the group billed as 'Paul Carrack's Noise To Go featuring Nick Lowe'.

Recorded in the closing months of 1982, and co-produced with Roger Béchirian, was Nick's next album, *The Abominable Showman*. Its sound reflected the studio wizardry of the period, and its title demonstrated a mania for punning wordplay. Working during that period in close proximity to gifted lyricists such as Elvis Costello and Chris Difford placed Nick in a competitive atmosphere in which an overworked lyric or title would some-times betray an otherwise decent song, a good example being 'Time Wounds All Heels', co-written with Simon Climie and Carlene Carter.

On the topic of 'clever-clever' lyrics, Costello recalls: 'If Difford, Lowe and I had dinner together, it was a case of who would be the first to make a play on words, and who would be the first to leave the room and write it down. The three of us, well, definitely in my case, were guilty of that, almost to a fault, and sometimes it got in the way and you learn to leave it out.'

'It's a cocaine thing as well,' says Nick. 'You think, "This is clever, sheer genius!" Sheer bollocks actually, but sometimes good. That's the awful thing about that drug, because occasionally you do bump into something worthwhile on the way out of the door. But the other day I was at my publisher's office and I saw a list of all the songs I've written. There were tons of titles, many of which I didn't recognise, with terrible punning title after terrible punning title. I didn't remember how the songs went, and there were pages and pages of them.'

The lead single on *Abominable*, released March 1983, was 'Ragin' Eyes', a jaunty, light rocker. Sadly, it is one of the few lively tracks on what is Nick's least memorable album. Listening to it some thirty years after its inception, one hears a number of frankly desperate attempts at a pop hit. The boy-band blueprint, 'Cool Reaction', written by Pete Marsh and Andy Howell of the Riviera-managed act Blanket of Secrecy, is a case of Nick compromising his work with inappropriate cover material.

'Nearly all of it in that period was rushed,' says Nick of the album's recording. 'I felt freaked out the whole time.'

There are a few notable tracks. 'Mess Around With Love' is a classic Lowe composition that dates back to the final days of Brinsley Schwarz, and its resurrection underscores the dearth of good new songs. 'Wish You Were Here', a duet with Paul Carrack, is honest-to-goodness soul music, and the ballad, 'How Do You Talk To An Angel' (which briefly featured in the *Born Fighters* documentary), anticipates the simpler, more direct songwriting that Nick would seek to perfect in the decades that followed, although its palm-court string arrangement saddles it with parody.

*

Prior to the release of *The Abominable Showman*, Nick and his band once again toured the USA, this time opening in sports arenas for Tom Petty & the Heartbreakers.

Nick's tour manager and sound engineer Brendan Walsh recalls: 'We would have all our gear in a U-Haul trailer, and after a couple of days we would have subverted the headline act's road crew. Our gear would then go on their truck and we'd get a decent sound-check. Nick and Paul and the guys were so friendly that everyone got on well. Tom Petty would appear in our dressing room looking for his crew, and gradually he started to hang out with us. Of course, there was that Brit thing, "We're not rock stars, we are chaps," and Tom would get the occasional break from being a rock star.'

Tom Petty, who became good friends with Nick and would later record a version of 'Cracking Up', was immediately recognisable in public and shunned the media spotlight. When the tour hit Boston, Massachusetts, and there was a night off between dates, Nick heard that soul star Wilson Pickett was appearing at Jonathan Swift's, a small venue close to Harvard University. He tried to persuade Petty to accompany him to the show, but the star declined, saying, 'I can't possibly go to a club, Nick, I'll be recognised and probably mobbed.' Nick suggested Petty go incognito, and eventually Petty agreed.

'I was meeting Tom in the hotel lobby. I couldn't wait to see his disguise, but when the elevator doors opened, out he stepped wearing his full regalia, including the top hat. He looked an awful lot like Tom Petty.'

Nick had spent much of the last eighteen months on tour, while Carlene had been pursuing her own career and was now promoting *C'est C Bon*, her debut album for Epic Records. The couple's schedules frequently clashed.

'We were both busy but we managed the best we could,' says Carlene. 'One of the nice things was that there was never any pressure about it. I never gave him a hard time about touring and he didn't hard-time me. If one of us was onto a song, we never gave each other any stick about it, like, "Hey, come and spend time with me." I know from my own history now that I've never found anyone else who actually really gets it the same way. They might say they do, but in the end it always comes back to, "You don't care about anything else but your music." But Nick and I juggled it fairly well.'

It seemed that one of the things holding Carlene and Nick together was the network of 'chaps and chapesses' who would turn up, often unannounced, day and night at Wellesley Road. I confess that I was an occasional visitor myself and recall spending one afternoon with Nick – he in dressing gown – watching the FA Cup Final on a small black-and-white TV in the kitchen. We drank some wine, and at half time I was sent out for reinforcements. After returning with three bottles of good French red, generously paid for by Nick, we watched the second half of the soccer match while devouring a very large piece of Stilton cheese. Carlene was upstairs snoozing.

It was clear that their marriage was under strain; neither partner had been entirely faithful, perhaps looking for love wherever he or she could find it, but certain indiscretions were uncomfortably close to home. Nick appeared to be in denial about this state of affairs and shut it out, bumbling around the house in a vodka haze, occasionally checking his 'to-do list' and sweeping the yard to get some fresh air. But some of those around him could see the picture more clearly. On the recent US tour, Noise To Go roadie Glen Churchman, a gentle giant possessed of an emotional streak who sadly died six months later, had been unable to hold it in any longer. After squaring up to a cop at LAX and having to be momentarily restrained by a phalanx of officers, he and the band boarded a jet upon which Churchman blurted out, mid-flight: 'I know what's been going on! And I don't know how you lot can just ignore it!'

Nick seemed oblivious to Churchman's outburst, but when they all returned to the UK, James Eller quietly quit the band and Nick reverted to bass for future shows. They wouldn't remain a quartet for long though; in May 1983, Nick was hired by Geffen Records to produce American singer-songwriter John Hiatt. Six tracks were required for an already half-completed album, which would be released that July as *Riding With The King*. The sessions took place at Eden Studios with Noise To Go providing the backing. The musical cohesion and camaraderie would lead to Hiatt joining the band to play a number of shows that year.

'We then had three lead singers,' says Martin Belmont. 'John Hiatt, Paul Carrack, and Nick – talk about luxury – but Nick sort of blew it. He was still getting drunk again and that put John off, so he hightailed it back to the States.'

According to Belmont, the breaking point for Hiatt occurred when the band played a European festival where Nick 'blew the gig'. Belmont says he wasn't present, having put his back out, although he could have been there; Brendan Walsh remembers a festival show at which an ailing Belmont performed 'gaffer-taped to a chair'.[18]

'John played guitar, so they could do without me,' continues Belmont. 'It worked as a four-piece, but not if one of them was incapacitated, which Nick was. That was it for John Hiatt.'

But Hiatt himself was no choirboy, and had been very much the party animal during his recent summer in London. 'John liked a drink too, but I don't think he could keep up,' says Walsh. 'We were really hard work for outsiders. You know that English–American thing, where the Americans don't really get it? You form this English mob for self-protection, and we were all extremely sarcastic, very London, and "far too pleased with ourselves", as Nick would say. John wasn't quite in there.'

John Hiatt now had his own album to promote, with shows lined up in California at which Ry Cooder would guest on guitar. He then returned to Europe and rejoined the Noise To Go. In December 1983, the band's European tour included a spot on German TV's *Rockpalast*. It was evident from Nick's appearance that he had been drinking heavily. With dark circles around his eyes, comically arched eyebrows, and his hair fashioned into the ubiquitous mid-eighties mullet, he looked, by his own admission, 'a bloated mess'. He could just about hold it together onstage and although his nimble bass playing was impressive under the circumstances, his general condition was a cause for considerable concern among his colleagues.

To paraphrase a line from 'Stick It Where The Sun Don't Shine', time was running out for Nick and his rotten racket. As Christmas approached, he was forced to confront his demons, and when he played London's Dingwalls on 23 December he had been seven days clean. His forswearing of the drink, and just about everything that went with it, had started, quite literally, with a bath after he had awoken one morning with an appalling hangover.

The family bathroom had been designed by the house's previous occupant, Sandy Sarjeant, former wife of Ian McLagan of the Faces. Carlene had loved its décor, especially the dark blue wall tiles, but as Nick turned on the bath taps he looked around the room, which he noticed was 'festooned in limescale'. What was once so exciting and luxurious was now in a state of disrepair, with fittings starting to come away from the walls. Lying in the bath, he began to think that the room had become a metaphor for his marriage. 'What am I doing here?' he asked himself.

'I got out of the bath and caught sight of myself in the long mirror. I looked like some creature I didn't recognise, really overweight, unhealthy and pink, and turning purple. I was bristly faced and jowly, with bags under my eyes and starting to go grey. I was radiating unhappiness. "An animal at bay" is the only way I can describe it. Then, almost as if an explosion had gone off, I said to myself, "This is it. Today is the day." I dried myself off, put some clothes on, and said, "It's clean-up time. Lose the booze and get yourself a new act."'

In May 1984, *Nick Lowe And His Cowboy Outfit* was released. The songs had been written and recorded in the period spanning Nick's drunkenness and sobriety. There was one moment of light relief when none other than former Shadows bassist Jet Harris – now a photographer – was hired to take some pictures of Nick in and around Chiswick. It was a truly surreal experience to be photographed, as a recording artist, by one's teen hero and early musical influence. All Nick can remember about the occasion was Jet's advocacy, as a recovering alcoholic, for Kaliber alcohol-free beer. 'We went to the pub and Jet drank several pints of it.'

Paul Riley, who worked on the early *Cowboy Outfit* sessions, recalls: 'I once refused to record Nick's vocal. I was co-producing and he was so out of it that he couldn't sing. I said, "Nick, let's not bother, you and your voice are just not here." He may not have agreed with me, but he later acknowledged that I was absolutely right.'

Also involved was Elvis Costello. 'It was the only time I produced Nick,' he says, referring to the song 'L.A.F.S.' (which stands for 'love at first sight'). 'I thought I was Willie Mitchell, the producer, with the horns, maybe even strings, but it doesn't really work. Nick doesn't sound right doing that, and I wasn't as insightful a producer of him as he was of me.'

Despite Costello's well-meaning production effort, the problem was there was simply no conviction in Nick's vocal on 'L.A.F.S.', or indeed much of *Cowboy Outfit*. It's a schizophrenic collection, with a few upbeat and optimistic sounds wrestling sluggishly with some overworked makeweights. 'The Gee And The Rick And The Three Card Trick' is a wordy piece of threesome innuendo, impossible to fathom. Singing it, Nick sounds jaded and uncommitted, as if he's simply going through the motions.

'God's Gift To Women', on the other hand, is an amusing country-style song, as is his version of the Springfields' 1961 hit, 'Breakaway', the spontaneous recording of which was pure fandom on Nick's part. Other outbreaks of sunshine include the rocking 'Maureen' and 'You'll Never Get Me Up (In One Of Those)', written by the air-travel averse Mickey Jupp.

The album's best-known song – 'Half A Boy And Half A Man' – sounded like a hit; in fact it reached number 53 on the UK singles chart. And if that sounds a little underwhelming, one only has to compare it with the lacklustre chart performance of Nick's immediately preceding 45s.

In Europe, 'Half A Boy' did even better than its UK showing, actually 'topping the charts' in the Low Countries. It cannot have hurt that Nick's records were now distributed in Europe by RCA, but, as Nick recalls, 'The week it went to number one we showed up in a grey industrial town on the Dutch border and there were, um – six people to see us! So I was starting to feel ridiculous and irrelevant.'

In August 1984, Nick and the Cowboy Outfit commenced a thirty-date US tour as the support act to Elvis Costello & the Attractions. However appreciative Nick was of the exposure, and however sympathetic the audiences, he was now imprisoned in a routine of album-tour-album, ad nauseam, and an endless string of interviews with which to contend. Tour manager Brendan Walsh recalls covering for Nick on a number of occasions: 'He had lots of phone interviews to do, mainly college radio stations, and they were often first thing in the morning. Nick would still be in bed, but I would be up and about. I'd heard him doing his interviews so many times that I had it down pat. They didn't know who they were talking to, just someone with an English accent, so I would be "Nick Lowe" for an hour.'

Nick's recording contract required him to deliver a new long-player annually, and although the cash advances came in handy, his ability or indeed desire to write commercial-sounding songs was waning. Joe McEwen, Nick's A&R manager at Columbia throughout the mid-1980s, comments, 'Although I personally loved many of Nick's songs on those albums, they didn't contain a radio-friendly track as strong as "Cruel To Be Kind". It became an issue.'

The wheels had started to come off around the time of *Nick The Knife*, and he was now feeling the first twinges of 'Come in No. 7, your time is up'. Because he'd produced a lot of records, in addition to being 'an artiste', he'd enjoyed the privilege of hanging out with record company people on the thirtieth floor – the business types in the organisation – and he knew how they viewed the talent. 'The suits' thought the artists were all morons and, in some cases, they were right, but they had very little respect for any of 'the turns', however bright. Nick admits there were occasions on which he had joined in the guffawing, and was under no illusions about his own role as an artist. He knew that the wheel was going to turn.

'I didn't have what it took to be one of those very rare people who could stay in pop decade after decade, like Sir Elton and Sir Cliff. You never actually know who buys their records, although many people do. But some of those record company executives talked about the talent in the most frightful way, even though the artists were the cash cows that were paying their wages. I overheard some awful stuff. I suppose the first time it struck me that my time was up was when I turned up somewhere, and instead of hearing, "Hey! Nick! In you come!" the guy on the door said, "Not so fast, mate, where's your pass?"

'It's very heady stuff when you are the toast of the coffee houses, but then suddenly you're not, even though you tell yourself you are. The hospitality continued for a little while, but in my heart, I knew it was all over.'

With or without the wristband, Nick still had a loyal following in the USA, with entertainment industry and media folk among their number. This would occasionally translate into a request for an advertising jingle – a Busch beer commercial comes to mind – and, occasionally, some music for the movies.

'I got asked to do stuff for films back then, most of which were turned down, but it was quite inspiring. I remember going out to Pinewood to see the directors of a movie called *Top Secret*. They told me it was "a bit surreal" – you don't know what era it is set in, but there's "a rock'n'roll guy like Elvis" as a spy. "OK – so you want something that's fairly corny, but with a little twist?" I took copious notes and wrote about three songs for them, but they all met with a resounding "nul points".'

At home, tensions between Nick and Carlene continued, exacerbated by two conflicting work schedules; Nick was touring heavily and Carlene was appearing in the musical *Pump Boys And Dinettes* at London's Piccadilly Theatre, alongside Paul Jones, Gary Holton and Kiki Dee. Occasionally they would both be home, but the mood was strained.

'I'd licked my wounds for a year and straightened myself out,'

Nick says, perhaps not appreciating the effect his heavy presence was having on those consigned to living under the same roof.

Carlene recalls him being short-tempered: 'He gave up the booze, but that's all he gave up. And he would sit at the kitchen table and play Solitaire and smoke cigarettes and listen to BBC radio, all the time. Tiffany or I would walk into the room he was in, and he would get up and move to another room. He just couldn't be with us. I think he needed his own space. The house was huge, so we could have definitely made that work, but he just wanted to be alone.'

The atmosphere at Wellesley Road was reflected perfectly in 'Indoor Fireworks', a then unreleased Elvis Costello song that Nick was soon to record. Of Nick and Carlene's domestic situation, Costello diplomatically comments: 'Nick and I certainly never talked about personal relationships and the only knowledge I have is of what was going on in my own life, but I know that in some ways the song was as true for Nick as it was for me.'

'Things work out the way they are supposed to,' reflects Carlene. 'I always have to believe that. And I think we were fuelled by a lot of intoxicating things, in every way. We just couldn't get past a certain point, and when the shit started falling apart, it really fell apart. It was both of us, it was not one or the other. I take responsibility for my part and I feel he takes responsibility for his. We tried.'

For Nick, the pain of sharing the same unloved house had become unbearable. One spring day in 1985, unable to suffer it any longer, he gave himself a good talking to. 'I'm going to put things in motion,' he told himself. 'I'm not going to do this any more. I'm going to get a divorce, I'm going to move out, and it's definitely going to happen today.'

Then he phoned his manager of ten years. 'You've got to help me get a flat,' he pleaded. 'I'm moving out.'

Jake Riviera was soon on the case; two weeks later Nick's cold war with Carlene had ended and he was now living in a Chiswick enclave known as Thames Village. It was actually less than a mile away from the house in Wellesley Road that the couple had shared for four years, but geographically 'across the motorway' and therefore symbolically distant, an elevated section of the M4 acting as his Berlin Wall.

CHAPTER 13

Superman's Girlfriend

'I love being on my own,' said Nick over a soft drink at a Chiswick pub in May 1985. 'Sunday papers strewn all over the place, kippers under the grill, and a good old black-and-white war film on TV.'

He had settled in quickly to his riverside flat and, having been sober for eighteen months, was capable of maintaining a calm domestic environment. It was, however, a lonely existence. 'I thought I'd moved into a swinging bachelor pad,' he says. 'But I was in fact living in an old folks' retirement complex. I was the youngest person there, but for a child of two.'

Following a lengthy period of abstinence, his appearance had changed dramatically and he was probably the thinnest he had been since the Fillmore trip some fifteen years earlier. During a show at Harlesden's Mean Fiddler, *Melody Maker* journalist Allan Jones, who hadn't seen Nick in a while, was genuinely concerned, leaning over and enquiring, 'Christ, is he all right? I hope he hasn't got some life-threatening disease.'

On the recording front, Nick had been working with studio engineer and co-producer Colin Fairley, who had mixed *Cowboy Outfit* the previous year.

'Nick pretty much gave me *carte blanche* on the sonic side of things,' says Fairley. 'It allowed him to concentrate on the arrangements and the actual performance of a song. When it came to mixing, he had very definite ideas on the vocal sound and level, plus the bass guitar was important. He didn't care too much for reverb.'

Nick's next album, *The Rose Of England*, released in August 1985, was an upbeat collection and a vast improvement on its immediate predecessors. Its title song, in which a mother weeps and wails for her young son who has gone off to war, unwittingly retells the experience of his great-grandmother Amelia Thatcher, and her young sons' modest roles in the American Civil War (see the Appendix). The song would later be covered by Graham Parker, as well as feted folk songstress, June Tabor. But as good as it is, 'The Rose Of England' would have been an outside bet as a 45 in a commercial marketplace that was dominated by Duran Duran.

Professionally, Nick was unhappy and getting unhappier because he felt as if he was on a treadmill, and he thought the records he was making were all 'piss poor'.

'These record labels don't really want me,' he thought, yet they were cracking the whip for more product. Then suddenly there came the word: 'Look, you're friends with Huey Lewis . . .'

Huey Lewis, then at the peak of his own recording career with his band the News, recalls: 'We were touring in Europe and I hooked up with Nick and Jake. They told me they had delivered Nick's new album, but the record company didn't hear a hit single. Would I mind producing a track? I said, "Of course, how about 'I Knew The Bride'?" Nick flew over to San Francisco, and we cut it.'

'It was a really fancy, expensive studio and Huey was in full flight. I hated having to ask him for this favour, but he did exactly what he promised he would do, which was to make a well-polished record. I also remember Jefferson Starship were recording in the studio next door. Actually, I think they come with the place. It was around the time they were doing "We Built This City On Rock And Roll". I recall Grace Slick and various other people, perfectly nice, behaving like they were from Mars. They'd come into the studio saying, "Man, we heard this rockin' sound comin' outta your room and we just had to come in, man, that's awesome, that rocks." To have these weeds come in with their ghastly pleasantries was so awful I almost threw up.'

'I Knew The Bride' was a curve ball, pitched into Nick's recording career from a highly commercial angle. He had appeased his record company paymasters by making an 'up-to-the-minute' version of what had previously been a minor hit for Dave Edmunds, and enjoyed working with his old pal Huey, but he suddenly found himself embroiled in that 'drum-machined, sharp-cornered noise' he was seeking to avoid. In the song's promotional video, he looks slimmer and healthier than of yore and the record's promotion reflected the confidence that Columbia Records still had in him.

'Bride' reached number 77 on the *Billboard* Hot 100 (and number 27 on their US Rock Chart), and stayed in the lower reaches of the hit parade for months. Not bad. 'We had Bob Clearmountain mix it,' recalls Joe McEwen. 'That was the formula back then. It got a lot of radio play and it's had an afterlife as a wedding song.'

By 1986, Nick was in musical limbo, stranded somewhere between his pop career and the artistic journey he felt compelled to take, if only he could put his hands on the roadmap. Paul Carrack had quit the band, and Bobby Irwin and his wife, Bianca, had gone to live in America.

'Columbia didn't seem to want me any more. I was on RCA for a while but I can barely remember it. It was as if I was being passed from one major label to another, tumbling down the totem pole. I was suddenly irrelevant. But the stuff I'd been replaced by was also terrible. I knew the end was coming, but when it came it was quite a shock. I'd had a pretty good crack as a producer, with a couple of hit records. I'd also had a few songs covered by other artists, and enjoyed a very good time. Perhaps I was supposed to go back to the biscuit factory, as most people do after their little go around, but I felt I hadn't actually done anything that was really good.'

During the following eighteen months, he would painfully slave over his next collection, recording and re-recording songs in what at times seemed like a futile attempt to capture the sounds he could hear in his head. He described it to others as, 'using the studio like a domestic tape recorder to purposely get a lo-fi sound'. He wanted the drums to be light, the vocal to be live, and any mistakes to be left in.

No matter how accomplished and sympathetic his musicians, the route was barbed with frustration. It would take him to Austin, Texas; Power Plant Studios, Willesden; and back to Rockfield in Wales to work with Dave Edmunds after a five-year impasse.

'I was starting to get this idea in my head that I should formulate a way of re-presenting myself. And in order for it to work I had to be forgotten. I needed to spend some time in the wilderness. I couldn't find anyone who knew what I was talking about. My long-term collaborators had either had to retire, or do something else because they were worn out with me and the way I was recording. Colin Fairley didn't understand that I didn't want that huge thumping drum sound. "Why are there all these microphones around the kit? Can't we get a sound like paper tearing?" I was trying to think up these ideas, but because I couldn't get anyone to help me with it, I was in danger of being talked out of it.

'"What? You mean you actually want to record the vocal while you play the guitar?"

'"Yes!" I wanted to go in and MAKE A RECORD, with the accidents and everything. No echo, nothing on it, ugly and hard to listen to. It wasn't like I was basking in it. I thought it was horrible as well, but there were moments. I remember cutting two tracks in Austin, "(You're My) Wildest Dream" and "I Got The Love", with Jimmie Vaughan from the Fabulous Thunderbirds on guitar. And Bobby Irwin, who was living in Texas at the time, playing a cardboard box. Then we did this weird reggae rockabilly thing with a strange groove, and the great and the good of the Austin music scene were crammed in. They thought it was mind-boggling, this sound. I was tearing my hair out. It was unconventional but it wasn't very good.'

Colin Fairley is not in complete agreement. 'I felt Nick was at his most creative on those Austin sessions,' he says. 'He is very highly regarded over there as an artist, which I noticed on a daily basis because he was recognised everywhere we went. We had a fantastic time, going to those Texan barbecues in ninety-degree heat and visiting Antone's blues bar, hanging out with Kim Wilson and Jimmie Vaughan.'

Interspersed with these sessions was another musical reunion, this time with Elvis Costello, who asked Nick to produce *Blood And Chocolate* alongside Colin Fairley. It was the first Costello album Nick had overseen since 1981's *Trust*.

'It was a "pistols at dawn" record, but only Nick could have made it,' says Costello. 'Even though he was already fed up with rock and roll, his own records didn't reflect the harshness. *Blood And Chocolate* was about six or eight years ahead of its time to some people's ears, like some sort of grunge record. Nick was really fantastic as a producer because he sensed that we could just about do two takes before we started fighting. It was like a Kinks record, we were so tense all of the time.

'I set a load of conditions. I don't know if Nick agreed with any of them, but he worked with them. One was that we didn't use headphones, just monitor speakers. The other key thing was it was a rhythm record and Nick was the fifth member of the band. He was hardly ever in the booth. He played rhythm guitar on nearly every track. He's such a good rhythm guitar player. He plays down his bass playing, which I have a whole other appreciation of, but he is the best rhythm guitar player I know. He swings, but he also has great time. And Pete Thomas didn't have great timekeeping then because he was still drinking, and Bruce Thomas was barely in the room. And I don't remember having any conversations with Steve Nieve at that time. He was pretty dark. We recorded it just before it all blew up, but Nick could catch that. It's the most unusual piece of Nick Lowe production.'

Although there was no shortage of requests for Nick's services, his career as a producer had otherwise stalled. Two years earlier he had produced 'agit-prop punk band', the Redskins ('ghastly racket'); he would go on to produce the Katydids; and in late 1985 he had worked with the Men They Couldn't Hang, a folk-meets-rock combo that had signed to Jake Riviera's Demon label and were somewhat in the style of the emerging Pogues. During these sessions the Men accompanied Nick on a recording of 'Wishing Well', which would find its way onto the Lowe album in progress.

By the autumn of 1986, he had been on the wagon for nearly three years. His self-discipline and clean living had helped to improve his look and frame of mind. He'd also taken the major step of learning to drive, passing his driving test on the second attempt at the relatively advanced age of thirty-seven. Before that, he'd had to ride his sturdy bicycle to the shops, or rely on friends and minicabs to ferry him around. He soon acquired a small car, which was convenient for nipping around town and running errands.

Having been 'off the sauce' for some time, he thought he could start behaving like a human again and have the occasional beer. While out strolling one evening, he popped into the Bell & Crown public house at Strand-on-the-Green, where curiosity got the better of him. A single pint of Fuller's ale took his head off and on the walk back home he was 'banging into everything on the towpath'. He had not intended to never drink again, but genuinely believed it was time to learn not to have two bottles of vodka at a sitting, or drink port, or the peach liqueur – 'whatever was in the cupboard'.

During this period, Nick continued to record tracks, mostly at the Power Plant with Colin Fairley engineering. Much of this material was recorded, only to be rejected, as the quest for an honest return to the music's roots continued. Nick was now taking his songs back to ground level; those that were dissected and rearranged, as he attempted to realise his vision, included 'Crying In My Sleep' and 'Love Gets Strange', the latter written by John Hiatt with whom he would soon be reunited.

In February 1987, the American band Commander Cody and His Lost Planet Airmen were in London. Nick was a close friend of Cody's former guitarist, Bill Kirchen, whose occasional group, the Moonlighters, he had produced at Am-Pro back in 1981. As the Airmen had a night off between dates, Nick invited them to dinner at a Greek restaurant near the Shepherd's Bush roundabout.

'I took a lot of people to Kleftico, including Johnny Cash and June Carter, but I don't think the proprietor really knew who they were. But anyway, I took the Airmen in there and we started getting stuck in, down in the basement. George aka Commander Cody didn't show up. I asked where he was and they said, "Don't worry, he'll join us later, he's with Margot Kidder." Margot was in town because they'd finished up post-production on the latest Superman movie and she'd been to Cody's gig at the Mean Fiddler the night before. I think she wanted the Airmen to play at the Superman wrap party and George probably said, "Well my dear, let's talk about it over dinner."

'After George and Margot had concluded their business they turned up at Kleftico, by which time the party was rocking. Margot sat next to me. I can't remember what I said to her, but I must have cracked a couple of jokes. We exchanged phone numbers and she invited me to a private party she was having at some restaurant. Then a couple of nights after that, her secretary invited me on a date on Margot's behalf. I thought it was a peculiar way of doing things, but I accepted the invitation. Of course, I was extremely pleased because I hadn't had a girlfriend or a date for ages, but I was starting to get my mojo back and I thought, "Man, this is really cool – blimmin' Superman's bird? Yes!"

'We fixed up a date and I started to think about what I was going to wear. Come the big day, I received an unexpected phone call from John Hiatt. I hadn't heard from him in ages. He had been through a hideous period, but he had survived. He said, "I'm back, and I want to make this record. I've managed to get Ry Cooder and Jim Keltner, and I've got Ocean Way Studio booked, and I want you to play bass." It was the dream call, but my immediate thought was, "I can't do that." I was getting better on the old bass, but Ry Cooder and Jim Keltner?! They were real heroes of mine, and it would have been the last straw if I'd got

237

out there and all my chops had completely gone. But my initial reaction was, "Fantastic! Now let me get my diary," which was of course totally empty. "Let me see now, when are we looking at?" thinking Hiatt would say, "In a month's time." But he said, "Well, actually there's a plane leaving in three hours."

'He explained that it had come together quickly, all on favours and hardly any money. Ry was only available for one day, and, "If he doesn't like it, he's not going to come back." I thought, "I'm not going to swim in these waters, I'm not capable of it. Plus, I've got a date tonight with Margot Kidder. And it's gonna do me a lot of good." So I said, "I'm really sorry, John, what a shame, but I'm . . ." I made some pitiful excuse, and he said, "Oh well, never mind, I'll have to get somebody else."

'About an hour later, just long enough for me to have missed this plane that Hiatt was talking about, I got a call from Jake Riviera. He was on a mobile phone in his car, which was very unusual at that time, and he'd heard that I'd turned Hiatt down. He was apoplectic with rage. He screamed, "You snivelling shit, I've had to listen to you whining about what a hard time you've had for the last three years, you fucking miserable worm, you've fucked up your career, you've fucked up your marriage . . ." He was very direct, as he was prone to be with me, and for which, I might add, I've had occasion to be grateful for. He went on, "Now you listen to me, you get your finger out of your arse, you pack a bag, there's another flight in two hours, and when you get to LA you go hire a bass and go straight to the studio and start fucking recording."

'I was really freaked out by the way Jake spoke to me. It scared the shit out of me and I knew I had to go. Well, of course I had to phone Margot. But I hadn't realised that blowing out "Lois Lane", and saying, "I'm really sorry, but I have to fly out to LA for an urgent recording session with Ry Cooder and John Hiatt," was actually rather erotic. I hadn't factored that in at all. It turned the gas up somewhat, because I think up until that point she thought I was a bit of a loser. But now she was excited. I told her, "It's only four days of recording, I'll be back in less than a week." She said, "OK. I'll still be here, I'll see you then." I thought, "Excellent!"

'So off I went to LA with my hand luggage. On arrival, I jumped into a cab and rented a bass guitar on my way to the studio. Then I sat down and we recorded "Memphis In The Meantime", which took about half an hour. And the next morning I returned to the studio and there was Ry Cooder. We did the record and it was an absolute turning point. Suddenly everything started crystallising, and I could see that these ideas I'd had . . . well, I wasn't alone, a lot of other people were in that place. I suddenly found I was having an open and easy talk with Ry, who is quite a shy man actually, which is why he has this reputation as a bit of a grump. And when I came back to London, Margot was waiting, which was very nice for a little while, but musically I felt born again. That's when I started plotting and planning.'

Constrained by time, Hiatt had needed to sing the songs live, while strumming his guitar, and simply get on with it. The 'band' – essentially drummer Jim Keltner – 'played quietly'. Nick's bass was subdued, possibly due to him treading gingerly on such hallowed ground, and the much-revered Ry Cooder (who in 2003 would be ranked eighth in *Rolling Stone*'s '100 Greatest Guitarists of All Time') had added his judicious slide guitar.

'That was the other thing,' Nick recalled. 'Keltner was so kind to me with Ry. He talked me up so that Ry didn't walk. But Ry liked my one-note-every-so-often kind of bass style that I had become rather keen on. Electric bass can rather screw up a good record if you're not careful.'

'It's my contention that rock ruined bass,' says Ry Cooder. 'But Nick was uncontaminated. That was evident from the upper left-hand corner. I checked out his right-hand technique, and it was very interesting. He wears a thumb pick, very *outré* in modern up-to-date bass players, and his right thumb makes an arc as he comes down on the string which delays the sound, just so. That's the hot tip in electric bass, the delay, and he squeezes out the note – a bit more delay right there – with the thumb pick. Now you got swing, can you dig it? He favoured an Ampeg SVT with an eighteen-inch cabinet, something I never had seen. Sounded like the Third Street Tunnel in downtown LA! Needless to say, I was gassed.'

Nick came back from California 'absolutely twanging'. The recording experience at Ocean Way had knocked him sideways and he saw that the idea he'd been carrying around in his head for a couple of years could be realised. He had also formed a bond with Ry Cooder.

'I had heard about Nick some years earlier,' says Cooder. 'How he and his band tore up a theatre in Australia, and how the manager cold-cocked the promoter and called him a kike. But that didn't worry me. When we were first introduced, on those *Bring The Family* sessions, right off I judged him to be a real straight arrow-type of cat with a good mind upstairs and plenty on the ball.'

All that remained for 1987 was to complete the album that would become *Pinker And Prouder Than Previous*, but not before undertaking a tour or two as opening act or rhythm guitarist for Elvis Costello, who appeared either solo or with his sometime band, the Confederates, which included guitarist James Burton and bass player Jerry Scheff, both of whom had been in Elvis Presley's touring band. Territories visited included the USA, Japan and Australia. Austin de Lone, who played keyboards as a Confederate, describes the experience as a 'musical wonderland with a rolling, rollicking cast and crew', and remembers Nick forgoing sushi in Japan in favour of dining on steak with James Burton.

This period also saw the birth of Nick's career as a standalone entertainer, with an acoustic guitar and a big grey quiff in its early stages of development. In San Diego, he deployed an almost Antipodean accent, telling the crowd, 'Don't worry, I'm not going folk on you. You will not be getting "Puff The Magic Dragon" or "Hang Down Your Head Tom Dooley".' He then almost apologised for the absence of backing musicians. Clearly, he had yet to perfect the type of patter that would become a hallmark of his later shows, but he nevertheless delivered cracking versions of 'From Now On', 'Heart' and 'The Rose Of England'.

That September, Dave Edmunds was hired to produce a solitary track for Nick's long-evolving new album. He and Dave had fallen out years ago but this was 'a sort of rapprochement', one of a handful that occurred in the decades following the demise of Rockpile. 'Lovers Jamboree', co-written by Nick Lowe and Paul Carrack, was the song that had been selected for this 'tentative hands across the ocean' with Edmunds. The session also brought Nick into contact with pianist and future collaborator, Geraint Watkins.

Dave Edmunds was still riding pretty high, having produced hits for the Stray Cats, the Everly Brothers and the Fabulous Thunderbirds, but Nick found him to be 'quite snooty', as if he was doing him a big favour.

'He wouldn't do anything that I suggested. He was still very good, but loud, just when I was starting to think that the loud thing was not going to get me anywhere. I was more interested in those fabulous little grooves you can get when it's quiet, which you can't get if you're just thumping away. It's tiring to listen to. "This take? Or that take? Which take? Is it the loud one, or the slightly louder one than that? Which one is it?" Frankly, I was starting to think he was a bit square. My thing is not a square thing. I don't know what it is, round maybe, but it's not a square thing.'

The new record was eventually released in February 1988, by which time Nick had vacated his Thames Village flat and moved into a small, early nineteenth-century terraced house in Brentford. With the exception of the Edmunds-produced track, *Pinker And Prouder Than Previous* broke all the rules of 1980s pop record-making. On the surface it sounded under-produced, but a great deal of work had gone into making it sound that way. Cardboard boxes for drums; Kim Wilson's distinctive blues harmonica, scratchy and asthmatic; Nick in the land of his forefathers, deep in the Cajun swamps.

'*Pinker* had its moments,' says Nick. 'A thing called "Cry It Out" . . . Jake Riviera's father had just died and he was obviously extremely upset. I'd never really seen him like that, but he really needed me in a way that he'd never done before. I was rather moved by this, the way he was so sad. He just wanted me to sit with him, while he wept. I said, "Just cry it out."'

Following their reunion, Dave Edmunds would produce Nick's next album, his first for Reprise Records, a division of Warner Brothers. A certain amount of financial investment was involved and neither Edmunds nor Reprise had any interest in making another *Pinker And Prouder*. That point had been made and sales were poor, but this didn't mean Nick was prepared to abandon his vision; he had a bunch of new songs, some of which could loosely be described as postmodern skiffle, and he was keen to get back to Ocean Way Studio in Los Angeles, if only to work again with Ry Cooder and Jim Keltner, plus guitarist Bill Kirchen.

'It was very difficult because Ry and Jim didn't dig Edmunds at all. I was rather frustrated by this because I was completely on their side. Ry is a great guy, but to use an overworked phrase, he doesn't suffer fools gladly. He always reminds me of "Mr Wilson" in *Just Dennis*, and appears to be quite grumpy. But he is a kind and lovely man, and extremely funny, and it takes a while to get to know him.'

The new album was recorded in two stages. The early sessions took place in March 1988 and yielded some strong numbers, including 'You Got The Look I Like', 'I Don't Know Why You Keep Me On' and 'What's Shakin' On The Hill'. Following a home demo session in July, Nick returned to Los Angeles to cut more tracks, such as 'Who Was That Man?'[19], 'You Stabbed Me In The Front' and the highly amusing 'All Men Are Liars', a song that name-checks the singer Rick Astley, who had a 'big fat hit that was ghastly'.

'We cut some good tracks,' concedes Nick. 'I thought "Shting-Shtang" was great – a one chord item, it's hard to do live.[20] But I was starting to get the bit between my teeth as to the way I saw it, and pennies were dropping all over the place. Dave did a pretty good job on a lot of it, although he wouldn't let me do my "Pinker And Prouder" thing. It was quite uphill because I couldn't persuade him to let me do the vocals live. Well, he'd let me do them, but he would be planning to make sure I had to re-sing them later.

'I remember Keltner saying, "Dave wants me to hit the drums so hard. He doesn't realise that I can play better and make this shit groove if I can just play at my own weight, otherwise you can get anyone to do this." Keltner got Ray Brown to play string bass on "What's Shakin' On The Hill". Ray's a very scary man. He came along and we all jumped to attention. I've still got the chart he wrote out for it, framed on my wall.'

Elvis Costello concurs on the challenge of recording in the presence of jazz giant Ray Brown: 'That was the only time I ever got completely in awe,' he says. 'Ray was the nicest man, but I was so nervous I couldn't play, I couldn't sing. Then, just as we were about to do the take, Ray says, "Nobody play any ideas." That's just like something Nick would say. Before you've thought about it, you've done it.

'When Nick was producing us once, he said to the engineer, "Turn the drums into one big maraca!" Just to hear Nick shouting, "Yesss!" in the control room will always live with me. You know what it's like in the studio, you burn out, you get headphone ears, you can't hear straight, and you get frustrated if the magic doesn't happen right away. But having Nick being the cheerleader, it doesn't matter.'

Nick is of the opinion that he 'overwrote' some of the songs on the album, which was titled *Party Of One*, and that there are too many clever phrasings, either lyrical or melodic. Today he tends to prune it down.

'I'll take words out so that it flows better and sounds like anyone could sing it. I don't think people are disappointed. I recognise where the good bits are, and I keep those in. "All Men Are Liars" was a phrase I heard on an early edition of *The Oprah Winfrey Show*. An outraged woman in the audience was shouting, "I tell you Oprah, all men are liar!" She kept repeating the phrase. "Are liar!" I knew it had to be a song. I wrote it quickly, but I rather think now that like a lot of my earlier songs there's too much lyric.'

> *All men, all men, all men are liars*
> *Their words ain't worth no more than worn-out tyres*
> *Hey girls, girls! Bring rusty pliers, to pull this tooth*
> *All men are liars, and that's the truth*

Clocking in at around three-and-a-half minutes, 'All Men Are Liars' is a bold and flagrant statement, laced with much amusing, internal rhyme, resolving with the conclusive pay-off, 'And that's the truth'. The knack of being able to write such stuff is a rare gift born out of considerable confidence, an acute sense of humour and much lateral thought. All men *are* liars; the theory may not be scientifically proven, but one suspects it is true. And packed in a three-minute song it makes for one hell of a premise. If in any doubt, just refer to one or two of Nick's nineteenth-century ancestors profiled in the Appendix.

By 1990, Nick and Carlene had been separated for five years and would soon divorce. Carlene had returned to the USA, signed with Reprise Records, and was in the process of recording *I Fell In Love*, the album that would re-launch her career as a 'New Country' star.

For Nick, the prospect of bonding with his musical in-laws was now marginal, not that the mutual respect had diminished. Johnny Cash was still proud of his stepson-in-law, whose song 'Without Love' he had recorded eleven years earlier. Furthermore, in 1982, Cash had written a lengthy letter to Nick in which he mentioned that he had been having discussions with Columbia Records about the possibility of Nick producing his next album. Although this never came to fruition, Cash was still excited at the prospect of cutting another of Nick's songs, an item which had been in endless gestation as its writer struggled to get beyond the opening verse.

Cash had always wanted Nick and Carlene to attend his shows whenever the Carter Family caravan rolled into London, and Carlene had often encouraged Nick to go along. He would occasionally get as far as the stage door, but come show time was likely to be found in a nearby pub. The prospect of getting up to join the company for a rousing 'Will The Circle Be Unbroken' was terrifying, but it did eventually happen – with Elvis Costello providing moral support – when Cash played London's Royal Albert Hall in May 1989. Nick looked rather uncomfortable onstage minus his guitar and therefore nowhere to put his hands, but later that night he went home to his Brentford lair and finalised 'The Beast In Me'.[21]

Five years later, Cash would give a television interview in which he recalled pestering Nick to finish the deeply confessional song: 'In 1979, June and I were in London staying with Nick Lowe and Carlene. Nick started the song while I was there. I said, "You should finish that, it's good" and he said, "No, it's a joke." I started this album [*American Recordings*, produced by Rick Rubin, released in April 1994] and I kept thinking he should finish the song and I should record it. So we called Nick Lowe and asked him to finish the song, and he did. He was a little shy about playing it for me. Here I am, father-in-law, and he didn't want to push songs to me. He almost refused to let me have it until we talked him into it.'

Cash had persisted for a decade or more and asked Nick every time he saw him, 'How is that song coming along?' Nick has since given a number of interviews to press and TV in which he recounts his all-night session working on 'The Beast', aided by 'at least three bottles of wine', only to wake up with a hangover and learn from Carlene that Johnny and June and their full entourage would be dropping by later that day to hear the finished song.

'They gathered round to hear me sing it. Whereas the night before I *had been* Johnny Cash, I opened my mouth and instead of [imitates Cash's deep voice] "The Beast In Me" coming out, there was this little weedy voice, "Oh the beast in me . . ." When I finished singing it, I was in bits. Then Cash said, "Sing it again!"'

*

Party Of One was released in February 1990, and is one of the few records on which Nick vocally 'testifies', sounding like a drowning man on 'You Got The Look I Like', presumably having been egged on by its producer, Dave Edmunds. Judicious use of echo on the 'you got it, you got it' hook bears his mark, as do the rockabilly work-outs, 'Refrigerator White' and 'Honeygun'. It was certainly Nick's most 'produced' album up until that point, and Warners got behind it.

In the period leading up to its release, Nick undertook a number of promotional activities. In June of the previous year he had performed for a staff gathering at the Warner Brothers headquarters in Burbank, where he introduced '(I Want To Build A) Jumbo Ark' with the comment, 'Here's something you don't see very often.' He then proceeded to accompany himself using a bass guitar, producing quite a unique, unorthodox blend. It was a trick he repeated a few months later on the MTV show *New Visions Rock*, where he also performed a rousing version of '(What's So Funny 'bout) Peace, Love And Understanding' alongside show host Nile Rodgers and his studio band (with Richard Hilton on piano and Larry Aberman on drums).

On 26 March 1990, he appeared on the BBC Two arts programme *The Late Show* performing 'What's Shakin' On The Hill', with guitarist Gary Grainger, drummer Peter Van Hooke and Paul Carrack on keyboards. It is a song that encapsulates the unexpected chill one might feel as *persona non grata* in the aftermath of a brush with success. It is the lament of the laminate-free outsider, excluded from hobnobbing with the in-crowd at a showbiz 'after party'.

> *That I someday may be joining in is just wishful thinking*
> *Cos admission's only guaranteed to favoured few*
> *There's a waiting list and plenty more*
> *In a long line leading to the door*
> *So I'll never know for sure, what's shakin' on the hill*

Though he 'longs so strong to be inside' he suspects he will 'forever be denied', but Nick's gloom wouldn't last for long; the day *The Late Show* was recorded at the BBC's Lime Grove studio, he met the programme's twenty-nine-year-old presenter, Tracey MacLeod – university-educated, erudite and with-it. It may have been Paul Carrack who persuaded Nick to speak to Tracey; perhaps Paul knew it would do Nick good. Following a drink in the green room, telephone numbers were exchanged and, within a couple of weeks, Nick and Tracey were dating.

'It got serious quite quickly,' says Tracey. 'I think that personally Nick was a bit lost. He'd had some relationships after his split with Carlene, but he was basically isolated from the world, living in Brentford and having this small group of people around him that were a mix of friends and entourage. Without getting into specifics, he seemed zombie-fied. When I started hanging out with him and we would do things together, it was like a light going on, and he gradually came alive again. He cut down on the alcohol. He had been drinking an enormous amount, partying a lot, often in the pub, and smoking forty Senior Service a day. It was pretty full-on.'

Nick confesses that he was slipping back into his old habits: 'Tracey saved my life in a way. I don't think that's overstating it. I was definitely regressing, and losing my self-worth. She put the brakes on that scene and definitely gave me back my self-respect. She grabbed hold of me and said, "Look, pal, come and have a look at this." She used to swim in a very high-class shoal of people in the arts, and introduced me to some of them. I sometimes felt out of my depth, certainly conversationally. I'm not a stupid person, but I didn't know what they were talking about most of the time. They were very witty. In my gang I'm quite witty, but with that lot I couldn't even get started.'

Nick and Tracey began to do the things that many couples

enjoy, such as visits to the theatre or dining out, and the occasional weekend away.

'We went to art galleries,' recalls Nick. 'These were places I would never go to, although I started to enjoy it. We went to France – she could speak French – but I'd never really had many holidays. I might have gone away once or twice with Jake Riviera. We would say, "I'm a bit knackered, let's go to Barbados." Jake and I would lie on the beach for ten days and come back again. But having a proper holiday, with someone you like, that was foreign to me, in more ways than one.'

'I think I introduced Nick to a different crowd of people, other than musicians,' says Tracey. 'I expanded his horizon socially, but not really culturally. He's an intelligent man and a great person to recommend a book to. I remember introducing him to the works of Patrick Hamilton, for example, who wrote *Hangover Square*. Nick would groove on it and buy the books, and read them all. I wasn't exactly *Educating Rita*, and for him to describe me as "a right brainbox", well that's just his shtick. He is always modest about his own intellectual gifts. "I'm not one for book learning," he might say. "I'm just a rock and roller, me."

'I can remember the first time we went on a weekend holiday, to a hotel in the New Forest, and I was pretty thrilled to be "going out with Nick Lowe". I knew some of his music, and all the work he'd done with Elvis Costello. I was with this person that I'd known about since I was a teenager, and really admired. There we were, in the hotel room, and he was sitting at a desk, furrowed brow, over a piece of paper, and he was writing, writing, writing, and I thought, "God, he's writing a song! Maybe he's writing a song about me!" When he went to the bathroom, I crept over to the desk and found he'd been doing the *Daily Mail* easy crossword.'

*

Nick had now turned forty and any idea of dragging out a career as 'Basher – I'm mad, me' had to be expunged. With the future uncertain, he welcomed the opportunity to become part of a new band that would epitomise mature roots rock, and a high level of musical credibility.

Just two years earlier, an album by the Traveling Wilburys had been one of the most successful in the history of Warner Brothers Records. The Wilburys were a super-group comprising George Harrison, Bob Dylan, Roy Orbison, Jeff Lynne and Tom Petty. In the void between the release of their triple-platinum *Traveling Wilburys Vol. 1* and its 1993 follow-up, Warners looked to its artist roster to examine whether another combination of elite musicians might emulate their success.

Cult hero Ry Cooder, a long-standing Warners act, was hardly a household name but his drummer of choice, Jim Keltner, *had* played on the Wilburys' debut. Cooder and Keltner occasionally toured and had at various times included in their line-up singer and songwriter, John Hiatt.

A picture was forming in the mind of Warner Brothers A&R executive, Lenny Waronker, 'the last of the great record men'. Cooder and Keltner had both played on Hiatt's *Bring The Family*, as had English bassist and Warners recording artist, Nick Lowe. Thus, the birth of 'Little Village' – named after an obscure Sonny Boy Williamson II recording – was more or less pre-destined.

The crack quartet agreed to give it a go, and much of 1991 was taken up with preparation for the recording of their debut album. For Nick, who was geographically remote from his new band-mates, this involved a 'Fedex and fax' pre-production process. Demo tapes and lyrics pinged back and forth across the Atlantic and recording sessions were punctuated by several flights to and from LA.

'I kept on coming and going until they started telling me I was playing great. Sometimes I would just stop playing. They liked that. When I didn't do anything at all.

'There was quite a bit of post-*Bring The Family* optimism when we started Little Village. We got together and rehearsed in the shed at the bottom of Ry's garden and became very excited by the tapes we made in there. Those tapes are really how it should have been, with Keltner's drum-machine stuff that was really wild and unlike anyone else's drum-machine stuff. We would finish recording early evening and I'd go back into town. I was staying at the Hollywood Roosevelt. They had this bar called the Hollywood Grill where they turned the room into a venue for higher-end acts, like Jimmy McGriff, Mose Allison or Kinky Friedman, who would play a cabaret-style residency for a week. I got very much into the routine and used to love going to the bar in the foyer and simply watching people. A kind of "Algonquin Round Table of LA" used to turn up, including Van Dyke Parks, Harry Dean Stanton, and Danny Hutton from Three Dog Night. They saw me there and they started to include me in their little salon. They were living it large and would all be smoking cigars – no one told them not to – but there was a new puritanism bedevilling showbiz in LA at that time and some of them were supposed to be on the wagon. One or two of these guys had organised this little routine with the waitress, who understood their code language. If they said, "A large 7 Up, if you please," it got them a vodka and tonic, and "I'll try a Coke," probably meant a brandy.

'Jimmy Webb was making a comeback, and when he did his residency at the Grill, the Wrecking Crew[22] members would all show up. I was in heaven, and I suppose because I was doing this thing with Ry, it had a certain cachet. I started to get quite friendly with Jimmy Webb and I would see him quite a lot when it was just the two of us. One night he told me he had this record coming out for which his record company was throwing a launch party. He invited me along, so we got a cab and turned up at this little joint. It was completely packed. I battled my way to the bar to get the drinks – "7 Up please" – and I looked over my shoulder and there, sitting all on his own, slumped at a little table, was Harry Nilsson. I hadn't seen him since that night in Mayfair. I thought now was the time to go and shake his hand and ask if I could buy him a drink and say, "You won't remember this, but I was a real asshole round at your flat one night." He was on his own so I thought it might be all right. The time had come. But when I turned around, Harry was gone.'

When the Little Village record was finished, the media was duly alerted and the band was launched. Journalist Chris Heim, writing in the *Chicago Tribune*, noted: 'Bassist, producer and songwriter Nick "Pure Pop For Now People" Lowe probably comes the closest to being a recognised name.' Although Nick probably never saw the clipping, he would have found it flattering, but embarrassing, to be viewed as having a higher profile than Ry Cooder, or indeed John Hiatt. Maybe this thing would have legs.

Promoting their 1992 album *Little Village*, they set out on a world tour. From seat D7 at London's Hammersmith Odeon on 26 February, Nick looked haunted and, frankly, terrified. He was playing just a mile or two from his own front door, and as many performers including rock veteran Keith Richards will attest, playing major cities other than one's own is child's play compared with working on home turf.

'Yes, I was nervous at Hammersmith. All my old mates were there. I've got some bootlegs from the tour and they are way better than the album, which cost Warners hundreds of thousands of dollars. I never play that Little Village record, but I have a great affection for those guys.'

The London shows were proficient but guarded and, like the *Little Village* album, oddly cold. Elvis Costello remembers the show he saw at Hammersmith as, 'twenty minutes of the best music I think I've ever heard, supernatural, as good as Little Feat in 1973. Then it all fell to pieces. But it was great to see Nick playing bass with those people, keeping company with musicians who can play at a higher level.'

The international tour schedule that followed provided Nick with an opportunity to meet, for the first time, his uncle Leslie. During the Second World War, Leslie Thatcher had followed in his father Louis's footsteps and gone into the theatre, using the stage name 'Dennis Thatcher'. He became a singer and as 'Peter Howard' crooned with the popular orchestras of Stanley Black and Jack Payne. In 1953, after several years living near London's Swiss Cottage, Leslie and his family emigrated to Canada, where he became a successful stage actor, as did his daughter, Nick's cousin, Wendy Thatcher.

'The old boy showed up when we played Toronto's Massey Hall that April. He was the black sheep of the family. He'd run away to Canada and become quite successful, and was many times married with children of a wide age range spread about all over the place. He looked a bit like me, with a beard, but several stone heavier. He died shortly after.'

Little Village played various European festivals in the summer of 1992, but these shows were to be their last, and there was no follow-up album. Nick is of the opinion that Warners were rather too generous in financing unlimited studio time, and because it was a democratic set-up, no one wanted to step forward into the spotlight.

'Hiatt did actually, but the poor chap got a lot of flak for it. Everyone said, "That John Hiatt, why doesn't he shut up?" But in actual fact, if he hadn't have spoken up, nothing would have got done. The record was really not very good, but the touring experience was great. I do remember a couple of the band members didn't like to be around smokers. Ry tried to stop the French from smoking. I said, "You're wasting your time, pal."'

Cigarettes aside, Ry Cooder has fond memories of working with Nick. He says, 'I so enjoyed his company "on the road", and that's a high compliment, since the road can scare you to death if you're in the wrong company. We'd get to the airport at the start of another impossible day, and Nick would curl up with his crossword puzzle book, end discussion, no crazy drama, no demands – no "Where's the broads? Where's the cash?" and that. What more can I say? He's a kind man, that's the top as far as I'm concerned. I'm happy to call him a good friend.'

Who knows what Little Village might have achieved given the space and time to develop, but as the operation came to its premature end, an exciting piece of news was about to make Nick's phone line rattle.

PART FOUR

The Second Coming

CHAPTER 14

Payday

Throughout Nick's early touring days, especially during the time that he was a successful record producer, aspiring musicians would frequently hand him their demo tapes, hoping to 'catch the selector's eye'. Often this would occur in a hotel lobby, as he was about to board the tour bus, or at a stage door, frazzled, having just played a loud and sweaty show.

At his most cruel, when asked by a young hopeful, 'Could you please listen to my tape?' he might put the cassette to his ear, rattle it a bit and throw it over his shoulder. But one day, a demo arrived that did pique his interest. The name on the box read 'Blair Forward' and it had been sent to him by the movie actor, Kevin Costner.

In the accompanying letter, Costner wrote: 'You are a fantastic producer and I'm writing on behalf of my friend Blair Forward who has done this demo. Maybe you could listen to it and produce him.'

Nick got the impression that he wasn't the only person on Costner's mailing list, but found Blair's music 'very eighties', with a brittle drum sound and a penchant for the Police.

Nick wrote a frank reply to Kevin Costner saying he didn't think the tape was very good, complete with a little critique of each track. He put it in an envelope and set it to one side with a view to having another look at it later, because he wanted his thoughts to come across in the right way. Then he promptly forgot all about it, until a couple of weeks later when he was sitting around with his mates and the Oscar awards ceremony came on television. Costner had won Best Director for *Dances With Wolves*, and Nick suddenly remembered the letter he had composed.

'I decided I wanted to post it, but I couldn't find it anywhere. I looked high and low. I asked everyone, including a couple of eccentric old ladies who used to do my garden. They might have posted it, they really might have – I read that P. G. Wodehouse used to throw his letters out the window and into the street, knowing that honest members of the public would pick them up and post them for him – but I don't know whether or not Kevin ever received my letter. Had he have done, I imagine him saying, "Man, that Nick Lowe is the only guy who has taken the trouble to write a little critique – haven't we got his tune on standby? Go on, get it in the film, he's a really good guy!" Or, "What is he on about? Take his song off the film!" Or, more than likely, he didn't get the letter.

'The little epilogue is that a few years later I was hired to play bass on half of Elvis Costello's *Brutal Youth* album – just the easy songs, mind you: Bruce Thomas played on the difficult ones. Elvis's producer, Mitchell Froom, was staying in a rented house in Kew, and we were rehearsing in Putney, so I used to pick Mitchell up every morning and the two of us would drive to the studio. One morning, I started telling Mitchell the story. "They all wanna be pop stars, these movie actors," he said. He then suggested that "Blair Forward" might be Kevin Costner's alter ego.'

*

The arrival of the Blair Forward tape coincided with the making of a Hollywood movie in which Costner would co-star with soul diva, Whitney Houston. Opening in US picture houses in November 1992, *The Bodyguard* became that year's second-highest-grossing blockbuster. Although barely audible during the film itself, Nick's 1974 song '(What's So Funny 'bout) Peace, Love And Understanding' – as performed by Curtis Stigers – was included on the astronomically successful souvenir album that went on to become the biggest-selling movie soundtrack of all time. Worldwide sales of around 45 million units have been reported.

There are a number of theories as to how Nick's relatively obscure song found its way onto this decidedly mainstream product. It falls to musician Curtis Stigers to tell the true story:

'I was the drummer in a high school band in Idaho in the early eighties,' recalls Stigers. 'Kids I hung out with turned me on to the music that had been coming out of the UK. Elvis Costello, Graham Parker, Squeeze and Nick Lowe, who I noticed had produced some of my favourite records. Years later, when I signed with Arista, my first album contained some hits, but there wasn't a lot of tempo. My souled-up, Sam and Dave-inspired version of "Peace, Love And Understanding" made for a great show-closer.

'In 1992, I was asked by Arista president Clive Davis to provide an up-tempo track for the soundtrack to a movie starring Kevin Costner and Whitney Houston. I submitted several songs that Clive rejected, the bastard! At the time, I was opening for Elton John and Eric Clapton in big venues. At Shea Stadium, Clive came backstage after my set and said, "What was that last song you played? That's the song! It's perfect for the movie."

'It was a gift to have the chance to record one of my favourites, a song associated with my hero Elvis Costello, and written by the mighty Nick Lowe. I had no idea it would go multi-platinum! Nick made a lot of money from it, and that makes me very, very happy. He called me after the cheques came rolling in and he told me I'd never have to pay for another meal in London. We've become friends, and that's beyond cool.'

For Nick, the *Bodyguard* moment was a timely reward after his quarter-century slog as one of music's best, yet largely unrecognised songwriters. 'I received a very big royalty cheque,' he told a number of interviewers, his glee just about concealed by his natural modesty. The number bandied about was 'one million dollars' and that turned out to be just the appetiser; broadcasting and residual royalties would provide a steady income stream for years to come.

Nick's piece of good fortune could not have arrived at a better time. With his major label pop career and Little Village behind him, and an aversion at that time to record producing and touring, he was in danger of giving up on trying to capture that elusive sound that was bouncing around in his head. Like so many musicians he could have easily faded into obscurity, doomed to work the small club circuit ad infinitum. Now, however, he was in a position to finance his own recordings and, more importantly, work at a dignified pace.

He needed a collaborator and one turned up in the now-enlarged shape of Bobby Irwin, who had been living in San Antonio for the previous seven years and playing drums in country bands. Nick and Bobby had stayed in touch and had shared many long-distance telephone conversations about music. When Bobby arrived back in the UK, it was observed he had 'gone native', and was speaking in a strange Spanish patois 'with a bit of West Indian thrown in'.

'When he first left England he was more of a soul guy and I was the country chap who had indoctrinated him into C&W.

Of course, in Texas he got way into it and learnt a lot, playing with some serious people, like George Strait and Ray Price. He had clearly overtaken me in the country-and-western stakes, the knowledge.

'When he returned to this country, he was what I'd been waiting for, and he knew exactly what I was talking about. He came to stay at my place and things started to get into gear. We spent a number of afternoons in the pub talking about what we were going to do. He would have bags of shopping – frozen food was defrosting and puddles of iced water were forming on the floor, and that's when he said, "I know the bloke we need to help us do this, it's Neil Brockbank."'

Nick related the above to me in May 2015, just a few days after Bobby Irwin had died. He started crying at the memory of Bobby's invaluable contribution to his musical rebirth, at a time when he was looking for a simpler, less contrived way of conveying his emotions in song and was done with 'stunt rhyming'.

Nick had also started to think seriously about becoming a solo performer. He constructed a set that would lend itself to that format and his musical confidence returned. Although he and Carlene were long separated, he stayed in touch with her family, mainly through his stepdaughter Tiffany, who would stay at the house and occasionally bring her grandmother, June Carter, to visit. Tiffany adored Nick, and he was proud of the fact she had chosen to stay with him and attend school in London. But Nick wasn't really equipped to be a parent at that point and found it difficult to cope with an independently minded teenager who was then hanging out with a wayward crowd.

Also, Nick's romantic relationship with Tracey MacLeod was coming to an end. 'I was madly in love with him,' says Tracey. 'And I was absolutely devastated when we broke up, but without getting into too personal a territory, I don't think it would have been possible for us to move on, to get married and have a family and those sorts of thing. It's what we wanted to do, but some part of me knew that I probably couldn't do it with him. As far as he had come, and his development into becoming a fully functioning human being and a member of the world, he was still very much in his own place. It was very difficult to make the break, but I knew I had to do it, so I was the one to finish it and he was very upset, and so was I.'

Tracey has many memories; during their time together she had witnessed Nick's songwriting methods first-hand and accepts that their social and domestic plans would have to be rearranged 'if the man came a-knocking', that is, if Nick had suddenly received divine inspiration.

'I'd arrive from work, having driven from the BBC arts department, where it was a high-intensity work environment, and occasionally when I got to Nick's he would have been writing and he was drunk. He would be jolly and amorous, and wanting to play me his new song. I thought, "Ooh gawd, I hoped we were going to have a nice evening," but it would be an evening about him, if he had really got into writing.'

Tracey would get to hear Nick's new song a few days later, and particularly remembers hearing 'Shelley My Love' for the first time.

'He had used my name, rather than "Shelley", which was lovely. But "Tracey" is not the most musical, or the most sing-able name, so he changed it to "Shelley", which is slightly less ludicrous-sounding. The writing went with the drinking, definitely. He would play the song again and again and again, probably with a few bottles of wine. By the time he played it to me, it was finished and he could play it brilliantly. It wasn't like you were getting the first crude version. He would know how he was going to sing it and perform it, and he would carry on until all the little tricks, or ticks, would be in place. When he first played me "Soulful Wind", and was doing that thing up and down the guitar frets, I remember thinking, "That's a bit fancy." And when he finished the song I thought, "Wow, that's fantastic."'

In January 1993, Nick commenced recording tracks for the album that would become *The Impossible Bird*. It was a fifteen-month process at a variety of unusual locations close to his Brentford home. Sessions started in the function room of the Turk's Head, a pub in Twickenham. He had previously hired the place to rehearse his new songs alone, remembering John Hiatt's comment that he never got anywhere until he started renting somewhere to work, a place in Nashville with a piano and an amp, and a few guitars.

Hiatt told Nick, 'If I hadn't written a couple of songs by the end of the day I'd feel bad.' But it took Nick a few months to write one two-minute song, never mind two-a-day. Some days he didn't feel like loading his gear into the car and driving to the Turk's Head, but he would still go there on the grounds of discipline. When he plugged his guitar into his tiny amplifier and sang, he found the room's acoustics extremely agreeable.

'You didn't need a PA system, you could sing out into the room, and in that little instant where the sound would come back to you, it was really inspiring. I'd written the songs at home, but when I sang them in this hall, it was almost like I was recording them. The kitchen staff thought I was a bit mad, singing on my own, and I felt embarrassed to start with, because they would stand and watch me on their cigarette breaks. "Who's this loser who rents this place to come and sing his own songs? He obviously can't get anyone to come and see him." I started going off the process when the pub changed hands and they would come in and start waxing the floor.'

Among the songs that Nick worked up at the Turk's Head was 'Where's My Everything?' Tracey MacLeod recalls its genesis: 'Weirdly, it actually came out of a little in-joke that we used to have. He'd be all grumpy, and go, "Where's MY cup of tea? Where's MY newspaper? Where's my this? Where's my that?" One time he couldn't think what he wanted, and he went, "Where's my . . . EVERYTHING?!" A light came on and he wrote this rather sad, heartbroken song about not having everything, but it came out of what was actually a lovely, harmonious time.'

'I think "12-Step Program" might have been Tracey's idea,' says Nick, referring to another new song, its full title appended with the bracketed 'To Quit You Babe'. 'I remember Tracey asking, "What about this 12-Step Program they're all going on about?" I feigned indifference, then I ran home and wrote it. But I had my heart broken, and suddenly in the midst of my abject misery came this flowering of some proper, soulful songs.

'I was in love with Tracey MacLeod. I'm much thicker than her, but we were totally devoted to one another, and we still are, in a way. She made me godfather to her first son. She was fantastic, she came along around the time I was in danger of going down the plughole again, and she really grabbed me and got me good. I adore her for her attention to detail. It was a dodgy time but she kept me focused. I've got a lot to be grateful to her for.

'The break-up was really, really awful, but I found that this fantastic, clear view came to me. I thought, "Man, I can write some seriously soulful stuff here." That's what I need. I didn't want to sing songs about being on the road again, or "here I am in a bar". I wanted to sing some grown-up shit, about being extremely pissed off, because I am. And I needed to put this across and really tell a story like a proper geezer, like all the people I admire. There was no point in just sitting around listening to my record collection. "You are going through this now, pal, where is your contribution?" Suddenly I thought, "I can do this."

'And Bob was back here, egging me on, and he also brought some people to the party – Neil Brockbank, who had worked with the producer Stewart Levine, and musician Geraint Watkins, who I didn't know very well. I always mistook Geraint's shyness and Welsh reserve for being rather snooty – but we were all in the same boat, looking for an opportunity to do something. But also, we didn't just want to do country and western, we liked pop as well. We wanted a very broad church and to use everything we've got. We were out of sync with the times, but very sure that together we could do something that would make a mark.'

For Neil Brockbank, meeting Nick and overseeing the recording process was a refreshing change following the style of production work he had been involved in during the previous decade. Digital trickery, and spending hours if not days analysing the kick-drum sound as part of a massive noise upon which the vocal would sit, was about to be replaced by putting the vocal performance centre stage with a view to capturing a live recording in which the musicians would fall in behind the singer, 'top down'. This was a total inversion of method, and relied on Nick knowing his own songs inside out.

'When it comes to the recording he's so ready,' says Brockbank. 'He's got the song under his fingers in every possible way and he can sing it in any tempo, so rehearsing his vocal at the Turk's Head, not even at home, was just brilliant, because it meant that there wasn't a note or a word that he hadn't already thought about twenty thousand times.'

'Neil joined us initially as a recording engineer, a co-producer really,' says Nick. 'He became totally part of it. It took us a while to get the little firm in place and we had a few people who fell by the wayside. We would take two steps forward and one step back, in an effort to try and thrill ourselves. Every so often we would record something and we couldn't believe we'd done it. It was so cool. And we'd listen back to it endlessly, and be so pleased. A good example would be "Trail Of Tears" [the Roger Cook song], and some of the very slow stuff we did, like "Drive-Thru Man", "Withered On The Vine" and "Lover Don't Go". It was so thrilling to play so slowly and keep a groove going.'

'Trail Of Tears' and 'Lover Don't Go' were the first two songs cut at the Turk's Head. Other nearby venues used for 'location recordings' were the Bonaparte Rooms, also in Twickenham, and the Old Cinema, just a few steps from Nick's front door. All of these buildings possessed the acoustic properties that were ideally suited to recording vocal performances.

'It was like recording inside a huge, old Martin guitar,' says Bill Kirchen, who had joined the team, from Texas, to add his electric guitar skills to the proceedings. 'Making that record made me realise what a really thoughtful pop theoretician Nick is. I asked him to send me the demos so I could work up some snazzy guitar parts, but he declined, saying. "If I do that, you'll make a meal of it," an expression I'd not heard before, but I got it.'

Whereas Neil Brockbank had previously seen Nick Lowe as a great songwriter and bass player, he now realised that he had also become 'a world class vocalist' and studio brain. Brockbank now sat alongside Nick, Bob and Geraint, all of whom would communicate in coded terms and adopt certain rules when it came to recording.

'"No Saturday afternoon guitar licks" became one of our red lines,' says Brockbank. 'No guitar *stuff*, no keyboard *stuff*, you know, that stuff musicians do because they learnt it in the guitar shop on a Saturday afternoon. Nick would use this word, "nonspecific", which I found really helpful. He wanted everything to be nonspecific, meaning you couldn't really nail it, but we all began to learn what he meant.'

Nick recalls feeling separated from himself during the sessions, because he and his colleagues would talk about 'Nick Lowe, the singer' in the third person.

'We used to talk about "the bloke". And when we were discussing a certain recording we might say, "You know that bit when he says . . . that middle bit, he should sound like . . ." as if we were talking about somebody else. And there was something rather crusade-y about it. We felt like we were on a mission and we were a rather fantastic secret society, all onto something. It was terrific fun and when it was happening it was like walking on air.'

Nick was still signed to Warners, but halfway through the recording sessions the label released him from his contract. Jake Riviera's Demon Records was conveniently still in business and picked up the record for release in the UK, but this left a void in America. Help was just around the corner.

On 12 June 1994, Elvis Costello & the Attractions played an outdoor show at Great Woods, Massachusetts. Nick had flown over from the UK 'to hang out' and, while relaxing backstage, was approached by Jake Guralnick, son of the eminent music biographer Peter Guralnick.

Jake Guralnick had previously written to Nick, care of Demon Records, enclosing a cassette of a new album by Sleepy LaBeef, knowing that Nick was a fan of the veteran rockabilly star. Jake and Peter Guralnick had co-produced the record and Jake was keen to get a quote for the sleeve from Nick. Some three months later, he was astounded to receive a five-page handwritten reply, asking detailed questions about the LaBeef album. The record had by now been released, although Guralnick remembers Nick's quote: 'Sleepy speaks, liars tremble.'

'It was the greatest day of my life thus far,' recalls Jake Guralnick. 'To receive a handwritten letter from my idol, Nick Lowe, telling me I had produced a fantastic record. I went up to Nick at the Elvis show and introduced myself as the guy who had written to him about Sleepy. He went crazy and started talking my ear off about the record. Then this guy walks over and he's the local rep for Warner Brothers. He says to Nick, "I'm really sorry we dropped you, I really liked the last record."'

Jake Guralnick's ears pricked up. He was then in the employ of Rounder Records, specialists in American roots music. He went to work the next day and informed his colleague, Glenn Dicker, that he had bumped into Nick Lowe.

'I said to Glenn, "I guess Nick got dropped by Warners." Our then business partner Chris Cote said, "Man, we gotta get that record." We had this little label, Upstart, distributed by Rounder, and we'd put out just one record at that point, but we had no money.'

Guralnick wrote to Jake Riviera at Demon with some background information on himself, Rounder Records and Upstart. He soon received a call from Nick's former A&R person at Columbia, Gregg Geller, followed by a copy of Nick's new record.

'It was a Friday and I listened to it all weekend,' continues Guralnick. 'I thought it would be like *Party Of One*, along those lines, but it was a totally new thing. Incredible. Jake Riviera had also been talking to other indie labels such as Hightone, but he told us he and Nick thought we seemed much cooler. We were young guys, about twenty-five. Jake called me and asked us to make an offer. He wasn't concerned with an advance, he just wanted the highest royalty rate we could afford, and he needed Rounder to guarantee the royalties if our offshoot label went out of business. We jacked up the royalty rate and made the offer. Our margin ended up being so small we went out of business. Our biggest record didn't make us any money!'

The Impossible Bird was released in November 1994, trailered by the single, 'True Love Travels On A Gravel Road', a cover of a song which Nick has since described as the perfect example of 'R&B meets country music'. Written by Dallas Frazier and A. L. Owens, it was previously recorded by Percy Sledge and Elvis Presley.

It was evident to Nick's long-standing fans that his reinvention was almost complete. As writer Paul Gorman succinctly puts it, 'He deliberately set about dismantling his reputation as the perma-grinning jack-of-all-trades.'[23]

The design concept for the album's artwork (of which there were at least two iterations) is credited to Valerie Boyd, who had been Nick's girlfriend in the mid-1970s and was now back on the scene and working as a photo researcher for the *Daily Telegraph*.

The very sound of Nick's new music would become the hallmark of his recordings over the next twenty-five years, or 'Act Two' as it would come to be known. The material on *The Impossible Bird* was so strong that it resulted in no less than three of its songs being covered by world-famous artists: Rod Stewart ('Shelley My Love'), Johnny Cash ('The Beast In Me'), and Diana Ross ('I Live On A Battlefield'). Nick had co-written 'Battlefield' with Paul Carrack back in 1989 for Carrack's *Groove Approved* album. The melody has a distinct Motown flavour, which might account for its appeal to Ms Ross, combined of course with Carrack's soulful vocal on what might be considered 'the demo'.

'I think a good song will be found,' reflected a hopeful Nick. 'What I do now is make my records sound as good as I can get them, but they're really glorified demos for my songs, that are recorded in such a way that people might say, "That's a good song but I can do it much better than that guy." Hopefully they'll cut my tunes, but I don't crave celebrity any more.'

This prompts the question: Are Nick's records simply vehicles for his songs, rather than artefacts designed to promote his career as a recording artist?

'What I hope is that both will happen. I hope people like my records because I do take a lot of trouble to make them sound like I've taken no trouble at all. I love performing, but the cliché is you don't get paid for going onstage, you get paid for the other twenty-two-and-a-half hours of the day when you've got to hold yourself together, travel to some town that you don't ever want to go to, stay in some crappy hotel, eat awful food, and be cold and lonely. Also, you can't just run to the bar like you could when you were younger and stay sloshed until show time – you've got to keep yourself together because the show is the high point of the day instead of the irritating interruption that it once was for me.'

In November 1994, with the help of the *Bodyguard* money, Nick went on the road with 'the Impossible Birds', comprising Bobby Irwin, Geraint Watkins, Paul Riley and Bill Kirchen. The tour commenced in Japan, playing five cities in late November, and reached London's Shepherd's Bush Empire on 10 December. It was a packed house and the local crowd got a taste of the way Nick's music was evolving, as would US and European audiences in the months to come.

It had recently been announced in the UK trade publication *Music Week* that Elvis Costello had split with his manager and business partner, Jake Riviera. The two men collectively stated: 'After 17 mighty, furious years we have decided to end our working relationship. We remain good pals and do not invite and will not welcome further questions on this matter.'

Nick was now Riviera's sole management client but in February 1995, when the Impossible Birds took their show to the

USA during what marked the twentieth anniversary of Nick's involvement with Jake, there was an unexpected deterioration in their business relationship.

It was the last thing Nick needed, now that his musical aspirations were finally being realised, but when he and the Impossible Birds played the House of Blues in New Orleans, Jake 'had the cob on'. It had been a good show in front of a reasonable crowd, and various people came backstage to pay their respects, including Graham Parker, Bob Andrews, several fans seeking autographs, and members of the support band.

'Jake began ranting. He started with, "That was a bit of a disappointment." I could see he was holding himself back. I replied, "Not now, Jake," and that was it. He went for me in a big way, and this was virtually in public. I told him I didn't want to hear it right now and to get the hell out. He replied, "I'm going, and that's the last you'll see of me."

'Jake had made a real statement, and when we got back to the hotel, he had checked out. And my feeling was that he wouldn't be coming back. I was quite relieved because I realised I was at a crossroads, and while we're at it [booking agent] Marsha Vlasic should go as well because she didn't get what I was on about either, still trying to get me on more rock-tastic shows and to play stadiums, and that was not what I wanted to do. I thought I would get a new agent, but I didn't know where to turn for help.

'After about three weeks had elapsed, Jake got in touch. He said he thought we should get together and discuss it, and he talked me round. In retrospect, I think we should have left it there. He used to have a go at me all the time; in fact in a way I needed it, but it wasn't very pleasant. He often had a point, but to have him come into the dressing room and start throwing his weight around, that had to stop. I don't think Jake ever got it, by which I mean the second half of my career.'

During this period Nick was hired to produce two tracks by country stars, the Mavericks – 'Blue Moon', for the soundtrack of the Tom Hanks movie *Apollo 13*, and 'True Love Ways', for a Buddy Holly tribute disc. Recording took place on 24 March 1995 at Nashville's famous RCA Studio B, birthplace of memorable hits from the Everly Brothers and Roy Orbison.

'We were all huge Nick Lowe fans,' says Mavericks' keyboard player, Jerry Dale McFadden. 'The idea of working with him was a dream come true. We often cut everything live and that was how Nick wanted to work. We had just one day to record, and we met up the evening before, for dinner. Nick was full of great stories. The next day [Mavericks singer] Raúl Malo couldn't be at the studio until the afternoon, so after we got the sound balance Nick suggested we put down "True Love Ways" and he would do the guide vocal. We started the song and I think we all had chills while recording, mainly because we were all hearing Nick's beautiful take on the Buddy Holly song in our headphones. Later Raúl came in and put his Malo magic on it, but I would still like to hear that rare version with Nick singing. Wow! We got to record a song with Nick Lowe.'

While in Nashville working on the Mavericks tracks, Nick met photographer Jim Herrington who was to become a long-term friend. As a late 1970s teenager, living in Charlotte, North Carolina, Herrington would hang out at his local record store where he heard the hot new music coming out of England.

'I was turned on to Elvis Costello, Dave Edmunds, and of course Nick Lowe,' recalls Herrington. 'Some years later, my first big photography job was Tom Petty. Tom took me into the fold for a couple of years when he was recording in LA. Tom and maybe Mike Campbell were going to pop next door to Ocean Way where Nick was recording, but unfortunately, they didn't ask me to go with them. I ended up living in Nashville and actually the girl at

MCA who was hiring me on the Petty stuff got transferred there. She was working with the Mavericks, with whom I became good friends. Their drummer, Paul Deakin, knew that I was a big Nick Lowe fan and told me Nick was back in town again to mix the songs. The Mavericks wouldn't be there, but I should just go along and pretend I was supposed to meet them. I went over to RCA Studio A, the big room, and acted dumb – "Is Paul here? Oh look, it's Nick." He's there with the engineer, and he asks, "Do you know any good record stores?" I said I did, so we got in the car and went driving around town, which of course for a lifelong Nick Lowe fan was quite a thrill. I took him back to his hotel and we traded phone numbers, and that was it. A month or two later I was at home in Nashville and the phone rings and it's Nick. He's back in town and he says, "Fancy a bit of dinner?"'

The cost of subsidising a road band had made a large dent in Nick's finances. For the foreseeable future, appearing solo with only an acoustic guitar for company was the sensible option. An appearance at London's Jazz Café in December 1995 delighted the capacity crowd and launched a series of concerts in the capital that would occur roughly annually at untested venues. Occasionally, a small band would be deployed.

Interspersed with these live appearances would be the release of a new album about once every four years. This was to become the pattern as Nick's visible work rate dropped. In a humorous twist on James Brown's famous epitaph, Jake Riviera described his client as 'the least hard-working man in show business'.

Playing solo in the intimate atmosphere of a small theatre, which would usually be sold out, he could structure his performance to incorporate the odd anecdote or an off-the-wall introduction. He was also very good at spontaneous ripostes to quell the occasional heckler, such as the time a request for

'Breaking Glass!' rang out from the stalls of a London theatre, delivered in a strong Glaswegian accent, to which Nick retorted, 'My, you've come a long way.'

This was the stand-up Nick Lowe, a role he played with grace and style. 'I much prefer him solo,' says Elvis Costello. 'Nick's poise as a singer, his maturity and his use of tone is beautiful. I can't believe it's this guy I've been watching since I was a teenager, and that incredible right hand on the guitar, the pulse of it, no matter how slow the tempo is, it's never ponderous, it's always right.'

Although Nick kept out of the public eye for long periods, he was now taking greater care over the writing and recording of new songs and exercising strict quality control. In the summer of 1996, recording resumed. Initially, he wanted to return to the function room at the Turk's Head, where many of his newer songs had been worked up and recorded, but this back-to-basics approach had to be abandoned.

'I thought I would save money by recording there, but what I hadn't taken into account was that in the evening the hall was used for various activities, like the aerobics club, wolf cubs, origami, so we had to take all the gear down each night and set it all up again the next day. It was very time-consuming. It would have ended up costing about the same as if we'd gone to Montserrat. I had been so sure about the way we recorded, for example doing the vocal at the same time as the track. Sometimes it worked fantastically, but it made it hard to do things over. We used to bring the stuff home and it sounded great, but we thought we could make it even better. So we went into the studio.'

Over the next two years Nick compiled songs for the forthcoming *Dig My Mood*, which was made in tandem with Geraint Watkins's *Watkins Bold As Love* using the same core musicians.

'Every few months Nick would tell us he had some songs ready and call a meeting,' says Neil Brockbank. 'He would say, "This is how it goes," and the boys would fall in behind him. We would then go into the studio. There was no instruction from Nick. They would just play what you hear on the record, with Nick singing live. They're listening in their headphones to the vocal that's actually going to be on the record. It's not a guide vocal, so this is, in a sense, like an Elvis Presley session or a Frank Sinatra session.'

Nick's songs were recorded in batches of three or four, often at topflight London studios such as RAK or the Townhouse, both of which had been used for *The Impossible Bird* mixing sessions. 'Going into the Turk's Head had been the key to establishing the ground rules,' says Brockbank. 'Once we'd done it, we never needed to go back there. We could go into a conventional studio, but we had to get there via the Turk's Head.'

Nick's friend, photographer Jim Herrington, was now traversing the US on 'self-assignment', which involved finding and photographing the living legends of country and rock and roll, such as Carl Perkins, Ray Price, Jerry Lee Lewis. 'No one was asking me to do it,' says Herrington. 'It became like a *Life* magazine assignment that I didn't actually have. I considered it to be serious work. I thought that it was of the utmost importance to document these people I thought were cool and valid. Admittedly, a highly subjective line-up.'

High on Herrington's hit list was Johnny Cash, and when Nick returned to Nashville, Jim got his opportunity. 'I took Jim over to Hendersonville,' recalls Nick. 'He got the full experience – the holding of hands and saying grace round the table, and June's stories about Elia Kazan, who had encouraged her to move to New York to study acting.'

'My dad turned me onto Johnny Cash's Sun recordings when I was very young,' continues Herrington. 'Cash to me was like bedrock under your feet, the top of the pyramid. I was a huge fan, so to go out there with Nick was a pretty big deal for me. I took every piece of photographic gear I owned, packed it in the trunk of my car, but by this time Johnny was getting quite ill and looked it. People in Nashville had told me he was very self-conscious about the way he looked and didn't like to be photographed any more. Of course, I can sympathise, but what a conundrum – here's my chance to get Johnny Cash! I never even opened the trunk. I didn't want to be the guy that Nick brought along who's suddenly taking photos.

'Johnny was as cool as cool can get. He obviously loved Nick, and he seemed to like me I guess, but as Nick insinuated, "He's my friend, my ex-father-in-law, and sometimes drinking partner, but there's still considerable awe." I felt it too. Johnny took us out in his jeep, just the three of us driving through the woods, back to the log cabin he used to write and record in. There's so many subtle ways I could have gotten the photo. I like to think I'm fearless with the camera, but I refrained out of respect for Nick, and for Johnny. I think Johnny himself would have said, "Jim, you fucked up, you could have photographed me but you didn't do it." It's my biggest, most profound photographic miss of all time.'

When *Dig My Mood* was released in January 1998, my brief assessment appeared in *Mojo*:

Nick Lowe Rocks But Gently? Possibly, except Lowe hardly 'rocks' at all here. This is not a complaint, but anyone anticipating a little shake and pop will require shock treatment as laser locates groove. 'Faithless Lover', the daring Jacques Brel-like opener, is a sparse mood piece, revealing a new eerie resonance in Lowe's voice. The tone veers even deeper into easy territory with 'You Inspire Me', a lush ballad that's clearly marked 'kd lang'. In fact many of these songs sound eminently coverable, especially 'The Kind Of Man That I've Become' – another ready-to-wear item for Johnny Cash. 'Time I Took A Holiday', complete with 'Groovin' intro, finds its author seeking 'somewhere quiet and not over-looked' so he and his baby can 'go get cooked', but elsewhere, the mood we're asked to dig is deep and foreboding. Not for the first time Lowe reiterates 'love's a hurting thing' ('What Lack Of Love Has Done') and doubts if he will ever find what he's looking for ('High On A Hilltop'), whilst the hilariously-titled 'Failed Christian', written by Henry McCullough, inspires a sud-den outbreak of Dylanesque warbling. Throughout the record, the vocal is set high in the mix, proudly occupying perhaps 70% of the picture, allowing the volume to be cranked up without any nasty drums annoying the neighbours. It's a mature sound from one of England's greatest singer-songwriters and although it's one step back from 'The Impossible Bird', it's several jumps ahead of the competition.

While drafting the review, I asked Nick a few questions over the phone and was told that Jake Riviera had taken the record to 'fourteen major labels' only to be turned down by all of them; Nick said he would like to have been offered a deal, but only because it would have been nice to say, 'Thank you very much, but no thank you.'

On the prospect of signing to, say, Virgin Records, he elaborated: 'If I'd signed a big contract I would have had to do all the things that I'm unwilling to do in order not to be seen as a bastard. You've got to do what they tell you to do. You've got to go and sit on the couch in the morning – it fills me with despair

– and do every crappy pop show and I'm not interested enough in it any more. I'd feel like a foolish old git.'

No doubt, at that time, labels such as Virgin would have been nonplussed by tracks such as Nick's cover of Ivory Joe Hunter's string-driven country confessional 'Cold Grey Light Of Dawn', or the gospel-tinged 'Lead Me Not', and indeed 'You Inspire Me', the album's standout song. Written and sung in a style that pre-dates rock and roll, it would have suited many vocalists of the Sinatra era. Nick in fact wrote it with his parents in mind, and played it to them in the company of his cousin Wendy Thatcher and her husband, who were visiting from Canada.

'I certainly think that music and entertaining runs in the family,' says Wendy. 'I remember us having dinner, and afterwards Nick sat at the table and played it to us. It was so simple and lovely.'

As my *Mojo* review mentions, 'You Inspire Me' cried out to be covered by k.d. lang, and one hopes there is still time.

'I think k.d. was in the frame at one point, and Bette Midler, but the trail went cold. The only well-known person to have recorded it is Engelbert Humperdinck. He sings it great, but the musical accompaniment is vile. Engelbert was doing it live. It was going to be a serious session, with an arranger and proper musicians. I said, "OK," and he sung it great, but the music was poor.'

In February 1998, Nick made a return appearance at the Jazz Café for the first of three London shows that year. In March, he visited Japan, accompanied by Geraint Watkins and Bobby Irwin, and in June he played with full band at London's Queen Elizabeth Hall, where country singer Jim Lauderdale opened the show. There was also a memorable concert in December at Her Majesty's Theatre, where Nick's opening act was Dan Penn and Spooner Oldham, much-revered writers of songs such as 'Cry

Like A Baby' for the Box Tops, and 'The Dark End Of The Street' for southern soul enigma, James Carr. This was Nick's kind of music – 'raceless, classless' – and he felt honoured to have Dan and Spooner on the bill.

One of the more revealing songs on *Dig My Mood* was 'Lonesome Reverie', in which the singer finds himself – post break-up – at ease with his solitude and enjoying the time and space in which to reflect. As he turns for home he is 'torn reluctantly' from his quiet musing.

'You go deep into this awful depression. Then you're riding on this wave of righteousness – "I'm so alone – this is fantastic! I'm so misunderstood! Where shall I go? I can go anywhere!" It was a great wave of down and then up.'

Would Nick miss that freedom to 'pick out a place to dine' – maybe over a crossword and a half bottle of wine – if ever he were a little less alone than he was at that point?

'Party-of-one style dining – I'd miss that! I've always found it very easy to be my own company. I have no trouble being on my own at all. In fact, I think it's something of a luxury to be able to be on your own. To be alone is different to being lonely of course, to state the bleeding obvious. That's probably why I have this music thing. To this day, if I'm sitting in an airport, if I've got to waste time, it's no problem at all.[24] Traffic jams, I laugh at them. I can always just go to this fabulous place and simply muse on things, especially if I've got a song on the go. Just lay it aside, and if you've got any time while you're waiting for someone, or walking somewhere, just dig the song out and have a look at it while you're doing something else.'

A case in point might have been a work-in-progress entitled 'Indian Queens', a highly descriptive and surreal tale that would appear on his next collection of songs.

Drinking and brawling I drifted south
Where I worked the rigs off Galveston
One day a shark took a diver's leg
And I dove in and drug him out
He said he'd leave me everything [long pause here when played live]
But he died before he could sign the will

'I did it driving back from Fowey in Cornwall, a little hung over [Nick owned a cottage there in the 1990s, which was rented out as a holiday home]. Indian Queens is a hamlet just off the A30, a well-known traffic black spot, and Yellowknife was Margo Kidder's hometown in Canada. I made the story up on that car journey, in my head. It was a four-hour drive and I went into a trance. I got very worried that I would forget it. That does happen. You have the tune so clear in your head, then it's gone. I always used to say, rather pompously – although I haven't made this up myself – that if I forget the song, then it's not good. But that isn't always true.'

By July 2000, Nick had written a number of new songs he considered worthy of being recorded. With Neil Brockbank, Bobby Irwin, Geraint Watkins and guitarist Steve Donnelly, he went into RAK Studios and tackled 'She's Got Soul' and 'Cupid Must Be Angry'. He was now on his way to making the album that many still consider to be his best.

CHAPTER 15

A Battered Sophistication

That's how I knew when the track was finished, when it felt like it wasn't my song.

September 2001 saw the release of *The Convincer*, an album that came relatively hard on the heels, at least in Nick Lowe terms, of its predecessor. Just as 'Faithless Lover' was track one on *Dig My Mood*, 'Homewrecker' was another low-key opener.

'Nick and I were absolutely at one on this,' says co-producer Neil Brockbank. 'It's like a little preamble while you're rustling your progamme and getting to your seat. We had wanted to start *The Impossible Bird* with "The Beast In Me", but Jake Riviera talked us out of it. He wanted a toe-tapper, but in a funny kind of way you don't know what loud is until you've heard quiet.'

'Homewrecker' was recorded in two sessions a week apart, each employing entirely different instrumentation and vocal microphones. The separate recordings were spliced together with an inspired and daring edit. 'What makes the edit convincing is the vocal,' says Brockbank. 'You don't notice any change in

281

weight or tone, and that's because he's taken the trouble to rehearse it ahead of time so that when he hits the studio he's nailed on.'

'*The Convincer* was "the convincer",' adds Brockbank, now confident that Nick's modus operandi was achieving its aims. Housed in a package assembled by Nick's girlfriend, graphic designer Peta Waddington, the album met with considerable critical acclaim and would go on to be regarded as the final work in a trilogy of introspective albums.

'People see it that way, which I do too,' Nick says. 'Those records *are* linked. We were all in on it, Bobby, Geraint, Steve, Neil. It was a mere detail that I was writing and singing the songs. It didn't sell in huge numbers, of course, but the people who got it really did get it. It was great to see more women at the shows, and homosexuals, and more young people. In fact, a lot of the grey ponytails melted away.'

The album contains two cover versions – 'Poor Side Of Town', a 1966 US hit for Johnny Rivers, and 'Only A Fool Breaks His Own Heart', co-written by Norman Bergen and Shelly Coburn. Nick first heard the latter, performed by Mighty Sparrow and Byron Lee, when it was burnt onto a CD for him by Jim Herrington. Bergen, who served his apprenticeship as a musical arranger for the likes of the Chiffons and Tony Orlando, 'started showing up backstage', and later came to London to record with Neil Brockbank at his Goldtop studio in Camden Town.

'Has She Got A Friend?' is more up-tempo, with instrumental echoes of the Everly Brothers, while 'Between Dark And Dawn' and 'Let's Stay In And Make Love' both occupy that spot where easy listening, country and soul music miraculously meet. Such recordings serve to remind us that there is no other songwriter, east of the Atlantic, working so successfully in this rarefied field.

The Convincer also contains one of Nick's most amusing songs in 'Lately I've Let Things Slide', its title a model of understatement that holds up a mirror to addiction. One can only imagine the reaction from his colleagues when he first demonstrated it for them at one of their planning meetings.

'It's all too painfully autobiographical,' confesses its writer. 'And as I've discovered, lots of other people recognise themselves in it. I love Arthur Alexander, he's one of my favourites, and I think of it as one of his type of songs.'

> *With a growing sense of dread, and a hammer in my head*
> *Fully clothed upon the bed*
> *I wake up to the world that lately I've been living in*
> *There's a cut upon my brow, must have banged myself somehow*
> *But I can't remember now*
> *And the front door's open wide, lately I've let things slide*

The song's middle eight and final verse diarise another lost day in the life of a committed drinker:

> *I go to the bin, I throw the laundry in, and pick out the cleanest*
>   *shirt*
> *Then I tell myself again, I don't really hurt . . .*
> *That untouched takeaway, I brought home the other day*
> *Has quite a lot to say . . .*

Johnny Marr, formerly guitarist and songwriter with the Smiths, and a Nick Lowe superfan, describes *The Convincer* as a soul record, despite the strong country influence that pervades many of the songs.

'You can listen to him and go, "Oh, he puts that song over like Johnny Cash," yet *The Convincer* is *soul*,' says Marr.

'Nick is an Englishman who has through time immersed

himself in American influences. Instead of "I'm A Mess", Al Green would have sung, "I'm broke up", say. Whereas years ago, Nick Lowe may have sung "Cracking Up", he can now sing, "I'm A Mess". Only an English soul guy like Nick can sing that kind of song with an acoustic guitar and do it authentically. He sounds like Memphis via Chiswick.'

A teenaged Marr had first entered Nick's realm back in 1980, when his then group, White Dice, had answered an ad in the *NME* and sent their demo cassette to Jake Riviera, who was talent spotting for F-Beat. Jake liked what he heard and offered the group a session at Nick's Am-Pro studio, with Paul Riley engineering. Although there is some divergence of opinion as to Nick's precise involvement in the session, Marr does recall seeing him get out of a cab outside the house and then 'wobble unsteadily' on the staircase. Perhaps it was Carlene who made a bigger impression that day, having greeted the group at the front door in her nightdress. 'Being in Nick's house was something else,' says Marr. 'I felt one step closer to something great.'

Marr's next Lowe encounter occurred in 1988 when he joined the Pretenders and Nick was hired to produce their version of 'Windows Of The World' for the *1969* movie soundtrack.

'We also did a version of Iggy Pop's "1969", with Nick producing. After the first take he pressed the intercom and said, "I know you're not gonna believe this, but that was the take." He was laughing about it because he was aware of his reputation as the "bash it down" producer, and allowed us to do a few more takes, but we ended up using take one. Nick was absolutely right. It was a great track. He suggested that his credit on the label should have been "Watched by Nick Lowe".'

On the very day that *The Convincer* hit US record stores – alongside Bob Dylan's *Love And Theft* and Jay-Z's *The Blueprint* – the world was shaken by the terrorist attack on New York's World Trade Center. In 9/11's immediate aftermath, Nick found himself in town to do promotional interviews. He stayed at the Soho Grand, where parts of the hotel had been commandeered by the New York City Fire Department to house their men and equipment during the clean-up operation at Ground Zero. Nick recalls the sight of 'dog-tired firemen with sunken eyes' trudging through the building as they returned each day from their grim task. That October, Nick played the London Palladium, where he opened his set with a sombre reading of the Chi-Lites' 'There Will Never Be Any Peace (Until God Is Seated At The Conference Table)'.

In 2002, Nick undertook a fifteen-date solo tour in America, but it was an otherwise quiet year. By now Jake Guralnick was his co-manager, working alongside Jake Riviera in '2 Jakes Management' and taking care of US operations. During his time looking after Nick's American record releases, Guralnick had worked closely with Riviera and had gradually become a trusted advisor.

Guralnick recalls: 'I said to Jake Riviera, "I see a lot of things you're not doing in America." The agent wasn't right for Nick, and they weren't really pursuing film and TV as much as they should have been. I just saw some opportunities and said to Jake, "Let me manage Nick for the US." I had a highfalutin proposal where Jake would bankroll me to have an office, but he told me I should work out of my house. Jake was my mentor and he got me started and everything I learnt was from him.'

Of Nick's recent US tour, Guralnick told *Billboard*: 'We were looking for venues that would be good for an acoustic show with promoters that would appreciate what we were trying to do.'

Those kinds of venues seemed rare, but there was one to be found in many key cities and they mapped out a future touring circuit for Nick and his increasingly solid fan base.

'The difference between Nick and other artists is that he never disappoints,' says Guralnick. 'He is "Nick Lowe" onstage, and offstage. He is a total pleasure to be around, appreciative, and completely brilliant. Everything about him is exactly what you want, and it opens doors. Everybody wants to do business with him.'

The year 2003 saw the passing of three people close to Nick. On 15 May, June Carter died in Nashville of heart complications. This was followed on 12 September by the death of her husband, Johnny Cash. Both of these sad events were preceded by the death of Nick and Penny's father, Drain, on 21 February 2003. He had been suffering from cancer and passed away, aged eighty-seven, in Watford General Hospital. Nick had been intermittently close to his dad and involved him in various flying-related activities such as the Confederate Air Force trip of 1981. There was also the time Drain flew on Concorde.[25]

'We were talking about it one day and Drain told me they were planning to take Concorde out of service. I said, "Really? Well in that case we'd better get on it!" Up until then, Concorde was out of reach and only people like David Frost and Joan Collins could afford it, but I was getting some success when I became a bit of a pop star and I was able to make grand gestures. Best of all, I was able to take Drain over to New York with one of his mates.'

Nick had always had a strange relationship with his father, who like most men of his generation – especially those who had fought in the war – found it hard to express their emotions. He had spent much of his Air Force life away from home and therefore seemed to his son like a figure that only existed in the letters he wrote home, and that Pat would recite.

'He certainly was a hero and I felt he was disappointed in me, because I so took after my mama. I just wanted to stay inside and sing Lonnie Donegan songs with her and harmonise on each word, rather than stand in a freezing cold garage handing him spanners while he changed the spark plugs on the car – the kind of stuff that boys are supposed to do with their dads. Although he may have been a disciplinarian, I can't remember him ever laying a finger on me, but he could be quite intimidating and distant, which probably stood him in good stead when he was honing his skills in the RAF. In fact, the RAF defined him.

'He would never tell me he loved me, and I could feel him stiffen when I insisted on giving him a kiss, even when he was an old man. I visited him in hospital when he was close to death. The nurses had had a go at shaving his moustache, but it was done rather badly and I didn't have the heart to tell him. I remember our last words. I told him I loved him, and he replied, "I love you too, old boy."'

Nick's girlfriend and future wife, Peta Waddington, remembers catching the music bug at an early age and developing an unshakeable love for Cliff Richard, even if his records were considered by some to be deeply uncool. Out of step with her 1970s schoolmates, her passion for an enormous variety of music ran deep. As a member of the school orchestra, her musical skills were modest, but she became 'a very accomplished fan'. She went on to study graphic design at college and upon moving to London landed a job as girl Friday at the Fitch & Co design agency in Soho Square. Exploring the surrounding area, Peta soon discovered that episodes of the *Jools Holland's Happening* TV show were being filmed at the nearby Astoria. It was at one of these shows, in 1990, that she first clapped eyes on Nick, 'suited, booted, and shock headed'.

Over the next ten years, Peta would occasionally notice him from the corner of her eye at random events, or driving his car in slow-moving traffic, and once, sitting a couple of rows in front of her at the theatre, his 'big, white plume of hair' obstructing the view. Peta also spotted Nick at the London screening of *The Man Who Invented Rock'n'Roll*, a documentary about Sun Records producer Sam Phillips, in 2000. In fact, Nick had also noticed Peta that night.

It was time for Miss Waddington to introduce herself. As is often the case in such encounters, she said something 'disappointingly idiotic' and walked away horrified that she'd made a poor impression, or so she thought. Her only recourse was to write Nick a letter, care of an address printed on the back of one of his record sleeves. As an accomplished graphic designer, Peta cheekily suggested that she might work on his next album sleeve. Two weeks later, to her astonishment, she received a handwritten reply.

An inciting moment had occurred when Peta was commissioned to create the artwork for *The Convincer*. The sleeve's photographer, Dan Burn-Forti, was the son of Dorothy Burn-Forti of Famepushers fame and the former co-manager of Brinsley Schwarz. Dan was a small child when Nick last saw him. Through their reacquaintance, a connection was made. In the years that followed, Peta and Nick's friendship endured and mutual admiration was established without the pressure of a serious relationship.

In 2002, Peta travelled to the USA to soak up Cajun music at its source and landed a spot on KBON radio, based in Eunice, Louisiana. She insists that investigating 'Swamp Pop' and spinning the local music was just a hobby, but it led to her being away for months at a time, messing around on a Louisiana escape, and coming home with her own rock and roll anecdotes. Maybe Peta and Nick did have a future.

Nick, meanwhile, had shown no interest in becoming a dad, but the hours he had spent poring over his late father's RAF flying log books may have brought home the realisation that he could easily become the last of the Drain Lowe family line.

One evening while Peta sat listening to more of Nick's stories, drinking after-dinner tea and passively smoking his Silk Cut cigarettes, he suddenly said, 'Now, are you sure you don't want to have a baby?' In 2004, much to the slight bewilderment of friends and family, Peta and Nick found themselves expecting a child.

On 14 March 2005, a palpable shudder ran through the audience at London's Barbican Theatre as Nick unveiled a new song entitled 'I Trained Her To Love Me'. It had real shock value and certainly succeeded in unnerving the more sensitive sections of the crowd, both male and female, as each successive line cranked up the audacity.

> *Do you see the way she lights up when I walk in the room?*
>   *That's good!*
> *And the skip in her step when we're both out walking in the*
>   *neighbourhood*
> *This one's almost done – now to watch her fall apart*
> *I trained her to love me, so I can go ahead and break her heart*

This was taking male conceit to a new level, confessing to a talent for attracting a string of easy lovers, only to cynically ditch them, one after another. The song's scansion and economy of lyric are impressive, even if the sentiment is dubious, especially when sung to a lilting Latin rhythm that sets out to seduce, only to deceive.

In the song's middle eight, he recalls one particular girl who 'cut up rough' and told him he only does it because he can, and would therefore 'wind up one lonely, twisted old man'.

Poo-pooing the girl's suggestion, he espies yet another candidate, prompting the keen couplet: 'Here comes a prime contender, for my agenda'.

If there was ever a song that cried out for a good, old-fashioned 'answer record' – maybe something along the lines of 'You Thought You Could Train Me To Love You?' – then this was a front runner. For although there was no shortage of women who were wont to swoon over Nick's suave personality, his days of training them to love him were now well and truly in the rear-view mirror. 'That sort of thing is no longer available to me,' he would say in interviews, having expressed his love for Peta Waddington, who had now given birth to their son, Roy. Born in February 2005, he was present, a babe in arms, at the Barbican show.

Nick was now partway through recording tracks for his next album, but its release was still over two years away. For co-producer Neil Brockbank, the process was prolonged by 'a couple of false starts'. Some years earlier, Neil had offered Nick his notice in the misguided belief that *Dig My Mood* could not be bettered. Thankfully, Neil's notice was declined. Then came *The Convincer*. But Brockbank was disappointed that none of these records was troubling the charts.

'I thought it was going to put Nick right back in the frame and we would have hits, maybe not Top 40, but we were gonna hit the album charts. But we never got close. Obviously, they were a huge critical success, but there was no response from the rude public. None at all.'

Keen not to make 'The Convincer Part Two', the new firm continued to gather at Nick's place to hear and critique his new songs. These sessions would involve frequent trips to the pub on the corner and 'lots of red wine' to aid critical assessment of the material on offer and stimulate frank discussion. Early songs that made it to the recording studio included 'Long Limbed Girl', 'A Better Man' and 'The Other Side Of The Coin' (which had already been recorded by Solomon Burke), but there was a feeling in the camp that everyone 'knew too much' about what the others could do, musically, and a danger that they might repeat themselves.

'The more time went on, the harder and harder it became for Nick to write songs he was happy with,' says Brockbank. 'He'd covered all the concepts and topics, and he went into an even slower routine of writing. That's why there was a long gap.'

Nick was of course dealing with his first experience of fatherhood and frequently travelling with Peta and Roy up and down the motorway between Brentford and Winchester, where Peta had a cottage at which the three of them spent much of their time. Somehow Nick still found the space to create, wisely retaining his Brentford house for work purposes. When the allure of the M3 motorway began to fade, it was time to buy a family home.

Peta and Nick searched west London for a suitable property, but ended up buying a place just around the corner. This meant, of course, that Nick could stroll from 'the old house' to 'the new house' as circumstances dictated.

Determined not to refer to the old house as a 'man cave', Nick permits the slightly less vulgar 'writer's shed' to describe its core function. Somewhat more comfortable than a rented office, and infinitely more efficient than a study within earshot of a busy family kitchen, it provided the perfect retreat that most writers crave. Nick knew he was fortunate to have this option, but stops short of calling it a luxury. It is where he does what he does to summon the songwriting process. This involves pottering around the house, occasionally staring out of the window, stroking his chin, and playing Patience, often with two or three games on the go. Lulled into a trance, a lyric or song idea will hopefully come forth. Plenty of time, not to mention solitude, is essential if the process is to work.

'A couple of hours in which to write is not long enough,' he maintains. 'You just about start to get somewhere, then you've got to stop. And the thought that you will have to stop kind of prevents you from getting anywhere really interesting, if you know, for example, you've got a domestic chore coming up. I don't want to blame anyone, but in order to write you've got to get into a frame of mind, and that's before musical notes, or words – note one, or word one – come along. It can take you a long time.

'I can look out of the window for hours. It's very difficult for people to understand. If they had a CCTV camera on me, they would just see some bloke standing in the middle of a room, going to make a cup of tea, then stopping halfway through. I loved that cartoon character that I think Robert Crumb used to draw. He was a fat bloke sitting in a chair viewed from several different angles, then one of him looking out of a window, from above, a human being sitting, standing – that's how I feel, quite a lot of the time. But if I had to sell the old house for financial reasons, yes, I would rent an office. I have to be completely on my own to do this stuff.

'Before I had the wonderful life I lead now, when I was a single man – on paper it sounds marvellous – I could come and go as I pleased, but I was living badly. I wasn't treating myself very well, but the upside of that is you can totally give yourself over to this peculiar thing that you have and that other people don't seem to have. It's wonderful, but it's very destructive. Everyone knows that about writers, and it can drive you mad – the tremendous highs then plunging into terrible troughs. I once heard someone describe it as "manageable doldrums". I don't get really bad low downs, the depths, but I have been like that in the past. When I was younger I didn't really get it; I didn't know what was happening, and sometimes it was simply a very bad hangover, but then you realise that these waves of emotion are part of the process. The elation is illusionary, and the terrible impending doom you can feel is just as illusionary as when you are on top of the world. You think you're a genius, you really do. You think you're in touch with something that is totally connected to the Almighty.'

On 12 December 2006, Nick and Penny's mother died at Horton Hospital in Oxfordshire, after a short illness. She had been in a residential care home for some time.

'Nick wouldn't ring Pat or go and see her,' says Penny. 'It's another sign of my mother indulging him. We found this incredible place for her, near where we live. It was like a five-star hotel. Nick came up and saw her on occasion but the visits got fewer and fewer, until they stopped altogether. Pat would never say a word about it, except she would comment, rather obliquely, "I wonder how Nick is, I haven't heard from him."

'I called Nick and said, "Look, you're not going to like this . . ." What he does is he goes absolutely silent, then he says, "Yes, OK, right, goodbye," and puts the phone down. But thank God Nick did eventually go up there, because she died shortly afterwards. It's almost as if he doesn't want to be confronted with anything nasty.'

'He doesn't like anything unpleasant, bad news or confrontation,' says his brother-in-law, John Perriss. 'If you say something about his parents such as, "This would have been great for them," all those rooms in his mind are closed off. He might say, "You're right, Pat would have been mad for it," but then the subject is closed and it's time to move on.'

Penny recalls Pat being entranced by her son's musical endeavours back in the early years, especially when the Brinsleys were signed by Famepushers: 'Mother was bursting with pride because they'd been "discovered", or so she thought. She did indulge him. I remember once when Nick was late for lunch and we were starving, Mum saying, "Can't we give Nick another five minutes?" I told her I thought he wasn't coming. Mum said, "Yes, he's probably very tired, I suspect he's got jetlag." I think we all fell about laughing because Nick had only been as far as Germany, and he'd been back for four days. She forgave him for an awful lot of things. Nick can be a charmer, but I've always been extremely proud of him.'

Of his parents, both now deceased, Nick remembers, 'They had been through the war. Not only did they realise that they'd survived, but they'd lost a lot of their old mates. They weren't very old and were now thrust into this world of tremendous optimism and everything was going to be fantastic. I remember, for instance, whenever I'd say, "We went to a junk shop and bought this great old table from the 1940s – look it's got the utility mark!" my mother's nose would wrinkle. "What do you want that old rubbish for? Look, we've got Formica tops here, they're so easy to keep clean." They thoroughly embraced all the new inventions and couldn't understand how my mates and I wanted the 1930s art deco. They thought the future was going to be so much better for their kids.

'Drain's fun-loving character wasn't present all the time; after the party had moved on he changed quite a lot. But he was very "hail fellow well met" with his mates, and very good company. Those Air Force guys had survived the war and it was pretty fantastic to still be flying jets in the 1950s and 60s, with the residual goodwill that the RAF enjoyed. And when they got together, they used to have a bloomin' good time. A lot of that rubbed off on me. I've always felt quite at ease in the military world. People always go on about, "Ooh I couldn't join the army, with all that marching up and down with a gun." I used to think, "No, actually, I could do that." It was something I grew up with and understood.'

Eventually, the new album was complete and *At My Age* was released in June 2007. Highlights include 'Hope For Us All', 'Rome Wasn't Built In A Day' and 'People Change', featuring vocal support from Chrissie Hynde. Promotional copies were accompanied by a press kit for which American record producer Bill Bentley wrote: 'Somewhere in London a musician carries the keys to the musical kingdom. In his Technicolor sonic scope are all kinds of sounds, from rock to country to soul to pop. Nothing is off limits, as long as it has a groove and goodness based in reality. The musician has been performing for 40 years, but is as fresh today as the first time he stepped onstage.'

Bentley's piece also described Nick as 'the headmaster of British rock', a phrase that has since stuck like glue to press releases and newspaper reviews around the world. The release of *At My Age* was preceded by an intimate concert at St Luke's Church in the City of London, where Nick's four-piece band was augmented with a horn section that included British jazz pioneer Chris Barber on trombone, alongside Matt Holland (trumpet) and Martin Winning (saxophone). The performance was filmed by the BBC for a television broadcast and the same line-up played a sold-out show at the Royal Festival Hall in October of that year, by which time 'I Trained Her To Love Me' had become a fixture in Nick's concert repertoire.

For some years, Nick had been accustomed to the relative comfort of flying first or business class because, he reasoned, '[my] butt's too big for coach'.[26] He remembers, with a little embarrassment, Neil Brockbank – in his role as tour manager – checking him in at airline desks as if he were royalty. 'This is Mr Lowe,' Neil would announce authoritatively. 'And these are his suitcases. He will be travelling in first class . . .'

In the spring of 2008, Nick boarded yet another plane for a solo tour of the USA. Although the pre-tour publicity made mention of the recent *Jesus Of Cool* reissue, Nick was more interested in giving a public airing to newer songs. 'People Change' was as good a mission statement as any, given the probability of a few older fans yearning in vain for a Rockpile reunion.

The opening act on the tour was the esteemed Canadian singer-songwriter, Ron Sexsmith, whom Nick later described as 'the last songwriter to know where the bucket to the melody well is stashed'.

'I asked them if I could ride in their car as I don't drive,' recalls Sexsmith. 'They were kind enough to allow me to travel with them. Neil was driving, Nick's next to him in the front, I'm in the back, and the guitars are in the trunk. I didn't know Nick – I'd only met him once before – but he was just so gracious and had many amazing stories.'

To melt the miles on journeys such as the 215-mile drive from Nashville to Atlanta, Lowe and Sexsmith would play a game they called 'Funny/Not Funny', in which two superficially similar entertainment acts were contrasted. 'Funny' artists were those that appeared to take themselves less seriously than the 'Not Funny' variety. As Sexsmith remembers it, 'It would be something like "Bing Crosby funny, Frank Sinatra not funny". But I can't remember the precise rationale. Maybe it was whether or not somebody had a sense of humour. We preferred people who did.'

*

Whether singer Daryl Hall would qualify as funny or not funny is unknown, although one suspects the former. He had long been a fan of Nick, and in 2008 invited him to appear in an episode of *Live From Daryl's House*, the monthly performance webcast through which Hall rose to the challenge of surviving a fast-changing record business.

'I needed to reinvent myself,' says Hall, who has had many artists appear and perform with him, including Smokey Robinson, Todd Rundgren and his long-term musical partner, John Oates. 'Nick was one of the first people I wanted on the show. We've known each other for a long time and we've kept in touch. My buddy, T-Bone Wolk [who played bass on Paul Carrack's *Groove Approved* album and many Hall & Oates hits], who is sadly no longer with us, was also good friends with Nick. It was the three of us, playing acoustic guitars and singing some of Nick's songs.'

The episode in question was filmed at Hall's London residence on Hammersmith Terrace, where a number of Nick's songs were recorded and filmed, including 'I Live On A Battlefield', 'Shelley My Love' and 'Cruel To Be Kind', the latter bringing obvious joy to the trio as their soulful harmonies filled Hall's big, empty basement room with its ideal acoustics.

'I am drawn to Nick's lyrics and his sensibility,' says Hall. 'I like his take on things. I wouldn't call him a purist because he's not, but he draws from some very pure sources. It resonates with me.'

As long ago as 1985, Daryl and Nick had started to write a song together, but it was never finished. In 2017, however, Hall confirmed that progress had been made and 'When The Spell Is Broken' was now finished and recorded for inclusion on his next solo album. 'I haven't even told Nick yet that I'm putting it on the new album,' says Hall. 'That's a long-time connection that's finally bearing fruit.'

*

The Hardly Strictly Bluegrass Festival takes place annually in San Francisco's Golden Gate Park. 'Hardly Strictly' was conceived by the retired banker and billionaire philanthropist, Warren Hellman, who at age seventy-four was still a budding banjo picker. In the autumn of 2008, Nick made one of his many appearances at the festival and appeared solo on the Rooster Stage, mid-afternoon under bright, hot sunlight. He confessed to the capacity crowd that the dark cashmere sweater he had chosen to wear was not his 'smartest move'.

He also appeared that week at San Francisco's Great American Music Hall, playing bass in the succinctly named 'Guitar-Bass-Drums', his musical colleagues being Ry Cooder and Jim Keltner, or 'Little Village with all the John Hiatt taken out'.

Elvis Costello played support and music celebrities present included Emmylou Harris and Bonnie Raitt. Two days of rehearsals – which Cooder apparently agreed to after initially suggesting that an extended soundcheck would suffice – resulted in a canny set list that was Lowe-catalogue heavy.

Opening a little hesitantly on the first of two nights with 'A Fool Who Knows', the trio soon acclimatised itself. A huge round of applause brought smiles to their faces and they were off. 'Gai-Gin Man' picked up the pace, with Keltner providing his trademark grooves. Then Lowe greeted the audience in typically self-deprecating fashion, pre-empting any criticism that his group might appear under-rehearsed.

'There will be train wrecks and car crashes,' he promised, but insisted that this would make for 'entertainment gold'.

Bracing themselves for an unpredictable show, the crowd became ecstatic as Cooder, a reportedly 'cantankerous old shrinking violet' famously reluctant to play live, took the stand for 'Fool For A Cigarette'. Why, we were all wondering, was this man not getting out more? His performance electrified the room, his face convulsing as he poured his story out and punctuated it with slide guitar stabs, rendering the $100 ticket price irrelevant – other than the fact that the money was going to a good cause.

The two-night stand was the second in a series of annual fundraisers in aid of the Richard de Lone Special Housing Project, and its plans for a purpose-built home for sufferers of Prader–Willi syndrome, a genetic disorder.[27] Richard, who suffers from Prader–Willi, is the son of Lesley and Austin de Lone, also known as 'Audie', the former member of Eggs Over Easy who several decades earlier helped to inaugurate the London pub rock scene and has since played keyboards on a number of Lowe and Costello musical outings.

'The Richard de Lone Special Housing Project is still moving along,' says Austin de Lone. 'But it is a long process. We were in a bit of a stall for a couple of years, but have now picked up the pace, and the pieces. We have been talking to a state senator and some others in the department of disabled services. The music community – the church of rock and roll – has been our backbone, with help from Nick, Elvis, Bonnie Raitt, Bill Kirchen, Buddy Miller, Jim Lauderdale, Boz Scaggs, Elvin Bishop, Jimmie Vaughan and others. As Prader–Willi is a rare syndrome and does not have the drawing power of something like breast cancer or autism, it is a harder push, but we are not giving up.'

In May 2009, Nick set out once again with Ron Sexsmith as his opening act, this time on a UK tour. It was the first time Ron had met Nick's band.

'We were all in a splitter van and those guys are hilarious,' recalls Sexsmith. 'Bobby Irwin was one of the funniest people I've ever met. I can be pretty funny at times, when I'm with my band, but around Bobby I didn't say a word. What am I gonna say? I can't compete, and they're all funny. I'd be laughing all day and Nick and I would always duet on that Louvin Brothers song, "My Baby's Gone".'

The Lowe/Sexsmith tour hit London on 18 May and played the Royal Albert Hall. An assortment of faces attended the after-show party, including Martin Freeman, Curtis Stigers, Jo Brand, Chrissie Hynde, Martin Chambers and 'punk rock' persons, Glen Matlock and Rat Scabies. With a capacity of around five thousand, the Hall was an ambitious venue ticket sales-wise, but it was pretty much sold out. The box office story could be quite different in the provinces, however, where shows were sparsely attended.

'They booked all these big rooms, but I don't think any of them were sold out,' says Sexsmith. 'I thought, "What's going on? It's Nick Lowe, with his band, why aren't you here?!"'

Ticket sales improved for Nick's 2009 summer tour with Ry Cooder. Playing a similar set to the one that dazzled audiences in San Francisco a few months earlier, Cooder and Lowe – with Cooder's son Joachim on drums, accordionist Flaco Jiménez and singer Juliette Commagere – packed every European hall they played, and later that year visited Japan, Australia and New Zealand.

On 24 September, preceding another solo tour in the USA, Nick took part in an edition of Elvis Costello's *Spectacle* TV series, recorded at New York's famous Apollo Theater. Other musical guests included Levon Helm, Richard Thompson and Allen Toussaint. Following a brief chat at the microphone with his host, Nick performed 'The Beast In Me', and left the stage to hear Costello describing him as 'England's greatest songwriter'.

On Sunday 5 September, 2010, Nick and Peta were married at Cambridge Cottage at the Royal Botanic Gardens, Kew.

'I didn't really get a proper proposal,' says Peta. 'If anyone ever asked us, he'd say, "Well, I guess it's an inevitability." It was

Roy really. He wondered why we weren't married, and that was part of the reason, and partly because we'd been together for ten years. I realised I didn't need a romantic proposal and ten is a nice round number. We thought we should get on with it and stop fannying around. Vanity played a big part in getting the show on the road – I figured we should do it while we still had all our own teeth.

'The wedding was quite low key. I think Nick was very mindful of the fact he'd been married before and we didn't need to make too big a deal of it. But it was a great excuse to have a party. The coming together of all our friends was lovely. We got very excited about getting married mainly because we had some fantastic music.'

Following the service and wedding breakfast at which best man Bobby Irwin gave a heartfelt and hilarious speech, there was an evening reception attended by many friends and associates. Paul Gorman was master of vinyl ceremonies, leading with the Lowe family favourite, 'We're Gonna Get Married' by Bo Diddley.[28]

No sooner had Nick put away his wedding suit than he was back to work. Following a get-together with Elvis Costello on 1 October for 'Costello Sings Lowe/Nick Sings Elvis', the 2010 fundraiser at the Great American Music Hall for the aforementioned Richard de Lone Special Housing Project, he set out on another US tour, this time 'with full band'.

CHAPTER 16

The Old Magic

23 October 2010, New York City

At the foot of Sixth Avenue, near the entrance to the Holland Tunnel, sits the City Winery. As the Saturday-night ticket-holders gather outside around opening time, they are strangely oblivious to the lanky, white-haired gentleman striding up Varick Street, carrying a clean white towel under his arm. He is on his way from a nearby hotel to perform the last of three sold-out nights at the venue.

The room is wide and woody, and has played host to some well-known artists from the fields of jazz, country and post-Woodstock legacy rock, including Mose Allison, Rosanne Cash, John Sebastian and 'Jethro Tull's Ian Anderson'. Ticket prices are $60 for table view, $35 for a barstool. Food and wine is served in the comfortable surroundings and the acoustics are good. The backstage facilities, however, are spartan, and visiting stars have to rely on front-of-house lavatories for that pre-show pee, thus any preservation of mystique is somewhat compromised.

Around 9.30 p.m., Nick takes the stage alone with his trusty

Gibson J-150 guitar[29] to croon the recently composed 'Stoplight Roses'. This is a song that warns every guilt-ridden cheapskate who has ever bought his partner some sad, scentless, gas-station flowers as a peace offering, not to get his story 'too straight'. It's a daring intro, and those paying attention are amused by the song's sentiment. The familiar 'Heart' and 'What's Shakin' On The Hill' follow, then the boys saunter on and join in the subtle intro to 'What Lack Of Love Has Done'.

Should any old-timers in the audience be challenged by Lowe's more recent material, he soon corrals them with a snappy 'Ragin' Eyes' and all is well with the air-punching, way-to-go set. Then, partway through the show, he introduces his band members.

'On bass, please say hello to retired babe magnet, Matt Radford. On guitar, please give a warm welcome to secret millionaire and tireless worker for charity, Johnny Scott. On piano, I'm pleased to introduce you to former child prodigy, Geraint Watkins. And what can I say about the next man? On the drums, would you please put your hands together for El Bandito, currently wanted for questioning by Homeland Security, Mister Robert Trehern [aka Bobby Irwin]!'

Nick appears extremely relaxed performing live, but confesses to being a little nervous beforehand.

'Sometimes you need a bit of that. It's always the fear that tonight is the night you're going to be found out; that you're actually kind of crap, and everyone is going to see it. I don't think this is uncommon among performers. You get a little frisson. Could this be the night you're gonna have no trousers on? But in the main, I'm champing at the bit. Once you're onstage and the game is all on, it's quite the reverse. It's terrific and I really enjoy it. It's the thing I know how to do. As with every entertainer, not everyone likes you – far from it in my case – but you know that the people who have come to see you want you to do your thing.'

And Nick's thing at this point is to continue performing well into his sixties and hopefully his seventies, just as Frank Sinatra or Leonard Cohen once did. Is it an addiction?

'Yes, I think so, although I can't compare myself to those people. If I didn't have an upcoming tour, or some public appearance to look forward to, I think I would quickly succumb to old age. When you're performing, you don't feel like you're any age at all. It's as if you exist in a bubble. Obviously there comes a time when the pipes go. I've already got arthritis in my hands, but everything still works, it's not a great problem. If someone like me doesn't perform or work, there doesn't seem to be any reason to be here. If I've been off the road for a while, I start to feel older and older. I start putting on weight and acting like some old git, instead of having a purpose, and being bright and interested and keen on meeting people. If I didn't do it, I would become very reclusive and wear carpet slippers.

'Nobody said to Duke Ellington, "Hey you're sixty-three, you can't do this any more, not that old swing stuff again. Move over, granddad, and give the youngsters a chance!" When you're younger you tend to pretend you're something else, but there comes a time when you say, "We're done now," and you have to welcome your uselessness and all the duff things that you do. And when you welcome it in, it takes a load off your mind and also it makes you feel fireproof. It improves your look, and the sound and the whole tone of what you do. Instead of trying to hide your age, you own up and it makes the cool stuff that you've figured out seem even cooler.'

'Nick Lowe is alone among rock stars in being better in his sixties than he was in his twenties,' says writer David Hepworth. 'With the records he's made in this century he's arrived at a musical persona which really resonates with a lot of people. It is the persona of a man in late middle-age belatedly coming to terms with what the rest of us would call real life. Maybe that's Nick, or maybe that's just his character. Because rock, as Bruce Springsteen said, retards adulthood and prolongs adolescence, Nick ended up doing things in his fifties that most of us did in our early thirties. He's the first rock star to make apology an art form.'

Nick's re-presentation as the artist who would grow old gracefully and embrace his sixties was probably 'a first' among the children of the 1960s pop-music boom, and the 1970s rock scene that followed. He has no desire to slavishly follow the latest trends in music, and celebrates advancing age with style and panache.[30] He views it as an asset, in stark contrast to his more 'rock-tastic' contemporaries who attempt to cling on to their youth and disguise the signs of ageing. He knows, of course, that you're 'never too old to rock', but it can reach a point where dressing up as one's younger self can start to look ridiculous.

'There's something about wearing the clothes that suit you at the age you are,' says Elvis Costello. 'Who would you rather be – Steven Tyler or Nick Lowe? Steven's a good character, but isn't that an awful lot of work before you go out in the morning?'

'This hasn't been done before,' says Pulitzer Prize-winning reporter David Segal. 'Rock is a young person's genre, and it was all about youth when it was born. But what do you do when the genre grows up? Do you try and stick with the young kids that defined the genre, or do you create something new? That's what Bob Dylan and Nick Lowe have done, in different ways, but they are the two men that are doing this with the most integrity and plausibility, and emerging with their artistic credibility intact.'

Segal recalls the time he gave Nick a tour of the *Washington Post* offices: 'You need ID to get past security, but Nick didn't have anything with him at all that had his name on it, but then I remembered I had a copy of *The Convincer* in my bag, with

Nick's face on the front. The guard let him in. We went up to the newsroom on the fifth floor. It was thrilling, because there were probably ten or fifteen people there who knew who he was and adored him. I remember walking up to [the *Post*'s Style section editor] Amy Argetsinger, who is a huge fan, and I introduced her to Nick. She couldn't believe it. Then I took him to my desk and a group of people huddled around and it caused a commotion, which is not an easy thing to cause in the newsroom.'

The Old Magic, released September 2011, saw Nick pull some more rabbits from the hat. It continued in a similar sonic setting to his previous albums recorded with the new firm, and in addition to the aforementioned 'Stoplight Roses' features introspective ballads with themes that might strike a chord with the more reclusive listener, such as 'I Read A Lot' and 'House For Sale'. There is also a cover of Elvis Costello's 'The Poisoned Rose' and a co-write with Geraint Watkins in 'Somebody Cares For Me', one of the more up-tempo items on the record.

In 'Checkout Time', Nick squares up to his mortality, fearful that his activities in a previous life may have compromised his chance of crossing the Jordan River and reaching heaven. 'Sensitive Man', a song that he has described as 'the Sam Cooke song that Sam Cooke didn't do', came to Nick when he was reading *Dream Boogie*, Peter Guralnick's epic biography of the late singer.

To help promote the album, Nick opened for 'alternative rock' band Wilco on the first leg of their 2011 US tour, playing venues larger than those to which he had recently been accustomed. Initially, Nick was surprised to be asked to appear with Wilco. As he later told *Houston Press* writer William Michael Smith, 'I thought it was a bold idea. Would their audience go for it? Would my audience come to a Wilco show?'

He needn't have worried; bonding with Wilco opened a number of doors for Nick, plus it was a chance for him to broaden his appeal, particularly with the younger demographic. He would also join the band onstage to perform favourites such as 'Cruel To Be Kind' or 'I Love My Label', and, together with soul star Mavis Staples, the Band's classic 'The Weight'. Staples would later cover Nick's composition 'Far Celestial Shore', produced by Wilco's Jeff Tweedy for her 2013 album *One True Vine*.

Nick also appeared at the Grammy Museum in downtown Los Angeles for a ninety-minute Q&A session before a standing-room-only crowd that included a number of music-biz people and musicians, including drummers Pete Thomas and Clem Burke. The event was reviewed in *Billboard* under the headline: NICK LOWE ENTHRALS GRAMMY MUSEUM CROWD.

A seven-song acoustic set was bookended by a discussion that included Nick's thoughts on various topics, such as his top two songwriters. 'Bob Dylan – the greatest,' came the reply, 'and Randy Newman is in there, but he's not as prolific.'

What were Nick's first thoughts about Elvis Costello's music? 'Too many words and too many chords.'

Rockpile? 'The reason I am here is because of Rockpile. I was a fan of Dave Edmunds. I went out of my way to make friends with him. It's hard to see him now. He's a lonely man.'

On ageing: 'As you get older, it's more fun to sing the blues. It cheers you up.'

Other notable Nick Lowe sightings included a return to London's Royal Festival Hall in June 2011, and a run of shows at the Leicester Square Theatre in March 2012, where he performed a version of Gene McDaniels's 1961 hit 'Tower Of Strength' and an unreleased original, 'Tokyo Bay'.

Later that month, Nick took the band to Australia and New Zealand, and then on to the USA in April. Touring-wise, 2012 was one of Nick's busiest years, and it ended with a fundraising show at his old school, Woodbridge, on 12 December, where his song introductions amused the audience. Of 'I Live On A Battlefield', which had been covered by none other than Diana Ross, he said: 'I'm afraid it really is a very poor version. But it bought me a new bathroom suite.' He also recognised some of his old school friends in the crowd and noted that they had brought along their partners. 'Don't worry, ladies,' he added. 'All of my songs are quite short, so if you don't like this one, there will be another one along in a couple of minutes.'

A few years earlier, Nick's retinue had expanded with the recruitment of tour manager John 'Kellogs' Kalinowski, a mild-mannered gent whose long experience in rock and roll touring went back to the days of the Paramounts and Procol Harum; Leon Russell and Joe Cocker's 'Mad Dogs' tour; the Kinks; Madness; and Van Morrison. It is almost impossible to think of a tour manager with a more diverse résumé, and his addition to the team relieved the pressure on Neil Brockbank, who could now concentrate on the out-front sound.

Kellogs introduced some subtle refinements to Nick's on-the-road experience, such as ensuring that a single glass of chilled white wine was waiting on a table in the wings when Nick stepped off stage. Tragically though, Kellogs died from a heart attack on 25 February 2013. At his funeral in Oxfordshire, which took place on a predictably rainy Thursday, Nick commented, 'When Kellogs was born, they broke the mould.' Armed with his acoustic guitar, he proceeded to sing to the congregation, his selection being the 1959 Cliff Richard hit, 'Travellin' Light'.

At the 2013 SXSW Music Festival in Austin, Texas, a panel of veteran musicians talked about Nick under the topic 'Lowe Common

Denominator'. Chris Stamey, from the dB's, remembered that in his band's early days, they 'stole everything they could' from Nick. Ron Sexsmith, acknowledging Lowe's personal and professional reinvention, said, 'He's done this beautiful thing, you know – created this almost whole new image.'

'He's definitely figured out a way to age gracefully a lot more than I have,' added longtime REM sideman Scott McCaughey, prompting laughs from the audience. 'I feel like I owe Nick my entire career,' said Kathy Valentine of the Go-Go's. 'If it wasn't for Nick Lowe, I don't think I would have ever had a context for how you could be a really cool bass player and songwriter, and just be such a personality.'

On the sartorial front, the *New Yorker* wrote about Nick's choice of spectacles under the heading: THE RIGHT FRAMES. Noting that Lowe had 'an uncommonly solicitous manner', writer Nick Paumgarten accompanied his quarry to a chic eyewear store in Lower Manhattan. Already wearing thick black frames, Nick wanted a new pair, telling the assistant, 'I'm hoping something is going to say, "I'm yours." I suppose I'm looking for a bit of show business, something that's a little flamboyant without being vulgar.'

When Nick found the frames of his fancy and placed an order, the assistant asked him for his email address. He confessed that he didn't have a computer, let alone email. 'What about Facebook?' she enquired. 'It's twerpy,' came the reply.

Never mind a computer, Nick didn't even carry a telephone, much to the frustration of his household. 'It drives me mad,' said Peta. 'What if there's an emergency?' He did eventually agree to carry a phone when on tour, but would either forget to keep it charged or, indeed, switch it on. He viewed the instrument like a landline that could easily be out of range, should it ring. And his first mobile device was an ancient model with big buttons 'suitable for seniors'. Despite the advances of modern technology, Nick liked to remain a Linked-Out kind of guy.

During 2012, 'Team Nick' in the USA – principally co-manager Jake Guralnick, PR Matt Hanks, and Glenn Dicker and the folks at Yep Roc Records – had suggested to Nick that he might wish to make a Christmas album. The idea was initially met with scepticism.

'It was always seen as rather tacky and sort of vulgar,' he would later tell Jim Sullivan at Boston news station WBUR. 'When the idea was suggested to me, my initial reaction was one of horror – that my record company could have thought that an artist of my stature could possibly wish to have their hands soiled by this terrible, commercial nonsense. But that feeling lasted for about a minute and ten seconds – as long as an early B-side.'

Nick and his colleagues soon got to work on the 'Seasonal Selection' and even thought they might 'festoon the studio with holly and Christmas cards to summon the energy of Christmas'. It would be an opportunity to rekindle childhood memories and sing one or two Yuletide oldies that deserved reviving.

If Nick's objective was to give the songs 'a brand-new suit of clothes', the exercise had to start with the undergarments. Roger Miller's father-and-son friendly 'Old Toy Trains' and 'Christmas Can't Be Far Away', written by Boudleaux Bryant and made popular by Eddie Arnold, were the starting points. And the recording of Roy Wood's 1973 UK hit, 'I Wish It Could Be Christmas Every Day', would involve 'knocking out every other chord to turn it into something else'.

He also put a call out to one or two musical associates, and this yielded the surreal 'Hooves On The Roof' from Ron Sexsmith, and Ry Cooder's lyric for 'A Dollar Short Of Happy', which when wedded to Nick's era-defying melody, possessed all the qualities of a standard from the golden age of song.

Quality Street – A Seasonal Selection For All The Family hit the shops in October 2013, just ahead of Thanksgiving and the holiday season. As far as new songs from the pen of Lowe were concerned, 'Christmas At The Airport' finds its narrator stranded in an air terminal that's in shutdown mode due to winter weather. The idea for the song arrived while Nick was nursing 'a terrible hangover' at Geneva Airport the morning after a late drinking session that followed a TV appearance with Mavis Staples. Nick was quick to point out that it was not Miss Staples with whom he was drinking, but members of her crew. By the time his plane landed in London, the song was more or less complete.

Another Lowe composition, and a highpoint of this turkey-free collection, is 'I Was Born In Bethlehem', in which Nick's lyrical powers are at their height. Speaking as 'the Son of God', *as yet unborn*, he reports on his family's search for an empty bed in downtown Bethlehem.

On the emotive topics of Christmas and religion, Nick recalled his childhood experiences in a memorable 2014 interview with Terry Gross for US National Public Radio's Fresh Air station.

'We had a really great time but you had to be happy with an orange and a couple of walnuts in your stocking,' he remembered. And the toys he received included 'the Dan Dare ray gun, the Davy Crockett hat, and the painting by numbers set', while the sound of Bing Crosby's songs permeated the family home.

When asked about the role that religion played, and if going to church was part of his Christmas as a child, Nick explained that his parents were not churchgoers, and in fact his father, Drain, was rather pained by the prospect of attending church, due to his RAF obligations that involved worship. 'I have a rather complicated relation to it,' he said. 'I have all the equipment to make me rather devout, I would almost say. I'm very interested in different religions and I know quite a lot about it. I love gospel music and I love going to churches, but one drawback is that I don't actually believe in God. It is quite a handicap.'

When it comes to song lyrics, there are countless examples of Nick Lowe's on-the-money rhyming couplets, a number of which appear in this book, by permission of the publishers. I personally witnessed his quick wit and lyrical skill at Eden Studios back in 1979 when I popped in to pitch some songs to Dave Edmunds, with whom I had previously co-written 'A1 On The Jukebox' (after Nick had very kindly delivered my crude cassette sketch to Dave). He liked my title, 'Monster-in-Law', but although I had an opening line, I was without the next bit. I cautiously recited my effort in front of Dave and Nick: 'I walked to the altar with the best intent.' With hardly a break in the metre I was suggesting, Nick immediately responded: 'In a three-piece suit with a 12-inch vent.'

Now, I don't know if he rhymed 'intent' with 'vent' and worked backwards, as one often does, or started by associating 'altar' with 'three-piece suit' and worked forwards, but it took him a mere nanosecond to deliver the line. This ancient memory prompted a discussion about songwriting, wherein Nick recalled his early days with Kippington Lodge, in which Brinsley was initially 'the star of the group' and the main writer.

'By the time we became "Brinsley Schwarz", Brinsley wasn't writing at all, and Bob could never finish anything. The hardest thing with songwriting is finishing it, so you can say, "Here's one, with a beginning, a middle and an end." Everyone has big ideas, but "finishing it" is what sorts the men out from the boys. There was no rigorous quality control in the group. It was more a case of, "Has anybody finished one?"'

Today, Nick says he has two theories about songwriting, the first being that he might be waiting for inspiration and someone visits, unannounced. He doesn't know the gender or the background of the visitor, only that he or she is a really good songwriter, far better than he is, and all they want is for him to perform one of their songs. They show him a couple of their efforts and they are really good. Then the person disappears. He doesn't know where they've gone, or if and when they'll ever come back, but if there's no sign of them after a month or two, he will know their style of songwriting so well that he can do a pretty fair approximation of it – close, but not quite as good. All his best stuff is therefore 'written by someone else'.

His second, more recent theory is that there's a radio in the flat next door, permanently tuned to a cool music station. It's left on day and night and he can hear it coming through the wall, although the sound is muffled and indistinct. One day the station will programme a great new song which he can hear through the wall clearly enough, but it's over before he can learn any of it. Knowing they might play it again at any time, he keeps a notepad ready so that with each play he can capture a little more of it, until he's got it all.

'It's more of a listening process than anything,' he says. 'And when I find I'm looking at a song that I feel I've had nothing to do with, a cover effectively, it's finished.'

Some of Nick's earlier songs, and indeed those of many writers, were conceived under the influence of mind-altering substances, or 'drugs' for short. These days, of course, nothing much stronger than coffee or the occasional glass of wine serves to jolly up the process, but I was curious to hear from Nick what he thought might be the appeal of intoxicants to artists, musicians and writers.

'I suppose, on reflection, the stuff I was mostly interested in back then were stimulants that helped me to overcome my shyness and get in touch with what I thought was a bottomless well of creative brilliance, which up until then I'd been denied access to. Most people know nowadays that if you ingest enough vodka and cocaine you become convinced that every room is lit by your presence, hangs on every word, and is fascinated by your wit and charm when the truth is, you're actually a sweating, crashing bore who can't shut his cakehole.

'It took far too much time and money I could ill afford for the penny to drop but it eventually did around the mid-1980s when I came to my senses and willed myself off everything, except tobacco, for two or three years. After that, I purposely re-established a relationship with alcohol, occasionally passionate but mainly business-like and platonic, which is still just about on today but could well follow smoking, which I quit when Roy turned up.

'I think in those early days I also found myself confronting my creativity and having it surprise me. I was surprised by stuff that I didn't think I knew about, or ideas that I didn't think anybody else had had before. That was exciting. Suddenly the decks are clear and the curtains go back. Lights, Camera, Action! The audience is in the house and your creativity is onstage. You can see something clearly. You're pulling it down straight from the source. But after a while you realise that it's an illusion. Well, it generally works once. Then you think it will work next time, so you keep on doing it, trying to chase it. You're having a pretty good time along the way, but ultimately, if you're lucky enough to survive, you realise that it is a chimera, and a fraud, and life is a lot more difficult than that.

'All those things that people say about cocaine are true. Like the first time you get high and try and make a record and it's fantastic. Everything works. It's the wonder drug. Let's do it again and make another fantastic record. And it never happens again, never. You can chase your tail and get close, but you can't finish it. If you just took a drug to turn you into Paul McCartney – AND John Lennon – then of course everybody would take it. And nobody would think that "Strawberry Fields Forever" was much cop.

'As the song goes, take it from a fool who knows.'

Throughout this story, much has been made of Nick's lyrical skills, his snappy couplets, his amusing turns of phrase and compelling song titles, but his tunes and musicianship should not be overlooked. He has, of course, confessed to borrowing one or two melodic hooks, either consciously or subconsciously, and some examples have been cited, but there is also much originality in his work.

Martin Belmont, who has played guitar on many of Nick's recordings and tours, tells us: 'He has a penchant for rhythmic oddities. One of the best examples is "I Love The Sound Of Breaking Glass", not for its chords, but because of its rhythmic construction and the way it ended up sounding, with Bob Andrews's insane piano. It's a pretty unconventional song, with irregular bar lengths, almost up there with some of John Lennon's famous short bars. It's not something Nick does to be clever. It's something that sounds good.

'Then there are other songs where it's all very straightforward, such as "Ragin' Eyes" or "Rose Of England" – what a fantastic song that is! The way he uses the chords to harmonise the melody is very conventional, but it works. The chords, or the harmony you put with a melody, can make or break it. I think the song has just three or four major chords and one minor chord, and they reinforce the melody, and the lyrics, and give the song a harmonic base to sit on. Nick's choice of chords is always great. I also like listening to his acoustic guitar playing because he uses his thumb, not a pick. It's an intimate sound and it goes with the kind of music he's making these days.'

Conversely, for electric bass, Nick uses a thumb pick, rather than his fingers. This style may have originated during his childhood years, learning to play ukulele banjo with a plectrum. Therefore, the transition to playing acoustic guitar without a pick and strumming with his hand is interesting.

'It's very much an American style of playing,' says folk-inclined singer-songwriter Reg Meuross. 'It's a trait of people who tend to know a lot of chords. They're not necessarily going for the best guitar sound, they're really going for the feel. That's always been Nick's thing.'

Greg Townson, guitarist with Los Straitjackets, says: 'When I heard Nick solo for the first time, even though the chords were very simple, something about his style threw me. I thought maybe he was in an open tuning or had dropped his low E string down to D. I asked him backstage if that was the case and he kind of laughed and said, "No, it's standard tuning." Later, I realised it was the voicings he used. Also, he uses his fingers, and that gives it a rich sound. He puts nail polish on, so that he can have a percussive attack if he wants, without the risk of breaking a nail. He doesn't like fancy chords, in general, but once in a while, if the song calls for it, he'll use a chord that goes beyond a basic triad. He never solos or plays too many melodies on the guitar. It's great because it keeps everything focused on the song and his voice. He's got a fantastic feel on the instrument, and "feel" is everything for Nick. I've thought a lot about his guitar playing, and it's very unique. Maybe some of it came from Johnny Cash, who only used the thumb on his strumming hand and kept it very basic.'

As regards 'chords', and guitar technique in general, this has been discussed by subscribers to the 'Nick Lowe Fan Club' group on Facebook; one 'Percy Thrillington' enquired about Nick's playing on 'Christmas At The Airport', and 'Joe Silver' replied (non-guitarists, look away now): 'If you're talking about, say, what he's doing at 0:26, it's an A minor chord. He's playing the A, at the fifth fret of the low E string with his thumb; E, at the seventh fret of the A-string with his third finger; A, at the seventh fret of the D-string with his pinkie; and barring the top three notes at the fifth fret with his index finger. Hope this helps!'

To which 'Thrillington' responded: 'half an octopus, half a man'.

There was a time, say around 2000, when Nick could exist quite comfortably on his residual royalties and the occasional tour, but sales of records had been in free-fall for years and the big corporations no longer shipped tonnes of plastic around the globe. Even *The Bodyguard* soundtrack had peaked.

'There isn't really a record business anymore,' reflected Nick back in 2012. 'But I'm one of the lucky ones because I've had a few of my songs covered, and people show up to see me do my shtick. For me, it's not as essential as it once was to keep the new records coming out.'

It is true that an evergreen song can continue to reward its writer with royalties long after the record has dropped off the chart. In Nick's case, there are two songs in particular, although their longevity was slightly underestimated back in 1982, when Martha Hume interviewed Nick, and asked, 'Which of your songs do you think they'll still be playing in twenty or thirty years' time?'

'My hit,' answered Nick, referring to 'Cruel To Be Kind'.

'I think they might play, perhaps, "(What's So Funny 'bout) Peace, Love And Understanding",' responded the prophetic Hume, citing a work that would one day be listed as one of *Rolling Stone*'s '500 greatest songs of all time'.

The music business had certainly changed since that interview, as had Nick's personal circumstances. Now, more than ever, he felt the impetus to work live. With the exception of London, ticket sales in the UK had been disappointing, and this resulted in more overseas appearances, primarily in the USA, and increasingly as a solo act.

Promoters are often prepared to offer an artist a similar fee for a solo show as they would if he or she were to turn up with a band. The ticket price would be more or less the same; if 'Nick Lowe' can command, say, $40 a seat, the price is not likely to increase that much simply because there are half-a-dozen musicians onstage. However much the singer would love to bring a band and feel the power of drums and amplification in the small of his back, the show would probably gross the same amount of cash. Touring solo, with an entertaining show, can provide an artist with a living, year in, year out.

Nick enjoys either approach; as he commented in 2012: 'There's something very seductive about playing live with a big gang of people, although some tunes work better acoustically. "Heart", which has a kind of reggae beat, is one of them, and "What's Shakin' On The Hill" is another. "What Lack Of Love Has Done" works better with the band, as does "Ragin' Eyes", although I do that one acoustically too. If you do those straight-ahead rock and roll songs and you don't mash it too much, you can score points. I'm looking forward to playing this acoustic guitar festival in Sweden, then America in about a month's time. It's a fairly long tour, all solo.'

Nick loved performing, but what he found frustrating was that although his shows could sell out in any number of cities in America where he might play multiple nights at a prestigious venue, it was often a different story nearer to home. His lengthy Euro jaunt of spring 2014, while profitable, found him playing 'rock on the rates' shows in obscure Dutch hamlets to tiny audiences, and even though his generous fee was guaranteed, the experience was further dampened by an unsympathetic support act that the local promoter had slotted in. In Nick's mind, there didn't seem to be much creative thought being put into the dates.

'I have to defend Jake Riviera on this,' says Jake Guralnick. 'Nick was in a financial position where he had to generate quite a bit of money because he'd set up his life in a certain way. And there's money in going to all these small markets in Belgium and Germany and Holland. Jake was doing what needed to be done for Nick, but this is maybe something that Nick misses. He goes out and has a tough time on the road and then it's like he's not remembering why four months earlier he agreed to it.'

Either way, Nick had a sneaking feeling that there might be a wider audience he could reach, even though he knew he would never go totally mainstream because, as he once mentioned in an interview, 'I don't have that Cher gene.'

His 2011 US tour opening for Wilco had been the eye-opener; the audiences were a little more youthful than he had been used to, and his act had gone down rather well. Also, there was a higher percentage of girls in attendance. As he told writer Mark Norris from *Buffalo Spree* magazine: 'A large number of younger people heard what I'm doing and realised it wasn't going to be some sort of history lesson, that it was going to be an entertaining evening. There was a seismic shift and suddenly they were all getting it.'

What, then, were Nick's chances of attracting a slightly younger crowd to his own shows? Maybe not on the same scale as Leonard Cohen, whose appeal began to cross the generational divide during the latter years of his life, but the same principle might apply in smaller venues. And by 'a younger crowd', Nick didn't mean teenagers; he meant people in their thirties and forties. Jake Riviera, who had now been managing Nick's career for thirty-nine years, did not share this aspiration.

'Jake latched on to something I said – my mantra about trying to attract a younger audience. It was working in America. They get it. People like Johnny Cash had three or four generations of fans. The younger crowd want to be there, but Jake wouldn't have it. I think he wilfully misunderstood it. He thought that the Christmas record was of no interest, but I thought it was good. I got frustrated, coming back from the USA where Jake Guralnick, and Glenn Dicker at Yep Roc Records, and my press officer, Matt Hanks, all help out. They get me to younger audiences, which is what I want. It's my fault too, because I hadn't worked on it, but Jake Riviera wouldn't accept there was a more youthful audience out there.'

Riviera no longer possessed the fire of yore, and after years of putting himself on the line and risking life and limb on behalf of his artists, was probably contemplating retirement. But Nick had not been burning with ambition either. Both men had plenty of distractions and, in Nick's case, a new young family.

One former associate with a fairly large axe to grind was of the opinion that 'Nick and Jake deserved each other'. In accepting much of the blame for his predicament, Nick acknowledged that there had been long periods in the previous twenty years when he had effectively ignored his fan base. The lengthy gaps between album releases were, he explained, down to the extremely slow songwriting process and, as the cliché goes, waiting for the muse to strike. Or, as Nick puts it, 'waiting for the bloke to knock'. And even when enough new material had been assembled, the delicate matter of capturing *the* performance on record added to the delays. But the passing of time no longer mattered, because Nick didn't have a major recording contract that demanded regular output, unlike in the mid-1980s when such pressure was blamed for some relatively lacklustre albums.

'It's not as if I have a huge audience waiting for the new one,'

Nick would say, modestly, but he *knew* he was good, and any time it looked as if his writing might be all washed up, he would always deliver the killer song – as had been the case with 'You Inspire Me', 'Lately I've Let Things Slide' and 'I Trained Her To Love Me' – and of course he did want his songs to see the light of day.

But the relationship with Riviera had been withering on the vine for a while.

'I think he had been getting fed up with me. I didn't have the heart to sack him, even though we were at the end of the road. I was rather hoping he was going to chuck it in. When we met, we used to get on each other's nerves. We never socialised any more, although he used to call me every day with updates. But often it was something I'd already heard from Jake Guralnick three days earlier.'

Nick had much to thank Jake for, not least of all the 1987 ear-bashing that resulted in him hooking up with Ry Cooder and Jim Keltner, which he acknowledges as the epiphany that sparked the second, crucial phase of his musical career. But although he knew deep down that Jake always had his back, the deed had to be done.

He returned from Europe on 1 May 2014, and while preparing for a three-night stand at London's Union Chapel the following week, did the unthinkable and terminated his business relationship with Riviera. After their four-decade ride, Jake no longer had to face the challenge that his client was putting in front of him.

CHAPTER 17

The Jesus of Cool

If Nick's personal ambition on the 1977 Stiff Records tour had been to front a band that 'looked strange', he certainly struck gold when he hooked up with Yep Roc Records label-mates, Los Straitjackets. With all due respect to the band's superior musicianship, their appearance is quite alarming. Nick of course played it deadpan, as if appearing onstage with four musicians wearing Mexican wrestling masks was nothing to get too worked-up about.

The 'Quality Holiday Revue' of December 2014, which featured a mix of Nick singing solo, Los Straitjackets playing some of their surf instrumentals and Nick being accompanied by the band, was an immediate success and set a pattern for further 'holiday revues' in the years to come.

Former Faces star and Rolling Stones sideman, Ian McLagan, was to have been the opening act on the bill, but he sadly died from a stroke, age sixty-nine, on the day that the tour opened in Minneapolis. There was no question of cancelling; the show had to go on, as no doubt McLagan would have wanted, and each night Nick paid tribute to his departed friend.

At Cleveland's Beachland Ballroom, he told the audience, 'Mac was an amazing guy, the archetypal Mod, and what we used to call "a groover", a kind of archaic expression nowadays, but that's what he was. He had this incredible gift of being able to spread goodwill around and cheer people up. The way I see it is, if we can't have him in person, we'll try our best to have him in spirit.'

'It was the first time we saw the leadership side of Nick,' says Straitjackets' guitarist Greg Townson. 'He tapped into the loss we were all feeling and helped bring us together. It was quite a dramatic way to start working together and it created a bond that wouldn't have been present at the start of our musical relationship otherwise.

'When we first rehearsed, the first thing he told us was not to listen to the old records. He wasn't interested in recreating the past. He wanted us to bring our own band sound to the arrangements and do something fresh. In other words, he wanted us to be ourselves with the songs. The great thing about Nick is that after every show, right after we came off stage, he'd give us some specific feedback on a couple of things we could try to do differently on the next show. It's always coupled with great enthusiasm for what went right that night. He kept saying it was getting good when he felt like he was part of our band.'

On 8 May 2015, Bobby Irwin died of cancer, aged sixty-two. He had been suffering for some time and was forced to intermittently vacate his drum chair with Geraint Watkins & the Mosquitos during their weekly residency at Tooting's Wheatsheaf public house. Bobby's death was not only tragic in itself, but also a major blow to the new firm, both musically and as simply good company.

'Bobby was extremely funny,' says Nick. 'He could make me howl with just a look and I would laugh so hard my face would hurt. He was wonderful to travel around the world with.'

At Bobby's funeral at St Stephen's Church, Twickenham, Nick took the lectern to deliver a eulogy for his fallen drummer and veteran musical partner. A few minutes beforehand, Bobby's brother Chris, who would sadly die within days of the funeral, had recalled their childhood moments and revealed that, as a sixteen-year-old school leaver, Bobby was employed by the Beatles at Apple as an office assistant to their publicist, Derek Taylor. This nugget came as a surprise, even to Bobby's closest friends in attendance. Then, Geraint performed a comforting 'It's A Wonderful Life' seated at the piano, with Martin Winning on sax.

Nick's own public address to the three-hundred-strong congregation was nothing short of high drama. Tears fell faster than the hailstone rain in the churchyard, which was punctuated by bursts of spring sunshine, just as Nick's emotionally charged speech was dotted with humorous asides that brought hearty laughter.

'I looked up the word "eulogy" before writing these notes,' said Nick. 'It is supposed to be brief. Well, I first met Bob in 1976 when I was recording at Pathway Studios in Stoke Newington.'

Within moments of recalling this encounter, Nick broke down in tears, unable to continue for a full minute. Time became suspended as mourners allowed him a moment to summon composure. Eventually, he mopped his eyes with a checked handkerchief and continued.

'I don't know how I'm going to get through this,' he said, thumbing his notes and looking as if he was about to return to his seat. The Reverend Jez Barnes stepped forward in support, his holy intervention persuading Nick to continue describing his unique musical partnership with Bobby.

Then Nick slammed the congregation with the nitty-gritty: 'Bob was larger than life. When he told a joke, it was as if he saw himself as a member of his own audience.' More laughter. And then, by emotional contrast: 'I don't know how I'm going to carry on without him.' Nick's son Roy popped up from the pews to deliver a fresh handkerchief.

'We spent many years touring the world as young musicians. There are of course stories that I couldn't possibly repeat in church, but I'm quite happy to give anyone a personal consultation later, if you wish.' More laughter amid the tears. Nick had done Bob proud, and returned to his seat to huge and sustained applause.

Recording engineer Neil Brockbank then read from Corinthians, and 'He Who Would Valiant Be' was sung by all. Following the service, many of us repaired to a nearby hostelry to toast Bobby's memory and exchange stories about the great man.

Within a few months it became clear that the loss of Bobby Irwin had effectively drawn a line under the way of working that Nick had enjoyed over the past two decades. He was not necessarily down, but had little interest in serving up 'another new dish' when his recent albums had enjoyed only modest sales. There were, of course, artistic milestones, but the public's appetite had to be weighed up against the cost of making those kinds of records.

'In a way, I think I'm done with that. I can't really see the point of it, and I don't have the drive to want to tell people something in a way that I think they haven't heard before. Also, I've done about six [albums] in a row now. They always get four- and five-star reviews – I can't remember the last time I got less than four or five stars – but stars in magazines don't sell the things. And even though my records eventually go into the black, they are so expensive to make. When we occasionally went into RAK, we really had to have our shit together to get our money's worth. But it was very relaxed as well. If we got fed up, we might say, "OK, I'm going home now," whereas we really should have ploughed on. I guess a new record would eventually make its money back over a number of years, but Bob's demise has finally brought the curtain down on an era we'd all got thoroughly used to.'

Although not always credited as such, Bobby Irwin was very much a co-producer alongside Nick and Neil Brockbank. His mere presence in the studio would have affected the outcome of any session, from his barrage of comic remarks that kept the mood up – 'I refuse to play the red-nosed buffoon any longer' – to the occasional sideways glance that might have prevented a lacklustre performance from making the cut.

Brockbank sums it up: 'When Bob died, I said to Nick, "I think we were making those records to please Bob," and Nick said, "I never thought of it that way but I think you're right." Bob was the arbiter. Nick and I would produce the records, but Bob was *producing us*. Even now, when I'm in the studio, I'm saying to myself, "What would Bob think?"'

It is impossible to overestimate Irwin's contribution to Nick's recorded output from *The Impossible Bird* through *Quality Street*. He was the magician's assistant, and a master of understated rhythmic accompaniment, as supplied on a minimal drum set. It didn't matter if the bass drum was a different colour to the tom-tom, or if the snare drum stand was a good fit. As long as his drums and cymbals were in approximately the right position, Bobby would hit them and make the whole thing swing. And 'swing' was what he was good at, in the studio, on the concert platform, or in a social situation *après* gig, but now the indispensable Irwin had checked out.

Since his 2014 hook-up with Los Straitjackets, Nick toured with the group annually, presenting the 'Quality Holiday Revue'.

Group members observed his on-the-road discipline for keeping himself in shape and getting rest, so that his voice was in good form.

'He likes to arrive shortly before the performance,' says Greg Townson. 'When he gets there, he's relaxed and we're often having a casual conversation right before we hit the stage. Somehow, he always manages a few humorous anecdotes related to wherever we're playing. He's a gracious bandleader and acknowledges all of us during the show.'

In 2016, Los Straitjackets recorded an album entitled *What's So Funny About Peace, Love And Los Straitjackets* on which they interpreted, instrumentally, thirteen Nick Lowe songs. Production was handled by Neil Brockbank. Townson recalls Nick's reaction to his group's demos for the record: 'He asked us not to be too strict with the melody to the songs, just the opposite of what you'd think a songwriter would say. Again – "don't be so reverential". He and Neil added a little background vocal part that Nick did in London later, as well as his son Roy's first appearance on record! He did a cymbal overdub. Of course, Nick also participated in the *Jesus Of Cool* parody cover.'

Another enjoyable diversion for Nick was performing with close friends, Paul Carrack and Andy Fairweather Low, in 'Lowe–Carrack–Low', to give the trio its informal yet succinct moniker. They made one of their earliest appearances in London at a 2015 benefit show for Henry McCullough, former guitarist with the Grease Band and Wings. McCullough had recently suffered a massive heart attack and was wheelchair-bound. The charitable event at Putney's Half Moon was organised by Dave Robinson, and also included performances by Graham Parker and Suggs from Madness. A fundraising auction took place, in which a 45-rpm-disc-shaped cheddar cheese – bearing 'So It Goes' c/w 'Heart Of

The City' record labels, and supplied by Dorset cheesemonger, Justin Tunstall – went for £600. Nick then took the stage to deliver a chilling version of McCullough's 'Failed Christian'. Paul and Andy soon joined in for an acoustic and harmony strum-along. Classic songs included Ray Charles's 'Crying Time', Bobby Darin's 'Things' and Johnny Cash's 'I Don't Hurt Anymore'.

It was easy to spot the trio's potential as a live attraction on the UK theatre circuit, and possibly on disc. Some recording had already been done at Carrack's home studio, but Nick felt the results were disappointing and were therefore shelved. Nick's agent, Paul Charles, suggested that they play some British festivals with a view to touring the following year.

'There is some motivation in "The Three Brexiteers", as I call them,' says Neil Brockbank, whose light-hearted nickname does not necessarily reflect his three colleagues' views on the UK's relationship with the European Union. 'What Nick is looking for there is a bit of Carrack's penetration of the English provincial market, and what Carrack's looking for is a bit more credibility. And "Fair" is along for the ride. He's great, and visibly thrilled to be on the planks with Nick and Paul. It's a very good show. Nick's got, what, four songs that are recognisable? Carrack's got six! Andy's got maybe three? "Bend Me Shape Me"; "If Paradise Was Half As Nice"; "Wide Eyed And Legless". Put it all together and it's hit after hit, then a couple of covers, then more hits. When Andy does "Paradise" the whole theatre is singing along. It's a very valuable property, and serious box office.'

Like many performers, Nick needs to get into character prior to a run of live shows, and it can take him several weeks to turn into 'Nick Lowe – the bloke who goes on tour'. During this period, he becomes absent-minded, balancing his gradual transformation with the everyday chores that require his attention and interacting with his family, or taking Larry the Whippet for his walk. It drives his nearest and dearest 'round the twist'. Occasionally he hears Peta say, 'You've already gone, haven't you?' Young Roy has even been known to enquire, 'Has Dad got the coat on yet?' – 'the coat' being shorthand for his father's mind having already left home.

The process is essential in order to become the person who can sail through flight delays, tolerate inclement weather and adapt to sudden schedule changes, in other words, to get from A to B and undertake C 'without touching the sides'. He also has to be able to deal with 'mad fans' who insist on a selfie in circumstances that require him – no matter how sincere he clearly is – to maintain a shit-eating grin until the shutter is pressed. And most importantly, to be able to save himself for that all-important live performance and be the guy that says, 'Hello Cleveland!'

Some of the time he is actually two different people because, when he returns home from a tour, the reverse process is required. It's a challenge to purchase the correct items at the supermarket when his head is still in performance mode. Or pick his son up from his football match without leaving the muddy boots behind, when, for the last three weeks, he has been the centre of attention in the eyes and hearts of adoring fans in the heady world of showbusiness. He knows he's not a household name, but after spending all that time in America with his 'small but perfectly formed audience', who pat him on the back and tell him how marvellous he is, he could be forgiven for thinking he's some kind of star.

After a few weeks back home, he will have shaken off 'the coat' to hopefully become 'Dennis', the man who can drive to the town hall and pay his council tax, because 'Nick Lowe can't do that shit'. But he has to keep 'Nick Lowe' on the back burner, ready for the next slice of action. Then it's time to shed a couple of kilos, update his wardrobe and review his set lists. 'What?!' he might say to himself. 'I've got to play that old song again?' Then he thinks, 'Man, that's a pretty good tune,' and finds himself singing it slightly differently, so that it doesn't sit there like 'a sludgy old piece of cake you've got to serve up to your people every night'.

'It's not the money,' he says. 'I have got to do it. Sometimes it confuses my family, people that have loved me and I have loved in return. They are sometimes confused and hurt by the fact that they seem to come second. It's a terrible thing to say, but it's the truth. Obviously, if there was a fire I wouldn't save my guitars, but there's something in me, I can't help it. But I have to be two people in order for me to be a responsible husband and parent, and less selfish than I really need to be. We've all seen people in the music business who treat their families like shit, and I didn't want to be one of those people, but I really can understand why that happens. You have to discipline yourself so that you don't cause mayhem in other people's lives, especially people who love you and realise that you are sort of elsewhere for quite a lot of the time.'

As much as he's a musician, he's also a thinker and confesses to sometimes 'over-thinking', especially when a call comes in requesting his participation in, for example, some music documentary or media event. He'll get a call from a guy who wants him to do something. He's not sure. Then he thinks it could be cool, but he'll remember having dealings with the guy before. He weighs up the pros and cons and always thinks first about what could go wrong. He looks at the downside, but might run out of reasons not to do it, and finds himself saying, 'On the other hand . . .'

Indecision also extends to releasing new records. There are always new songs in development, and one or two of them may meet his self-imposed high standards, but then of course they have to be recorded properly, and so further indecision sets in. As he told Iowa City writer and illustrator Cheryl Graham, when discussing the fact that in 2016, anybody with a laptop computer can make a record, 'Yeah, they can knock one out, and it'll be pretty good, but "pretty good" is the new shite.'

Disinclined to make a new long-playing record, he was pleased to be presented with studio alternatives and invitations to collaborate on songs in Nashville, although the first time he returned there after a long absence, he confessed to being terrified by the prospect of working with the pros. But suddenly his old skills returned, and he found himself thinking, 'Maybe I should do some producing again, because I'm pretty good at this, knowing how somebody else's music should go, and people seem to listen to me.'

Suddenly, the fact that he was in his mid-sixties didn't seem to matter. His new publishers, Big Deal Music, were proactive and, with offices in New York, Los Angeles and Nashville, ideally placed to hook him up with other writers. Big Deal's senior vice president in Nashville, Dale Bobo, had long been a fan, and stops just short of calling Nick 'a musical hero'.

Bobo made it his mission to seek out people for Nick to work with. Aiming high, the first person he approached was Bob DiPiero, a Nashville Songwriters Hall of Fame inductee and writer of fifteen number one country hits, with songs recorded by artists such as Reba McEntire, Vince Gill and Tim McGraw.

'DiPiero got back to me within moments,' says Bobo. 'He told me he'd always been a Nick fan and it made him happy that he was going to get to write with him.'

Having set up the meeting with DiPiero, and sessions with other top writers such as Tommy Lee James, Al Anderson and, via his New York colleagues, Dan Auerbach from the Black Keys, Bobo would pick Nick up from his hotel in the morning and drive him to the place of work. This was usually a home studio, often in a little house with a garden, just outside of town, or at an office with recording equipment and an interesting selection of guitars. Work commenced mid-morning and by mid-afternoon, a song, maybe two songs, were written.

It is not uncommon in Nashville for a professional studio demo to be recorded immediately after a writing session, as was the case with Al Anderson's 'Good Girls Love Bad Boys', co-written with Nick. At Legends Studio, for example, a new song can be recorded for a fixed fee, with house musicians who will learn it in a matter of minutes, give it a quick run-through and, when the engineer hits the record button, usually capture it on the first take. 'Those session guys will do you a shit-hot demo in about, er, thirty minutes,' confirms Nick.

Dale Bobo appreciated that Nick's professional reputation would often precede him in Nashville: 'When we got to the writing room, you could see these people were excited to be there with Nick. People here are by and large up on their music history and they know who he is.'

Long-term Nashville songwriter Bill Lloyd concurs. With his own musical credentials straddling modern country and power pop, Lloyd represents the local ear-to-the-ground musician who grew up listening to the music coming out of Britain in the late 1970s.

'My friends and I started reading about Nick Lowe in the cool rock magazines of the day,' recalls Lloyd. 'We saw his name attached as producer to Elvis Costello. It was love at first listen. Nick's music was a blueprint for the thing I was going for on the Foster & Lloyd records, and his hilarious twisted lyrical side was a big plus.'

Of course, it does help to have worked and hung out with some familiar names, such as Elvis Costello and Chrissie Hynde.

As Elvis Presley's original drummer, D. J. Fontana, once quipped, 'It's not what you know, it's who you knew.' And there is no doubt that Nick's former marriage to Carlene Carter – and its direct connection to the Johnny Cash and June Carter saga – rings bells in Music City. Those local songwriters who had not followed the story, but suddenly learnt about it from a chance remark, can get quite excited.

'What's that? You knew Johnny Cash?!'

'Many of the songwriters I've met in Nashers work in duos,' says Nick. 'I'm the third element that comes into the room, and of course everyone's looking for the fourth element, which is the song. And nobody I've met with has been able to tell me what it is I'm supposed to bring to the party. Do you bring a title? A verse? Some people will tell you, "Don't bring anything."

'I might have come to town with a few half-finished songs in my saddlebag, not to punt them, but to have something to produce if I'm asked, "What you got?" On one occasion, I had a pop thing that I thought was a pretty good idea, maybe a little too mature for Justin Bieber, but his kind of feel, with an insistent melody. But I'd painted myself into a corner with it. The duo I was writing with liked it and, boy, did they go to work on it. "OK right, we're gonna do this, we're gonna do that." Their necklaces and bracelets were shimmering, and I'm looking at this brilliant thing that's quickly taking shape, and I'm thinking, "Yes! This is what I've come to Nashville for."'

On the subject of songs taking shape, Jake Guralnick recalls, 'I was in LaGuardia Airport with Nick. We were having a coffee and he took out a notebook and started writing stuff down – it was the lyrics to "Tokyo Bay". I'd never been there when he was writing. Usually I imagine him at his place in Brentford, thinking about a new song. He talks about going into a trance, and I was witnessing it. It was like he went somewhere, wrote some stuff down, then he was back with me and said, "What time is our flight?"'

'He's so brilliant,' says Chris Difford. 'I remember going to his house in Brentford once. We had a few beers and I asked him if he was writing. He said he had one or two ideas on the boil, and I immediately knew that he was slowly brewing a potion of clever and charming lyrics that would document his love life and his way in the world. Each Lowe album is another log on the fire that glows brightly with wonderful images and brings warmth to my life. He is a storyteller from the deep within. "Stoplight Roses" – only he could see that and put pen to paper; "Hope For Us All"; "What's Shakin' On The Hill"; so many great songs that chill me. I wish that I would take my time and see the world from his armchair, with his eagle eye of wry humour.'

Carlene Carter: 'He is a great songsmith. He taught me so much about writing songs. Not actual teaching, but being around him and with him, I learnt a lot about the sound of words, the percussive quality of syllables. As far as John [Cash] was concerned, Nick was a good writer, but Nick was very conscious of not wanting to appear to be pushing his songs to John. He knew "The Beast In Me" was right up John's street, but that song took a long time to finish.'

Chrissie Hynde: 'How do I rate Nick as a songwriter? He's one of the greats, and I'd put him up there with the rest of the great songwriters. There aren't that many . . . Neil Young, Bob Dylan, Lucinda Williams, Ray Davies . . . I'd put Nick up there with them. I hold him in the very highest regard.'

Ry Cooder: 'Nick and myself – we're of a generation lucky to come up in the happy golden age of pop songs: intro, verse, chorus, half an instrumental verse, chorus, and out; things we took to be an integral part of life, but gone now for the most part.

Three chords and the truth, as per Harlan Howard [who wrote country hits including 'Heartaches By The Number', 'I Fall To Pieces' and 'Pick Me Up On Your Way Down']. Back in our days from youth, the songwriter was the key man – or woman, let's be fair. Can you imagine the Everly Brothers without Boudleaux and Felice Bryant? Songwriters were good storytellers and good poetry men. I rate Nick as a real songwriter, and that's the reason he is a good musician and fun to work with. He plays the song, not just the notes, and his bass-player timing is the best. "Time is all you got," in the immortal words of the late, great Milt Holland. Nick pulled my coat to some very good white songwriters, an area in which I was deficient. We had some good talks about Johnny Cash, Carl Smith, and so many others.'

Huey Lewis: 'I hope he lives and writes songs for ever. He's a treasure, and a real authentic songwriter. When Huey Lewis & the News played Shepherd's Bush Empire a few years ago, I asked Nick if he wanted to sit in. He said, "I don't rock any more." But Nick can do whatever he wants. He's a genius. He's brilliant and he's funny, wonderful, generous and a sweet guy. They don't come any better than Nick Lowe, period. Britain ought to be proud of him.'

To acknowledge and summarise Nick's musical abilities, he is a highly accomplished bass player; his rhythmic aptitude on acoustic guitar would propel any rock and roll band; he can sing lead and layer harmonies; and is a natural and gifted writer of both lyric and melody. It's a skillset that awards him at least 'triple threat' status as an artist, and this is before one takes into account his ability to entertain.

So why isn't Nick Lowe more well-known? Why does he remain a cult-throb, singing only to the choir and maybe a couple of stragglers in the churchyard? Why haven't any of his recordings this century scraped even the lower reaches of an album chart? Why, in the UK, has he been unable to fill modest venues in the provinces?

True, his last smash hit was back in 1979, although the mention of 'Cruel To Be Kind' usually rings a bell or two. His more recent music, however, is virtually unknown beyond a loyal band of followers, despite its undeniable crossover appeal. His fans are mystified, yet one senses an air of protectiveness surrounding their favourite music maker. Do they really want him to be discovered by the masses? What if his face did appear in the media every day? Would the hoi polloi even *get* 'I Trained Her To Love Me'? Is he the secret his fans would rather not share?

Perhaps the secret itself doesn't want to be shared; Lowe maintains his outsider status to the point of immaculacy, and maybe that suits him. For answers, we must look to the man himself. He would sure like to sell more records but only up to a point, and not if it means prostituting himself on chat shows and social media. The royalties would come in handy, but not if there was too much glad-handing involved. As his former manager Dave Robinson told writer Michael Bonner for an article in *Uncut*: 'He's the perfect example of an Aries. Aries like power without responsibility, they're very creative. I call it panicking in the face of success. But I think he realised when fame might come it could fall on him to do a large amount of work. He didn't want to do that. Nick would always slope off before success.'

But it goes deeper than being workshy or having an aversion to publicity. Maybe if we go back to the aftermath of the British Empire, a bygone era during which segments of the working middle classes gained access to the English public school system, we might find some pointers. This is where we may come into contact with 'toffs', and experience the affectations of the privileged idle rich. To these guys, everything was 'a bit of a fag' [too much like hard work]. It was satirised in the Billy Bunter stories and portrayed in TV's *Dad's Army*, specifically the character 'Sergeant Wilson', as played by John Le Mesurier, and later Bill Nighy. Wilson, nonchalant and slightly distant, behaved as if he was above life's day-to-day mundanities. It's a trait that is often accompanied by useful qualities such as stoicism in the face of adversity and quick-wittedness in a tricky situation, but it also manifests itself in demonstrable modesty and an abhorrence of the unseemly, especially aggressive self-promotion.

Of course, Nick knew how to *produce* hits, as exemplified by his work with the Pretenders and Elvis Costello, but writing hits he found less straightforward. To help solve the riddle I spoke with the writer Peter Silverton, who has a keen insight into what makes Nick tick. He first saw him perform with Kippington Lodge at a church hall in Wadhurst, East Sussex, and often interviewed him for *Sounds* during the Stiff Records and Rockpile era. Silverton has been a true fan of the Lowe oeuvre ever since, and helped to identify a number of obstacles that have stood between the artist and commercial success.

I listened to Silverton's theories, the first being that although Nick talked expansively about 'pop music' in the mid-1970s – probably because 'pop' was a dirty word and therefore it appealed to the contrarian in him[31] – he didn't really know how to consistently write a real pop record. Real hits were written by people such as Nicky Chinn and Mike Chapman, the songwriting and production duo behind the likes of Sweet and Mud.[32] Nick also aspired to cynicism in his songs, typical examples being 'Music For Money' and 'I Love My Label', but Nick didn't have a cynical bone in his body compared with Chinn and Chapman, who cleverly manipulated the teen market with slick recordings and juvenile lyrics, such as 'Does anyone know the way to block Buster?' That's not quite as snappy as Nick's story [in 'So It Goes'] of remembering 'the night the kid cut off his right arm', an opening line worthy of the Band, whose chief songwriter, Robbie Robertson, was the truly authentic model to which Nick had aspired during his formative years. But authenticity plays no role in the act of making hits, and it is the same with irony.

It is hard to think of many hit singles that take a genuinely ironic stance. Randy Newman's 'Short People' is a rare example. But, as Silverton points out, Newman had his biggest hit with 'You've Got A Friend In Me', from the movie *Toy Story*, and the public at large didn't get 'Short People'.

'They saw "Short People" as a novelty record,' says Silverton. 'To me, Nick's irony is so very clear in "(What's So Funny 'bout) Peace, Love And Understanding" by Brinsley Schwarz. The song is structured around irony. Does he really mean it? Doesn't he really mean it? Is it funny? Is it not funny? That bit in it where he talks about "more peace and love for the children of the new generation" – it's an obvious joke. It could have been a hit record and that is the bit that got in the way. People don't want a gag like that in their record. If they want a gag, they want "Ernie (The Fastest Milkman in the West)". Nick put that gag in there.

'You'd go and watch the Brinsleys in a pub and they'd do the Shadows dance. That was self-referential and ironic, and it goes down brilliantly with about two hundred fans, but it would go over the heads of the general public. The problem with irony is that it tells the wider audience that they don't get the joke. They know that the joke is at their expense, because irony in a pop record says to them: "This is not really what you think it is; you thought you were buying a pop record; actually, you're buying something which has an ironic take on pop records," which also means that the status of all the other pop records that they've bought is downgraded. They perceive it as patronising, I think, and Nick's "pop records" were "pretend pop records".

'But the thing about Elvis Costello's version of "Peace, Love And Understanding" is that he really meant it. He wasn't playing with anger. That's why his version goes in a totally different direction, because he's really angry about it, and he means it, whereas Nick couldn't mean it at that point. Although today when Nick sings the song, he does mean it. He has had to come all the way round to be able to reclaim his own song, which was reinvented for him by Elvis.'

And then came 'Cruel To Be Kind', with added Dave Edmunds, and it was a hit.

'Edmunds is bereft of irony and cynicism, at least in his music,' continues Silverton. 'But he knows how to make hit records. His production techniques were clever, but not clever-clever. Nick was smart, and Edmunds was not smart, in that way. He's a talented Welsh guitar player who likes being in pop music and spending a lot of time in his Jaguar, or in the studio. Nick is a smart man in a business that is not really full of very smart people. And he hooked up with a smart person like Jake Riviera, and took advantage of the brutalities of Jake's language and persona.

'Nick's shtick – his ironic self-deprecation – is inherently a lie, but it knows that it's a lie. It's a way of moving through life as if nothing really matters, while everyone else thinks it does. David Niven played the same trick. Life just happened to him. "No, I just knocked that together," he might say. It's the cult of the amateur. When Nick was producing the Damned, he was probably saying, "Well, I just found myself here." But it requires a lot of drive, and low cunning. And I think there's a lot more cunning in Nick then he would ever admit to. I don't think even he knows it. The thing is, you go into the music business with the intention of becoming a pop star. You may say, "This doesn't really matter," but it does. You pretend it doesn't matter, and some people think what you're saying is the truth, but it's not. It distances you from the music business, so that when it turns out you're not a pop star, you've got somewhere to hide. If your record flops, you say, "Actually, I'm not that serious about it," therefore it doesn't matter that it's not a hit. There is that side of Nick – he really cares about what he does, but he pretends he doesn't.'

Despite Nick's profile management strategy, there were still pockets of influential media folk who were quietly monitoring his accomplishments, variously describing his live performance as 'nearly devastating', and his status in the world of popular music as approaching 'god-level'. He remains important to the tastemakers and switched-on critics, not to mention his many fans, because in addition to being a superb songwriter, he came along at a time when much of rock music had become pretentious and overblown, and here was Nick revelling in the three-minute song and bringing his music to their attention via a tiny London-based record label – Stiff Records – that helped change the rules.

Although not yet inducted into any Halls of Fame, he had attracted the attention of the American Association of Independent Music (A2IM), an organisation founded in 2005 to support and improve the business of boutique record labels that make and sell the sounds of musical pioneers, mavericks and outsiders.

The term 'independent' had been a misnomer, hijacked in the 1980s by music publicists who sought to align their clients with the edgier side of contemporary music, when in fact the 'independent label' in question was often a discreetly bankrolled offshoot or imprint of a major record company.[33] 'Indie', as it became affectionately known, was, in the minds of many consumers, *a musical genre*! A2IM sought to redress the balance.

For a good example of an authentic 1970s independent label, one needs to look no further than Ork or Beserkley in the USA, or Chiswick and Stiff in the UK, and even further back, Andrew Loog Oldham and Tony Calder's Immediate Records. Stiff Records was, of course, where Nick Lowe was launched as a solo artist. Although historically one or two major labels have distributed his music, Nick had remained independent in spirit and deed throughout much of his recording career. Since 1994's *The Impossible Bird*, he had consciously avoided links with large corporations and chosen to plough his unique furrow. It is therefore fitting that in 2017, A2IM, through its 'Libera' programme, inducted him as an 'Independent Icon'.

'Few artists get better with age,' stated a press release. 'Nick Lowe is the exception.'

According to the *New York Times*, Mr Lowe spent much of the 1970s 'busy not fitting into three successive movements: pub rock, punk and new wave. As the inaugural artist and house producer at Stiff Records, he helped create the blueprint for the modern indie label, and helmed historic early recordings for the Damned, Elvis Costello, and the Pretenders, among others. More recently his releases on Yep Roc Records have heralded a bona fide second coming.'

Nick was due to accept the prestigious award on 8 June 2017 at an industry event in New York City, alongside singer-songwriter and feminist icon Ani DiFranco, who was being presented with a Lifetime Achievement Award. But just nine days before the ceremony, he received the devastating news that Neil Brockbank, his co-producer and right-hand man on the road, had died suddenly at the age of sixty-six. Everyone in Nick's circle was shocked. It transpired that Neil had become a victim of lung cancer. He had probably been carrying the disease around in his body for some time, but it failed to surface until around 20 May, when symptoms loudly presented themselves. An email from Neil as recently as 18 May informed me that he had just fired up his old computer to look up some tour-related trivia, but had otherwise 'been ill'.

Neil's unexpected death – almost two years to the day since the passing of drummer Bobby Irwin – was yet another blow to the old firm. In the forty-eight hours that followed, Nick wrestled with the prospect of undertaking his overseas commitments minus the presence of his loyal batman, and confessed to feeling nervous. Imminent events included the important A2IM award ceremony and a series of shows around New York State that would follow. There was also a trip to Japan, for which Neil had been studiously arranging the work permits and immigration papers, such was his crucial role. Nick knew that he could not shirk from his responsibilities. Fortuitously, Neil's own right-hand man, twenty-seven-year-old Tuck Nelson, a London-based native of Boise, Idaho, was ready to take care of Nick, his road guitar and the out-front sound on the upcoming dates.

'I hadn't done any tour managing before,' says Nelson. 'But I had done some onstage sound for Nick. I sort of knew his act, but I didn't know the "special effects" that each song required. I wasn't yet "part of the show", like Neil had been. I had to learn it, but luckily that mostly occurred in Japan, so I guess, at first, I got away with it. I felt like, "Who the hell else is gonna do it? Of course, I'm gonna do it!"'

At the PlayStation Theater on Times Square, Nick handled the A2IM event with aplomb, graciously accepting his award. Previous winners included Arcade Fire and the Arctic Monkeys. When he was introduced, the entire audience rose to its feet in recognition of his crucial role in modern popular music and his 'iconic' status.

Following an introduction from Sound Exchange CEO Michael Huppe, Nick told the crowd, 'I am simply another ageing gent from across the sea who fell in love at a very early age with the wonderful music that this great nation has given the world. I was lucky to have the opportunity to go out and try and make something out of my love and hobby and along the way managed to make one or two good records and hundreds of terrible ones, but of course nobody remembers those, which is why I am standing here this evening.'

He then performed 'Lately I've Let Things Slide' and 'Cruel To Be Kind'. As the locals might say, you could 'feel the love' in the room.

The following night, Nick commenced another run of sold-out shows at the City Winery. The venue's dinner service was still being wrapped up as he walked onstage, bang on 9 p.m., without any fuss or introduction. The waiters and bus boys were sensitive to his solo acoustic performance and moved around in a hushed manner as he delivered his most bruising, personal songs. Although the distant rumble of a subway train below the Winery's foundations was an occasional, ambient distraction, you could otherwise have heard a toothpick drop.

He opened with 'People Change' and 'Stoplight Roses', followed by one of his entertaining welcome speeches, worked out in advance, not improvised, because these days, he admits, he's 'not good enough to just wing it'. After confirming his name, he commented that on such a beautiful day, 'New York might actually be the greatest city on the planet.' Loud applause. He thanked everyone for coming out, and the next night remarked that, 'last night's crowd were unusually handsome and elegantly dressed, but frankly, looking at the house tonight, I thought last night's lot were a bit seedy'. Laughter.

'I've devised a programme here, which I hope is going to meet with your approval. I want to do a few things that I haven't done for a while, or in some cases never done. Well, there's the odd new tune. But rest assured that the whole set will be balanced on the cornerstones of several of my most well-known works. It would be rude not to. I mean, if you went to the time and trouble to go and see, say, Billy Joel in concert, and he didn't play, er, "We Didn't Start The Fire", you wouldn't be very pleased, would you? It's exactly the same with me, it's only a question of scale. So, I intend to keep them coming, jukebox style.'

Enchanted by Nick's comedic patter and his songs of love and loss, highlights of which were the unreleased 'Blue On Blue' and 'Crying Inside', the audience sat in reverential silence, except of course for the inevitable participation that always accompanies 'Cruel To Be Kind'. His set, with encores, clocked in at eighty minutes, and although this was brash New York, and Nick was almost fifty years into his musical career, it was suddenly as if we were watching 'Nickie', the precocious twelve-year-old, strumming his ukulele banjo to entertain his parents' friends in a cellar bar somewhere in Germany, smiling, beguiling and knowing exactly when to leave us wanting more.

EPILOGUE

Since winning the A2IM Independent Icon award in June 2017, Nick Lowe has continued to write and record new songs, tour consistently and undertake endless rounds of promotional activity.

In October 2017, he was interviewed by *GQ* editor-in-chief Jim Nelson for the American TV series *Speakeasy*. Broadcast the following month, the sixty-minute discussion saw Nick answer numerous questions and perform three songs. Nelson's introduction talked of Lowe being 'a wildly creative force in music for a half-century . . . a legendary songwriter, producer and recording artist with a singular style, a searing wit and a whole lotta soul, the creator of three-minute masterpieces that have stood the test of time . . . longevity like his is one thing and rare enough, but along the way he's also managed to innovate, to continually reinvent himself . . . [his] ageless, timeless balladeering and dark, moody pop, to me, only confirms his status as the modern-day Cole Porter.'

In the spring of 2018, Yep Roc Records released Nick's first new tracks in over four years, recorded with Los Straitjackets at the Diamond Mine Studio in Queens, New York. Two original compositions – 'Tokyo Bay', written around 2011, and the more recent 'Crying Inside' – were accompanied by the Gibb brothers' 'Heartbreaker' and the Cliff Richard favourite, 'Travelin' Light'. As the EP went into production, a semi-surprise party was being organised for Nick to celebrate his fifty years in entertainment.

Invitations went out to just about everybody who had participated in his musical and personal journeys. The party took place in late April at Mayfair's historic Scotch of St James nightclub, pretty much the joint where 'swinging London' was invented back in the mid-1960s. The ground floor bar was packed, as was the basement dance floor where DJs Wendy May and Mark Lamarr spun an inspired selection of tunes. Around 10 p.m., Nick gave a modest speech which was followed by a skiffle-style sing-song. Lyric sheets were handed out and the crowd sang along, the first number being Tennessee Ernie Ford's 'Sixteen Tons'.

Among those present, mingling with close family members, were Nick's former band-mates Brinsley Schwarz and Billy Rankin, plus many other musicians including Chrissie Hynde, Geraint Watkins, Chris Difford, Bill Kirchen, C. C. Adcock, Rat Scabies, Clive Langer and Paul Carrack. The painter Humphrey Ocean looked on, as did film critic Mark Kermode, broadcaster Robert Elms and actor Martin Freeman. Nick would have loved to stay at the party all night, reminiscing with those who had played major or minor parts in his life, but the road was calling once more. Within seventy-two hours, he and his trusty assistant Tuck Nelson were on a flight to Tokyo.

Per Gessle, songwriter and, alongside Marie Fredriksson, one half of Swedish hit-makers Roxette, had flown in from Stockholm for the party, describing Nick as one of his 'all-time musical heroes'. Gessle would later confirm that he and Nick had been collaborating in the studio on a song entitled 'Small Town

Talk'. And collaboration was to feature more and more in Nick's songwriting; there was 'When The Spell Is Broken', written with Daryl Hall (admittedly a 1985 vintage), and a number of more recent Nashville co-writes, all in the pipeline.

Under the circumstances, what were the chances of Nick completing that fully fledged new album his fans were crying out for? Wasn't an EP enough? Clearly not. In June 2018, Nick was back in the USA, once again touring and recording with Los Straitjackets. At Danny Blume's studio in upstate New York, they recorded a number of songs for future release. Perhaps a long-playing record was being assembled in instalments.

In May 2018, the American writer Mark Binelli had travelled to London to spend several days with Nick and interview him for a major *Rolling Stone* feature. The long-established magazine was in the process of switching from fortnightly to monthly publication and repositioning itself to appeal to a younger readership, but there was still space for an in-depth interview with a legendary, evergreen musician. The seven-page piece, entitled 'SAINT NICK', ran in the December 2018 edition and saw the reporter visiting Nick's home in Brentford and nearby locations, such as the Royal Air Force Museum in Hendon. In his overview of Nick's fifty-year musical career, Binelli observed: 'Lowe possesses a talent, common among a certain strain of middle-class Brits, of marrying congenital self-effacement with supreme confidence, with neither personality trait ever quite overriding the other.'

Immediately after Christmas, Nick flew to Chicago for a number of dates including a New Year's Eve show with Los Straitjackets at SPACE, in Evanston, Illinois. This was preceded by solo shows at the same venue on 29 and 30 December. 'On the first night I was still getting over the recent seasonal festivities,' confesses Nick. 'It was as if "Dennis" was on stage for the first couple of songs, but luckily Dennis knows Nick Lowe's act and, as I recall, he made a reasonable fist of it.'

Yep Roc had hinted on its website that new recordings would appear in the spring of 2019, and in May the label issued Nick's next mini collection, comprising 'Love Starvation', 'Blue On Blue' and 'Trombone', along with a cover version of 'Raincoat in the River', first recorded by Sammy Turner in 1961. In the run-up to the EP's release, there was a string of US east coast shows with Los Straitjackets.

It was also announced that Nick would appear as special guest of Mavis Staples at Nashville's Ryman Auditorium on 15 May, in a show celebrating the soul and gospel legend's eightieth birthday. This would be followed by an early summer UK tour for 'Nick Lowe's Quality Rock & Roll Revue Starring Los Straitjackets', including a headlining appearance at Suffolk's Red Rooster festival. This would be the longest UK tour Nick had undertaken in many years – around twenty dates. There was also talk of an appearance at west London's Ealing Jazz Festival in July. 'Lovely,' said Nick. 'I can get there on the bus.'

Having now reached an age at which many performers start to slow down or turn grouchy, Nick remains excited and positive about all of the forthcoming work in his schedule, including songwriting exploits in such places as Nashville. 'I'll definitely keep going there until they think I'm a dead loss,' he says. 'You know how it goes, you've got to stick your baited hook in the harbour in order to catch the fish that might be swimming by. So, who knows?

'This thing, music, is totally in charge of me. I sort of *am it*, in a way, so if it wasn't there now – if it was suddenly surgically removed – there wouldn't be anything to me at all. I would be hollow. Everything that I know comes from the music.'

APPENDIX
All Men Are Liars – The Untold Story

Nick Lowe had music and entertainment in his blood, having received much encouragement from his mother, Pat, who had spent her childhood in the backstage world of travelling performers where she was unavoidably exposed to the greasepaint and razzmatazz of showbiz.

Nick's maternal grandmother, Muriel Blanche Kelly, later known as Blanche, was born in Bury St Edmunds, Suffolk, on 17 December 1893. Her father, Patrick Kelly, hailed from Preston, Lancashire, and joined the army at the age of twenty-six as a private in the 3rd Royal Lancashire Militia, based at Fulwood Barracks near his home town. Periodically the battalion would travel to Warley Barracks in Essex for training, and it was during one of these excursions that Patrick met his wife-to-be, Anne Mary Phillips, who hailed from Perth, Western Australia.[34] Following Patrick's discharge from service, his family were to lead a nomadic life as he chased employment and worked various jobs, often menial in nature. In the late 1890s the family moved to Patrick's home county of Lancashire, where Muriel's sister, Florence Kathleen, was born in 1899. Within a few years, the Kelly family moved once again, this time settling in Lambeth, south London, where Patrick took a job as a lodging house caretaker to supplement his army pension.

London was the perfect base for Muriel. Wishing to pursue a career in the theatre, she took full advantage of the capital's opportunities and within a short time was appearing in *Mam'selle Champagne*, a musical burlesque that toured the provinces before opening at London's Oxford Theatre in June 1914. A review in *The Stage* described it as: 'a bright and breezy piece, full of action, colour, melody, and fun'. Some aspects of the show, however, 'called for the blue pencil': 'The ladies' costumes are a trifle too short – if the word can be applied to skirts slit almost to the waist and displaying hip fleshings'. The critic did, however, describe Muriel Kelly, in the role of 'Sadie', as 'an attractive queen of the boulevards'.

By July, Britain was embroiled in the Great War, but music hall was thriving. That month, twenty-year-old Muriel appeared at the Empire, Leicester Square in *Partners*, assisting American comedy duo Fisher and Green, and causing, according to one report, 'hearty merriment'. The following May, Muriel was one of seven all-singing, all-dancing girls in the musical burlesque *Nurses* at Southampton's Palace Theatre. Playing opposite her, in the part of 'Ralph Ellery', was a twenty-four-year-old actor by the name of Louis Victor. Thrown together in the production throughout its run, Muriel and Louis became lovers.

The actor and entertainer Louis Victor – the grandfather Nick Lowe never knew – was born Louis Victor Don Clan-Alpine Thatcher on 25 September 1891 in Bedford Park, west London. The early lives of Louis's parents were as dramatically different as their meeting was unlikely, yet it is from their marital union that we see glimpses of the character and creativity of Nick Lowe, who was – until the story was unearthed during research for this biography – substantially unaware of his maternal lineage.

It is a fascinating story. Readers are invited to take two separate journeys into the past to discover a hitherto secret bloodline. The second of these will be to the medieval terrain of the Austrian Tyrol. But first, come with me, if you will, to the mid-nineteenth century farmlands of New York State, USA.

On the southern outskirts of Syracuse, 185 miles west of the New York State capital Albany, lies the hamlet of Fabius. It was to this verdant region, once home to the Onondaga Indians, that a peddler named Elijah Johnson Thatcher came in 1839, following his discharge from the US Army.

Born 1799, in Hartford, Connecticut, Elijah was the son of the Reverend and future missionary, Gamaliel Thatcher, born 1772, and his wife Sally (née Johnson), born 1777.[35] Elijah Thatcher's wife Amelia (née Stone), born 1824, gave birth to five children, the eldest of whom was Don Clan-Alpine Thatcher, born 1842 in Fabius. On leaving school at the age of sixteen, Don worked briefly as a door-to-door huckster, or 'travelling salesman' as his father would describe him in the US census of 1860. But young Don's commercial career was rudely interrupted by the outbreak of the American Civil War.

In the spring of 1861, to assemble an army tough enough to tackle the troublesome Confederates in the south, recently inaugurated US president Abraham Lincoln launched a call-to-arms urging able-bodied men from all walks of life to 'rally round the flag' and sign up to a Union Army (the Nick Lowe composition, 'The Rose Of England', eerily echoes Lincoln's call-to-arms). Don Thatcher, then eighteen years old, heard Lincoln's clarion call, and had no hesitation in following in his father's footsteps, for Elijah, an army veteran, had died just ten weeks earlier.

On 22 May 1861, Don enlisted at Syracuse with Company I, New York 12th Infantry Regiment. Military records reveal that he was five-foot-six in height, with blue eyes and a fair complexion. Whether or not he was one of the more charismatic soldiers in the platoon is left to the imagination, but his name is mentioned several times in the diary of Lewis Bramer Jr, a member of the 12th Infantry regimental band.

Military activity in the region was slow to materialise and Don was frequently mustered in and out of service as tensions rose and then subsided. In September 1862, his younger brother, Fitz, also signed up and joined Company F, New York 14th Regiment, by which time Don had seen action at the Battle of Malvern Hill.[36]

Don was among hundreds in General George B. McClellan's Union force who were injured in action. After recovering from a gunshot wound to his left forearm in Lincoln General Hospital, Washington, DC, he was released from active service on 25 January 1863, 'by reason of physical disability'. Don stayed with the army and took a desk job in Washington, working in the adjutant general's office until 1865, when, within weeks of Abraham Lincoln's assassination, he was discharged with a modest army pension. He was twenty-three years old.

Four thousand miles away in another land and, culturally, another orbit, the Swiss-Austrian Von der Trave family were clinging to the last *guldens* of their vanishing wealth. Domiciled in the castle of Lichtenfels, in the picturesque mountains of the Austrian Tyrol, the Von der Traves could trace their origins back to the sixteenth-century reign of Charles V, Holy Roman Emperor and Archduke of Austria. This once great dynasty had gradually sold off its forests and farmlands, and its holdings in the cotton and wool trades, to provide each of its young heirs with an education befitting his or her nobility. By the end of the nineteenth century their fairy-tale castle would lie in ruins.

The head of the family was Count Francis Charles Caspar Von der Trave, an engineer by trade. His son, Baron Charles Ignatius Caspar Von der Trave, had been born in 1824 in Rorschach, Switzerland. Upon his father's death, the young baron enjoyed the hereditary title of count but his financial status was considerably less grand. Like his forefathers, Charles would spend profligately to bestow upon his children a classical education.

In 1852, as a 'Professor of Music', Charles travelled to London to explore opportunities in the world of sheet music publishing, and while there devised and sold arrangements for pianoforte, including works by Mendelssohn and Schubert. Trading as 'Charles Albert Caspar', he may have sought to ingratiate himself with the Royal Society of Musicians, whose premises were in Lisle Street, Soho. Although there is no record of Charles becoming a member of the Society, he did cite a Lisle Street address when he married Mary Frances Coad, the twenty-seven-year-old Cornish daughter of Richard and Martha Coad, residents of South Hampstead, London.

Mary Coad was seven months pregnant when she married the baron at a London register office on 1 February 1853. The couple set up home at 1 Stanley Terrace in Stockwell, south London, where Mary gave birth to a daughter, Alberta, on 25 April.[37]

Baroness Alberta Mary Frances Caspar Von der Trave would become the most resourceful member of the family, having been provided with the finest cultural grounding that Europe could offer. She had studied modern languages in Stuttgart and Paris, and at the age of sixteen was sent to Weimar in Germany to become a pianoforte pupil of Franz Liszt, the eminent Hungarian-born composer who dominated European music in the mid-nineteenth century.

Alberta's life was to be one of constant reinvention as she followed diverse career paths. By her mid-twenties she was giving piano recitals as 'Alberta Caspar' in London and other English cities. In August 1878, the *Yorkshire Post and Leeds Intelligencer* noted: 'Mademoiselle Caspar has played before every crowned or princely head that has visited the Exhibition, and if the compliments of royalty carry weight with them, she has no reason to be dissatisfied; for all our illustrious guests, including His Royal Highness the Prince of Wales, have had occasion to express to her their warm appreciation of her magnificent talent.'

This was the grand age of creativity, invention and anything-is-possible *joie de vivre*. It was also the dawn of photography, but long before silent movies would kick-start the film industry, it was art – as in big paintings reflecting Victorian life – that drew the masses. Such pictures were the movies of their day and the public, many of whom were illiterate and relied on bold imagery for information, flocked to galleries to witness the unveiling of major works.

No one was more swept along by the excitement than Alberta. In 1880, while living with her parents in Angell Road, Lambeth, she began to explore various techniques for colourising mono-chrome photographs. It was a medium that moved her to promote 'Crystoleum', a process whereby a photographic print was pasted on to a piece of glass and the tissue of the paper later removed, leaving only an ink outline of the subject, which was then filled in with colour. This early form of painting by numbers became popular with Victorian ladies of leisure who aspired to decorating their homes with designs of their own hand.

Sensing the commercial opportunities afforded by the supply of artists' materials to a growing market, Alberta gave talks on art and held painting demonstrations at the Marshall & Snelgrove department store in Oxford Street. To publicise the Crystoleum concept and enrol students, she produced a pamphlet, its blurb assuring 'entire novices' that they could quickly master the technique.[38] The popularity of Crystoleum, soon to be described in advertising material as 'The Grandest Light of the Century', started to attract international attention, particularly from America.

Alberta had also taken a keen interest in the artworks of the Pre-Raphaelite Brotherhood, especially one of the movement's pre-eminent founders, Edward Burne-Jones, whose work with stained glass would further inspire her business instincts. In an attempt to recreate Burne-Jones's masterpieces, Alberta invented 'The Method of Imitating Stained Glass' for which she obtained a British patent in 1884. Flexing her entrepreneurial skills, Alberta sought to patent her invention in the USA. In February 1885, she took a train to Liverpool where she boarded the steamship *Oregon*, arriving in New York on 9 March.

Alberta's business activities moved swiftly,[39] but the American trip was to have far greater consequence; while promoting her painting methods in New York and awaiting the outcome of her patent application, Alberta was reunited with an American man she had previously met in Paris, former Union soldier Don Clan-Alpine Thatcher.

Since his injuries at the Battle of Malvern Hill and the army desk job in Washington, DC, Sergeant Don Thatcher had gone through some major life changes. By 1865, he had returned home to Onondaga County and married local schoolteacher Rosemond Millard Bogardus, three years his senior and daughter of a farmer, Henry P. Bogardus. It would be a rocky marriage, disrupted largely by Don's work ethic; with little prospect of employment in the aftermath of the Civil War, he and his brothers travelled to New York City in search of opportunities. By 1866, Don and his brother Frank (aged twenty-four and nineteen respectively) had set up a grocery store on New York's Lower East Side. Within two years they were joined by their brother, Fitz. Together they established 'D. C. Thatcher and Brothers', with two further branches on Eighth Avenue.

Meanwhile, their widowed mother, Amelia, had moved west to Illinois with younger siblings Edward and Ella in tow. When Don's New York grocery business folded after just three years of trading, he and his brothers re-joined their family in Chicago and Don was reunited with Rosemond. In 1869, he worked at the Dining Saloon on Randolph Street, and the following year he and Rosemond travelled south to St Louis, Missouri, then the fourth largest city in the USA.

Described in mid-nineteenth century pictorial brochures as the 'Metropolis of the Mississippi Valley', St Louis's downtown shops and restaurants were flourishing. Don took a job at the Metropolitan Dining Hall, becoming its manager in the summer of 1871, and within two years had moved on to the Grand Central Hotel, where business opportunities awaited him. He went into partnership with a consortium of local businessmen and, for a while, the hotel thrived. The 1870s, however, would be a decade of economic recession and the financial crisis of 1873 heralded what became known as 'the long depression'.

Don was then living with Rosemond at the Everett Hotel, but they soon fell out, leading the *St Louis Post-Dispatch* to report that Rosemond 'cowhided him on a public street in St Louis'. In 1879, separated from his wife, Don was forced to file for bankruptcy and was soon reduced to taking lowly employment at various local catering establishments.

Impecuniosity did not prevent Don from gadding about. The *Post-Dispatch* article also stated that 'it was his custom to make money in America and go to Europe and spend it'. He had visited Belgium and France, where he 'mingled with people of prominence'. Such persons included Alberta Caspar, whom he courted and later proposed to, having met with her family in London, where he conveniently failed to mention his marriage to Rosemond.[40]

Following the 'Windsor Hotel court case' of 1883 in which Don faced charges,[41] he fell out of favour with the St Louis business crowd and returned to Chicago, and thence to New York, where his estranged wife now kept an apartment in Brooklyn. Although Don had been separated from Rosemond for some years, he had remained on good terms with her stepbrother, civil engineer Oliver Hoyt Bogardus, who offered Don a room at his family home in Syracuse. Among the many engaging characters Don ran into in New York was an electrical engineer by the name of Charles Adams-Randall, a former assistant to Thomas Edison, inventor of the phonograph. Adams-Randall had subsequently become an inventor nonpareil, a genius one might say, and would soon conceive, among other contraptions, the jukebox.[42]

Don Thatcher was spellbound by the inventor's technical skills and sought to emulate him. Luckily, the brilliant Adams-Randall was happy to support Don's nascent creativity while recruiting him as a representative to oversee his patent applications in London. Like the jukebox, this was music to Don's ears, given his designs on Alberta. On a visit to England, he gave his occupation as 'Engineer' on the ship's passenger list and, upon arriving in London, took lodgings in Cromwell Road, South Kensington. He soon patented some simple inventions of his own.[43]

Back in New York, Adams-Randall was working on his 'Electro-Mechanical Time-Stamp', an ingenious device that facilitated the printing onto packages and documents the precise time of their receipt. On his next visit to London, Adams-Randall found Don and Alberta happily ensconced in the Caspar household and, apparently, married. Before long, Adams-Randall was walking out with Alberta's younger sister, Evelyne, but this cosy tableau was threatened by the fact that both he and Don had wives in the background.

To further encourage his future brother-in-law, and perhaps cement his own relationship with Evelyne, Adams-Randall made Don a shareholder in 'The Electric Date and Time-Stamp Company Limited'. Its principal asset was slowly gaining acceptance as a useful business tool and needed to be promoted in Britain. In the spring of 1889, advertisements were placed in the *Glasgow Herald* and other publications offering shares to investors, but the company failed to win sufficient contracts and went into liquidation within two months.

To salvage his Time-Stamp, Adams-Randall looked to America. Requiring a representative to oversee its US patent application, he despatched Don to New York and joined him there that November. But the mailroom equipment business was not uppermost in Adams-Randall's mind; having proposed to Evelyne in London, and with a spring wedding planned, there was the small matter of Phoebe, the existing wife from whom he had been separated for seven years. Desperate for a quick divorce he conspired to 'commit adultery', openly spending one night with an un-named woman at an address on West 34th Street.[44]

Among God's creatures man must be
The most slimy and slippery
There stands the naked ape in a monkey suit
Behind the little moustache he grew, the shifty brute

Nick Lowe, 'All Men Are Liars'

In addition to promoting her patents, Alberta continued to compose, and enjoyed good notices in the press. A notice in the *Manufacturer and Inventor* of December 1890 reported: '"Forest

Echoes", by Alberta Caspar, has already attained a well-deserved success with all the leading bands, and the present arrangement for the piano is a dainty and characteristic composition of great merit. "Crystoleum Galop", arranged by Alberta Caspar, is a really irresistible Galop de Concert, its rhythm and tuneful melody set every pulse moving, and the air lingers in one's memory for some time.'

When another of her sisters, Eugenie, married a civil engineer named William de St Martin in London on 9 February 1891, the witnesses were again 'Mr and Mrs Don C. Thatcher'; however, a formal record of their own marriage remains elusive.

Alberta was pregnant at this point, and gave birth to a son on 25 September 1891. He was christened 'Louis', perhaps as a reminder of the epic commute that his father was in the habit of undertaking roughly twice a year, between his life in England as a failed inventor and his intermittent business activity in Missouri. It was a trek that gives real meaning to the song 'You Came A Long Way From St Louis'; the steamship crossing between England and the eastern seaboard of America took an average of eight days, and the onward rail journey from New York to St Louis, on the 'Nickel Plate Road', a further fifteen hours.

When Don disembarked at the newly constructed Union Station, with its magnificent 65-foot barrel-vaulted ceiling in the Grand Hall, he had truly arrived. But in London he was little more than a Bedford Park novelty who attempted to carry off the rank of 'Major, US Army (retired)' – a conceit that went unchallenged in the pre-information age. By day, he worked as a caretaker in a Liverpool Street EC2 tenement building, returning to Chiswick each evening by Underground train. In London, he watched the infant Louis take his first steps, but Don's heart was in the USA where he still enjoyed a high profile among the Missourian catering fraternity.[45]

*

On 27 May 1896, a tornado hit St Louis. Fortuitously, for most of its inhabitants, the storm petered out just south of the city centre where Don was planning to open his next enterprise, the new Thatcher Restaurant. It would be located at the ten-storey Century Building, then under construction on Olive Street, but on 17 August, as Don stood watching workmen applying the finishing touches to the building's stone facade, he was startled by an approaching team of horses. Standing dangerously close to a deep excavation on the sidewalk, Don stepped onto a scaffold board that was laid precariously across one corner of the hole. He lost his balance and fell 25 feet into the sub cellar, breaking three ribs and suffering severe internal injuries. Rushed home and comforted by heavy doses of morphine, he died two days later.

In the aftermath of Don Thatcher's death, the St Louis media was alive with related stories. Having recently travelled to Missouri with five-year-old Louis in tow, his widow, Alberta, was forced to put to one side her articles about 'pen painting in oils' for *The Queen* magazine in London, and focus her attention on the catering business. She was now the new manager of the Thatcher Restaurant, but an unexpected skeleton came out of her late husband's closet in the form of Rosemond, described in the press as 'D. C. Thatcher's Other Helpmeet'.

'How good or bad a man actually is, is rarely known until after his death', declared the *St Louis Post-Dispatch* on 10 September. 'His good qualities are usually set out in his obituary. His evil attributes develop in the police courts. Whether there was evil in the life of Don C. Thatcher will probably become known when Mrs Rosemond M. Thatcher arrives in St Louis to claim the estate of the deceased as the lawful widow.'

Rosemond, now living in Michigan, threatened to sue her late husband's estate, protesting that she was Don's legal wife of some thirty years and therefore entitled to his 'fortune'. But there was actually very little money in the pot and any implications in the press that he had been a bigamist were dispelled by attorney Marshall F. McDonald, who robustly stated that Don had 'secured a divorce in 1886 on statute grounds'. Nevertheless, Rosemond had been using the name 'Mrs Don C. Thatcher' for three decades. Failing to extract a settlement, she sued the owners of the Century Building, where Don had died, for damages in the amount of $5000, a case she lost. Whether or not Don and Rosemond were ever legally divorced is unproven, but she did become the recipient of his $2 per month army pension until her own death in February 1899.

Even more bizarre than the emergence of Rosemond was the fact that prior to Don's death, Alberta's brother, Cecil, had arrived in St Louis from Europe, via Australia and San Francisco. At Alberta's insistence, Cecil had been encouraged to involve himself in their restaurant business, despite the fact that he had previously pursued a career in medicine, funded largely by his high-spending father.

Cecil 'Percy' Caspar Von Der Trave – now 'Count Von Lichtenfels' – was thought to be a valuable asset to the Thatcher business, not least of all in public relations terms. He certainly possessed basic bookkeeping skills, having worked as an accounts clerk in the London offices of the Bass brewery; as soon as he was installed in the Thatcher business, however, he started to display abnormal traits. Eventually the authorities took an interest in his erratic behaviour and – at Alberta's behest – took him into custody.

Cecil was placed in a detention cell at the St Louis City Hospital and confined to the 'insane ward', where he attracted the attention of the doctors when he claimed to have 'hypnotic powers'. Sceptical at first, they allowed him to experiment on his fellow inmates, and he seemingly used his hypnotic powers to becalm violent or upset patients, as reported in the *Troy New York Daily Times* of 12 April 1897 under the headline HANDY IN A HOSPITAL. 'I should have no fears in emulating Daniel in his lion's den act,' commented Cecil. 'I could control the brutes with a look.'

Alberta and seven-year-old Louis returned to England in 1899, after Alberta's mother, Mary Frances Caspar Von der Trave, had died in Brentford, Middlesex, at the age of seventy-four. Now widowed, Alberta lodged with the Adams-Randall family, who were living in Battersea. Although both of her sisters had 'married well', Alberta was now a single parent with no independent means. With her creative instincts still sharp, she hoped that some of her inventions would come good. In 1903, she registered a patent application for 'Improvements in and Means for Removing and Preventing Wrinkles on the Face', and in 1906, 'An Improved Water Closet Seat'.[46] But Alberta was only one of many aspiring inventors who collectively filed tens of thousands of patent applications every year, rather creating the impression that this was the Edwardian equivalent of buying a lottery ticket, the necessity for cash being the true mother of invention.

Far more promising than any of Alberta's patents was the acting talent of her son, fast gaining experience as an entertainer. In Alberta's eyes, Louis was a child prodigy and she would become his mentor.

In July 1905, she took him to the USA aboard the steamship *New York* with a large troupe of British actors and actresses who were due to appear with the popular American actress and singer Edna May, in *The Catch of the Season*. Thirteen-year-old Louis, billed as 'Master Victor', played the part of 'Bucket' in the show's three-month run at Daly's Theatre on Broadway.

Having returned to England and now trading as 'Madame Victor – variety agent' from her four-room apartment at Broadway Hall in Hammersmith, Alberta managed Louis's early stage career, billing him as 'The Dude-Venile'. She would also cast Louis as the lead member of many interchangeable adolescent song-and-dance troupes, or 'kiddie acts', such as 'The Komedy Kids' and 'The Six Nippy Nippers'. He was soon described in early twentieth-century entertainment publications as 'The Juvenile Transatlantic Comedian' – or perhaps, 'Half A Boy And Half A Man'.[47]

But the promising lad was fast outgrowing his juvenile persona; it was in the 1909 production of *The Arcadians* that Louis, now seventeen years old, first attracted encouraging notices in *The Stage*. The show toured extensively for two years, playing Aberdeen, Glasgow, Hull and Sunderland before crossing the Irish Sea in August 1911 for a week at Cork Opera House.

We now return to Southampton's Palace Theatre, where Louis first met Muriel – now customarily referred to by her family as 'Blanche'. *Nurses*, the show in which Louis and Blanche appeared, soon transferred to the London Coliseum where it was revamped and renamed *Pick Me Up* under the auspices of famed producer, Sydney Blow. The production toured throughout the summer of 1915, and when it ended its run in October, Louis and Blanche joined the cast of another Blow production, *Brides*. By the time that show reached London in January 1916, Blanche was five months pregnant and took a break from performing while Louis continued in Blow's next production, *Sugar And Spice*.

With the arrival of their firstborn imminent, Louis and Blanche were keen to name the day, but theirs was a business that left little time for matrimonial niceties. *Sugar And Spice* was installed at the Bradford Empire when, on 28 April 1916, just three hours before curtain up, their shotgun wedding took place, witnessed by the show's principal lady, Claire Romaine, and male co-lead, Gilbert Childs. That evening the tireless Louis was back on the boards. His son, Leslie Victor Thatcher, was born ten days later.

The boy was barely one month old when his father was called up to join the British Navy at the midway point of the Great War.[48] During Louis's absence, Blanche juggled their son's parenting with occasional stage performances and was assisted at home by her mother-in-law, Alberta, who doted on Leslie and would later encourage his theatrical leanings.

As the war was drawing to a close, Louis found himself stationed in Kent, where he appeared at the Gymnasium Theatre, Chatham, in *Mother Goose – A Sailors' Pantomime*. Three years later, he found himself in court for non-payment of salary to an actor under his production wing – a case he lost – and while he was appearing in *Patches* at the London Palladium, Blanche became pregnant with their second child, a daughter, to be christened Patricia.

During the mid-1920s, Louis and Blanche enjoyed one of their longer-running successes, *Paradise Alley*, a British version of the American musical comedy. Louis would forever sing its main refrain around the house: 'I want to be king of the kids, king of the kids in Paradise Alley, I want to share all the joys, of the girls and boys, with their homemade toys.'

Meanwhile, his own kids – Leslie and Patricia – were farmed out to the Actors' Orphanage, such were the demands of the theatrical profession.[49]

Alberta continued to run her agency, now known as 'Victor Troupes (are in all the best productions)', promoting, among others, the 'Eight Wonder Kiddies'. She now operated from an address in Brook Green Road, Hammersmith, although a snippet in *The Stage* reported: 'Victor's will shortly be opening offices in the West End district.'

But sadly, it was not to be; Nick Lowe's great-grandmother died on 17 April 1927, aged seventy-three. She had led a most eventful life, encompassing an education in Europe as a student of Franz Liszt; business ventures promoting Crystoleum and various patents; and ten years with Nick's great-grandfather, Don Thatcher, the American Civil War veteran and restaurateur who frequently hopped between London and St Louis, Missouri.

In the early 1930s, Louis Thatcher changed his stage name to 'Bobby Victor' but still found himself trading on his old reputation when going through a thin patch. Seeking professional engagements, he advertised his availability in the trade press as 'Lieutenant Commander Juvenile – expert feed character'. His big break eventually came in 1932, when he landed a part in the film production of J. B. Priestley's *The Good Companions*. Under the name of Robert Victor, he played the part of 'Nobby – a lorry driver'.

Louis's brush with celluloid was brief. Having previously lived in a series of rented rooms in and around London's theatreland, he and Blanche had now relocated to Brixton, south London. But the couple would soon separate, allowing Louis to spend much of his time in the pubs and clubs of Soho seeking work, but opportunities were sporadic.[50]

Now reduced to scratching around for a living, Louis's enthusiastic drinking got the better of him and he is remembered in family folklore as 'incredibly talented, but bone idle, and a drunk'. Estranged from Blanche, Louis died from cardiac failure and acute bronchitis on 2 November 1945, at a flat in Betterton Street, Covent Garden, which he had shared with an actress named Lilian Palmer.

Acknowledgements

This biography could not have been written without the help and input of numerous people who know and love Nick Lowe's music and have been happy to reminisce. I am indebted to the following persons for granting me interviews, many of which were face-to-face, the remainder being over remote communications when geography was a factor. I would therefore like to thank: Danny Adler, Roberta Bayley, Martin Belmont, Dale Bobo, Aldo Bocca, Shirley Brilleaux, Neil Brockbank, Roland Brockman, Dez Brown, Chris Buisseret, Clem Burke, Roger Buswell, Carlene Carter, Andy Cheeseman, Graham Chignall, Andy Childs, Ry Cooder, Elvis Costello, Brian Dandridge, Chalkie Davies, Austin de Lone, Chris Difford, Colin Fairley, Barry Farmer, Gregg Geller, Ian Gomm, Jake Guralnick, Daryl Hall, Martin Hampson, Steve Hampson, David Hepworth, Jim Herrington, David Hipkins, Eryl Holt, Chrissie Hynde, Jerry Jaffe, Tim Jenkins, Vic Keary, Bill Kirchen, Barry Landeman, Andrew Lauder, Huey Lewis, Bill Lloyd, Tiffany Lowe, Tracey MacLeod, Joe McEwen, Jerry Dale McFadden, Johnny Marr, Reg Meuross, Tuck Nelson, Jack O'Hara, Penny and John Perriss, Ian Pollock, Paul Riley, David Segal, Ron Sexsmith,

Peter Silverton, Curtis Stigers, Wendy Thatcher, Greg Townson, Peta Waddington, Brendan Walsh and, of course, Nick Lowe.

Certain sections of the text, mainly in the period 1969–1973, are based on research and interviews for my book *No Sleep Till Canvey Island – The Great Pub Rock Revolution* (published 2000, 2003), and related contributions from: Bob Andrews, Ricky Blears, Dot Burn-Forti, Glen Colson, Dai Davies, John Eichler, Chris Fenwick, Charlie Gillett, Nigel Grainge, Alan Marcuson, Graham Parker, Billy Rankin, Jake Riviera, Dave Robinson, Rat Scabies, Brinsley Schwarz, Pete Thomas and Terry Williams.

For providing crucial information, putting me in touch with certain hard-to-reach individuals, or general support and encouragement I thank: Eli Attie, Peter Barnes, Roger Béchirian, Stuart Bell, Valerie Boyd, Paul Bradshaw, Christian Brown, Jack Cheng, Russell Clarke, Mike Cloy, Dave Cronen, Katherine De Francis, Lesley de Lone, Glenn Dicker, Gloria Di Pietro Nicholl, Paul du Noyer, Dave Edmunds, Pete Frame, Chris Gabrin, David Gentle, Lesley Glover, Paul Gorman, Mike Halpern, Didz Hammond, Matt Hanks, Bobby Irwin, Allan Jones, John Kalinowski, Nigel Kerr, Mark Kidel, Neill King, Peter Knock, Larry LeBlanc, Ian Luck, Pia Meijer, Annette Milnes, Jonathan Morrish, Shilah Morrow, Peter O'Brien, Christopher Onions, Ciaran O'Shea, Devorah Ostrov, Eddie Piller, Peter Redburn, Alan Robinson, Claire Robinson, Larry Rohter, Cynthia Ross, Genevieve Schorr, Henry Scott-Irvine, Robert Segarini, Esa Seppänen, Charles Sharman-Cox, John Sheets, Michael Shelley, Keith Smith, Greg Sowders, Stacy D, Dave Steinfeld, Stuart Sullivan, Lance Swanson, Trevor Tall, Gill Taylor, John Tobler, Elizabeth Tucker Thomas, Michael Weaver, Sammi Wild, Richard Williams, Rachel Woodmansee and Mal Young.

For assisting in copyright matters I thank: Dave Ayers, Martin Costello, Jenn DiChiara, Jonathan Kyte, Suzanne Metrick and Chris Thompson.

Various publications in the British Library proved useful, although I was able to conduct a great deal of genealogical research on the Internet. This would have been unthinkable a couple of decades ago, but today the abundance of historical data available online leads one to imagine that it really is 'all out there', if you wish to search for it and occasionally get lucky. My discovery of Nick's American and Austrian antecedents was a significant turning point and absorbed me for two years or more as I reconstructed their incredible story. And while doing so, I did discover one trivial yet highly amusing fact: in my 2010 book, *Ian Dury – The Definitive Biography*, I noted that Ian once lived in Digby Mansions, Hammersmith – flat number 54 to be precise. By almost unbelievable coincidence, 'pub rock-wise', Nick Lowe's great-grandmother, Alberta Thatcher, gave her address in a 1906 patent application as 54 Digby Mansions, Hammersmith. Maybe Ian found some of Alberta's old notes.

I would especially like to thank those who not only helped with my research but went the extra mile and tolerated my pestering. These are they: former Woodbridge School pupil and photographer Tim Jenkins, for hooking me up with many 'Old Woodbridgians' who shared memories of their schooldays with Nick; Paul Riley, for granting me access to the Nick Lowe tape library and tape box information sheets; Rod Melvin for his late-night Soho piano tickling to help reconstruct the tune that Nick's mother once put funny words to – and Louis Barfe for swiftly identifying said tune from my crude recording; photographers Dan Burn-Forti, Chalkie Davies, Ken Friedman, Gijsbert Hanekroot, Jim Herrington, Andy Phillips and Ebet Roberts, with a special mention for Roberta Bayley, Barry Landeman and Clare Morris for exceptional photo assistance; Peter Silverton for his perceptive analysis of the Lowe creative psyche and career stance; and Peta Waddington for her organisational skills, attention to detail, and invaluable filtering and sifting.

Last but not least: heartfelt thanks to my family, and to Julian Alexander, my literary agent at Lucas Alexander Whitley, London; Sarah Lazin, my literary agent at Lazin Books, New York; Andreas Campomar and Claire Chesser at Constable, London; Howard Watson, copy editor; and Ben Schafer at Da Capo Press, USA.

And, once again, thank you Nick for sharing your memories.

Lyric Reprint Permissions

The author is grateful to the music publishers detailed below for permission to reprint song lyrics from the following works:

'All Men Are Liars' – Written by Nick Lowe – Used by permission of BMG Rights Management (UK) Ltd

'Bay City Rollers We Love You' – Written by Nick Lowe – Used by permission of BMG Rights Management (UK) Ltd

'Marie Provost' – Written by Nick Lowe – Used by permission of BMG Rights Management (UK) Ltd

'What's Shakin' On The Hill' – Written by Nick Lowe – Used by permission of BMG Rights Management (UK) Ltd

'Indian Queens' – Written by Nick Lowe – ©2003 Used by permission of Big Deal Notes (ASCAP) All rights reserved. International Copyright Secured

'Lately I've Let Things Slide' – Written by Nick Lowe – ©2001 Used by permission of Big Deal Notes (ASCAP) All rights reserved. International Copyright Secured

'I Trained Her To Love Me' – Written by Nick Lowe and Robert Trehern – ©2004 Used by permission of BMG Rights Management (UK) Ltd and Big Deal Notes (ASCAP) All rights reserved. International Copyright Secured

'Born A Woman' – Written by Martha Sharp – Used by permission of Shapiro Bernstein & Co Ltd (PRS)

Select Bibliography

Books

Anger, Kenneth, *Hollywood Babylon* (Straight Arrow Press, 1975)

Birch, Will, *No Sleep Till Canvey Island* (2016) [eBook]

Costello, Elvis, *Unfaithful Music & Disappearing Ink* (Viking, 2015)

Demoriane, Hermine, *The Tightrope Walker* (Secker & Warburg, 1989)

Hynde, Chrissie, *Reckless: My Life* (Ebury Press, 2015)

Jones, Allan, *Can't Stand Up For Falling Down* (Bloomsbury Publishing, 2017)

Keegan, John, *The American Civil War* (Vintage, 2010)

Paxman, Jeremy, *The Victorians* (BBC Books, 2010)

Tyla, Sean, *Jumpin' In The Fire* (Soundcheck Books, 2010)

Newspapers and magazines

Abrams, Bobby, 'Nick Lowe: A Candid Interview', *Bomp!* (January 1979)

Frame, Pete, 'Bringing Brinsley', *ZigZag* (May 1970)

Kent, Nick, 'The Rockpile Tapes', *NME* (30 July 1977)

Murray, Charles Shaar, 'Springtime for Basher', *NME* (18 March 1978)

Rachlis, Kit, 'Two from Rockpile', *Rolling Stone* (18 October 1979)

Rohter, Larry, 'Return of the Man Who Used to Rock', *New York Times* (13 September 2011)

Russell, Steven, 'Nick Lowe: Back in Detention Again', *East Anglian Daily Times* (24 November 2012)

Segal, David, 'The Lowe-Key Approach: An Aging Rocker's Graceful Segue', *Washington Post* (14 October 2001)

Silverton, Peter, 'Nick Lowe: Jesus of Cool', *Sounds* (25 February 1978)

Thomson, Graeme, 'Nick Lowe: An elegant elder statesman of rock', *The Herald* (14 July 2007)

Waddell, Ray, 'Nick Lowe Hits the Road in Support of Convincer', *Billboard* (15 June 2002)

Ward, Andy, 'The Survivors: Nick Lowe', *GQ* (31 October 2011)

Weiss, Peter, 'Neil Brockbank: w/Nick Lowe & Geraint Watkins', *Tape Op* (November/December 2011)

Windolf, Jim, 'Nick Lowe on Songwriting', *Vanity Fair* (20 March 2009)

Worthington, Cal, 'Everyday Life in Rural California', *ZigZag* (July 1976)

TV and film

BBC Four Sessions at LSO St Luke's, BBC, dir. Janet Fraser Crook (2007)

Born Fighters, dir. Peter Carr (1979)

Concert for Kampuchea, dir. Keith McMillan (1980)

Don't Ask Me Questions: The Unsung Life of Graham Parker and the Rumour, dir. Michael Gramaglia (2013)

Elvis Costello: Mystery Dance, dir. Mark Kidel (2014)

If It Ain't Stiff, It Ain't Worth A Fuck, dir. Nick Abson (1977)

Punk Britannia: Pre-Punk 1972–1976, BBC, dir. Andrew Dunn (2012)

Rockpile: Live at Rockpalast, dir. Christian Wagner (1980)

Spectacle: Elvis Costello with..., season 2, episode 3, dir. Alex Coletti (2009)

Websites and podcasts

chordmaster.org

elviscostello.info

livefromdarylshouse.com

nicklowe.com

nicklowebiography.com

'KLRU-TV: Nick Lowe interview with Evan Smith', overheardwithevansmith.org (2012)

'Johnny Cash & Nick Lowe – The making of "The Beast In Me"', YouTube.com

'Nick Lowe – Cruel to Be Kind promo', dir. Chuck Statler (1979),
    YouTube.com
'Nick Lowe with Nile Rodgers' New Visions Rock, VH-1 (1990),
    YouTube.com
'Word Podcast 168 – with Nick Lowe', mixcloud.com (15 April 2011)
'Nick Lowe: The Fresh Air Interview with Terry Gross', npr.org
    (15 September 2011)
'Nick Lowe Brings His Quality Holiday Revue to America' with Terry
    Gross, npr.org (22 December 2014)
'Speakeasy: Nick Lowe interview with Jim Nelson' (2017),
    YouTube.com

Social media

Nick Lowe, facebook.com/NickLoweOfficial
Nick Lowe Biography 2019, facebook.com/NickLoweBio
Nick Lowe Fan Club, facebook.com/groups/349514205430765/
Nicklowebiography, instagram.com/nicklowebiography
Nick Lowe Biography 2019, twitter.com/nicklowebio

Blogs and online articles

Anonymous, 'Van Morrison Drummer Bobby Irwin Dead at 62',
    suncoastvanfans.blogspot.com (2 July 2015)
Christgau, Robert, 'Nick Lowe Consumer Guide Reviews',
    robertchristgau.com
Friedman, Roger, 'Costello's Ex-Manager Goes Nuts', foxnews.com
    (28 June 2003)
Graham, Cheryl, 'Nick Lowe: the man you don't know, who made the
    songs you love', littlevillagemag.com (4 October 2016)
Mackie, John, 'Q and A with Nick Lowe', canada.com (6 October 2007)
Murray, Noel, 'Interview with Nick Lowe', avclub.com (11 December
    2011)
Persson, Lennart, 'Nick Lowe and Kevin Costner', abcnyheter.no
    (11 October 2007)
Persson, Lennart, 'Let it be peace!', abcnyheter.no (9 January 2009)
Taylor, Luke, 'The Current's Guitar Collection: Nick Lowe, Gibson
    J-150', thecurrent.org (10 December 2014)
Windolf, Jim, 'The Style and Substance of Nick Lowe', wwd.com
    (26 November 2013)

Select Discography

Kippington Lodge

Kippington Lodge released five singles on the Parlophone (EMI) label between 1967 and 1969, the first of which was released before Nick Lowe joined the group in February 1968.

'Shy Boy' c/w 'Lady On A Bicycle' (October 1967)
'Rumours' c/w 'And She Cried' (March 1968)
'Tell Me A Story' c/w 'Understand A Woman' (August 1968)
'Tomorrow Today' c/w 'Turn Out The Light' (December 1968)
'In My Life' c/w 'I Can See Her Face' (April 1969)

Session musicians augmented Kippington Lodge on their early recordings, 'Tell Me A Story' being the first recording on which it is believed group members played their instruments.

Kippington Lodge – Shy Boy: The Complete Recordings 1967–1969 is a 15-track CD compilation released by RPM Records in 2011.

Brinsley Schwarz original albums on United Artists

Brinsley Schwarz (April 1970): 'Hymn To Me', 'Shining Brightly', 'Rock And Roll Women', 'Lady Constant', 'What Do You Suggest?', 'Mayfly', 'Ballad Of A Has-Been Beauty Queen'

All compositions by Nick Lowe except: 'Hymn To Me' (Lowe-Andrews-Rankin-Schwarz)

Despite It All (November 1970): 'Country Girl', 'The Slow One', 'Funk Angel', 'Piece Of Home', 'Love Song', 'Starship', 'Ebury Down', 'Old Jarrow'

All compositions by Nick Lowe except: 'Piece Of Home' (Andrews)

Silver Pistol (November 1971): 'Dry Land', 'Merry Go Round', 'One More Day', 'Nightingale', 'Silver Pistol', 'The Last Time I Was Fooled', 'Unknown Number', 'Range War', 'Egypt', 'Niki Hoeke Speedway', 'Ju Ju Man', 'Rockin' Chair'

All compositions by Nick Lowe except: 'Dry Land' (Gomm), 'One More Day' (Gomm), 'Range War' (Gomm), 'Niki Hoeke Speedway' (Ford), 'Ju Ju Man' (Ford), 'Rockin' Chair' (Gomm)

Nervous On The Road (September 1972): 'It's Been So Long', 'Happy Doing What We're Doing', 'Surrender To The Rhythm', 'Don't Lose Your Grip On Love', 'Nervous On The Road (But Can't Stay At Home)', 'Feel A Little Funky', 'I Like It Like That', 'Brand New You Brand New Me', 'Home In My Hand', 'Why, Why, Why, Why, Why'

All compositions by Nick Lowe except: 'It's Been So Long' (Gomm), 'Happy Doing What We're Doing' (Lowe-Andrews), 'I Like It Like That' (Kenner), 'Home In My Hand' (Self)

Please Don't Ever Change (October 1973): 'Hooked On Love', 'Why Do We Hurt The One We Love?', 'I Worry ('bout You Baby)', 'Don't Ever Change', 'Home In My Hand', 'Play That Fast Thing (One More Time)', 'I Won't Make It Without You', 'Down In Mexico', 'Speedo', 'The Version (Hypocrite)'

All compositions by Nick Lowe except: 'Hooked On Love' (Gomm), 'Don't Ever Change' (Goffin-King), 'Home In My Hand' (Self), 'Speedo' (Navarro), 'The Version (Hypocrite)' (Marley)

The New Favourites Of Brinsley Schwarz (July 1974): '(What's So Funny 'bout) Peace, Love And Understanding', 'Ever Since You're Gone', 'The Ugly Things', 'I Got The Real Thing', 'The Look That's In Your Eye Tonight', 'Now's The Time', 'Small Town Big City', 'Trying To Live My Life Without You', 'I Like You I Don't Love You', 'Down In The Dive'

All compositions by Nick Lowe except: 'I Got The Real Thing' (Lowe-Gomm), 'Now's The Time' (Clarke-Nash), 'Trying To Live My Life Without You' (Williams), 'I Like You I Don't Love You' (Lowe-Gomm), 'Down In The Dive' (Lowe-Schwarz)

Brinsley Schwarz compilation albums

Brinsley Schwarz's Original Golden Greats (United Artists, March 1974): 'Shining Brightly', 'Country Girl', 'Starship', 'Funk Angel', 'Nightingale', 'Ju Ju Man', 'Happy Doing What We're Doing', 'Surrender To The Rhythm', 'Don't Lose Your Grip On Love', 'Hypocrite', 'It's Gonna Be A Bring Down', 'Run Rudolph Run'

All compositions by Nick Lowe except: 'Ju Ju Man' (Ford), 'Happy Doing What We're Doing' (Lowe-Andrews), 'Hypocrite' (Marley), 'It's Gonna Be A Bring Down' (Gomm), 'Run Rudolph Run' (Berry)

15 Thoughts Of Brinsley Schwarz (United Artists, July 1978): '(What's So Funny 'bout) Peace, Love And Understanding', 'There's A Cloud In My Heart', 'Nightingale', 'Hypocrite', 'Funk Angel', 'I Like You I Don't Love You', 'Rockin' Chair', 'Shining Brightly', 'Country Girl', 'Surrender To The Rhythm', 'Hooked On Love', 'Don't Lose Your Grip On Love', 'The Ugly Things', 'Nervous On The Road (But Can't Stay At Home)', 'Home In My Hand'

All compositions by Nick Lowe except: 'Hypocrite (Marley)', 'I Like You I Don't Love You' (Lowe-Gomm), 'Rockin' Chair' (Gomm), 'Hooked On Love' (Gomm), 'Home In My Hand' (Self)

Surrender To The Rhythm is a 20-track CD compilation released by EMI Records in 1991.

Hen's Teeth is a 22-track CD compilation released by Edsel Records in 1998. It includes tracks from Kippington Lodge, and Brinsley Schwarz as 'The Hitters', 'Limelight', 'The Brinsleys' and 'The Knees', the last of which was in fact the group Man, not Brinsley Schwarz.

What IS So Funny About Peace Love And Understanding? (BBC radio recordings) is a CD released by Hux Records in 2001.

Cruel To Be Kind (BBC radio recordings) is a CD released by Hux Records in 2004.

It's All Over Now collects together eleven of the tracks produced by Steve Verroca in 1974 and released on various formats by Mega Dodo in 2017.

Brinsley Schwarz singles on United Artists

'Shining Brightly' c/w 'Hymn To Me' (May 1970)

'Country Girl' c/w 'Funk Angel' (October 1970)

'Speedo' c/w 'I Worry ('bout You Baby)' (August 1973)

'I've Cried My Last Tear Over You' c/w 'It's Gonna Be A Bring Down' (March 1974)

'(What's So Funny 'bout) Peace, Love And Understanding' c/w 'Ever Since You're Gone' (June 1974)

'Everybody' c/w 'I Like You I Don't Love You' (January 1975)

[as The Brinsleys] 'There's A Cloud In My Heart' c/w 'I Got The Real Thing' (March 1975)

[as The Hitters] 'Hypocrite' c/w 'The Version' (April 1973)

[as Limelight] 'I Should Have Known Better' c/w 'Tell Me Why' (January 1975)

Nick Lowe original albums

Jesus Of Cool (Radar, March 1978): 'Music for Money', 'I Love The Sound Of Breaking Glass', 'Little Hitler', 'Shake And Pop', 'Tonight', 'So It Goes', 'No Reason', '36" High', 'Marie Provost', 'Nutted By Reality', 'Heart Of The City' (live)

All compositions by Nick Lowe except: 'I Love The Sound Of Breaking Glass' (Lowe-Bodnar-Goulding), 'Little Hitler' (Lowe-Edmunds), '36" High' (Ford)

Pure Pop For Now People (Columbia, USA, March 1978): 'So It Goes', 'I Love The Sound Of Breaking Glass', 'Tonight', 'Marie Provost', 'Heart Of The City', 'Rollers Show', 'They Called It Rock', 'No Reason', 'Little Hitler', 'Nutted By Reality', '36" High', 'Music For Money'

All compositions by Nick Lowe except: 'I Love The Sound Of Breaking Glass' (Lowe-Bodnar-Goulding), 'They Called It Rock' (Lowe-Edmunds-Rockpile), 'Little Hitler' (Lowe-Edmunds), '36" High' (Ford)

Labour Of Lust (Radar, July 1979): 'Cruel To Be Kind', 'Cracking Up', 'Big Kick, Plain Scrap', 'Born Fighter', 'You Make Me', 'Skin Deep', 'Switchboard Susan', 'Endless Grey Ribbon', 'Without Love', 'Dose Of You', 'Love So Fine'

All compositions by Nick Lowe except: 'Cruel To Be Kind' (Lowe-Gomm), 'Switchboard Susan' (Jupp), 'Love So Fine' (Lowe-Rockpile)

Labour Of Lust (Columbia, USA, July 1979): 'Cruel To Be Kind',
  'Cracking Up', 'Big Kick, Plain Scrap', 'American Squirm', 'You
  Make Me', 'Skin Deep', 'Switchboard Susan', 'Dose Of You',
  'Without Love', 'Born Fighter', 'Love So Fine'

All compositions by Nick Lowe except: 'Cruel To Be Kind' (Lowe-Gomm), 'Switchboard Susan' (Jupp), 'Love So Fine' (Lowe-Rockpile)

[Rockpile] *Seconds Of Pleasure* (F-Beat, October 1980; Columbia, USA,
  October 1980): 'Teacher Teacher' (Pickett-Phillips), 'If Sugar Was As
  Sweet As You' (Tex), 'Heart' (Lowe-Rockpile), 'Now And Always'
  (Lowe-Rockpile), 'Knife And Fork' (Hennie-Anderson-Barge),
  'Play That Fast Thing One More Time' (Lowe), 'Wrong Again'
  (Difford-Tilbrook), 'Pet You And Hold You' (Lowe-Rockpile), 'Oh
  What A Thrill' (Berry), 'When I Write The Book' (Lowe-Rockpile),
  'Fool Too Long' (Lowe-Rockpile), 'You Ain't Nothin' But Fine'
  (Soileau-Simiens)
Includes a bonus EP *Nick Lowe & Dave Edmunds Sing The Everly
  Brothers*: 'Take A Message To Mary' (Bryant-Bryant), 'Crying In The
  Rain' (Greenfield-King), 'Poor Jenny' (Bryant-Bryant), 'When Will I
  Be Loved' (Everly)

Nick The Knife (F-Beat, February 1982; Columbia, USA, February 1982):
  'Burning', 'Heart', 'Stick It Where The Sun Don't Shine', 'Queen Of
  Sheeba', 'My Heart Hurts', 'Couldn't Love You (Anymore Than I
  Do)', 'Let Me Kiss Ya', 'Too Many Teardrops', 'Ba Doom', 'Raining
  Raining', 'One's Too Many (And A Hundred Ain't Enough)', 'Zulu
  Kiss'

All compositions by Nick Lowe except: 'Heart' (Lowe-Rockpile), 'My Heart Hurts' (Lowe-Carter), 'Too Many Teardrops' (Lowe-Carter), 'One's Too Many (And A Hundred Ain't Enough)' (Lowe-Wilson), 'Zulu Kiss' (Lowe-Ceiling)

The Abominable Showman (F-Beat, June 1983; Columbia, USA, June
  1983): 'We Want Action', 'Ragin' Eyes', 'Cool Reaction', 'Time
  Wounds All Heels', 'Man Of A Fool', 'Tanque-Rae', 'Wish You Were
  Here', 'Chicken And Feathers', 'Paid The Price', 'Mess Around
  With Love', 'Saint Beneath The Paint', 'How Do You Talk To An
  Angel'

All compositions by Nick Lowe except: 'We Want Action' (Lowe-Carter), 'Cool Reaction' (Marsh-Howell), 'Time Wounds All Heels' (Lowe-Carter-Climie), 'Paid The Price' (Martin)

Nick Lowe & His Cowboy Outfit (F-Beat, May 1984; Columbia, USA, May 1984): 'Half A Boy And Half A Man', 'You'll Never Get Me Up (In One Of Those)', 'Maureen', 'God's Gift To Women', 'The Gee And The Rick And The Three Card Trick', '(Hey Big Mouth) Stand Up And Say That', 'Awesome', 'Breakaway', 'Love Like A Glove', 'Live Fast, Love Hard, Die Young', 'L.A.F.S.'

All compositions by Nick Lowe except: 'You'll Never Get Me Up (In One Of Those)' (Jupp), 'Awesome' (Lowe-Profile), 'Breakaway' (Springfield), 'Love Like A Glove' (Carter-Eller), 'Live Fast, Love Hard, Die Young' (Allison)

The Rose Of England (F-Beat, August 1985; Columbia, USA, August 1985): 'Darlin' Angel Eyes', 'She Don't Love Nobody', '7 Nights To Rock', 'Long Walk Back', 'The Rose Of England', 'Lucky Dog', 'I Knew The Bride (When She Used To Rock'n'Roll)', 'Indoor Fireworks', '(Hope To God) I'm Right', 'I Can Be The One You Love', 'Everyone', 'Bo Bo Skediddle'

All compositions by Nick Lowe except: 'She Don't Love Nobody' (Hiatt), '7 Nights To Rock' (Trail-Innis-Glover), 'Indoor Fireworks' (Costello), 'Everyone' (Ball-Rue), 'Bo Bo Skediddle' (Piers-Walker)

Pinker And Prouder Than Previous (F-Beat, February 1988; Columbia, USA, February 1988): '(You're My) Wildest Dream', 'Crying In My Sleep', 'Big Hair', 'Love Gets Strange', 'I Got The Love', 'Black Lincoln Continental', 'Cry It Out', 'Lovers Jamboree', 'Geisha Girl', 'Wishing Well', 'Big Big Love'

All compositions by Nick Lowe except: 'Love Gets Strange' (Hiatt), 'Black Lincoln Continental' (Parker), 'Cry It Out' (Lowe-Profile), 'Lovers Jamboree' (Lowe-Carrack), 'Geisha Girl' (Lawton-Williams), 'Big Big Love' (Stewart-Carroll)

Party Of One (Reprise, February 1990): 'You Got The Look I Like', '(I Want To Build A) Jumbo Ark', 'Gai-Gin Man', 'Who Was That Man?', 'What's Shakin' On The Hill', 'Shting-Shtang', 'All Men Are Liars', 'Rocky Road', 'Refrigerator White', 'I Don't Know Why You Keep Me On', 'Honeygun'
NB bonus tracks on 1995 reissue (Demon Records): 'You Stabbed Me In The Front', Rocket Coast'

All compositions by Nick Lowe except: 'Rocky Road' (Lowe-Kirke)

[Little Village] *Little Village* (Reprise, February 1992): 'Solar Sex Panel', 'The Action', 'Inside Job', 'Big Love', 'Take Another Look', 'Do You Want My Job', 'Don't Go Away Mad', 'Fool Who Knows', 'She Runs Hot', 'Don't Think About Her When You're Trying To Drive', 'Don't Bug Me When I'm Working'

All compositions by Cooder-Hiatt-Keltner-Lowe

The Impossible Bird (Demon Records, November 1994; Upstart Records, USA, November 1994): 'Soulful Wind', 'The Beast In Me', 'True Love Travels On A Gravel Road', 'Trail Of Tears', 'Shelley My Love', 'Where's My Everything?', '12-Step Program (To Quit You Babe)', 'Lover Don't Go', 'Drive-Thru Man', 'Withered On The Vine', 'I Live On A Battlefield', '14 Days', 'I'll Be There'

All compositions by Nick Lowe except: 'True Love Travels On A Gravel Road' (Frazier-Owens), 'Trail Of Tears' (Cook), 'I Live On A Battlefield' (Lowe-Carrack), 'I'll Be There' (Price-Gabbard)

Dig My Mood (Demon Records, January 1998; Upstart Records, USA, January 1998): 'Faithless Lover', 'Lonesome Reverie', 'You Inspire Me', 'What Lack Of Love Has Done', 'Time I Took A Holiday', 'Failed Christian', 'Man That I've Become', 'Freezing', 'High On A Hilltop', 'Lead Me Not', 'I Must Be Getting Over You', 'Cold Grey Light Of Dawn'

All compositions by Nick Lowe except: 'Failed Christian' (McCullough), 'Cold Grey Light Of Dawn' (Hunter)

The Convincer (Proper Records, September 2001; Yep Roc Records, USA, September 2001): 'Homewrecker', 'Only A Fool Breaks His Own Heart', 'Lately I've Let Things Slide', 'She's Got Soul', 'Cupid Must Be Angry', 'Indian Queens', 'Poor Side Of Town', 'I'm A Mess', 'Between Dark And Dawn', 'Bygones (Won't Go)', 'Has She Got A Friend?', 'Let's Stay In And Make Love'

NB a limited-edition bonus EP for retail promotion contains: 'There Will Never Be Any Peace (Until God Is Seated At The Conference Table)', 'Different Kind Of Blue', 'Mama Said'

All compositions by Nick Lowe except: 'Only A Fool Breaks His Own Heart' (Bergen-Coburn), 'Poor Side Of Town' (Rivers-Adler), 'There Will Never Be Any Peace (Until God Is Seated At The Conference Table)' (Record-Acklin), 'Mama Said' (Dixon-Denson)

Untouched Takeaway (live) (Yep Roc Records, USA, 2004): 'What's Shakin' On The Hill', 'Faithless Lover', 'I Live On A Battlefield', 'You Inspire Me', 'Cruel To Be Kind', 'Indian Queens', 'Let's Stay In And Make Love', 'Shting-Shtang', 'The Beast In Me', '(What's So Funny 'bout) Peace, Love And Understanding', '12-Step Program (To Quit You Babe)', 'Dream Girl', 'Without Love', '14 Days', 'Tombstone Every Mile' (Bill Kirchen lead vocal), 'Shelley My Love', 'I'll Be There'

All compositions by Nick Lowe except: 'I Live On A Battlefield' (Lowe-Carrack), 'Cruel To Be Kind' (Lowe-Gomm), 'Dream Girl' (Crutchfield-Crutchfield), 'Tombstone Every Mile' (Fulkerson), 'I'll Be There' (Price-Gabbard)

At My Age (Proper Records, June 2007; Yep Roc Records, USA, June 2007): 'A Better Man', 'Long Limbed Girl', 'I Trained Her To Love Me', 'The Club', 'Hope For Us All', 'People Change', 'The Man In Love', 'Love's Got A Lot To Answer For', 'Rome Wasn't Built In A Day', 'Not Too Long Ago', 'The Other Side Of The Coin', 'Feel Again'

All compositions by Nick Lowe except: 'I Trained Her To Love Me' (Lowe-Trehern), 'The Man In Love' (Feathers-Claunch-Cantrell), 'Not Too Long Ago' (Stampley-Kilgore), 'Feel Again' (Virgin)

The Old Magic (Proper Records, September 2011; Yep Roc Records, USA, September 2011): 'Stoplight Roses', 'Checkout Time', 'House For Sale', 'Sensitive Man', 'I Read A Lot', 'Shame On The Rain', 'Restless Feeling', 'The Poisoned Rose', 'Somebody Cares For Me', 'You Don't Know Me At All', 'Til The Real Thing Comes Along'

All compositions by Nick Lowe except: 'Shame On The Rain' (Hall), 'The Poisoned Rose' (Costello), 'Somebody Cares For Me' (Lowe-Watkins), 'You Don't Know Me At All' (West)

Quality Street (Proper Records, October 2013; Yep Roc Records, USA, October 2013): 'Children Go Where I Send Thee' (Trad arr. Lowe), 'Christmas Can't Be Far Away' (Bryant), 'Christmas At The Airport' (Lowe), 'Old Toy Trains' (Miller), 'The North Pole Express' (Copyright Control), 'Hooves On The Roof' (Sexsmith), 'I Was Born In Bethlehem' (Lowe), 'Just To Be With You (This Christmas)' (Bon), 'Rise Up Shepherd' (Trad arr. Lowe), 'Silent Night' (Trad arr. Lowe), 'A Dollar Short Of Happy' (Lowe-Cooder), 'I Wish It Could Be Christmas Every Day' (Wood)

The Quality Holiday Revue Live (Yep Roc Records, USA, November 2015): 'A Dollar Short Of Happy', 'Ragin' Eyes', 'Christmas At The Airport', 'Not Too Long Ago', 'Linus And Lucy', 'I Love The Sound Of Breaking Glass', 'Sensitive Man', 'Somebody Cares For Me', 'The North Pole Express', 'Half A Boy And Half A Man', 'I Wish It Could Be Christmas Every Day', 'Children Go Where I Send Thee', 'I Was Born In Bethlehem'

Reissues: remastered and expanded versions of *Jesus Of Cool*, *Labour Of Lust*, *Nick The Knife*, *The Abominable Showman*, *Nick Lowe & His Cowboy Outfit*, and *Party Of One*, and remastered versions of *The Rose Of England* and *Pinker And Prouder Than Previous* were released by Yep Roc Records between 2008 and 2017.

Nick Lowe compilation albums

16 All Time Lowes (Demon Records, September 1984): 'Born Fighter', 'Marie Provost', 'American Squirm', 'Skin Deep', 'When I Write The Book', 'Little Hitler', 'Cruel To Be Kind', 'Heart Of The City', 'Switchboard Susan', 'I Love The Sound Of Breaking Glass', 'Big Kick, Plain Scrap', 'Cracking Up', 'Without Love', 'Nutted By Reality', 'So It Goes', 'They Called It Rock'

Nick's Knack (Demon Records, March 1986): 'Ragin' Eyes', 'Dose Of You', 'One's Too Many (And A Hundred Ain't Enough)', 'Now And Always', 'Endless Grey Ribbon', 'Burning', 'Wish You Were Here', 'Love So Fine', 'Mess Around With Love', 'My Heart Hurts', 'Basing Street', 'Raining Raining', 'Stick It Where The Sun Don't Shine', '36" High', 'Saint Beneath The Paint', 'Let Me Kiss Ya'

Basher (Demon Records, September 1989): 'So It Goes', 'Heart Of The City', 'I Love The Sound Of Breaking Glass', 'Little Hitler', 'No Reason', '36" High', 'Marie Provost', 'Nutted By Reality', 'American Squirm', '(What's So Funny 'bout) Peace, Love And Understanding', 'Cracking Up', 'Big Kick Plain Scrap', 'Born Fighter', 'Switchboard Susan', 'Without Love', 'Love So Fine', 'Cruel To Be Kind', 'When I Write The Book', 'Heart', 'Stick It Where The Sun Don't Shine', 'Ragin' Eyes', 'Time Wounds All Heels', 'Tanque-Rae', 'Maureen', 'Half A Boy And Half A Man',

'Breakaway', 'She Don't Love Nobody', '7 Nights To Rock', 'Long Walk Back', 'The Rose Of England', 'I Knew The Bride (When She Used To Rock'n'Roll)', 'Lovers Jamboree'

NB the CD version omits seven of these tracks.

The Wilderness Years (Demon Records, 1991): 'Fool Too Long', 'Let's Go To The Disco', 'Everybody Dance', 'Bay City Rollers We Love You', 'Allorolla Part 1', 'Rollers Show', 'Heart Of The City', 'Halfway To Paradise', 'Truth Drug', 'Born A Woman', 'Endless Sleep', 'Shake That Rat', 'I Love My Label', 'I Don't Want The Night To End', 'So Heavy', 'Keep It Out Of Sight', 'Heart', 'I Got A Job'

All compositions by Nick Lowe except: 'Everybody Dance' (Lowe-Adler), 'Halfway To Paradise' (Goffin-King), 'Born A Woman' (Sharp), 'I Love My Label' (Lowe-Profile), 'Keep It Out Of Sight' (Johnson)

The Doings (Edsel Records, August 1999) is a 4-CD collection of tracks from 1976–98. Discs 1–3 contain a total of 66 previously released tracks. Disc 4 contains these rarities: 'Pet You And Hold You' (live 1982), 'Cracking Up' (live 1982), '(What's So Funny 'bout) Peace, Love And Understanding' (live 1982), 'Baby It's You' (duet with Elvis Costello), 'Don't Think About Her' (1989 demo), 'Rocky Road' (1989 demo), 'Losin' Boy' (1994 home recording), 'Love Is After Me' (1994 home recording), 'Lonely Just Like Me' (1994 home recording), '36" High' (live 1994), 'Raining Raining' (live 1994), 'Without Love' (live 1995), 'Lover Don't Go' (live 1995), 'Dream Girl' (live 1995), 'I'm Coming Home' (live 1995), 'I'll Give You All Night To Stop' (1995 studio outtake), 'Soulful Wind' (live 1998), 'She Don't Love Nobody' (live 1998), 'Cruel To Be Kind' (live 1998), 'Half A Boy And Half A Man' (live 1998)

All compositions on disc 4 by Nick Lowe except: 'Pet You And Hold You' (Lowe-Rockpile), 'Baby It's You' (Bacharach-David-Williams), 'Rocky Road' (Lowe-Kirke), 'Losin' Boy' (Giles), 'Love Is After Me' (Hayes-Porter), 'Lonely Just Like Me' (Alexander), '36" High' (Ford), 'Dream Girl' (Crutchfield-Crutchfield), 'I'm Coming Home' (Horton-Franks), 'I'll Give You All Night To Stop' (Hunter), 'She Don't Love Nobody' (Hiatt), 'Cruel To Be Kind' (Lowe-Gomm)

Quiet Please . . . The New Best Of Nick Lowe (Proper Records, March 2009; Yep Roc Records, USA, March 2009) is a 2-CD and limited-edition DVD collection that contains a total of 49 previously released tracks. The DVD contains nine rarely seen videos and an entire 2007 Belgian concert.

The Brentford Trilogy (Proper, July 2009) is a 3-CD set comprising the original albums *The Impossible Bird*, *Dig My Mood* and *The Convincer*.

Nick Lowe singles and EPs

[as Tartan Horde] 'Bay City Rollers We Love You' c/w 'Rollers Theme' (United Artists, June 1975)

'Keep It Out Of Sight' c/w '(I've Been Taking The) Truth Drug' (Dynamite, Holland, 1976)

[as The Disco Bros.] 'Let's Go To The Disco' c/w 'Everybody Dance' (United Artists, 1976)

'So It Goes' c/w 'Heart Of The City' (Stiff, August 1976)

[as Tartan Horde] 'Rollers Show' c/w 'Allorolla' (United Artists, Japan, 1977)

EP: [The Disco Bros.] 'Let's Go To The Disco, Everybody Dance' c/w [The Tartan Horde] 'Bay City Rollers We Love You', 'Rollers Show' (United Artists, Holland, 1977)

Bowi EP: 'Born A Woman', 'Shake That Rat', 'Marie Provost', 'Endless Sleep' (Stiff, May 1977)

'Halfway To Paradise' c/w 'I Don't Want The Night To End' (Stiff, October 1977)

'I Love The Sound Of Breaking Glass' c/w 'They Called It Rock' (Radar, February 1978)

'Little Hitler' c/w 'Cruel To Be Kind' [Brinsley Schwarz version] (Radar, May 1978)

'American Squirm' c/w '(What's So Funny 'bout) Peace, Love And Understanding' [as Nick Lowe and His Sound] (Radar, October 1978)

Live at The El Mocambo EP: 'I Love The Sound Of Breaking Glass', 'Shake And Pop', 'Heart Of The City' (Columbia, Canada, 1978)

'Cracking Up' c/w 'Basing Street' (Radar, June 1979)

'Cruel To Be Kind' c/w 'Endless Grey Ribbon' (Radar, August 1979)

[Rockpile] 'Wrong Way' c/w 'Now And Always' (F-Beat, September 1980)

[Rockpile] 'Teacher Teacher' c/w 'Fool Too Long' (F-Beat, November 1980)

'Burning' c/w 'Zulu Kiss' (F-Beat, February 1982)

'My Heart Hurts' c/w 'Pet You And Hold You' (live Cleveland 1982) with free single 'Cracking Up' (live Cleveland 1982) c/w '(What's So Funny 'bout) Peace, Love And Understanding' (live Cleveland 1982) (F-Beat, April 1982)

'Ragin' Eyes' c/w 'Tanque-Rae' (F-Beat, April 1983)

'Half A Boy And Half A Man' c/w 'Awesome' (F-Beat, May 1984)

'L.A.F.S.' c/w '(Hey Big Mouth) Stand Up And Say That' (F-Beat, July 1984)

'I Knew The Bride (When She Used To Rock'n'Roll)' c/w 'Darlin' Angel Eyes' (F-Beat, July 1985)

'What's Shakin' On The Hill' c/w 'Cruel To Be Kind' (Reprise, April 1990)

'All Men Are Liars' c/w 'Gai-Gin Man' (Reprise, August 1990)

[Little Village] 'Solar Sex Panel' c/w 'Do With Me What You Want To Do' (Reprise, March 1992)

[Little Village] 'Don't Go Away Mad' c/w 'Big Love' (Reprise, May 1992)

'True Love Travels On A Gravel Road' c/w 'In The Middle Of It All', '12-Step Program (To Quit You Babe)', '(What's So Funny 'bout) Peace, Love And Understanding' (Demon, November 1994)

Live! On The Battlefield EP: 'I Live On A Battlefield', '36" High' (live Tokyo 1994), 'Without Love' (live Chicago 1995), 'Dream Girl' (live Houston 1995), 'In The Middle Of It All' (Upstart, July 1995)

You Inspire Me EP: 'You Inspire Me', 'Soulful Wind' (live Tokyo 1998), 'She Don't Love Nobody' (live Tokyo 1998), 'Cruel To Be Kind' (live Tokyo 1998), 'Half A Boy And Half A Man' (live Tokyo 1998) (Demon, June 1998)

'Lately I've Let Things Slide' c/w 'She's Got Soul', 'There Will Never Be Any Peace (Until God Is Seated At The Conference Table)' (Proper, November 2001)

'Go 'Way Hound Dog' c/w '(I've Changed My) Wild Mind' (Yep Roc, November 2011)

'Tokyo Bay' c/w 'Crying Inside', 'Heartbreaker', 'Travelin' Light' (Yep Roc, April 2018)

'Love Starvation' c/w 'Blue On Blue', 'Trombone', 'Raincoat In The River' (Yep Roc, May 2019)

Endnotes

Introduction

1   *Labour Of Love – The Music Of Nick Lowe* (Telarc 2001); *Lowe Profile – A Tribute To Nick Lowe* (Brewery Records 2005); and *Lowe Country – The Songs Of Nick Lowe* (Fiesta Red Records 2012).

Chapter 2

2   In Mafraq, Drain and his fellow servicemen looked forward to putting on the 1956 Christmas entertainment, dubbed the 'Hi and Lowe' show. One Sergeant L. R. Baldwin wrote a special song with the refrain: *'Sing "Hi", sing "Lowe", wherever you go, Groupy Lowe's Air Force will never say "No".'*

Chapter 3

3   Although Lonnie Donegan famously recorded some rousing rockers, usually based on the songs of American folk and blues legends, he also had a penchant for comedy numbers, of which 'Lively' is an example. One can only imagine an eleven-year-old Nick Lowe mimicking Donegan's novelty song about petty criminals, with semi-spoken 'jokes' such as: *'I sung this song at a policeman's dance, but I was only singing for coppers.'*

4   The Combined Cadet Force (CCF) is a Ministry of Defence-sponsored youth organisation in the United Kingdom. Its aim is to 'provide a disciplined organisation in a school so that pupils may develop powers of leadership by means of training to promote the qualities of responsibility, self-reliance, resourcefulness, endurance and perseverance'.

5   Known to car enthusiasts and collectors as 'The King's Car', or 'The Hussein Jaguar', the 1955-built Model XK140 has changed hands many times and was last seen, resprayed green, in California.

Chapter 5

6   Chartwell, also known as Wellchart, was founded by Jerry Perenchio (died 2017) whose associated company, Chartwell Artists,

managed, among others, Andy Williams, Johnny Mathis and Glen Campbell. The music publishing rights of various Famepushers acts, including Brinsley Schwarz, Ernie Graham and Help Yourself, were assigned to Chartwell in 1970, but were all later acquired by Nick Lowe's subsequent publisher, Plangent Visions Music, for a relatively modest sum. The Chartwell catalogue included the subsequent hits '(What's So Funny 'bout) Peace, Love And Understanding' and 'Cruel To Be Kind'.

Chapter 6

7   Andrew Jakeman was born in Edgware, Middlesex, in February 1948. He had worked briefly for an advertising agency, sung in a local beat group and spent time in Paris, where he became a road manager and translator of lyrics for a French group called Les Variations. His early occupations and business activities included road manager for Darryl Way's Wolf; record shop assistant; stallholder at Kensington Market; candle maker; and van driver for *Time Out* magazine.

Chapter 7

8   Former hit group the Troggs were captured on tape in the studio control room, arguing about how a hit record should be made. The covert recording circulated around the music business, much to the amusement of all who heard it. It includes the group's singer, Reg Presley, thinking out loud in a broad accent: 'Drummers . . . I shit 'em.'

9   The origin of the phrase can be traced back to Shakespeare – *Hamlet*, Act 3, Scene 4: 'I must be cruel only to be kind,' spoken by Hamlet to his mother. Nick may have read *Hamlet* at school, but a more plausible source is the obscure 1965 record by Unit 4+2, 'You've Got To Be Cruel To Be Kind'.

Chapter 8

10   Nick's first song covers were Teddy Raster's version of 'Brand New You Brand New Me' (1972), and Dave Edmunds's version of 'She's My Baby' on *Subtle As A Flying Mallet* (1975).

Chapter 9

11   The band's name is often associated with 'Rock Around The Rock Pile' – a song from the 1956 jukebox movie, *The Girl Can't Help It*. However, when Dave Edmunds toured North America in 1969, he visited a club in Toronto called Rockpile. It stuck in Edmunds's mind and he named his 1971 album after it. When he and Nick formed their band some years later, it was automatically assumed to be 'Rockpile'. Writer Larry LeBlanc confirms: 'The Rockpile [club] was on the corner of Yonge and Davenport approx. 1968–1972.'

12   Born Marie Bickford Dunne, Ontario, Canada, 1896.

13   Pirate DVDs have circulated and in 2018 it appeared on Amazon Prime, although to what extent this was with the blessing of its makers is unknown.

Chapter 10

14   Mastering engineer, George 'Porky' Peckham, would inscribe cryptic comments at the centre of his record pressing lacquers, 'A Porky Prime Cut' being the most common.

Chapter 11

15   *This is Spinal Tap* is a 1983 satirical movie that lampoons

the stereotypical British rock band touring the USA; the lovable character Nigel Tufnel, played by Christopher Guest, is a brimming font of pseudo-profound observations, delivered in a 'Mockney' tone of voice.

16 The tape of 'We Oughta Be Ashamed' (written by Earl Montgomery and George Jones) was deemed lost for years. Elvis Costello recalled: 'The track was not in the CBS archive, not listed anywhere, so Steve Berkowitz went to the House of Cash – this was not long after John died – and by sheer chance they were clearing the archive and there was this tape, an Ampex reel from Am-Pro. It was like handling a religious artefact.'

Chapter 12

17 Martha Hume's interview appeared on *An Interrogation of Nick Lowe (alias Nick the Knife)*, a 1982 promotional LP on Columbia Records.

18 Belmont's back problem surfaced earlier that year; in Santa Barbara on 18 April 1983 he performed chair-bound.

Chapter 13

19 'Who Was That Man?' was Nick's response to the King's Cross Underground station fire of November 1987 in which thirty-one people died, including a man who could not be positively identified for sixteen years, and was known as 'Body 115'. He was eventually identified by a rare 'clip' in his brain that had been installed during an operation for an aneurism in 1980. His name was Alexander Fallon.20 A very good live version of 'Shting Shtang', featuring a superb guitar performance by Steve Donnelly,

appears on *Untouched Takeaway* (Yep Roc Records, 2004).

21 'The Beast In Me' was also the name of a 1963 Broadway musical by James Costigan (book) and Don Elliott (music). As well as being recorded by Johnny Cash, Nick's own recording of 'The Beast In Me' can be heard over the closing credits of the pilot episode to the hit TV show *The Sopranos*.

22 A group of elite LA session musicians that played on many hit records in the 1960s and 1970s.

Chapter 14

23 Paul Gorman, in the booklet that accompanies Lowe's *The Brentford Trilogy* CD box set.

24 Nick would often occupy himself with a *Codewords* brain-teaser book, writing at the top of each puzzle his tour location.

Chapter 15

25 As well as flying Drain and his friend on Concorde, Nick generously financed a return flight from New York to London for Rockpile tour manager Andy Cheeseman, to enable him to attend his brother's UK wedding, mid-tour.

26 As mentioned to reporter David Segal in an interview for the *Washington Post*.

27 For further information, please visit www.pwsausa.org/international

28 Other records played at Nick and Peta's wedding party included 'The Snake' by Al Wilson; 'Soulful Dress' by Sugar Pie DeSanto; 'Pickin' Wild Mountain Berries' by Conway Twitty and Loretta Lynn; and 'December, 1963 (Oh, What A Night)' by the Four Seasons.

Chapter 16

29 In 2018, Nick commented, 'For the last two years I've favoured the "Western Classic", which is a reissue of the original J-200 designed by and made for singing cowboy Ray Whitely in the 1930s.'

30 In 1998, Nick told Salon TV's John Milward: 'The number of contemporary artists who appeal to me is infinitesimal.' In the same interview, he stated: 'As long as my body holds out, I'll be grooving when I'm seventy, and not some sort of horrible spectacle.'

Chapter 17

31 In a 1978 interview with Bruce Kessler from Houston radio station KTRU, Nick said, 'I dreamt up this slogan "Pure Pop For Now People". I used the word "pop", on purpose, to irritate people.'

32 Nicky Chinn and Mike Chapman teamed up in the early 1970s to form one of the UK's most formidable pop songwriting teams, creating hits for Sweet ('Ballroom Blitz'), Mud ('Tiger Feet'), Suzi Quatro ('Can The Can') and others. By 1974 they had scored over two-dozen Top 40 hits, including five chart toppers.

33 Renowned rapper Talib Kweli referred to it as 'fake indie' during his performance at the 2017 A2IM awards ceremony in New York City. Kweli admitted that his early records were bankrolled by a major label and made to look 'independent'.

Appendix

34 Patrick and Anne were married on 8 April 1888 in Bury St Edmunds. Their first two children, Winifred, born 1889, and Louisa, born 1891, both died at young ages and Muriel became the eldest of their four surviving offspring. At the time of Muriel's birth, the Kelly family lived in Suffolk while Patrick was stationed at Warley as a quartermaster sergeant with the Army Pay Corps.

35 In the late eighteenth century, the Reverend Thatcher travelled extensively throughout the eastern states preaching the gospel as an Episcopal Pastor, and later became Rector of Christ Church, Ballston Spa, near Saratoga Springs. Gamaliel Thatcher was appointed a missionary in 1805, a short time before his death at the age of thirty-two.

36 On 1 July 1862, on what was to be the climax of the 'Seven Days Battles' that ended the Peninsula Campaign, Confederate General Robert E. Lee launched a series of assaults on the robust Union position on Malvern Hill, Virginia. Although both sides were evenly matched in number, with around 55,000 soldiers each, the Confederates suffered far greater casualties, losing over one-tenth of their men while achieving no strategic advantage.

37 The couple would have five more children over the next sixteen years – Eugenie Victoria, born 1855; Evelyne Anna, born 1863; and Cecil 'Percy' Arthur, born 1866. Their last two children – Mabel Violet, born 1867 and Carl Bernhard, born 1869 – both died at a young age.

38 One such novice was Mrs Lizzie Holmes Goggs, who soon became a partner in Alberta's enterprise. But as Crystoleum was taking off, Goggs broke away from the firm and attempted to publish

Alberta's pamphlet as her own work. In the summer of 1882, Goggs commenced trading as 'The Crystoleum Company' at 500 Oxford Street, advertising Crystoleum classes at her premises. By the end of the year, Alberta and Goggs were at war, each side taking out press advertisements claiming that they were the true originator of the medium. To protect her rights, Alberta commenced legal proceedings via her solicitors, Lidiard & Co, seeking an injunction in the Chancery Division of the High Court. The action, *Caspar v. Goggs*, sought 'to restrain Mr & Mrs Goggs from selling or disposing of the book entitled *A Guide to Crystoleum Painting*'. On 25 April 1883 in the High Court, the Honourable Mr Justice Pearson found in favour of the plaintiff, Miss Alberta Caspar. She immediately published a fuller version of her original manuscript from the Regent Street premises of 'The Original Crystoleum Company', sole registrants of 'Crystoleum, Crayonium and Email Vitre in Great Britain and France'. Within a year, James and Lizzie Holmes Goggs had filed for bankruptcy in the High Court. Alberta, meanwhile, sought to further protect her invention by applying for a patent, which was granted in October 1884. A review in *The Bookseller* in December of that year endorsed Alberta's publication, *Crystoleum*, an original copy of which is in the British Library.

39   Alberta had previously made contact with an American artist named Eugene Pearl through whom she met with an attorney, Phillips Abbott, who immediately filed a US patent application for the 'Stained Glass' invention (with one half assigned to Pearl, later to become a patent lawyer himself).

40   Following Don Thatcher's death in 1896, an extensive report of his marital circumstances, including his courtship of Alberta Caspar, appeared in the *St Louis Post-Dispatch* of 12 December 1897.

41   In 1883, Don Thatcher appeared in court in St Louis to answer charges brought by the State of Missouri in respect of the 'embarrassments of the Windsor Hotel Company'. Although it appears to have been a fairly minor case, the proceedings attracted the attention of the press due to a bizarre incident that occurred in the courtroom. When state attorney Frank J. Bowman called Thatcher's attorney, Mr Chester Krum, 'a liar', Krum retaliated, striking Bowman with his cane. A fight broke out in which 'Bowman had his two hands full of Krum's whiskers, while Krum had his hands full of Bowman's hair . . . Detective Stiles grabbed them both by the legs and Mr Thatcher seized them by the collar'. The case was adjourned.

42   Born in 1846 in Massachusetts, Charles Adams-Randall had spent time in England, first visiting London in 1872 to seek protection under British Patent Law for his invention 'Improvements in Telegraphic Printing Apparatus'. In 1888, Adams-Randall conceived not only the 'Electro-motor Velocipede' – or, as it later became known, 'the moped' – but also, in its embryonic form, the jukebox. Although the invention of the first 'coin-operated phonograph' is generally attributed to Louis T. Glass, who unveiled his nickel-in-the-slot machine in San Francisco in 1889, Adams-Randall

had filed a patent application for his 'Automatic Parlophone' in England the previous year, and he is regarded by some jukebox enthusiasts as the originator of the concept. He continued to thrive as an inventor and later patented, among other devices, one of the first 'electro-massage vibrators', and the 'Portable Stereophone', a forerunner of stereophonic headphones; his patent was cited by Koss, and later Sony when their 'Walkman' was patented in the 1970s. He also established the Randall Telephone Manufacturing Company, and in 1912 publicly predicted a telephone device that would allow 'under-seas conversation' over a 5000-mile route, i.e. transatlantic telephone calls. It was not all plain-sailing for Adams-Randall. On 27 December 1885, he was travelling from Boston to New York aboard the *Boston Flyer*, when, at Pelhamville, Westchester County, New York, the train derailed on a high embankment. The locomotive and the postal car shot down the steep slope, killing the driver and injuring many. The sleeper carriage that was occupied by Adams-Randall overturned, but miraculously stayed on the embankment. He escaped with minor injuries.

43 Don's 'Portable Egg Case' was the subject of an application in 1887, as was his 'Liquid Fuel Cartridge', both reported in the *Patent Journal and Inventor*. He had also sought to patent a 'Type Writer', for which drawings exist, although the first typewriter had been around for a decade or more.

44 On 12 March 1890 – fourteen days, in fact, before his divorce from Phoebe was made absolute – Charles Adams-Randall married Evelyne Caspar Von der Trave in London, with 'Mr and Mrs Don C. Thatcher' as witnesses.

45 Don's significant contribution to the fast food business was acknowledged in an article in the *St Louis Republic* under the headline: 'How much it takes daily to feed hungry St Louisans – Birth and Growth of the Downtown Dining Habit and the Men Who Have Helped It Along'. It reported: 'Don Thatcher has made and lost two fortunes in the restaurant business in St Louis, and returned for the third time and introduced a combination of lunch counter service and dinner a la carte, giving all the rapidity of the former with the elegance of the latter. This idea quickly made his third fortune, and of course other competitors came in to imitate him.' On 8 December 1893, however, Don was arrested and charged with 'swindling his former associates out of $5,000' – money it was alleged he collected in England when delivering a patent on behalf of real estate broker John V. Hair of Chicago. In 1894, Don bounced back to become the proprietor of Thatcher's Silver Grill on North Seventh Street, where he employed a staff of thirty men. His army of employees, many of whom were in the Waiters Union, confronted him over his use of non-union labour and threatened to strike. Don's reaction was to fire them all and hire an all-female workforce, whereupon the sacked men vowed to 'march in a body to the restaurant' to 'see how the girls do'.

46 'An Improved Water Closet Seat' incorporated a rolling device

impregnated with disinfectant that passed over a revolving toilet seat, similar in concept to the design that would appear in Japan nearly a hundred years later.

47 Although Nick Lowe had no knowledge of his grandfather's 'Dude-Venile' stage persona, his mid-1980s composition 'Half A Boy And Half A Man' is an uncanny pen portrait.

48 Louis cannot have been certain of what occurred while he was at sea, but in 1918 he filed for divorce, citing Blanche's adultery with a Romanian-born actor named Dolf Wheeler. Louis knew that Blanche and Dolf had appeared together in *Peaches* at various northern playhouses during the previous winter, but despite his suspicions he eventually dropped the proceedings and was soon reunited with his wife.

49 The Actors' Orphanage was established in 1896 by Kittie Carson, wife of the editor of *The Stage*. Its mission was to improve the welfare of young or unemployed actresses, and the destitute children of parents connected with the theatre. Patrons later included Sir Noël Coward and Sir Laurence Olivier.

50 In 1942, Louis appeared in *Sweeney Todd* at Ipswich Hippodrome, and in December 1944 he was named as the producer of *Cinderella* at Swansea Empire. He had spent much of that year publicising his new 'melodrama', *Brides In The Bath*, based on the crimes of George Joseph Smith, in which 'at least two of Smith's infamous murders will be reconstructed, showing how Smith drowned his unfortunate victims'. There is, however, little evidence of this grisly show reaching the stage.

Index

393